WALTER HOWARD FRERE

WALTER HOWARD FRERE
C.R., D.D., LITT.D.
Seventh Bishop of Truro

Walter Howard Frere

HIS CORRESPONDENCE
ON LITURGICAL REVISION
AND CONSTRUCTION

EDITED BY
RONALD C. D. JASPER, M.A., B.D.

WIPF & STOCK · Eugene, Oregon

Wipf and Stock Publishers
199 W 8th Ave, Suite 3
Eugene, OR 97401

Walter Howard Frere
His Correspondence on Liturgical Revision and Construction
By Jasper, Ronald C. D., M. A., B. D.
Copyright©1954 SPCK
ISBN 13: 978-1-61097-237-6
Publication date 7/01/2011
Previously published by SPCK, 1954

CONTENTS

FOREWORD — vii
INTRODUCTION — xi

Part One
LITURGICAL REVISION IN ENGLAND

CHAPTER I. EARLY DAYS — 3
CHAPTER II. THE ADVISORY COMMITTEE ON LITURGICAL QUESTIONS — 26
CHAPTER III. THE REARRANGEMENT OF THE CANON — 56
CHAPTER IV. INITIAL WORK IN THE CHURCH ASSEMBLY — 83
CHAPTER V. THE HOUSE OF BISHOPS. CANON AND RESERVATION — 95
CHAPTER VI. THE FINAL STAGES — 126
CHAPTER VII. IN OPPOSITION — 147
CHAPTER VIII. EPILOGUE — 179

Part Two
LITURGICAL REVISION IN OTHER PARTS OF THE ANGLICAN COMMUNION

THE LAMBETH CONFERENCE 1920 — 193
JAPAN — 198
SOUTH AFRICA (1) — 203
SOUTH AFRICA (2) — 228
NORTHERN RHODESIA — 230
HEBREW CHRISTIANS — 246
SOUTH INDIA — 249
CEYLON — 253

APPENDIXES

I. *Membra Disiecta* (listed individually, p. 258) — 259
II. THE ENTHRONEMENT OF DR. LANG AS ARCHBISHOP OF CANTERBURY — 298

INDEX — 313

FOREWORD

WHEN I was invited to write a Foreword to this book I could only consent on the understanding that I wrote as one who owes all the knowledge he has of liturgies to Walter Frere. I had the privilege of getting to know him when he was approaching the height of his influence and I was at an age when one is most impressionable. When I first came to Mirfield he was already that which he remained to the end of his life—a man devoted to God in Holy Religion. This devotion pervaded his whole life. It was not put on one side, even for a time, when he accepted the Bishopric of Truro: it was just a natural thing for him to return to Mirfield when he resigned the See: there had been no break in his Religious Life.

It was impossible to live with Walter Frere without being impressed by the fact that what he really lived for was worship; as Fr. Talbot wrote of him: 'Worship was to him the first of interests and the most usual of habits.' He strove to make his whole life an act of worship. At church, in the study, at recreation, at meals—he was always the essential worshipper. Hence his regularity, his industry, his self-giving —it all tended to God. In his conception of worship there is no doubt about the primacy of the Eucharist: that was the crown of all that he tried to do. At the end of his life, when he could only shuffle along a corridor to an improvised chapel, he would say: 'This is just what I long for: it is meat and drink to me.' We are not surprised then to find that the studies in the latter part of his life were mainly connected with topics connected with the Eucharist; between 1930 and 1935 he published three volumes of studies in the Early Roman Liturgy, and his last great work on *The Anaphora* was published in 1938, the year of his death.

In view of the place which the Eucharist occupied in his life, his attitude towards the 1928 Revision of the Liturgy is a matter of great interest. He was aware that there were grave defects in the Liturgy of 1662. For years he had been thinking out plans for a Revision. Several parts of the Church overseas had undertaken such a task and he was often consulted by them, but he was sure it would have been better if the Church at home had produced a revised Liturgy first, thus providing an example for others to follow. Be that as it may, when the Church at home did set itself to the task of Revision, Frere was well equipped to assist in the work. He considered the 1928 Book to be an improvement on the 1662; but he was not satisfied with it and was so certain that there was room for further improvement that he finally voted against it. He had a mind that could hold fast to certain principles of liturgical propriety, but at the same time he believed in experiments. One thing he had desired ardently was the provision of an alternative rite which would satisfy those who supported the Western tradition. This he failed to secure, but once the 1928 Book had obtained the official sanction of the Church he authorized its use in the Cathedral at Truro and elsewhere in his Diocese. At the end of his days in the improvised chapel mentioned above it was the 1928 Rite that he liked the celebrant to use.

As far as I remember there was no change in the way he celebrated the Eucharist from 1913 until he died. He did not genuflect at the Consecration; he made a low bow. After communicating, if not himself celebrating, he would make a genuflection, not towards either Host or Chalice, but where he had been kneeling. His idea of the Real Presence was more Eastern than Western: that our Lord was present in the Eucharist he was convinced, but that would seem to have been enough for him.

What has been said so far gives only one aspect of the worshipping Frere. He was without doubt a saint. A saint is a man who loves God supremely; and that love impels him to the consecration of all his powers and faculties to promote the glory of God, and also to an active charity towards men. A saint does not consider that he is giving glory to God by despising what God has created or by ignoring his own gifts. Frere was endowed with a positive galaxy of gifts, natural as well as supernatural. It was interesting to note how thoroughly he revelled in his studies, or how increasingly he responded to the appeal of music. His social gifts were apparent in any assembly whether of educated people or artisans, and his rich sense of humour would often break down barriers. He loved the beautiful things in creation. All these gifts were used and enjoyed and so dedicated to God. In a way we find them all in his worship—the underlying principles, the bringing of the people to take their part, the appropriate music, and the enrichment of a reverent ritual.

His was a busy life: his industry was really tremendous, and yet he was never too busy to give help. If you went to ask his counsel upon some matter and found him pen in hand writing one of his books, when he had finished the sentence he would put down the pen and turn to you, and you felt that the one important thing in the world at that moment was your problem. Such demands were frequent.

One final word about the amazing work he did with individuals. For the most part, I suspect, they sought him, not he them. He apparently considered it no part of his business to get into touch with the man in the street: he practically never initiated a conversation in the train, but got down to his book at once. But he had a way of making what appeared to be a casual remark to someone, a remark which haunted the individual and ultimately produced results which were signal and permanent. He had at times to deal with sad cases which caused him pain: he was like a rock in the question of right and wrong but was nevertheless very understanding. And so a persistent love and care, the provision where possible of new work, or the provision where needed of substantial help were always moving him. He made every excuse for the sinner and won many back to a holy life. There was something in his make-up which produced an almost heroic patience. He could see a very long way into the future. This patience made him content to wait both in his dealings with individuals and in the hopes for the success of something which he had planned: he was never in a hurry.

His name is surely to be included in the list of those who proved themselves to be a light of the world in their generation.

BERNARD HORNER C.R.

INTRODUCTION

IN some respects this book represents the fulfilment of Bishop Frere's own wish. A bundle of his longer and more important letters were left with the late Father E. K. Talbot at Mirfield accompanied by a characteristically minute note in Frere's own handwriting to the effect that at some future date they might be worth publishing. This is not to suggest, however, that Frere wrote them—or indeed any letters—with the possibilities of future publication in his mind. On the contrary, the evidence points in the other direction. They were often the products of a mind already exercised in all manner of problems. They lack the polished and measured style of his published works; grammar and style are often at fault. Frere was simply talking with his pen.

Nevertheless, he undoubtedly realized that these imperfect literary compositions would one day prove to be valuable documentary evidence of liturgical developments within the Anglican communion of his day. It was almost inevitable that the part he played in the Revision movement should be a leading one. The subject was close to his heart: it had taken possession of him as a student and had inspired his liturgical studies. One might say that he applied himself to the task with a sense of vocation. He affords a striking parallel with Dr. A. J. Maclean, Bishop of Moray, Ross, and Caithness, one of his great friends and correspondents, who was engaged on a similar task in the Scottish Episcopal Church at the same period, but with happier results.

The main purpose of this book is therefore the provision of important documents, which must speak for themselves. No attempt has been made at a critical survey of Frere's contributions to liturgical reform. In the two main sections of the book I have merely tried to set letters and memoranda in their context, rather on the lines of the late Dean Hutton's edition of the letters of Bishop Stubbs. There the Dean described his aim thus: 'It was thought that the letters of Bishop Stubbs, and the letters to him that have been preserved, would do something to show what he was and what part he played in the literary and ecclesiastical history of his day. I was asked to collect them and to add such an account of his life as should make them intelligible to those who did not know him.'[1] I have tried to do the same for Frere

---

[1] W. H. Hutton, *The Letters of William Stubbs* (1904), Introduction, p. v.

in this one particular sphere, though undoubtedly in a far less able manner.

In reproducing these letters, I have adopted the principle that inaccuracies, whether in grammar or in detail, must remain. To have done otherwise would have obscured the real Frere. It will also be noted that in his letters to other people the conclusions are nearly always missing. This is due to the fact that they have been taken, not from the originals but from carbon copies, in which signatures and concluding personal remarks such as Frere would add in his own hand rarely appeared.

Of the man himself these documents reveal much. There was, first and foremost, his sincerity of purpose and saintliness. Then there was his wide range of knowledge and firm grasp of detail. There was his ability to see things objectively and in the widest possible context. Unquestionably, too, he had his own axe to grind and he was not incapable of holy guile: but at the same time he respected views other than his own. Indeed the late Bishop Guy Warman wrote: 'I do not think everyone esteemed his considerateness as it deserved'. No one could possibly deny that he lived out most faithfully the two Frere family mottoes—'To preserve what has been handed down by those who have gone before' and 'Brother loves brother'.

Finally I should like to thank all those people who have helped me with this volume in any way. Fr. Bernard Horner, Bishop Frere's literary executor, and other members of the community at Mirfield furnished the bulk of the material and spared neither time nor trouble to facilitate the work. Dr. J. H. Arnold has been ready at every turn with help and advice. Professor Claude Jenkins has read the whole script and saved it from many errors and weaknesses. Without the initial support and encouragement of the Dean of Lincoln, the Rt. Revd. Colin Dunlop, the book would never have been written. The Revd. A. Grainge has been entirely responsible for the onerous task of compiling the Index. I must also acknowledge my indebtedness to many other people who either furnished information, loaned me letters, or gave me permission to reproduce letters: the Archbishop of Canterbury, the Archbishop of York, the Bishop of Winchester, the Bishop of Chichester, the late Bishop of Lichfield, Bishop Michael Furse, the late Bishop Guy Warman, the Dean of Westminster, the Dean of Chichester, Canon C. H. Leeke, Canon A. F. Smethurst, the late Canon J. H. Srawley, Canon G. W. Broomfield, the Revd. C. P. Shaw, Mr. Michael Sadleir, Mr. William Urry, Dr. Hugh Dalton,

Introduction

Mr. E. G. P. Wyatt, Mrs. W. Temple, Miss P. L. Wingfield and Professor Agnes Headlam-Morley, Mrs. Stuart Houston, Miss M. P. Crighton, Miss C. M. Cobb, Miss M. C. S. Mills, and the Editor of the *Church Times*. If there are any whom I have omitted or have been unable to contact, I hope they will forgive me.

R. C. D. JASPER

August 1953

I

EARLY DAYS

THE subject of Prayer Book revision had not merely occupied Frere's mind since his student days; it had also provided the stimulus for his liturgical studies. This was revealed in his Preface to *Some Principles of Liturgical Reform*, where he stated that even as a student at Wells Theological College he had become convinced that before long the Church would be compelled to face the problem of liturgical reform. 'The subject fascinated me, and liturgical study became an occupation which I have tried to pursue, however intermittently, ever since.'[1] It was fortunate that at the very outset he found a sympathetic spirit in the Principal, the Revd. E. C. S. Gibson, who himself played an important part in the work of Prayer Book revision until his death in 1923. Their regard for one another was considerable: Gibson thought Frere 'the most brilliant and polished scholar I have ever had the privilege to train',[2] and he frequently turned to him in later days for criticism and advice on revision matters.

Frere's notebooks show that he prepared himself for his liturgical studies by mastering the details of the Reformation in England, of which the Prayer Book was the child.[3] Once this was achieved, he soon bit deep into his subject and the first-fruits of his labours appeared in 1894—*The Winchester Troper* and the first volume of *The Sarum Gradual*. By the time his edition of Proctor's *History of the Book of Common Prayer* was published in 1902, his reputation as a liturgical scholar was established. This was evinced in 1904, when the Royal Commission on Ecclesiastical Discipline called him as an independent witness to give evidence on historical questions connected with the rites and ceremonies of the Church.[4]

The report of the Commission was finally published on 21 June 1906, and the second of its recommendations drew an interesting letter from Frere to Dr. Gibson, now Bishop of Gloucester, who had been one of the members. The recommendation read as follows:

'Letters of Business should be issued to the Convocations with instructions: (*a*) to consider the preparation of a new rubric regulating

[1] W. H. Frere, *Some Principles of Liturgical Reform* (London, 1911), Preface, p. v.
[2] C. S. Phillips and others, *Walter Howard Frere. A Memoir* (London, 1947), p. 30.   [3] Ibid., pp. 121–2.
[4] *Report of the Royal Commission on Ecclesiastical Discipline, 1906*, Minutes or Evidence, vol. i, p. 115.

the ornaments (that is to say, the vesture) of the ministers of the Church, at the times of their ministrations, with a view to its enactment by Parliament; and (*b*) to frame, with a view to their enactment by Parliament, such modifications in the existing law relating to the ornaments and fittings of churches as may tend to secure the greater elasticity which a reasonable recognition of the comprehensiveness of the Church of England and of its present needs seems to demand.

It would be most desirable for the early dealing with these important subjects that the Convocations should sit together, and we assume that they would take counsel with the Houses of Laymen.'[1]

Frere preferred to effect changes by means of canons rather than by rubrics. The action of lawyers had changed the whole significance of the latter; 'originally the most elastic of things', the rubric had become 'the most rigid'. As he emphasized in great detail a few years later in his *Principles of Liturgical Reform*, the rubric was, correctly, not directive but suggestive—a reminder concerning some point of law or custom.[2] Abandoning any hope of getting lawyers to see the meaning of rubrics in their original sense, he felt that it was best to regulate worship by means of the regular pre-Reformation method. In the present circumstances the most hopeful means of procedure, although by no means the best, was to secure the enactment of certain rubrics which would in themselves give a loophole for procedure by canon. This would, however, ensure that details of worship would not be debated in Parliament, for canons would only need the consent of the Crown.

Frere to the Bishop of Gloucester　　　　　　　　　　16 October 1906

My dear Bishop,

... My point about the canons is briefly this. The rubric, which was originally the most elastic of things, has now become the most rigid, because the lawyers interpret Prayer Book rubrics as if they were part of a Statute, and in the sense of the twentieth century rather than in the sense of the sixteenth or eighteenth century. Therefore merely to make fresh rubrics is to forge fresh chains for ourselves and our successors; for we shall never get the lawyers to take a different view of the matter so long as we are under an Act of Uniformity at all. At every opportunity therefore, I think we must proceed along some other line, which extracts our rules to a large extent from the stiffness of civil law. Procedure by canon I think meets this need. It is in fact ideally more satis-

---

[1] *Report of the Royal Commission on Ecclesiastical Discipline, 1906*, Report, p. 77.
[2] *Some Principles of Liturgical Reform*, p. 105.

factory that worship should be governed by canon and modified from time to time by canon. It emphasizes the right relation between Church and State, because the canons will not require Parliamentary sanction but only the sanction of the Crown. At the same time it is clear that since the rubrics have statutory authority, nothing can take their place except something which has equal authority: in other words, if we are to proceed by canon, Parliament must give us leave to proceed by canon, and say that it is prepared to treat our canons as modifications of the rubric under the Act of Uniformity.

It seems to me then that there are three possibilities.

(a) An Act of Parliament to say that the Church may proceed from time to time by canon to reform and alter the rubrics, and that such alteration shall have the force of law on receiving the royal assent. This is probably more than Parliament would ever assent to; therefore

(b) An Act of Parliament to say that certain scheduled rubrics may be amended by canon, delimiting a certain field in which the Church is allowed its freedom. If this is also more than Parliament is likely to grant because it does not know exactly what is going to take place, there is the alternative

(c) To enact certain rubrics which should in themselves give a loophole for procedure by canon. For example, to re-enact the Ornaments Rubric with an addition saying, 'or such ornaments as shall from time to time be defined by canon'; to add to the rubric about the Athanasian Creed 'or otherwise as shall be decided by canon'; to add somewhere at the end of Morning Service a rubric to say 'that such combination of Morning Prayer, Litany, and Holy Communion shall be considered allowable as Convocation may hereafter by canon determine'. The same sort of loophole may be made in a good many places. The Church would still be under rubrics which had their binding character under an Act of Uniformity, but there would be secured by the rubric a certain measure of liberty. This seems to me the most hopeful of the three, though not the most desirable.

In favour of this procedure, I think, is the fact which everyone feels— that it would be simply impossible to have the details of public worship discussed in full on the floor of the House of Commons. In some form or other that must be avoided. If detailed rubrics containing these new provisions were presented to Parliament, it is to my mind inconceivable that Parliament would not discuss them. Even though it did not and the rubrics as now amended went through, we should very soon find ourselves in exactly the same difficulty; because further amendments will be wanted and there will have to be the same recourse to Parliament. Whereas if the liberty is given to proceed by canon, it is given once for all, and so long as we are established the canonical procedure will be available. For example, in the case of the Ornaments Rubric it will be far better not to have to decide at once and with finality as to certain of the points involved. After ten years' time Convocation will much more seriously decide some of the points, or it can leave others to be decided as they are raised, if it has perpetually running the power to proceed by canon.

The vexed question of the censer might simply be avoided for the present. Convocation might simply leave it out; might simply define at the moment the most pressing points as regards ornaments, leaving the rest to be raised later as occasion demanded. This would give breathing space, much to be desired at the present time, and prevent us from arriving at hasty decisions: while at the same time it would retain for the Church the possibility of altering its decisions which needed to be considered, modified, or added to.

It should be emphasized, of course, that the canons would be inoperative without the sanction of the Crown; that is to say, that the State as represented by the Prime Minister or Cabinet would practically have a veto on anything that Convocation did. It can hardly be said therefore that the Church would be acquiring a dangerous licence. Its liberties would still be hemmed in by Letters of Business on the one hand and the assent to canons on the other. In fact this measure of liberty is really a very small one to ask for. I doubt whether we shall ever get more as long as we are established, but I do hope we might get this.

In the following year Frere was consulted by the Bishop of Lichfield, Dr. Legge, on behalf of the Upper House of the Convocation of Canterbury. A Committee of that House had been appointed to discuss the subject of the Daily Offices. Its Report was confidential and was never published; consequently it was probably discussed by the House 'in Committee', no record of the debate being printed or kept. Frere's Memoranda on permitted abbreviations of the existing order and alternative forms of service are therefore valuable evidence as to the scope and nature of the Committee's work. They are also of interest as being his earliest recorded views on Prayer Book revision. That the Bishops

Early Days

thought fit to consult him on these matters indicates his established reputation as a liturgical scholar.

Frere to the Bishop of Lichfield   4 *July* 1907

My dear Lord Bishop,

Will you allow me to put down some of the suggestions which I ventured to bring up, I fear in a very confused form, the other day?

It is advisable, I think, that in the case both of Morning and Evening Service, there should be

(a) Permissive abbreviations of the existing Order.
(b) An alternative Service; perhaps also it is advisable
(c) To have some abbreviation made once for all, and not merely permissive.

Under heading (a) I should suggest as follows:

1. The 'Dearly Beloved' at Morning Service to be omitted on all weekdays provided it is said once on a Sunday. Or it might be better to make this not permissive, but merely prescribe 'Dearly Beloved' at Sunday Evensong.

2. I don't favour any alternative form of Confession and Absolution nor any abbreviation of these.

3. The Lord's Prayer following might be omitted by permission; or I would *rather* take it out altogether in view of the fact that its proper place is after the Creed as the climax of the Service. Its position at the beginning had a meaning once when it was a private prayer introductory to the service, but it has long lost that meaning and I would far rather see it disappear altogether from this position.

4. As regards the Venite I should suggest its curtailment—permissive, or, as I should prefer, compulsory, by the omission of the closing verses. I should also suggest that a hymn may be used as an alternative to the Venite between Advent and the octave of the Epiphany, between Septuagesima and Trinity Sunday, and on all Red Letter Days. This would give an opportunity for striking the special note of the service by a hymn at the beginning of the service. I would on the same ground make special permission for the permissive use of the hymn in the same position at Evensong.

5. As regards Canticles I do not suppose it would be wise to make much change at the present moment for such special occasions as Holy Week; but I think it might be well that a Penitential Canticle should be given as an alternative to the Te Deum and Benedicite, as, for example, the Song of Hezekiah or one of the Penitential Psalms.

6. I think it would be well to make the Athanasian Creed an addition to the service on the days when it is used; not an alternative to the Apostles' Creed but a Canticle to be sung or said before it. This would simply be a return to previous use from 1549–1662. If this were at all likely to be a permanent arrangement, I should suggest that on these days the Canticle took the place of the Benedictus. But I don't think it would be that at all, but merely a stage towards the disappearance of the Quicunque from use in popular services. I am assuming in this view that it retains its usual form. If it were found possible to remove the clauses objected to or the framework of anathema (which seems to be the most hopeful way of dealing with the matter), I should like then definitely to prescribe it as an alternative to the Benedictus, and get rid of the psalm which is at present the alternative.

7. I think it might be well to provide a Collect to be used on Black Letter Saints' Days, or at any rate to authorize the use of the All Saints Collect with the insertion of a special saint's name; but it is rather by the way.

8. As regards the five prayers, I think they might well be reduced to four by making the first two coalesce more or less, and this section of the Service with Occasional Prayers and Thanksgivings might be a good deal enriched by additional forms for various needs of the Church—all optional in their use except those that belong to special seasons and occasions, such as the Ember Prayer, Rogation Prayer, or perhaps the Prayer for Parliament. Personally I would sooner that the Prayer for Parliament was transposed into a prayer for all sorts of governing bodies, County Councils, and Parliaments in the Colonies as well as our own, and that its use was purely optional like the rest and not confined to the particular times when our own particular Parliament is sitting. This collection of intercession and thanksgiving would then be available for use with the Litany.

9. As regards the Litany, I should suggest that the Amen be added before 'O Lord, arise, help us', and that should be the usual close of the Litany with St. Chrysostom and the Grace to follow; the omitted part being preserved as an intercession in time of trouble and placed with the other intercessions and thanksgivings, provision being made that this should be used as desired in conjunction either with the Litany or on other days with the prayers after the anthem.

So much then as regards the normal form of Morning Prayer, and the same thing really concerns Evening Prayer.

Early Days

Under heading (*b*) I should provide three alternative schemes of service.

1. A compressed form of Morning Service to take the place of Morning Prayer and Litany in their full forms when they immediately precede a celebration of Holy Communion. This therefore would be available for use on Sundays, Wednesdays, and Fridays. It should, I think, be made clear that it is an *Alternative Service*, and is to be used in its entirety and without further additions: that is to say, it is not a minimum form of service towards which others may approximate, but a form of service which people may take or leave as it is. If they do not use it, their alternative is to use the full service (with such abbreviations as shall there be expressly permitted). Unless this is made clear, everybody will make their own selections from the materials and there will be something like chaos. For this service I would prescribe as follows: Begin with 'O Lord, open thou our lips' and go on as at Morning Prayer to the end of the Benedictus (or other equivalent). Then I should suggest, though with less confidence, the use of 'The Lord be with you' followed by the Lord's Prayer, the versicles, and the third Collect. Then should follow the Litany (or it might be attached directly to the Benedictus, though not I think so suitably); in this way a shorter number of clauses should be provided, having regard to the intercession which is going to follow in the Communion Service in the Prayer for the Church Militant: it should end with the Lesser Litany 'Lord have mercy upon us, Christ have mercy upon us, Lord have mercy upon us', and its petitions should be taken also as the equivalent to the Kyrie at the beginning of the Communion Office; so that as soon as they have been sung, the celebrant would say the Collect for the day and then proceed to the Epistle and Gospel.

There is plenty of precedent for this combination of Litany with the Communion Service, and it has immense practical advantages, I think. The Lord's Prayer will then be used twice only in the Morning Service, one Creed will be said, the Prayer for the King will be reduced, and the special intercessions will not be so much duplicated. This ought to provide a short form of service taking from an hour to an hour and a quarter without sacrificing anything except repetitions.

2 and 3. As alternative forms for evening use, it would be well, I think, to provide a service on the lines of the ancient Vespers with the psalms in order and the Magnificat as a single canticle; and a service on the lines of Compline with fixed psalms, having the Nunc dimittis as its fixed canticle. These should be alternatives, either of which might be

used as well as Evensong. I don't think it would be necessary to follow rigidly the order of service in the old Latin Service. The saying of the psalms, of course, would go on at Evensong, or, if preferred, at the Vesper Service. The saying of fixed psalms would be the peculiarity of the Compline Service. At the same time, I should provide several sets of psalms which might be substituted for the ordinary psalms of the day either at Morning Prayer or at Evening Prayer. The American sets seem to me very good. I think this would meet most of the cases, and would provide for the orderly reading of the psalms, to which we are pledged by the Preface, but yet allow some deviation from its rigidity when occasion demanded it.

As regards lessons there would be no alteration practically. The ordinary lessons would be read at full Evensong if the full Service was used, and then at the additional Service for the Short Evensong or the Compline Service any other lesson may be read. On the other hand, if the two shorter Services were used instead of the one full one, one lesson of the Lectionary should be read at each. It seems to me very important to preserve in all ways the continuity of psalm singing and Bible reading. The Shortened Services Act did immense harm and was violently contradictory to the whole spirit of the Prayer Book Services in interrupting this orderly method. I hope no arrangements will now be made to disturb that, beyond such a small thing as I have suggested, namely, the provision of one or two alternative sets of psalms. It would indeed be well if a revision of the Prayer Book now included the repeal of the Shortened Services Act.

. . . I hope I am not troubling you overmuch with all this. My only desire is to lighten your labours if it may be so; and if this is really troublesome please put it all into the waste-paper basket. . . .

At the same time Frere was being consulted on the subject of Vestments. In February 1907 a Sub-committee of the Upper House was appointed to draw up an historical memorandum on the Ornaments of the Church and its Ministers. It was composed of Dr. John Wordsworth, Bishop of Salisbury, who was Chairman; Dr. Browne, Bishop of Bristol; Dr. Robertson, Bishop of Exeter; Dr. Gibson, Bishop of Gloucester; and Dr. Chase, Bishop of Ely. They met four times and at the end of June drew up a Draft Report, *Draft Report on the Ornaments of the Ministers*, no. 416, which was submitted to a few experts for criticism before being presented to the whole House. This Draft was of some eighty-eight pages, containing three chapters and an appendix. The first chapter was an historical sketch of the origin, development, and sym-

Early Days

bolism of liturgical costume; the second dealt with the Ornaments Rubric; the third with the ornaments of a bishop of the Church of England; and the appendix discussed the term 'Vestment'. The Bishop of Gloucester wrote to Frere on 6 July asking for his views on their work; Frere's reply was both lengthy and valuable. His main criticism was connected with pages 49 to 51 on 'Subsidiary Ornaments in the Church' from which the following is an extract:

Ornaments that are subsidiary. It has been decided in Liddell *v.* Westerton that some articles not expressly mentioned in the Rubric but subsidiary to the service are permissible. (See Moore's *Special Report*, p. 156, and Brooke's *Six Privy Council Judgements*, p. 74.) Under this head, organs, hassocks, &c., are allowed. But how far does this principle carry us? That any 'ornament' or article made use of must be honestly subsidiary to the service, and not used to introduce a ceremony not provided for in the book, would seem to follow not only from the words of the Act of Uniformity, but also from the following facts.

1. The Preface of the Book of 1549 contained the following clause (only omitted in 1662): 'Furthermore by this Order the Curates shall need none other books for their public service but this book and the Bible, by the means whereof, the people shall not be at so great charge for books, as in time past they have been.' This seems to prohibit the use of any ornament accompanied by a form of words not found in the Prayer Book, since otherwise some other book beside the Bible and Prayer Book would be needed.

2. By 3 and 4 Edward VI, cap. 10, the possession of any of the ancient service books was forbidden, the books themselves being ordered to be recalled, defaced, and destroyed. Clearly, then, the use of 'ornaments' for the regulation of which any of these books was required was prohibited.

The bearing of these two considerations on the use of such ornaments as the censer, the bason for washing the priest's hands, the sacring bell, the processional cross, and other ornaments which were certainly in use up to 1549, and are not in so many words prohibited in the Rubrics of the Book of Common Prayer is obvious.

(a) *The Censer.* The fumigatory use of incense outside the service was by no means uncommon in the seventeenth century. There are, for instance, the well-known notices of it in Herbert's *Country Parson*, chap. xiii, and Evelyn's *Diary* (Easter Day 1684). It was thus used not only on great festivals to sweeten the Church but also on other occasions, when the Church had been rendered insanitary, from funerals or other causes (see the examples in *The Case for Incense*, p. 159). With such use the Ornaments Rubric has nothing whatever to do. With regard to the ceremonial use of the censer during the service it may be noted that, according to the *Sarum Missal*, incense was used at the Introit (*Miss. Sar.* 581, ed. Dickinson), at the Gospel (*ibid.* 592), and at the Offertory (*ibid.* 593), and on two out of these three occasions certain words were to be said in connexion with its use. Since no directions for the use of such words or for censing are contained in the English Prayer Book, it is evident that for the use of the censer at these points of the service reference would have to be made to disused service books such as the *Sarum Missal*, which, as we have seen, were not needed by the curate, and were ordered to be destroyed. It would appear, therefore, that the censer is not a legal ornament of the Church. Against this conclusion (which is strengthened by the fact that censers are not seldom mentioned as 'monuments of superstition' to be destroyed, in episcopal Injunctions and Articles), there is very little to be said save the fact that a censer was included in the furniture of Bishop Andrewes' Chapel, and according to Prynne was used 'at the reading of the First Lesson' (*Canterbury's Doom*, p. 122); there was also one in Cosin's Chapel at Peterhouse (ibid., p. 73), and there was some use of incense before the actual service began at the dedication of an altar at Wolverhampton in 1635, where 'was incense burning which perfumed the whole Church', and the clergy are said to have come in, every one of them with 'a paper in his hand, which they termed a censer, and so they went up to the altar, reading it as they went, for they looked often on it' ('A Quench Coal', quoted in *The Case for Incense*, p. 163). There is also the solitary case of the Bodmin Inventory in 1566, where a censer is included among the goods and ornaments 'to be used and occupied to the honour of God in the same Church'. (See *The Case for Incense*, p. 157, and cf. *The Case against Incense*, p. 71.)

(*b*) *The Bason for washing of the priest's hands*. The use of this was ordered by the ancient service books, which contained words to be used by the priest at the time of the washing of the hands (*Miss. Sar.* 594). Since no directions for this were contained in the English Prayer Book of 1549 (or in any subsequent book), it is obvious that if it is used now recourse must be had to some other book than the Book of Common Prayer; consequently the considerations urged above would seem to show that it is not a legal ornament. There is, however, some evidence of a limited use of it being made in the seventeenth century, viz. by Bishop Andrewes in his chapel (*Minor Works*, p. 156; cf. *Canterbury's Doom*, p. 123), and at the consecration by him of Jesus Chapel, Southampton, 1620 (Sparrow's *Collection*, p. 395; Harington's *On Consecration of Churches*, p. 168, 1844), and at the consecration of an altar at Wolverhampton in 1635 ('A Quench Coal' quoted *Hierurgia*, vol. ii, p. 178).

(*c*) *The Sacring Bell*. There are no directions for the use of this in any of the English Prayer Books, and consequently, on the principles

Early Days

stated above, its use at the Sanctus or Consecration would seem to be excluded. It was treated as a 'monument of superstition' in Elizabeth's reign, and questions as to its destruction are sometimes found among Visitation Articles (e.g. Grindal's for York in 1571, Aylmer's 1577, and Sandys' 1578: see *Report of Ritual Commission*, pp. 408, 418, 423). A hand bell is, however, mentioned in the Bodmin Inventory of 1566 (see above); and the 'ringing of hand bells in many places' is mentioned among the 'points of Popery' remaining in the Church of England in a Puritan complaint in Elizabeth's reign (quoted *Hierurgia*, vol. i, p. 259).

(*d*) *The Processional Cross*. If this is simply carried at the head of the procession on entry into or departure from the Church, its use would seem to be neither more nor less illegal than the wands of churchwardens, or the verges carried before bishops, deans, and other dignitaries in Cathedral churches.

Frere declared the principle of 'Omission is prohibition' to be fallacious and defended the appeal to tradition. His comments were largely concerned with a defence of the use of incense. 'I am not arguing that the Prayer Book postulates incense; I am only arguing that it is impossible to disprove the admissibility of incense from Prayer Book rubrics.... On no grounds is it likely that provisions about incense would be found in the Prayer Book rubrics, and therefore their absence proves nothing.'

Frere to the Bishop of Gloucester   22 *July* 1907

My dear Bishop,

Many thanks for your letter and the draft Report. I have been looking carefully at some points in connexion with it, and have one or two suggestions to make; and in particular I want, if I may, to call your attention to certain passages connected with pages 49–51, which seem to me quite unworthy of the rest of the Report, and likely to do serious harm....

Pages 49–51. The whole of this argument reads to me like a piece out of a Privy Council Judgement—full of legal subtlety but destitute of any real knowledge of the matter in hand. It is only in another form the old dictum 'omission is prohibition'; and it rests, I think, upon three fundamental fallacies, which, if you will allow me, I will set out briefly.

1. There is no sign of any consciousness of the distinction in importance between the private prayers of the celebrant and the public

prayers. As you know very well, in some later missals for convenience sake such private prayers were inserted, though not by any means in all. The whole of these were omitted in the Prayer Book. Their presence or absence is of no special significance, and nothing can be argued from their absence. They surround other matters besides the incense and the washing of hands: there is, for example, the blessing of the deacon and the reading of the Gospel. If they are omitted in connexion with the incense, for which no rubrical direction is given, they are omitted also in connexion with the Gospel, which is retained, and with the Oblation, which in some form is equally necessitated. Their omission therefore in the Prayer Book is non-significant.

2. The passage leaves the whole matter of tradition out of account. It may be true that the first Prayer Book was meant to supersede a necessity to any further book, but it was not meant to be self-sufficient or to supersede tradition. It expressly postulated the existence of the tradition where its own influences were insufficient. The arguments one and two of page 49 are therefore to my mind quite unsound. The Edwardian priest was absolutely dependent upon tradition for many things that he was obliged to do, and the Prayer Book encouraged him in being so. He could not have gone through a service without it. And are we seriously to suppose that the Prayer Book forbade him to say private prayers because it no longer printed the ones which he had been accustomed to say before the service and at various points through it? If you rest your case upon the connexion of the ornaments with the form of words, which I contend to be invalid, the case not only breaks down at that point, but at this point too. The priest was confessedly to do many things according to tradition; it cannot be said, therefore, that the absence of directions in the rubric in itself prohibited him from swinging a censer in the usual way and saying his usual private prayers over it.

3. The argument fails because it is based on a misconception of rubric. Rubric has never been a complete directory: it was not so in medieval days, still less was it in the first Prayer Book, or indeed in any subsequent Prayer Book. The rubrics of the first Prayer Book do little else but direct in some particular points where changes are to be made in the usual custom. They least of all therefore can be said to be complete.

Paragraph (a) about the censer recalls to me a part of Dibden's speech at Lambeth which I thought at the time, and think more clearly since, as being unworthy either of his learning or of his candour. Did he know

Early Days 15

the condition of rubrics with regard to incense in medieval services? If so, it was unfair of him merely to cite the Sarum Book. If he knew of no other than the Sarum Book, then he was arguing from very insufficient premises, considering the position in other and more normal medieval service books; for Sarum was exceptional in the fullness of its rubrics, and indeed many English books were exceptional in that they contemplated the full ceremonial which was customary in great churches, rather than, like the Prayer Book, the minimum ceremonial which was to be used everywhere. Rubric being then of this character, to argue in any sense as to the disparity between the medieval rubric of English books in their fullness and the rubric of the Prayer Book in its meagreness is entirely misleading.

But further, what is the effect of this sort of argument in connexion with the York Missal?

(a) At York there is no prayer or blessing of incense at the Introit: there happens to be a word or two of rubric to say that the priest is to cense the altar.
(b) At the Gospel no mention of either lights or incense.
(c) The acolyte censes the choir at the Creed, but there is no incense mentioned at the oblation.

The first argument will be therefore—as there are no formulas of blessing incense there can be no blessing of incense: which doubtless is untrue. Secondly, as there is incense expressly mentioned only at the Introit and Creed there is none to be used at the Gospel and Offertory: which again no doubt is untrue. Further, as regards lights, there is no mention of portable lights at all, therefore there were none: which also is untrue.

Take Hereford: no mention of incense at the Introit at all nor at the Offertory. At the Gospel the deacon is ordered to cense only the middle of the altar and not the lectern. There is no mention of lights. In other words the Hereford Book, like the Prayer Book, only thinks it worth while to insert a rubric where it does something unusual. At Westminster no mention of incense at all: Westminster therefore and the Prayer Book are on the same lines. But what is sauce for the goose is sauce for the gander so far as the bare contents of the rubric are concerned; and if that is what you are going to judge by, you cannot make any distinction between them.

Now let me try and make my point quite clear. I am not arguing that the Prayer Book postulates incense; I am only arguing that it is impossible to disprove the admissibility of incense from Prayer Book rubrics. If I wished to prove that incense had been abolished at the Reformation, I should be very sorry to stake my contention on such a weak line of argument as this seems to be. I cordially agree that you cannot say that the Ornaments Rubric authorizes the use of incense; therefore what remains? Surely the true position is this, that the case so far as rubric goes is not proven; there is no rubric enjoining it, there is none forbidding it. Its admissibility or the contrary must be determined by other considerations. If its omission from the medieval rubrics did not mean that it was not to be in use, still less does its omission from the Prayer Book rubrics mean this; for medieval rubric was always permissive, while the rubric of the Prayer Book is, so far as it goes, mandative. The pre-Reformation service book told you, roughly speaking, the bulk of what went on in a big church and left you to adapt your own usages to it. The Prayer Book rubric told you what must go on everywhere and its provisions are a minimum which could be enforced at law. If then the authors of the Prayer Book had wished deliberately to maintain the use of incense in certain places, I still conceive they would not have put it in the rubric, because they could not have put it there unless they meant to insist upon it everywhere, which no one would have supposed to have been the case. In other words, this is a case where the argument *ex silentio* is particularly dangerous, as on no grounds is it likely that provisions about incense would be found in the Prayer Book rubrics, and therefore their absence proves nothing. Surely the only appropriate conclusion to be drawn, as well as the most politic one, is that incense is a matter neither forbidden nor enjoined. It cannot therefore be claimed as essential by clergy, since they have no rubric to back them (such as is claimed in the matter of vestments), nor can it be said that the use of it is contrary to the rubrics: in other words, the bishop may give leave for it or he may not.

To come to further points on page 50. There are instances of the retention of censers after the monuments of superstition had disappeared in 1559. Like other things of the same sort from the point of view of 1559, they were things which might be destroyed as superstitious in one place, but retained elsewhere in the hope of a reaction which might bring them into use again. That is why they, like the chasubles, did not all disappear at one point in 1559, but kept dropping out during the first ten years of Elizabeth's reign as it became more and more clear that such things were not going to be used in practice, though people had cherished hopes that they would be retained. It should be mentioned, I think, that Bishop Andrewes consecrated a

Early Days

censer for Worcester Cathedral. His use of it was no hole-and-corner affair, but his form of consecration of church plate was current among people interested in such things. The censer in the Bodmin Inventory of 1556 is not solitary, strictly speaking, because there are cases also in the Lincoln Inventories of the censer remaining and it was only by degrees they disappeared.

Paragraph (b). What I have said about the connexion with the priest's private prayers above applies here. The hand washing did not depend upon the fact that this or that particular prayer was inserted or was omitted in late missals. The prayers disappeared in the Prayer Book as all the other priest's private prayers did, but their disappearance in itself has no special significance. I think with regard to this and the proceeding, the value of the evidence of the Caroline Divines is very much understated and undervalued. If you consider how very little there is of any sort about ceremonial things, the amount that we can know about the Caroline practice is really remarkable, and it seems clear to me that Andrewes did not by any means stand alone. We know that he was a leader and that others modelled themselves upon him, that Laud followed his liturgical arrangements and again was a leader of men. The half dozen instances or so that may be amassed really represent, I have no doubt, a widespread practice on the part of humbler people whose records are unknown: indeed the Puritans would not have troubled themselves to make all the fuss they did unless it had been so.

Paragraph (c). The Sacring Bell. There are no directions for this as far as I know in any of the missals; therefore by this argument its use would seem to be excluded before the Reformation as well as after, which is absurd. Its use, of course, depended not at all upon rubric, but upon the orders of bishops and their councils from 1240 onwards. This is a further warning as to the dangers of arguing from rubric.

In all that I have said I do not at all mean to contend that it is reasonable to suppose that early Elizabethan bishops would for a moment have sanctioned incense: I am quite convinced that they would not. That is quite a different thing from saying that if they had wanted to, or if the temper of the day had made it desirable, they would have been precluded from doing so. My whole point is that the question is an open question, which the early Elizabethan bishops would have decided in the negative, but on which bishops in the present time, I am perfectly confident, can equally decide the other way if they think fit; and all these attempts to prove such points to be excluded by the rubric are bound to fail. They all rest upon some form of the dogma 'omission is prohibition', which dogma is quite inconsistent with known facts. I hope very much some modification may be made of this, otherwise I am sure it will damage the Report as a whole.

Frere then went on to criticize the section of the Report which attempted to define the meaning of 'Ornaments', using as authorities the Privy Council Judgement in the Liddell *v.* Westerton case and Forcellini's *Latin Dictionary*. He was prepared to accept neither: the Privy Council had made a pathetic attempt to define what they did not understand by referring to an ordinary Latin dictionary, instead of seeking the use of the word in technical liturgical language. The relevant passage in the Report read:

Definition of 'Ornaments' (pp. 40–41)

In the judgement of the Judicial Committee of the Privy Council in Liddell *v.* Westerton a distinction is drawn between 'ornaments' and 'decorations or embellishments', and it is laid down that 'the word "ornaments" applies, and in this Rubric is confined, to those articles the use of which, in the service and ministrations of the Church, is prescribed by the Prayer Book of Edward VI (Moore's *Special Report*, p. 156; Brooke's *Six Privy Council Judgements*, p. 51)'.

For this reference is made to Forcellini's *Dictionary*, the word *ornamentum* being there said to be used *pro quocumque apparatu seu implemento*, ibid. Reference should also be made to Durandus, *Rat*, lib. i, c. 3, 'De picturis et cortinis et ornamentis ecclesiae', and lib. iii, 'De indumentis seu ornamentis ecclesiae, sacerdotum atque pontificum, et aliorum ministrorum', and to Lyndwood, *Provinciale*, lib. 1, tit. 10.

It is further said in the judgement in Liddell *v.* Westerton that the word 'ornaments' in the Rubric 'is confined to such things as in the performance of the services the Minister was to use. . . . The Rubric to the Prayer Book of 1 January 1604 adopts the language of the Rubric of Elizabeth. The Rubric to the present Prayer Book adopts the language of the Statute of Elizabeth, but they all obviously mean the same thing, that the same dresses and the same utensils or articles which were used under the First Prayer Book of Edward VI may still be used. None of them therefore can have any reference to articles not used in the services, but set up in churches as ornaments, in the sense of decorations. . . . Their Lordships therefore are of opinion that although the Rubric excluded all use of crosses in the services, the general question of crosses not used in the services, but employed only as decorations of churches, is entirely unaffected by the Rubric.' (Brooke, pp. 53, 55.)

If the distinction is strictly to be observed, candles standing upon the altar or superaltar, whether lighted or unlighted, would not be 'ornaments' any more than altar crosses or vases; but if the lighting were to take place during the time of service, or if they were carried about, being thus actually used in the service, they would become 'ornaments', and the question of their legality would come into consideration under this Rubric.

Frere wrote of this:

It seems to me undesirable to put into the foreground the Privy Council's distinction in Liddell *v*. Westerton. It was no doubt a pathetic attempt to define what they did not understand by a reference to a dictionary, of all places—an ordinary Latin dictionary. I wonder that the lawyers are so pleased with it as they are. Of course the only real way to arrive at the meaning of the word 'ornament' is to do as the Report does and consider its use in technical liturgical language. Would it not be better first to do this, and then merely to allude to the Judicial Committee's attempt by the way? A proper definition of ornament drawn from liturgists—Lyndwood and contemporary usage—would be of real value, and to do this is far more consonant with what the Report does elsewhere than to revive legal dicta which had better be buried. Should it not be treated as you are treating the word 'vestment', as one into which a proper historical inquiry is to be made with a view to establishing its exact meaning?

Finally he dealt with the following Appendix:

On the Meaning of the Term 'Vestment'

It is commonly assumed that the term 'vestment' in the Ornaments Rubric of 1549, so frequently referred to in the Report, means a chasuble with its appurtenances, i.e. with amice, stole, and maniple or fanon; but this seems uncertain. The word 'vestment' is variously used, and sometimes it is used comprehensively for a whole set or suit, including more than the chasuble, amice, stole and fanon; e.g. in a constitution of Archbishop Gray of York (1250) we read, 'Vestimentum ipsius ecclesiae principale, videlicet casula, alba munda, amictus, stola, manipulus, zona, cum tribus tuellis; corporalia et alia vestimenta pro diacono honesta, juxta facultates parochianorum et ecclesiae; cum cappa serica principali, pro principalibus festis; et cum duabus aliis, pro choris regendis in festis supradictis'. It may be doubtful how far *videlicet* in this passage extends, but at any rate the alb is included under the term, and possibly the whole set of 'ornaments'. Again, in a constitution of Archbishop Winchelsea (1350) we have, 'Vestimentum principale cum casula, dalmatica, tunica, et cum cappa in choro cum omnibus suis appendiciis, frontale ad magnum altare cum tribus tuellis, tria superpellicia, unum rochetum', &c., where again it may be doubtful how much the word is intended to cover. On this passage the gloss in Lyndwood should be noted: 'Appendiciis sc. amictibus, albis cingulis, manipulis, et stolis' (*Prov.*, p. 250), where *albis cingulis* should probably be *albis, cingulis*, as the alb is not elsewhere mentioned (cf. Bonner's Articles given below). In Bonner's Articles of Visitation (1554) we have a 'principal vestment with chasuble, a vestment for the deacon and subdeacon, a cope with the appurtenances, that is to wit, an amice, albe, girdle, stole, and fanon, the high altar with apparel in the front and other parts thereof, three towels, three surplices, a rochet', &c., where he seems generally to be following Winchelsea with the gloss in Lyndwood (Cardwell, *Doc. Annals*, vol. i, p. 151). Other instances, given in *Essays on Ceremonial*, De la Mare Press, 1904, p. 246, are these: 'Item a red vestment, embroidered with lions of gold, of red satin; that is to say, a chasuble and a tunicle to the same, with two albs, two amices, two stoles, two fanons, and two girdles lately mended, and a cope thereto powdered with lions' (St. Mary-at-Hill, London, 1486). 'Item, unum vestimentum rubeum de velveto, texto cum imaginibus pondratis cum perlis: viz. cum una casula, duabus tunicis, tribus albis, tribus amictibus, cum stolis et fanonibus pertinentibus eidem, cum una bona capa ejusdem secta (?) et duabus aliis capis quasi ejusdem operis sed sine perlis, cum altari de eadem secta, et ridellio de sindone rubea' (St. George's College, Windsor, 8 Ric. II).

This comprehensive use of the word is well established; but it cannot be the use in the rubric, because the alb is mentioned separately, and the cope is given as an alternative for the 'vestment'. If then the term includes anything more than the chasuble it can only be the amice, stole, and fanon: and it is asserted that this meaning of the term is very common, as well as a use including the *alb* in addition. The instances, however, cited in *Essays on Ceremonial*, page 246, scarcely bear out this statement, as in all of them the word would seem to be actually a convertible term for chasuble. Thus in the first example given, 'Item six vestments with their albs and all other things pertaining thereto', the word 'chasubles' might well be substituted for 'vestments'.
So also in the following:

'A vestment of purple velvet, with the alb and all thereto belonging.'

'Item ii. vestments with albs. Item ii. without albs.'

'Item i. vestment of blue bawdkyn and red, with lilies, and a corporas of the same, lacking stole and fanon.'

None of these examples, except perhaps the last, really illustrate the use of the word in the Rubric, and it does not seem to be established

Early Days

that 'vestment' with 'alb' mentioned separately, and 'cope' given as an alternative, in a document with the precision and directive force of a rubric, means more than the actual chasuble. If it is taken to mean chasuble, amice, stole, and fanon, then cope must be given the same extended meaning, and be taken to signify 'cope with the appurtenances'. But no notices of the use of amice, stole, or fanon under the first Prayer Book of Edward VI, or in the reign of Elizabeth, have been produced; and had these articles been actually used it is improbable that they would have escaped the notice of the Puritans. The grey almuce, which had been dropped on the appearance of the first Prayer Book of Edward VI (Wriothesley's *Chronicle*, vol. ii, p. 16; Grey Friars' *Chronicle*, p. 59), and the use of which had been to some extent revived in Elizabeth's reign, was vehemently objected to, being regarded as one of the 'grosse points of popery evident to all men in the Church of England'; and, if the use of this, which had no doctrinal significance, was attacked by the Puritans, would they have failed to animadvert on the use of amice, stole, and fanon, had such use existed, when the cope was worn? It should also be noticed that Archbishop Harsnett and Bishop Creighton are not represented in their monuments with these ornaments, though they have a cope, alb, mitre, and pastoral staff.

Of this Appendix Frere wrote:

May I say I think it is possible to arrive at something more definite than you have. No doubt the use of the word is very varied.
    (a) It is like the word 'suit' as implying a whole set of vestments for three ministers or for two.
    (b) It is used as meaning a chasuble with or without the appurtenances. Sometimes the alb is expressly mentioned as being there or being not there; sometimes there is mention that the appurtenances are wanting. . . . In Bishop Barnes's *Ecclesiastical Proceedings*, Surtees Society, vol. 2 . . . in the Appendix No. 2, I struck on a set of inventories which illustrated these usages: 'vestment' with the alb mentioned; 'vestment' with the alb expressly excluded; 'vestment with the appurtenances'; 'vestment lacking all things belonging thereto'; and 'vestment' without any qualification.

The appurtenances I think no doubt are amice, girdle, alb, stole, and fanon. This satisfies all the varying uses, describing the garments for one single person and not three ministers. If you wished to be more precise you might mention the presence or absence of any particular one of the appurtenances. In the rubric it was desirable to mention the alb if for no other reason in order to give it its two adjectives.

 . . . There ought to be a comma after 'cope' I am certain.[1] The appurtenances referred as always to the group of minor things belonging to the set of 'vestment' which are quite rightly defined as being amice, alb, girdle, stole, and fanon. I don't think there is much doubt that both Winchelsea's and Bonner's definition of the vestments ends with *appenditiae* and fanon, i.e. a list of the appurtenances in the English. A cope standing by itself has no appurtenances; at least I cannot find any instance of one. The term 'vestment' in the larger sense (meaning a suit for the three ministers, and a cope as a processional alternative to the chasuble for the celebrant) or in the more restricted sense (meaning the complete dress of the celebrant) constantly has the phrase 'with appurtenances'. If anyone questions this definition I should merely ask him to prove, if he can, the use of a chasuble and alb without amice, stole, girdle, and fanon. I have never come across the smallest intimation that such a combination was in use. Underlying all the superficial differences of definition there is one unchanging custom and this is decisive as to what is meant. The latter part of [the Appendix] seems to me to be written under a misapprehension. No one would be found objecting to the use of amice, stole, and fanon, simply because they were included in 'vestment'. They were not worn with cope but only with chasuble (except possibly in pre-Reformation days the stole) and they probably disappeared in exactly the same degree as the chasuble disappeared.

With regard to that point I should be sorry to say as clearly as is said on page 54 that there is no trace of the chasuble in Elizabeth's reign. There are phrases in Puritan correspondence I think which (I quite agree) are probably exaggerations, but which unless they are exaggerations seem to imply the use of a chasuble. There are instances also in which the chasuble is retained in Inventories. I think here and elsewhere it is important to note these instances of retention, though they are but very few. They were retained for some time and retained in some cases with sanction, because it was not clear what was going to happen; at any moment a turn in the tide might come and then without any change of law they would come back into use. It is significant that the old ornaments were still in dispute in spite of the great outburst of iconoclasm at the beginning of the reign. This is strong proof that they were legal; as Parker said very accurately: 'They serve not to use at

---

[1] 'Cope with the appurtenances.'

these days.' But in some quarters there was a great reluctance to destroy them as long as there was any chance of their coming back again into use. All this I think in fairness ought to be said more clearly than is said. We are apt to look at the doings of the first ten years of Elizabeth's reign too much in the light of subsequent knowledge and too little from the point of the people who lived in it. We are apt therefore to discount rather than to emphasize every survival of those days: consequently such survivals seem to us like mere bits of folly which the whole course of history has shown to have been foolish; but to some men of the time they were legal ornaments which it seemed to be a wise thing to keep, in view of another revulsion which might come at any moment. And after all, was not the man who expected the law to be kept more within his rights than the person who expected it to be, as in fact it was, ignored?

The Official Report was finally published on 23 January 1908, and it is interesting to compare it with the Draft and note how much Frere's comments and criticisms were taken to heart.

On the section dealing with Subsidiary Ornaments the Report did not show any change of ground—the original thesis was maintained. A new section was incorporated, however, in answer to Frere's point of view. While admitting that in some minor matters such as the termination of collects some knowledge of traditional usage was presupposed, and that there were cases where the directions were obviously incomplete, it maintained that the publication of the Prayer Book in English involved a fresh start and the directions contained therein were intended to be complete. Moreover, the section 'Of ceremonies, why some be abolished and some retained' speaks only of these two classes, those abolished and those retained—a classification apparently intended to be exhaustive, leaving no room for a third class, those permitted but not enjoined.[1]

In the section on Ornaments, Frere's comments produced important modifications. All reference to Forcellini's *Dictionary* was omitted, and although Liddell *v.* Westerton was quoted, it was merely used in support of definitions drawn from the liturgists Durandus and Lyndwood.[2] Frere's advice was also taken in the Appendix and the final paragraph claiming the absence of vestments in the reign of Elizabeth was deleted, although the clear statement that there was no trace of the chasuble in Elizabeth's reign was retained on page 69.[3]

---

[1] *The Ornaments of the Church and its Ministers.* Convocation of Canterbury, Report 416 (1908), pp. 59–61.   [2] Ibid., pp. 50–51.
[3] Ibid., pp. 69, 108–9.

In 1911–12 there appeared two works which epitomized Frere's views on Prayer Book revision. The first was his book *Some Principles of Liturgical Reform* and the second was an article in *The Church Quarterly Review* for October 1912 entitled 'The Reconstruction of Worship'. In the latter he pointed out that the desire for liturgical reconstruction was world-wide, and not merely confined to the Anglican Communion. What was needed was a long period of authorized experiment, during which not only would there be some effort to satisfy the growing desire for enrichment and greater convenience in the traditional methods of service, but also an effort to provide the Church public with opportunities for acquiring sufficient knowledge and information on these matters to enable them to arrive at instructed judgements.

In the former Frere prefaced his suggestions with a plea that revision should be undertaken by skilled hands. 'The serious work will only begin when the Convocations decide that it is at least as crucial a matter to revise the Prayer Book as to retranslate the Bible; and therefore are content to place the initial responsibility in the hands, not of a Committee of Convocation, which, except in the Upper House, contains few of the scholars who are most competent for the work, but a body of revisers gathered and empowered for the purpose.'[1] His principal suggestions, nearly all of which occur somewhere in his letters, were as follows:

1. A fixed date for Easter.
2. A revision of the Calendar, together with the provision of Collects, Epistles, and Gospels for Lesser Feasts.
3. Proper psalms for Mattins and Evensong every Sunday.
4. Weekday arrangements for psalms and lessons to be based on the ecclesiastical and not the civil year.
5. A return to the old conception of rubrics: some directive, reminders of positive ecclesiastical laws concerning the services; others suggestive and elastic, giving hints to recall the approved customs of the Church. The provision of any necessary new laws should be by means of Canon Law, thereby dispensing with the hampering force of civil endorsement.
6. *The Sunday Morning Service*
    (i) To achieve completeness without undue length, elements repeated in duplicate or even more frequently should be omitted.
    (ii) *Mattins and Litany*
        a. A revision of the Introductory Sentences.
        b. Daily repetition of the Penitential Opening unnecessary.

[1] *Some Principles of Liturgical Reform*, p. 8.

Early Days

    c. The Venite, when used as an Invitatory, to end at verse 7.
    d. The reintroduction of Old Testament Canticles as alternatives to the Te Deum on weekdays in Lent.
    e. The prayers at the end of the Litany to be removed and set with the Occasional Prayers and Thanksgivings.

  (iii) *Holy Communion*
    a. A restoration of psalmody in the position of the old gradual.
    b. As a temporary measure, until further liturgical study and agreement on eucharistic doctrine had been achieved, the permissive use of the following rearrangement of the Canon: Comfortable Words, Prayer of Humble Access, Sursum Corda, &c., Preface and Sanctus, Consecration Prayer, Prayer of Oblation, Lord's Prayer.

7. The establishment of Compline as a second and more popular Evening Service.
8. A revision of the order for Adult Baptism, based on primitive services.
9. A restoration of the service of Unction.
10. Permission to use the 1549 Burial Service.

II

THE ADVISORY COMMITTEE ON LITURGICAL QUESTIONS

FRERE's suggestion for a committee of experts was partly met in 1911. On 5 May in the Upper House of Canterbury Convocation, Archbishop Davidson suggested the need of a body of experts to edit and co-ordinate the proposals which would ultimately issue from the various Houses, both Northern and Southern; it should be a small body and representative of all schools of thought.[1] As a result, on 6 July the Upper House unanimously agreed to the proposal of Dr. Gore, Bishop of Birmingham: 'That the Archbishop be requested, in conjunction with, if possible, the Archbishop of York, to arrange for the appointment of a Committee of scholars of acknowledged weight, whose advice can be sought with regard to liturgical and other proposals with which Convocation is now dealing, and that Committees of this House be instructed to ask for such advice in all appropriate cases.'[2] The Archbishop announced the names of those appointed to serve on 15 February 1912—Dr. Robertson, Bishop of Exeter (Chairman); Dr. Chase, Bishop of Ely; Dr. Gibson, Bishop of Gloucester; Dr. Drury, Bishop of Ripon; Dr. Maclean, Bishop of Moray and Ross; Canon [A. J.] Mason; Professor Swete; Dr. Frere; Dr. Brightman; Dr. Gee; Dr. Dawson Walker; Archdeacon Burrows; Dr. Guy Warman; Canon Morley Stevenson; Canon Christopher Wordsworth; and the Revd. H. A. Wilson.[3] In November four more members were added—Canon J. N. Dalton; Dr. Percy Dearmer; Prebendary Jackson; and the Revd. Claude Jenkins, the Lambeth Librarian, who was asked to act as Secretary to the Committee.[4]

The first meeting was arranged for 7 October 1912 to consider problems arising from the deliberations of the July session of Convocation. Three questions were submitted:

1. The liturgical position of Evensong on Easter Even.
2. The division of the Litany when followed by Holy Communion.
3. A proposed form of service for late Evensong.

The meeting was finally postponed until 22 October and Frere, doubtful of his ability to attend, wrote lengthy Memoranda on these

[1] *Chronicle of Canterbury Convocation*, 1911, pp. 300-1.
[2] Ibid., pp. 406-7.
[3] Ibid., 1912, pp. 11-12.
[4] Ibid., pp. 501-2.

questions and also on alternative forms of Mattins and Evensong. He eventually managed to be there, but his notes were still used as a basis for discussion, and many of his proposals were ultimately accepted.

Frere to the Bishop of Exeter   8 *October* 1912

My dear Bishop,

    I am sending some memoranda on the subjects of the points submitted to the Advisory Committee. I venture to do so partly because I am doubtful as to whether I can be present. The change of date has affected me unfortunately, because on 22 October I am in the middle of a mission at the Parish Church at Walsall. But further, hoping in spite of that to come, I have thought well to send some considerations in advance as it seems to me that if the Committee is to do its work at all profitably some memorandum at least, and perhaps a brief from all such members of the Committee as are disposed to write them should be sent in beforehand and circulated; otherwise our time may just be wasted in profitless discussions for want of preparation in advance.

Memorandum 1

Alternative Form of Mattins

(*a*) It is not quite clear whether 'All standing' is the best beginning. Uniformity counts for a great deal, and people are accustomed to saying the opening versicles kneeling. Probably, therefore, kneeling is better. Similarly, uniformity is desirable about the form of opening. The outline of Compline as drafted begins with the Invocation, and if it is adopted there, it might well be adopted at the beginning of the alternative Mattins and Evensong: followed by a brief pause it seems to give the most suitable opening leading up to the versicle, but if that is not adopted probably one of the opening sentences should be prescribed. This is a practical matter, since while people are waiting in church it is convenient that some sentence should be said to indicate the opening of the service before the versicle which calls for an immediate response from them.

(*b*) After Benedictus. Following medieval precedent there are two alternatives open. First, to proceed immediately to the Collect, preceded only by the Salutation. Secondly, on ferial days to say versicles with the Lord's Prayer and Creed, and then proceed to the Collect. As the purpose of this form is to be short, I would suggest that it is preferable to follow the former of these two, and say immediately after the Benedictus the Collect preceded by 'The Lord be with you' and perhaps succeeded by a closing versicle such as the old one 'Let us bless the Lord'—'Thanks be to God'.

(c) The Collect also needs consideration. The precedents indicate either that the Collect of the day was used (in medieval times) or else that there was a fixed Collect belonging to the Service. On some days after the Collect and closing versicles supplementary memorials were said. These are represented in our service by the Collects for Peace and Grace. Should the alternative form of Mattins have a fixed Collect or a variable Collect? It certainly should have a Collect which stands as *the* Collect, and if others are added they should be added as memorials, following ancient precedent. If it is desirable (in view of the fact that the Collect of the day will shortly be said at the Eucharist) that that variable Collect should not be said there, then the best thing will be to have a fixed Collect for the Collect of this Mattins. I venture to suggest that the simplest way of choosing the Collect for this purpose is to take the old Collect for Prime, now the Collect for Grace. This is particularly appropriate if the service is said early, as it probably generally will be: but if it is desired to make it available for a later hour in the day, or if it is wished to keep the Collect for Peace in use in such a service, then put the two Collects for Peace and Grace as alternatives, probably putting the Collect for Grace first, because that is suitable for an early hour of the day.

Memorandum 2

Alternative Form of Evensong

(a) The plan adopted with regard to the Collects here should be uniform with that adopted for the alternative Mattins. If, as is suggested above, it is taken in its shortest form, namely, the Collect said immediately after the single Canticle, then the service will be so short that there seems no reason why the occasional prayers, &c., should not be additional, as in the ordinary Evensong.

It certainly does seem undesirable that the formal service itself should be left without a Collect and should merely tail off into occasional prayers, whereas it is quite suitable that those should be said as supplementary to the Office Collect when the Collect has once brought the main service to its proper climax. I would therefore change the place of the words 'or' and 'and' thus—'ending with the second *or* third Collect *and* at the discretion of the minister', &c.

(b) It seems desirable to find some other name for this service than

Shortened Evensong. It is practically the old Vespers service, and might perhaps be called so, though that term is only a modern one.

Presumably it is meant to begin, as the alternative form of Mattins begins, with some versicles and, I hope, with the Invocation if it is adopted as above.

Similarly, at the end, it would be better to have the Collect appropriate to the service immediately after the Magnificat, preceded by the Salutation, and followed by its closing versicle, and so end, except that the additional prayers might be added.

Memorandum 3

Form for a Late Evening Service

1. The opening should be uniform with the rest; Invocation if it is used elsewhere; also it would seem to be better not to have 'Alleluia' but to have the Prayer Book equivalent of it, 'Praise ye the Lord'—'The Lord's Name be praised'.

2. I would make the six verses of the thirty-first Psalm optional. They are in the Secular Compline, not in the Benedictine one.

3. The prayers that follow are in the drafted form misplaced, and need reconsideration. The old Compline service consisted of two parts—the Office technically speaking, with the Lord's Prayer and a few versicles, ending with the Benediction. There was also a brief penitential service, which in the English forms of Compline follows here, and in the Roman form (in part) precedes the main office and follows the little evening lesson or collation. This arrangement is entirely thrown into chaos in the draft. The versicles that lead up to the Benediction are inserted in between the Confession and the rest of the little penitential office, so that the Benediction neither ends the little office itself nor the office in the larger sense. Its position is meaningless. It seems desirable to replace the versicles so that they follow the Lord's Prayer and lead up to the little Benediction, and then to take (according to English custom) the little penitential service consisting of some form of confession and absolution with further versicles and the Collect proper to the Office—'Lighten our darkness' or 'Visit, we beseech thee'.

4. The position of the Creed requires consideration. It is in accordance with the Prayer Book position at Evensong, but not the old position of the Creed at Compline. For uniformity's sake it had better stay where it is.

5. The character of the Confession and Absolution also needs some consideration. The Prayer Book has not retained anywhere the mutual

confession and absolution which belongs to Prime and Compline. It has made it much more of a ministerial or even sacerdotal function than it was; it was more allied to a mutual apology of people who have lived together for the day and wish to acknowledge the failures of the day mutually before it closes. There is all the difference here between family prayers and sacerdotal service, and I confess that I should regret to see the family prayer element taken out of it and the other introduced. It is not a position in which uniformity with the Prayer Book Morning and Evening Service is at all necessary, or I would say desirable. In fact, if any change in its character were made, I would sooner take out the special piece said by the officiant and make it less sacerdotal rather than more so.

6. The versicle 'We will lay us down and take our rest' has got into the wrong position. It should not come between 'O Lord, hear our prayer', which is traditionally the last of the choir versicles, and the Salutation, which is the officiant's versicle, 'The Lord be with you'. I do not understand why the words 'in peace' are omitted.

7. If it is desirable to add further prayers besides the Collect proper to the office, they should be added after the little versicle 'Let us bless the Lord', with which the Office proper ends. Many better Collects, I think, could be found than the one on page four of the leaflet, which is a very clumsy thing hashed up out of Collects for the first Sunday after Epiphany and the twenty-first and twenty-second Sundays after Trinity. It seems a model of what should not be allowed to exist. There are many beautiful Collects available. The benedictory form at the end seems hardly necessary when the earlier one is taken into account.

Memorandum 4

The Litany

(a) It is undesirable that the words 'After Morning Prayer' should be omitted. It may be necessary as a concession that the Litany should be said in the afternoon or evening, but its right place should first be indicated and the other be treated as exceptional. It would be preferable to devise some way of showing that it should precede the celebration and that it is rather the preliminary to that than the sequel to Morning Prayer. But if this cannot be done then it would be better to keep the words 'After Morning Prayer'.

(b) It is difficult to say exactly what should be done at the end. The Prayer of St. Chrysostom is particularly appropriate when Holy Communion is to follow immediately. Probably this was the original intention which led to its insertion here. The piece that most clearly and easily can be omitted is from 'O Lord, arise' to the end of the prayer 'We humbly beseech thee, O Father'. If everything from the Lord's Prayer onward is omitted, careful provision should be made to clear up the way in which the Litany joins on to the Eucharist, for it leaves the Litany in itself unfinished, and the method of connexion with the Eucharist should be indicated. The two problems of the Litany and the beginning of the Eucharist are really inseparable. Probably for ordinary purposes the best curtailment is to set an 'Amen' and the Grace at the end of the Collect 'O God, merciful Father'.

Memorandum 5

1. In the ancient days there was no Evensong belonging to Easter Even at all. In early days not only did the Vigil absorb the time of Lucernarium but also the service said at the ninth hour. There was no Eucharist except that which followed the Vigil. The Vigil began after None and continued through the night. The Liturgy was not to be completed till after midnight. Thus there was no Mass or Vespers on Easter Even. The Mass of that day is the Vigil Mass performed at night, with peculiar features of its own distinguishing it from the proper Easter Mass at which people communicated.

The Vigil Service is essentially a penitential service. The prayers are said in prostration. The Easter Service has not begun, nor does it begin except by slow degrees after midnight.

2. Several tendencies combined to alter this state of things. The feeling for the Vigil observance went, and people wished to have the whole thing earlier. Again, as the obligation to the Breviary Offices grows, it seems strange to have no Vespers. The result is a continual struggle between those who wished to keep the service in its right position and those who wished to anticipate it; and also a variety of use between those who said, 'There are no Vespers on Easter Even', and those who tried to import into the existing service some representations of Vespers. In the Frankish edition of the *Ordo Romanus* in the ninth century one can see both things, for the writer preserves the old Roman discipline of having no Vespers, but says his own people do not observe this. That succeeded in introducing into the close of the Mass some bits to represent Vespers—an Alleluia antiphon with a short psalm—116 (117), also an antiphon with Magnificat. The service more or less in this form was observed in England in the tenth century, according to the *Regularis Concordia* and also in the later diocesan uses,

although in the interval Lanfranc in his Statutes for the Benedictines has still further enlarged the Vespers, making it into a full service with even a hymn, and separating it off from the Mass instead of making the post-communion of the Mass to serve also as the Collect of the Vespers. From this it will be evident that there is no ancient or medieval precedent for a Festival Evensong. This occasion is in fact the great exception of the year. Easter begins with the Vigil Mass after midnight. No doubt this is an intentional following of the scripture lines.

3. In the Prayer Book services Holy Week has lost all its distinctiveness and is planned out in monotonous uniformity with the rest of the year. Easter Even lost its connexion with Baptism, lost its Vigil and its Vigil Service, and, indeed, everything else that belonged to it. It, however, gained certain things, and among them a distinctive character for the services that were given to Holy Saturday as commemorative of our Lord's death and burial. In the symbolic sense only was any connexion with Baptism left; but this connexion was maintained, and the thought of our Lord's burial is dwelt upon not only in Collect, Epistle, and Gospel, but also in the Lessons. The revisers who carried this through at various dates were amply justified in what they did, and any attempt to make a first Evensong of Easter Day to be said in the afternoon or evening of Saturday is going against every tradition alike of the primitive, the medieval, and the Reformation periods. The tendency to do so has probably not been developed by any sound liturgical instinct, but merely by the pressure of ladies who wish to decorate the church. Such decoration should be postponed, and the penitential aspect of the church preserved at least until the evening of the Saturday.

It was unfortunate that after regular meetings from 1912 until January 1914 the Committee was neglected. No further meetings were held until October 1915, and only then as the result of agitation by some of its members. A hint that all was not well appeared on 20 February 1914 when the Upper House of Canterbury unanimously adopted Report 481, which embodied the House's answer to be returned to the Letters of Business. When the question of comparison and correlation of these proposals with those of the other Houses of Canterbury and York was raised, the Bishop of Exeter requested a statement on the position of the Advisory Committee. 'Some time ago his Grace appointed a number of persons who were supposed to be more or less experts in liturgical matters whose advice and counsel would be available. Some questions had already been sent to that Committee, and answers had been returned, some of which had been adopted, if not all. In view of the expectations which had been raised in many minds at the time when the appointment of the Committee was publicly announced, and of the implied assurance that everything which ultimately proceeded from the House would have, to some extent, the imprimatur of a body of experts as something which at any rate they could pass, he thought that perhaps there were some outside the House who would feel that the Committee of Experts had not, so far, discharged all the functions in view of which it had been originally appointed. As the person who had been honoured by being elected Chairman, he felt obliged to ask whether it was considered by the House that the Committee should be discharged.' The Archbishop assured him, however, that the work of the Committee was by no means over and demands would be made upon it in the future.[1] In spite of this statement the Committee remained inactive for the rest of that year. It was Frere who was partly, if not wholly, responsible for its return to work in 1915. On 7 September 1915 he wrote to the Bishop of Moray and Ross, 'At last Lambeth has yielded to a small bomb and summoned us again', while he revealed to the Revd. H. A. Wilson ten days later that he himself had written a very strong letter to the Archbishop (of which unfortunately there is no copy among his papers): 'When I wrote to express views of this kind, or even bluntly to say that I thought we were being used as dust in the eyes of the public, the letter had the effect at any rate in part of our being taken off the shelf, and called together for this coming meeting'.

The trouble lay in the functions of the Committee. The Archbishop was determined to limit its sphere of action; it was to discuss and comment on just those points which were submitted to it by Convocation. It was not at liberty to initiate proposals itself. If Convocations were agreed upon a point and were not disposed to submit it to the Committee for comment, the Committee could do nothing. To a body of experts such a state of affairs was intolerable. The Archbishop, however, seemed determined that, for better or for worse, all initiative must remain in the hands of the Convocations—a situation which Frere had prophesied in his *Principles of Liturgical Reform* would not bring good results.[2] The Bishop of Exeter, as Chairman of the Committee, was in a difficult position: his loyalties were divided; he was a sick man; and the whole business caused him much unhappiness.

On 30 April 1915 the Archbishop wrote to the Bishop of Exeter advising him that the Committee would soon be asked to recommence its labours and at the same time emphasizing the limited terms of reference.

---

[1] *Chronicle of Canterbury Convocation*, 1914, pp. 201–3.
[2] *Some Principles of Liturgical Reform*, pp. 7–8.

The Archbishop of Canterbury to the Bishop of Exeter   30 *April* 1915

My dear Bishop of Exeter,

You are Chairman of the Advisory Committee on Liturgical Questions (popularly known as the Committee of Experts), which has dealt with Rubrical and Liturgical questions specifically referred to it by the Upper House of Convocation. The help thus given has been of the greatest value, and we owe cordial thanks to the members of the Committee for placing at our disposal their learning and wisdom in these matters. We are now approaching the end of the consideration of the long series of liturgical recommendations emanating from one or both Houses of our Convocation. These recommendations are still in a provisional stage, as further steps will be required before they can be regarded as authoritatively endorsed by Convocation as a whole. In these circumstances I venture to hope that you may find it possible to invite the members of your Committee to consider whether any of the recommendations which we have thus made seem to them to call for protest as being liturgically faulty to such a degree as would make the reconsideration of the question in Convocation desirable. I am anxious, however, to make it clear that I am not inviting the Advisory Committee to take in hand a revision of all our work. This would be to constitute your Committee a new House of Convocation or even Tribunal of Appeal. All I am anxious for is that if, in the view of those who have given learned consideration to these subjects, something which Convocation has provisionally said or done is markedly at variance with what your experts regard as liturgically right, you should kindly call my attention to the point with a view to the possible reconsideration of the particular recommendation in question.

It is for you in your wisdom as Chairman to judge how the request I have made can be most satisfactorily complied with without our placing on the shoulders of your Committee an unreasonable burden or inviting prolonged and detailed labours by men whose hands (to use a common phrase) are already overfull. If you feel that you can help us in the way that I have suggested, I am sure that you will kindly take such steps as you feel to be appropriate and practicable.

I am,

Yours very truly,

Randall Cantuar.

The Joint Committee of both Upper and Lower Houses of Convocation appointed in 1914 to harmonize the Resolutions arrived at by both

Advisory Committee on Liturgical Questions

bodies had already presented their Report (487) in January 1915. This contained 162 Resolutions, of which 94 had already been substantially adopted by the Upper House. The Upper House debated and accepted this Report with certain amendments in February and April 1915 and produced their results in Report 487B. On 19 July the Bishop of Exeter sent a circular letter to members of the Advisory Committee, calling a meeting for 19 October to discuss this Report: he enclosed with it a copy of the Archbishop's letter to himself.

My dear Brother,

I hereby give notice that the Advisory Committee will be called together on Tuesday, 19 October, at 2 p.m., and will be expected to sit if necessary through the week until Saturday at 1.

The business will be to consider possible objections for Prayer Book Revision comprised in Report 487B, which is enclosed herewith.

You will see that what is before us is the text of the alterations and additions *proposed*, and that it will be out of order to make suggestions in regard to points not dealt with in the Report; but this would not in my judgement preclude suggestions *alternative* to those in the text of the Report. At the same time at this stage of the proceedings—and in view of the possibility that, before the final reply of both Convocations to the Letters of Business is adopted, the recommendations in Report 487B may have to undergo some reduction in volume—I think it desirable that we should keep within the narrowest possible limits any suggestions of the nature of redrafting.

In order to prepare the detailed Agenda, I request that all members who have proposals to make shall send them to the Secretary, the Revd. Claude Jenkins, Lambeth Palace Library, not later than 18 September. All suggestions should bear the number of the paragraph in the Report to which they relate. I would add that supposing any given paragraph or paragraphs are *not* made the subject of any objection or suggestion by our Committee, this fact will not be taken to commit us to unqualified approval of the proposed change as ideally right, but only to acquiescence in it.

Very sincerely yours,
A. Exon.

N.B. In Report 487B there are a few paragraphs which do not in their present form come within the scope of our reference. These are Sections 1, 2, 3, 7, 20, and the first paragraph in Section 35: 'The Committee . . . in language'.

There was an undoubted sting in the tail of this letter. The paragraphs to which the Bishop of Exeter referred involved important but highly controversial subjects—Concerning the Service of the Church, the Recitation of the Psalter, the Lectionary, the Ornaments Rubric, the Quicunque Vult, and special Collects, Epistles, and Gospels. They were considered to be beyond the scope of the Committee's terms of reference because no final decisions on them had yet been reached. Nevertheless, as the ensuing letters show, these were matters about which members of the Committee felt deep misgivings and on which they particularly desired to express themselves.

The Bishop of Moray and Ross to Frere   8 *August* 1915

My dear Walter,

. . . What I wanted to write to you about was the Advisory Committee, which is at last to be unmuzzled again at the eleventh hour—too late, I fear, to do much good. I wanted to consult you as to whether we could not persuade the Chairman to let us discuss the *principles* of the Psalter and Lectionary;[1] for as to the former, at least, and partly as to

---

[1] The recommendations in Report 487B on the Psalter and Lectionary were as follows.

     (a) *The Order how the Psalter is appointed to be read*

The Joint Committee reported as follows:

1. Both Houses recommend that the existing monthly course be retained, the Upper House for use throughout the month, the Lower House on weekdays only.

2. Both Houses recommend that the provision of Proper Psalms be extended, but the Houses differ as to the amount of extension that is desirable.

  (a) The Upper House provides a table of additional Proper Psalms to be used on Advent Sunday, Christmas Eve, the Epiphany and its Eve, Palm Sunday, the Monday, Tuesday, Wednesday, Thursday and Saturday before Easter, the Eves of Ascension Day and Whitsunday, Trinity Sunday, the Feast of St. Michael and All Angels, and All Saints' Day. It also provides selections of psalms from which choice may be made at festal seasons, and on Rogation Days, the Dedication Festival, and the Harvest Thanksgiving.

  (b) The Lower House desires that Proper Psalms shall be provided for all Sundays and Holy-days in the year. (A complete table has been prepared by a Committee, but has not been considered in detail by the House.)

3. The Upper House has prepared a table of 21 selections of psalms to be used at the discretion of the Minister instead of the psalms of the day on any day for which proper psalms are not appointed. It desires that one of these selections shall be used on the last day of months which contain 31 days.

4. The Lower House approves the principle of making certain omissions from

the latter, the proposals made seem to me against all good liturgical principles—breaking up the course of psalms once a week by omitting those which would fall on a Sunday and substituting others for them (proper ones for every Sunday); and the total abolition of any course of Sunday lessons by letting the Minister pick and choose between a considerable selection. There is no objection to special psalms for every Sunday if the weekday course is continuous, as in your *Principles of Liturgical Reform*: but what the Lower House proposes is to introduce a confusion which we are doing our best to get rid of in the case of the

the Psalter as used in public worship. The Upper House meets the difficulty felt by some persons in the recitation of certain passages by the provision of the selections mentioned above.

(The Joint Committee are unable to harmonise the recommendations mentioned above.)

5. Both Houses desire that steps shall be taken to secure a revision of passages in the Psalter in which the language is obscure or misleading.

The Upper House resolved that His Grace the President be asked to arrange for a conference between the two Houses or representatives of the Houses.

(b) *The Lectionary*

The Lower House recommended—

That it is desirable that the Lectionary should be revised, other Lessons from the Old Testament, more profitable for members of congregations generally, being substituted for some of the first Lessons now appointed on Sundays and on weekdays; and that a larger choice of alternative Lessons both from the Old and New Testament for Sundays, Holy-days, and Eves of Holy-days be provided.

A Committee of the Lower House presented two Reports, Nos. 475 and 485.

On the presentation of the first Report the House approved—

I. The adoption of the ecclesiastical weeks in preference to the calendar months as the framework of a Church Lectionary.

II. The principle of selecting second Lessons as well as first Lessons for every Sunday.

The Table of Lessons was referred back to the Committee.

The Second Report contained a revised Table, and the following Resolutions were carried:

1. That this House approves generally the Table of Lessons submitted by the Committee.

2. That this House desires that permission may if possible be given for the experimental use of the Table of Lessons for two years before its final adoption or incorporation in the Book of Common Prayer.

3. That the Prolocutor be requested to convey the above Resolution to his Grace the President and their Lordships of the Upper House.

The Joint Committee recommended that the Upper House be asked to give consideration to the above-mentioned Resolutions.

The Upper House resolved that his Grace the President be requested to refer the proposed Table of Lessons to a Joint Committee of the two Houses for consideration both in regard to general principles and in regard to details; and that power be given to the Joint Committee to confer with any similar Committee appointed by the Convocation of York.

Lectionary. I understand the Bishop of Exeter proposes to rule out discussion on psalms and lessons, as the two Houses have not yet agreed: but surely if the Advisory Committee is to be of any use, it is to advise on principles *before* the Houses have made up their minds, not afterwards when it is too late. Do you agree?

As a matter of detail, we (in Scotland) have found your suggested division rather too complicated, and that each portion is too long. So our latest idea is to divide the Psalter for the week-day course into five weeks, and to keep the present Prayer Book portions exactly as they are, which will simplify matters considerably. Only Sunday will be a *non dies* as far as that course is concerned. I will explain this in more detail when we meet. I shall hope to be at the Committee in October.

Yours affectionately,
A. J. Moravien.

Frere to the Bishop of Moray and Ross   7 September 1915

My dear Bishop,

... As to the Advisory Committee. At last Lambeth has yielded to a small bomb and summoned us again, as you say, but I fear not to much purpose. Their line seems to be only to ask our advice when it is too late to adopt it. The Psalter and Lectionary are crucial instances; and unless they are prepared to allow us to discuss them, I for one don't feel inclined to go or take any further bother about it at all. Not that there are not other points which are of importance; but if the dealings with the Committee are of this sort, what good is it our doing anything? Of course I entirely agree that one of the biggest blots in the proposals is with regard to the Psalter, and a Committee like ourselves ought to make every possible protest. Do write strongly to the Bishop of Exeter. I am doing what I can in a letter to him, but I fear it is altogether his fault. It is part of the Lambeth diplomacy to make everything as ineffective as possible.

I am interested to hear of your new plan for the Psalter in Scotland, keeping the division into sixty portions. When I have got a little clearer, I want to write further about one or two points, so that we may have a little concerted action as to what resolutions are sent in. I am very much inclined to propose boldly that there should be an alternative Communion Office—the first Prayer Book or something closely modelled upon it. This, I think, would come within our terms of reference; and as the Bishops at present have excluded practically every effort to reform our Office, I see no other way than this of raising the whole question of its general inadequacy. But I want to get this quite clear in my head and one or two other points, and will write again in a day or two. I am only just back from holiday....

The Bishop of Moray and Ross to Frere 9 September 1915

My dear Walter,

Many thanks for your letter. I wrote to the Bishop of Exeter about a week ago urging the importance of the Advisory Committee discussing things like the Psalter and Lectionary *before* Convocation had made up their minds. In reply he asked me to draft motions which I would like them to propose, and that he would do his best to get them into the agenda if it was at all feasible....

I agree that we ought to concert some line of action beforehand....

I doubt if a proposal for an alternative Communion Office would be in order. But anyhow I hope we should do something better than the 1549 inverted Invocation, for which the Egyptian fragment is no real justification....

Yours affectionately,

A. J. Moravien.

On the same day Frere also wrote to the Bishop of Exeter in the same strain.

Frere to the Bishop of Exeter 9 September 1915

My dear Bishop,

I have been trying to see my way clear about the meeting of the Liturgical Advisory Committee. I notice that you say in a postscript to your letter that certain sections are excluded from our consideration. Among them are two of the most important questions—the Psalter and the Lectionary. Considering the importance of these, it seems a great pity if it is really inevitable that when the Committee meets for what I suppose will be its most important meeting, we shall not be able to discuss these.

The proposals about the Psalter seem to me (and I do not stand alone upon the Committee) to be the most objectionable of all those that are definitely made by the Upper House, whose advisers we are. Are we to understand that our advice is not to be given until the matter is settled? If this is the method, and this is not the only side which points in that direction, the work of the Committee becomes of no value. When a matter is once settled, what is the good of giving advice?

I am venturing, therefore, though with much diffidence, to write and ask whether this ruling is really inevitable. So far as I understand the Archbishop's letter, it might be taken to mean that our Committee was invited to consider any of the recommendations made by the Upper House, not necessarily those to which the Lower House had agreed. But you will know more than I what the Archbishop's intentions are, and probably have good reasons for your ruling which I don't know.

In writing this, of course, I quite understand that we are still only at an early stage, and the matter may be said to be still fully open for discussion and suggestion. At the same time, I don't think it can be denied that so far as the Convocations are concerned, there is a tendency to regard their part of the work as closed, and to be impatient with any suggestion that is not already included or in accordance with their draft recommendations; so that practically so far as the initiating of proposals is concerned, it is almost too late for any advice now to get a hearing; and it will be even worse in a few months' time, when all the outstanding questions between the different Houses of Convocation have been settled. So I plead for leave to consider all these matters now, or else that the Committee should not be asked to advise about them at all; in which case, for the credit of the Committee, it should be publicly stated that they have not advised about the matter. Even as it is, I think the Committee is likely to incur certain criticism which it does not deserve, for it may be supposed to have a hand in a number of proposals here, which it has never in fact had the opportunity to discuss and is now only asked to look at from the point of view of a third reading, instead of, as I submit, being called in at the second reading and committee stage. As it is, I cannot but regard the whole scheme as a tithing of mint and cummin, only neglecting the weightier matters of the law. But if we are only asked whether mint and cummin should be tithed, we can only say 'Yes'.

Please forgive my quarrelsomeness, but I had hopes of our being of some use, when I saw that we were to be allowed to sit again; and I find these hopes much curtailed by your postscript even further than by the letter of the Archbishop. I am quite content simply to put this before you and leave the matter until we actually meet, so long as I may submit one or two proposals on these sections, and be prepared to have them ruled out by you at the time if they are found to be ultimately inadmissible. . . .

Other members of the Committee also protested to the Bishop of Exeter and their united efforts proved effective. On 16 September Dr. Robertson wrote to Frere announcing concessions on the points raised.

The Bishop of Exeter to Frere   16 *September* 1915
My dear Dr. Frere,

    I have thought over your letter very carefully, as well as another from the Bishop of Moray and Ross.

    With regard to Section 3 of Report 487B, I am not quite clear that we are not in a position to discuss it, as the Upper House at this moment has nothing before it with regard to the Lectionary. What has happened is that the President has appointed a Joint Committee to report upon the Lower House proposals.

    I think the best way of getting any suggestions you have on the Lectionary effectively considered, would be to communicate them personally to the Bishop of Ely, who is Chairman of the Joint Committee appointed to deal with the matter.

    Section 2, dealing with the Psalter, stands substantially on the same footing, as the matter is referred to a Conference of the two Houses for Report; but, in this case, the Upper House did adopt certain general principles with regard to proper psalms, &c., and I have decided provisionally to admit to the Agenda Paper two motions by the Bishop of Moray, dealing with these points. I am not absolutely clear that they are strictly in order; but what I think will meet the case will be to deal with them after we have disposed of the motions which are certainly in order.

                        Believe me, with kind regards,
                              Very sincerely yours,
                                        A. Exon.

That Frere and the Bishop of Moray and Ross were not alone in their doubts as to the value of the Committee in its fettered condition is evident from another letter which Frere received from the Revd. H. A. Wilson in reply to a request for comments on a list of suggested points to be raised at the next meeting.

The Revd. H. A. Wilson to Frere   15 September 1915

My dear Frere,

Many thanks for your letter and its enclosure.

I am afraid that I have not given so much attention to the Resolutions which we are to be asked to consider as I might have done, if it had not escaped my notice that we were asked to communicate any points we wished to raise by 18 September. But I have been regarding the matter less from the point of view of one who thinks of raising questions about the Resolutions than from that of one who is rather doubtful whether he should not withdraw altogether from the Committee.

It has all along seemed to me that we stand in some danger of being supposed to have advised, or at any rate to have passed, what may be proposed by the Convocations with regard to a considerable number of important matters about which we have never been consulted at all, but about which it might be reasonably supposed that if we were not definitely consulted we would probably have had, in some way or other, an opportunity of expressing our opinion.

I do not know how far this was in the minds of those who devised the forming of a Committee: but I am not free from suspicion that it may have been thought convenient to have such a body to act as a screen; not asking it any questions about certain important matters but allowing it to be supposed that all that was proposed, and all omissions to propose things, had in some sense received its support.

You are more acquainted than I can be with the proceedings and probably with the motives of the personages concerned, and can therefore judge better than myself how far my suspicion is justified. But I confess it is rather strengthened than removed by the Archbishop's letter to our Chairman, and by the apparent desire to exclude certain matters on which I think outsiders would probably suppose that we would have something to say. Of course, if there is real need for doing so, we can clear ourselves by explaining what our position has been: but I don't like manifestos, and I hope there may be no need of one.

I have not definitely made up my mind (I should like, for example, to have some talk with Brightman before doing so), but my present inclination is to attend the meeting on 19 October, though I should probably be content to leave the raising of points to others who will deal with them more effectively—indeed it is practically too late for me now to send notice of anything to Jenkins. Of the points you mention, there is one which 'as at present advised' I am afraid I should not agree—that of requiring assent to the Nicene Creed at Confirmation.

I am not sure that a proposal to restore I Edward VI is practically the best way of raising the point which I take we both have in view—but it would raise it. As to all the other points, I do not think I need say anything; where I do not agree, I do not disagree strongly, and am, I think, open to conviction.

Very sincerely yours,
H. A. Wilson.

Frere replied with a most revealing letter, of which mention has already been made.

Frere to the Revd. H. A. Wilson   *17 September 1915*

My dear Wilson,

I entirely sympathize with what you say. I doubt altogether whether the Committee is not doing more harm than good. But when I wrote to express views of this kind, or even bluntly to say that I thought we were being used as dust in the eyes of the public, the letter had the effect at any rate in part of our being taken off the shelf and called together for this coming meeting: so I felt bound to make the best of this opportunity. But my hopes have been dashed a good deal by the way in which this particular meeting is managed, as you say; and I wrote in protest to the Chairman expressing a good deal of what you say. . . . To this I have an answer this morning saying that the Lectionary is certainly beyond our scope, but that the Psalter may possibly be admitted and two questions on it by the Bishop of Moray, if and when the things which are plainly in order have been dealt with. That, of course, is a small point as compared with the whole attitude of the Bishops to their Committee, which is like that of a weak vicar to his parish council, as far as I can see; namely, that he consults it when he has made up his mind, and about things that don't matter, with the result that the council is not a great success. I think this may well show whether we can so far carry on any Committee work of this kind or not. I quite think with you, we may think it best to withdraw unless we have the promise of better handling or some hopes of better things. We shall see. . . .

On the same day Frere sent in a list of proposals to the Secretary with a covering letter. His list was a long one, and he expressed a desire to be relieved of much of the burden of moving them all.

Frere to the Revd. Claude Jenkins 17 September 1915

My dear Jenkins,

    Here is my list of proposals. I have struck out two or three because I hear from the Chairman that No. 3 is inadmissible, and that No. 2 will be raised by the Bishop of Moray if it is found to be admissible. Possibly some of these points may be raised by other people, in which case don't put them down to me. I hope Brightman will send in something, and his points are likely to coincide: indeed I much hope you will be able to relieve me of a good deal of this by distributing it among people who have similar motions: otherwise I shall be a perfect nuisance to the Committee. . . .

His proposals were as follows:

The Psalter

2.1. It is preferable that the Psalter should be said in course of weekdays only.
  2. Proper psalms should be provided for all Sundays and Holy-days and some seasons such as Easter week.
  3. Provision should be made where necessary for first evensongs. Otherwise the course shall be preserved and not destroyed by allowing selections to be substituted.
  4. In accordance with the proposal of the Lower House, certain omissions should be made from the Psalter as used in public worship.

(These proposals were left out in order that they might be dealt with by the Bishop of Moray.)

The Lectionary

3. Support should be given to the following two points in Report 475 of a Committee of the Lower House.
  1. The adoption of the ecclesiastical weeks in preference to the calendar months as the framework of a Church Lectionary.
  2. The principle of selecting second Lessons as well as first Lessons for every Sunday.

(These proposals were those left out as being inadmissible.)

Advisory Committee on Liturgical Questions

The Calendar

4.1. 2 January. It is not desirable to alter English tradition as to the day of the Name of Jesus.
  2. 7 March. The companions of St. Perpetua should be referred to.
  3. 29 June should be the day of St. Paul as well as St. Peter.
  4. 14 September should be St. Cyprian and not Holy Cross Day. The latter should be kept on 3 May.
  5. St. Faith should not be omitted on 6 October.
  6. 6 November. Martyrs should be added to the title 'Saints and Doctors of the Church of England'; especially the Marian Martyrs, though it would be preferable to give them another day, e.g. 16 October.

Rules for Feasts and Fasts

5. The number of Vigils should be cut down.

The Order for Evening Prayer

17. It would be better that the Confession and Absolution at the beginning of Evening Prayer should be unlike Morning Prayer.

The Litany

21. The placing of the War Prayers apart from the Litany among the Occasional Prayers, at the same time giving permission to insert them at the end of the Litany.
25. In the place of the phrase 'Lords of the Council and all the nobility' should be inserted 'Members of the High Court of Parliament' or some phrase dealing with assemblies ecclesiastical and civil throughout the Empire.

Collects, Epistles, and Gospels

34.1. The second Gospel for Christmas Day should be St. Luke ii, 1–14.
35.1. The old Gospel for Ember Days should be restored at each of the four seasons.
   2. The rest of the additional Collects, Epistles, and Gospels need reconsideration in view of ancient precedent and the present need of a fuller use of Holy Scripture and Holy Communion.

Holy Communion

36.1. Some alternative form of Holy Communion is urgently needed. This should be the 1549 Order or some modified form of it.

2. There should be no modification of the first rubric at the head of the service.¹

40. The Summary of the Law should not be permitted as a substitute for the Ten Commandments.

Baptism

72.1. No modification should be made in the rules about sponsors.

2. The formal inquiry whether the child has been baptized is a desirable safeguard and should be kept.

100. An alternative form of Baptism of Adults should be provided.

101. The Rubric should continue to require Adult Baptism to be administered on a Sunday or Holy-day.

Confirmation

116.1. The terms 'Godfather, Godmother' should be banished here if they are banished from Adult Baptism; otherwise the terms will seem to imply that a baptismal godparent is required and one who stood as such for an infant.

2. No address should intervene between 'Our help' and the laying on of hands.

3. Candidates should rehearse or declare their assent to the Nicene Creed, which should be recited in the Conciliar and not the Liturgical form.

Matrimony

117. No modification of the rubric dealing with the publication of banns should be made.

Burial

144. Some provision should be made for the case of cremation.

153. It is urgent that the Order of 1549 or some modified form of it should be authorized as an alternative.

Both the Bishop of Moray and Ross and Dr. Brightman sent Frere their criticisms of his proposals. The former expressed his general agreement with them, with the exception of some comments on those connected with the Psalter.

The Bishop of Moray and Ross to Frere   14 September 1915

My dear Walter,

... I now enclose my ideas on your proposals. I hope you will keep your first two Psalter motions together, so that we don't vote on them

---

¹ 'So many as intend to be partakers of the Holy Communion shall signify their names to the Curate, at least some time the day before.'

separately—certainly not 2 before 1—and I would cut out the word 'preferable'. We must be very plain, I think, in stating not only where we should ourselves prefer this or that course, but where we consider a liturgical principle to have been violated. . . .

Yours affectionately,
A. J. Moravien.

Then followed Frere's list of proposals, with the Bishop's comment—mostly 'Yes', and in a few cases 'No opinion' or 'Perhaps'. The only comment of note is on the Psalter, as mentioned above.

1 and 2. I don't think this is stated clearly or emphatically enough. It is essential in my view that if proper psalms are appointed for Sundays as suggested in 2, then the weekday course should be as proposed in 1. The two must stand or fall together.

2. I am against proper psalms for all Holy Days, both for other reasons, and because this would constantly interrupt the course. (This does not apply to proper psalms in the octaves of certain great festivals, as these would not, if arranged properly, interrupt the course.)

3. I think proper psalms should only be appointed for first Evensongs on great festivals. I agree that the 'selections' should not be allowed.

4. Yes.

Brightman's letter was in his own inimitable style. He expressed approval of most of Frere's points: his criticisms of the remainder were terse and vehement.

The Revd. F. E. Brightman to Frere   18 *September* 1915

My dear Frere,

For the most part I agree with your points—and no doubt some of them I should propose myself. Only I haven't yet drawn up any list. I came away from Oxford without my papers and have been unable to get them: and have only been able to get from Jenkins his copy of the 'Resolutions' without the covering letter, so that I forget what was to be excluded from discussion.

But there are two or thee of your points I do not agree with.

2.4 (*The Psalter*). I should like to know exactly what the Lower House means. (The Lower House approves the principle of making certain omissions from the Psalter as used in public worship.) I quite desire the omission of certain psalms from the Sunday and Festal course; and possibly certain groups of verses from one or two psalms. But I don't want a general expurgation; nor perhaps any omission from the weekday complete course.

6 (*The Lectionary*). I can't remember anything about St. Faith: so I can't say anything about this.

Why 16 October (for the Saints, Doctors, and Martyrs)?

36 a (*Alternative Order of Holy Communion*). I don't agree with you at all. It seems to me that at almost any sacrifice we ought to continue to 'say the same thing' at the altar. If the other people will not consent to the reconstruction of the Canon, it seems to me it must be left for the present, much as I should desire 1549.

36 b (*Holy Communion. First Rubric*). 40. (*Omission of the Summary of the Law*). 116. 2. (*Place of Address at Confirmation*). These I agree with, with limitless emphasis.

100 (*Alternative Form of Adult Baptism*). I don't understand what you want here.

116, p. 48 (*Candidates to recite the Conciliar form of the Nicene Creed at Confirmation*). I don't agree with you at all. It is a very serious matter which ought not to be dealt with merely en passant in a liturgical revision. Hitherto the laity have been initiated on the basis of the Apostles' Creed, and it would be a considerable thing to alter this: and at least it ought not to be done *obiter*, but as the result of a definite and independent consideration of the thing on its merits. And I cannot conceive why the Conciliar form should be used.

The whole thing is depressing enough. I should like to amend nearly every line. It does not seem to me to be done with any real care or appreciation or knowledge of real needs.

I hope you will cut up *English Rite* without fear or favour.

Yours affectionately,
F. E. Brightman.

In the following week the Revd. Claude Jenkins sent a copy of the Draft Agenda to Frere and asked for his advice about it. He was obviously not satisfied with it, and it seems that hardly any members of the Committee had sent in any comments or suggestions.

Advisory Committee on Liturgical Questions

The Revd. Claude Jenkins to Frere 24 *September* 1915

Eruditissime,

I send you a proof of the Agenda, because I want you to see that, apart from misprints introduced by the printer, I have represented your motions correctly.

I also want you of your great benevolence to say which of the unholy lot of amendments I have put down you would advise me to cut out of the proof. My Lord of Exeter has not seen them yet, and I expect I shall be exceedingly unpopular if they all stand: he will probably cut out a lot anyhow on the ground that it cannot be said to be liturgically wrong to use a collect less good, shall we say, than might be imagined. I think some of them are very, very poor; but I don't want to waste the Committee's time: only that if they are going to acquiesce it should be deliberately, not by default.

I should be most honestly grateful for criticism.

I have had nothing from Brightman and have written to him on the chance that he may after all send something.

I shall hold back the proof till I hear from you further....

Yours ever,
Claude Jenkins.

Frere replied as follows.

Frere to the Revd. Claude Jenkins 28 *September* 1915

My dear Jenkins,

I am returning the proof. I have been spending such time as I could get today in going over bits of it. It certainly is unfortunate that you and I should figure so much, but I am not sure whether a printed apology from you is the best way of getting over the difficulty; and personally I should feel rather happier if you left out the first sentence of your note, though, of course, it is true enough. I wonder if we still cannot get some of the other members to figure upon the Agenda more. I am writing to Christopher Wordsworth urging him to do something. I had a letter from Brightman on the subject of my suggestions, and while differing from some of them, he says he would probably himself be prepared to propose some. From his comments, which are mainly those of dissent, I gather that he would be in favour of Section 36. ii (Rubric): Section 40, page 35: and Section 116, page 47, paragraph v. So I am writing to ask him whether he will take those off my hands.¹ If he will, I think it will be a relief both to you and to me to have other names on the list. He may, of course, be willing to take up more of the points; and if he sends in things, as I hope he will, for other than those which are down to one of us, it would be far better if he did them. I will tell him to write to you, though of course one never knows whether he will or not.

I am inclined to think, on going over your list, that the things which are criticisms of the wording of the rubric are hardly worth having in when there is so much else. . . . I suppose the Draft Report does not profess to have done anything more than make jottings to be put into more accurate language later on. I think we shall a little bit waste powder if we concern ourselves merely with the wording of rubrics.

As to the wording of collects, I hardly know what to say, except that I gave them up as hopeless and came to the conclusion that it was best to say nothing about them at all. But I like your page 5 and argument drawn from the Proper Prefaces, so I hope you will express as adequately as you get the opportunity the dissatisfaction that most of the collects provide.² They really would be very bad as extempore prayers most of them, and are quite unfit for print, let alone recitation. . . .

I hope this is in time to be of some use, but what will survive Herod in the shape of the Bishop of Exeter I really don't know. I gather from your letter that you have got another copy of the proof, and therefore I am sending this to Brightman as a stimulus, charging him to send it on to you, though without delay. . . .

On the same day Frere wrote appeals for proposals to Canon Wordsworth and Dr. Brightman. The first met with no response, but the second was surprisingly successful.

¹ Sec. 36. The first rubric in the H.C. Service to be retained as it is, as against the proposal in the Report to delete the words 'at least some time the day before'.
Sec. 40. The Summary of the Law should not be permitted as a substitute for the Ten Commandments at H.C.
Sec. 116. At Confirmation no address should intervene between 'Our help' &c. and the laying on of hands.

² Jenkins wrote in a note to the Agenda: 'From our experience in regard to Proper Prefaces it seems probable that a reconsideration of some of the collects might produce alternatives which Convocation would be willing to accept. The Collect for the Transfiguration taken from the Scottish Book does not represent the principal reason for which some of us desire its commemoration: the Thanksgiving for Seasonable Weather might well be improved; and as a hospital chaplain I most earnestly hope that we may find better prayers for the sick, for hospitals, and for those who minister to them. The collects following are not submitted as alternatives, but in the hope that some member of the Committee may be able to put into a worthier form what they try to say.'

Advisory Committee on Liturgical Questions

Frere to the Revd. F. E. Brightman   28 *September* 1915

My dear Brightman,

Many thanks for your letter of 18 September. Jenkins has sent me a proof of the document that is going out, and I am sorry to find that he and I are almost the only people who figure on it. I hope you will let me take out my name from some of the places and insert yours instead. I have marked on slip 3 and 4 three motions with which I gather from your letter that you are heartily in sympathy. Will you undertake these instead of me? And do send in other things. There is just time I expect, and really the Committee will be reduced even to a lower state of futility if there is nobody but Jenkins and me alternating with an occasional bit of Maclean. Do what you can, and that speedily; and write to Jenkins as soon as you can, sending him on this proof: possibly I ought to have returned it direct to him. But I have written to him to say what I am writing to you, and I know he has written to you in something of the same sense: so I do hope you will step in some of the breaches and that speedily. . . .

The results of this appeal are indicated in a further letter from Jenkins.

The Revd. Claude Jenkins to Frere   4 *October* 1915

Eruditissime,

. . . I have received your proof from F. E. B. today and have sent the revise to the printers to be struck off. You will be fairly astonished when you see it, for Brightman has sent in a series of criticisms huge in number and covering nearly the whole ground.

I am profoundly glad and have cut out the apologetic note from my first sentence. I inserted it because it seemed ὕβρις in me to be taking up so much space. I am so glad you agree about the collects and Brightman writes just as strongly: he has proposed emendations for many of them but does not seem satisfied that some of them can be mended.

Your point about wasting powder is one which I feel strongly in some cases; but we are up against a great difficulty. I think I could spot one Bishop who will raise the question of the paragraph in the Archbishop's letter about our not being asked to undertake a revision of the whole of their work. If that is done and the Bishop of Exeter inclines to it, we shall have to proceed by way of general resolutions; but as the present motions are drawn, it is very difficult to rule any individual one out of order. The Bishop writes that he hesitates about some of them, but does not indicate which.

What I am afraid of is this: on some big questions, e.g. the alternative service of Holy Communion, we are almost certainly going to be beaten, as the Upper House will not give way now that the Bishop of London[1] has gone over. If that is so, there is a very real danger that the things we most care about not having come off, there should go through as the product of revision—with the 'acquiescence' at any rate of our Committee—the really deplorably mediocre stuff which most of the rest is. And as for the rubrics, so far from those being rough jottings as they ought to be, they are what will actually appear in the new annexed book unless cause is shown to the contrary. So far as my opportunity of judging goes, those of the Bishops who are not utterly bored with the whole subject—which is to them even as dilapidations—are rather pleased with their work; and some of them are by no means prepared to welcome criticism on it.[2] It was quite clear at the last meeting that some of them were inclined to be restive under some frank expressions of opinion as to their ideas of a Proper Preface; though they laughed when Canon Dalton boomed forth in a big voice, 'Episcopi Anglicani semper pavidissimi'. However, clearly the result was an improvement; though I know that the Bishop of Exeter dreads a repetition of the strain. I think he is really very ill. I am awfully sorry about it. I am perfectly certain that he doesn't want to force things through as some of them do.

The strong point in our position is the Archbishop's attitude: he objects to change unless it can be shown to be justified and of primary importance. But if, on a subject where he has no special knowledge, people whose knowledge on that subject he respects say that such and such a thing which it is proposed to do ought not to be done, you may be certain that it will not be done. If, on the other hand, they say such and such a thing ought to be done, he will go as far with them as other considerations make it possible, and do his best to make them possible. In a case where he has special knowledge, he will follow his own judgement, while welcoming all manner of criticisms so as to be certain that he has not overlooked any point.

[1] Dr. Winnington-Ingram.
[2] In the light of this remark, it is interesting to note what the Bishop of Norwich, Dr. Pollock, conceived the functions of the Committee to be. On 5 July 1916 in the Upper House he claimed it to be 'a body which was appointed for the minor function of preventing the House from making slips in diction, and so on'.

So that if we are driven to general resolutions, there is still hope. Only in that case, the people on either side will make just all the difference.

F. E. B. says he is prepared to die in the last ditch for some of his motions, so that the struggle will at least be heroic.

Yours ever,
Claude Jenkins.

When the Committee met from 19 to 23 October the proposals were entirely in the hands of the Bishop of Moray, Brightman, Jenkins, and Frere. As Frere had hoped, many of his own suggestions were taken off his hands by the other three. The meeting was a great success for this little group, largely as a result of some plain speaking led by Frere. On this Dr. Claude Jenkins provides the following note.

'Frere and I sat nearly always side by side (sometimes with Morley Stevenson between us) and though we usually talked sitting at a large table, he stood up at the fourth or fifth meeting and made an impassioned protest that though we were a body of people who were supposed to have devoted a good deal of time and thought to liturgical questions we were not being allowed to consider any of the matters which to liturgists constituted the main points of interest in any scheme of Prayer Book Revision by way of enrichment or otherwise. He was backed up by three other liturgists present, viz. H. A. Wilson, F. E. Brightman, and the Bishop of Moray and Ross—whether or not there had been previous discussion I don't know. The English Bishops were rather startled; although the matter dropped for the moment, there was rather less disposition to raise questions if 'x' were strictly within our terms of reference.'

Scarcely any of the group's proposals were ultimately rejected, though two of Frere's did not find acceptance: (17) a plea for different forms of Confession and Absolution at Morning and Evening Prayer; and (116) the declaration of assent by confirmation candidates to the Nicene Creed in the Conciliar form.

The findings of the Committee were drawn up in a Report which was submitted to the Upper House of Convocation. It was, in the words of the Bishop of Gloucester, 'a microscopic scrutiny' of Report 487B,[1] and bore striking testimony to the Committee's dissatisfaction with Convocation's attempts at Prayer Book Revision. The Report was in four sections. The first two contained some 160 points dealing with liturgical and textual details; the third dealt with matters of drafting, while the fourth contained a list of certain questions upon which the Advisory Committee were willing to give advice should the Upper

---

[1] *Chronicle of Convocation*, 1917, p. 19.

House desire it. The sting here, too, was undoubtedly in the tail: the Bishops were being asked to listen to the advice of experts on a large range of subjects outside the terms of reference.

This was once more largely the work of Frere. On 20 October he had proposed 'that it is urgent that some alternative form of the Order of Holy Communion be provided', but his proposal was ruled out of order. The Chairman, however, suggested that they should send up with their Report an intimation of their desire to be allowed to consider such questions as this—a proposal to which all members except the Bishop of Ripon, Dr. Drury, agreed.[1] Before the conclusion of the meetings the subject was discussed again when the Bishop of Moray raised the question of the Psalter course. Frere thereupon produced a list of subjects on which the Committee might express its readiness to be consulted, and the Bishop of Ripon, his opposition to the plan now overcome, himself moved a resolution to this effect.[2] The following conclusion was therefore inserted as the fourth section of the Report:

That this Committee would be glad to offer their advice on the following points, should the Upper House be willing to receive it—

1. Principles of Psalter-recitation and of the Lectionary at Morning and Evening Prayer.
2. The use of the Quicunque Vult.
3. The use of an alternative Order of Holy Communion.
4. The use of a general alternative Order for Burial.
5. The restoration of some form of Holy Unction.
6. The provision of an alternative and briefer formula for use by the Bishop at Confirmation.
7. The Lectionary of the Holy Communion.
8. The provision of psalmody for the Holy Communion.
9. The correction of the misplaced words in the Preface.
10. The restoration of 'Holy' in the Nicene Creed.
11. The use of Antiphons in the Occasional Offices.
12. The provision of a substitute for Te Deum in Lent.
13. Processionals for the Great Festivals.
14. The Order for the Consecration of Churches.[3]

The presentation of the Report suffered considerable delay, due mainly to the illness of the Bishop of Gloucester, Dr. Gibson. Finally on 5 July 1916, rather than wait any longer, the Upper House agreed that the Joint Committee of the two Houses should consider it and report at the

[1] *Minutes of the 7th Meeting of the Advisory Committee*, 20 Oct. 1915, p. 6.
[2] Ibid., 23 Oct. 1915, pp. 18-19.
[3] *Report of the Advisory Committee on Liturgical Questions upon the Resolutions of the Joint Committee* (487B), pp. 22-23.

next session of Convocation.¹ This was done and on 8 February 1917 the Bishop of Gloucester, now recovered, was able to present Report 487C to the Upper House. Only Sections 1 and 2 of the Advisory Committee's proposals were considered. It was thought inadvisable to study the details of drafting in Section 3 at this stage, while Section 4 had been clearly beyond the competence of the Joint Committee to consider—that was a question purely and simply for the Upper House. Of Sections 1 and 2 the Joint Committee had agreed absolutely or substantially to 113 of the Advisory Committee's points: in 11 others they had framed a resolution in consequence of the advice given, though differing from it in some measure; in 5 others a decision was deferred in view of matters still being discussed by Convocation; while in the remaining 31 cases the Joint Committee had refused to accept the advice given.² The House then considered the Report and accepted it with the exception of one important point. Against the advice of both the Advisory Committee and Joint Committee the Summary of the Law was retained as an alternative to the Ten Commandments in the Order for Holy Communion.³

The Upper House also unwisely disregarded the Committee's offer of advice on the questions in Section 4 with the single exception of the Athanasian Creed. The Committee recommended its use as a Canticle instead of the Venite on certain occasions—verses 30 to 39 on Christmas Day and the Feast of the Epiphany, and verses 3 to 27 on Whit Sunday and Trinity Sunday. The Upper House approved of the suggestion but the Lower House rejected it, and the proposal was dropped.

With the publication of Report 504 in 1917 and Report 515 in 1918 the Canterbury Convocation's proposals for Revision were completed and the Advisory Committee was summoned no more. Its life, on the whole, had not been a happy one: its usefulness had been restricted by the severe limitation of its terms of reference: and some of its most valuable advice had been rejected. Nevertheless, some good results were achieved and its contributions to the Revised Prayer Book were not unimportant—the Table of Occurrences, the Order of Compline, the Invitatories to the Venite, the additional Proper Prefaces, the re-arrangement of the latter portion of the Litany, the wording of some of the Additional Prayers, and the form of recitation of the Ten Commandments. In all this work Frere's share was considerable. Not only did he lay the foundations for the proposals on Compline and the Litany, as we have already seen, but the Committee's brief Minutes make it clear that he played a leading part in the work on the Table of Occurrences, the Invitatories to the Venite, and the Proper Prefaces.

¹ *Chronicle of Convocation*, 1916, p. 469.
² Ibid., 1917, p. 19.   ³ Ibid., pp. 32-35.

III

THE REARRANGEMENT OF THE CANON

CONCURRENTLY with his work on the Advisory Committee Frere was busily engaged with the problem of the Canon in the Communion Office. His dissatisfaction with the 1662 Canon was clearly stated in his *Principles of Liturgical Reform*:

'It will probably be recognized that the present state of our liturgy at this point is gravely at variance, both with the oldest and most universal liturgical tradition, and also with the practical needs of the Church today. . . . Our present Consecration Prayer stands baldly in isolation from all that belongs to it. On one side the Prayer of Humble Access separates it from the Preface and Sanctus, with which it is intimately connected by right; and, on the other side, the whole act of Communion separates it from the Prayer of Oblation and the Lord's Prayer, which also are, when rightly placed, integral parts with it of one whole. . . . There is a wide divergence at present between the Latin West and the more primitive East as to the doctrine of Consecration. . . . Until this doctrinal point is nearer a settlement, it would be inopportune to take any steps towards the reinsertion of the Invocation of the Holy Spirit in either of the positions which it has come to occupy. . . . But the present state of our Order is doing harm, and hindering worship. Standing in its isolation as little more than a recital of the Institution, our present Consecration Prayer is more Roman than Rome. It ties the act of consecration more narrowly to the Words of the original administration than any other Christian liturgy has ever done; and it encourages, therefore, inevitably the habit of looking upon the consecration in the narrowest and most partisan way. . . . There is a simple and small step in the right direction which can be taken easily, and will not carry us farther than we are at present able to go. . . . The restoration may at first be only optional and experimental; nothing need be altered in the Book as it stands: only in the Codicil permission should be given for the rearrangement of the order as follows:

1. Comfortable Words.
2. Prayer of Humble Access.
3. Sursum Corda, &c.

The Rearrangement of the Canon

4. Preface and Sanctus.
5. Consecration Prayer.
6. Prayer of Oblation.
7. Lord's Prayer.'[1]

The matter was first raised in July 1913 by Canon Dalton, who asked Frere to support a Resolution on the rearrangement of the Canon at a meeting of the Advisory Committee. Frere did not agree with all the contents of the proposal and reminded Canon Dalton that in any case it was unconstitutional for the Advisory Committee to discuss matters which had not been submitted to it for consideration.

The Revd. Canon J. N. Dalton to Frere   21 July 1913

My dear Frere,

On Monday next after we have settled about the Proper Prefaces, would you feel inclined to second the Resolution I enclose? It goes only one step further than what you recommend in your *Liturgical Reform*, in that I venture to bring back the general intercession to the Canon, and place the Prayer of Humble Access after, instead of before, the Prayer of Consecration.

I am sure we must not attempt any change in the actual wording of the Prayers now. But the rearrangement of their order I do hope we shall obtain.

If you, with Wilson and Brightman, were agreed in what recommendation should be made to their Lordships, I hope our Committee would be unanimous, and that something might come of it; and I would fain hope that the enclosed might be adopted.

Your very sincerely,
J. N. Dalton.

Frere to the Revd. Canon J. N. Dalton   23 July 1913

My dear Canon,

Of course I sympathize with the main purpose, but I have two difficulties.

First, that I think the intercessions had much better be kept where they are, in the old position before they were transferred to the Anaphora. Secondly, that I think the 'Order of Communion' section should

[1] *Principles of Liturgical Reform*, pp. 187–91.

be all kept together. I am indifferent as to whether it comes before the Sursum Corda or immediately before Communion; but I am very unwilling to split it up and put part of it in one place and part in another. In other words, I think the Prayer of Humble Access ought to follow the Comfortable Words. I hope that if the Prayer of Oblation follows the Prayer of Consecration, as it certainly should do, the Amen of the former may be omitted, and *Wherefore* may be prefixed to the latter. This is so simple that it could be done by rubric, leaving the Prayer Book printed as it is. For (*v*) it is important I think to have no Amen, so as to make sure that the two prayers coalesce into one, and (*b*) this coalescing is more effectively done by the transitional word, *Wherefore*.

I am afraid I probably shan't be able to come up on Monday. It is difficult to get away from here in any case then, and I have two sets of people to see on that day. I wonder if the Chairman will let you bring this in without invitation from my Lords? We certainly want an opportunity of expressing our minds on this, which is the most valuable and necessary of all forms of the Communion Office. But get Exon to move the Bishops to ask for an opinion. Then give it, not squeeze it in unasked.

Yours sincerely,
W. H. Frere

Canon Dalton did not succeed in raising the subject at the meeting of the Advisory Committee, but before long it came to the very front in the Revision movement. On 9 February 1914 the Lower House of Canterbury Convocation agreed by 79 votes to 8 'that the Prayer of Humble Access should be removed from its present position, and placed immediately before the Communion of priest and people; that the "Amen" at the end of the present Prayer of Consecration should be omitted, and that the Prayer of Oblation should follow at once (prefaced by the word *Wherefore*), and then the Lord's Prayer.'[1] This was, in effect, proposing a compulsory alteration in the Communion Service. The Joint Committee of both Houses accepted this proposal in January 1915, but with the modification that it should be a permissive and not a compulsory rearrangement.[2] On 28 April, however, the Upper House completely rejected it by 15 votes to 5,[3] whereupon Frere drew up a Memorandum deploring their decision.

[1] *Chronicle of Convocation*, 1914, pp. 152–61.
[2] *Report of Joint Committee Canterbury Convocation No. 487*, 1915, section 59, p. 28.
[3] *Chronicle of Convocation*, 1915, pp. 273–95.

A Crisis in Prayer Book Revision   23 April 1915

On Wednesday in last week the Bishops sitting in the Upper House of the Convocation of Canterbury rejected by 15 votes to 5 a proposal brought before them by the Joint Committee concerned with Prayer Book Revision couched in the following terms: 'Permission shall be given for the rearrangement of the Canon as follows: The Prayer of Consecration shall be said immediately after the Sanctus, the *Amen* at the end being omitted; the Prayer of Oblation shall follow at once (prefaced by the word *Wherefore*), and the Lord's Prayer; then shall be said the Prayer of Humble Access, followed by the Communion of Priest and People; after the Communion shall follow the Thanksgiving, the Gloria, and the Blessing.'

The proposal is not a new one: it had previously been accepted by the Lower House on the recommendation of its own Committee; and from thence it passed into the proposals of the Joint Committee. This past history seemed to promise that the proposal would be adopted; more especially as it deals with one of the worst blots on the present Book of Common Prayer. Its rejection, therefore, is somewhat of a surprise; for Revision without some attempt to remove this blot is almost like 'Hamlet' with Hamlet left out. It would not be respectful to comment on the speeches of those Bishops who gave their grounds for voting in the majority. We may confine ourselves, therefore, to noting the fact of the decision, and pass on reluctantly to consider its significance.

The Church of England has at present the worst liturgy in Christendom.

1. Its defects since 1552 have continually been felt. The principal point now proposed, the reunion of the Prayer of Oblation with the Consecration Prayer (from which it was divorced in 1552) was prominent in two ways in the early seventeenth century; for (*a*) some bishops (and others too no doubt) were accustomed in celebrating Holy Communion thus to restore the Prayer of Oblation to its proper position: and (*b*) in the Scottish Book of 1637 the matter was authoritatively and more satisfactorily handled, for the new Canon or Consecration Prayer was then made on sound traditional lines, from which, of course, the present Scottish Liturgy descends.

2. The defects are not merely those of liturgical form. The present truncated Consecration Prayer, ending as it does with the recital of the Words of Institution, tends to inculcate a doctrine of consecration

which is exaggeratedly Roman and Western in its character. If, as is probably the case, the Roman Canon is, next to our English Rite, the most unsatisfactory of liturgies, the two are alike also in the fact that our prayer emphasizes and wildly exaggerates one of the least satisfactory features of the Roman Rite, i.e. the unbalanced prominence of the Words of Institution.

3. Further, the divorce of the Prayer of Oblation has another unfortunate doctrinal effect. The divorce of oblation from consecration tended to encourage a habit of distinguishing between sacrifice and communion, instead of keeping the two in close touch, according to the sound teaching of St. Augustine, clearly expressed by our Canon before it was dismembered.

4. The present Order is also very undesirable on practical grounds. The dislocation of the Canon, from which our rite suffers, has given rise to the habit, which spreads in spite of all protests, of the celebrant importing large sections of the Latin Canon in order to fill the hiatus caused by the postponement of the Prayer of Oblation till after Communion. As long as the dislocation is continued that habit will go on; it has increased in the last half-century by leaps and bounds. It is obviously incongruous and even grotesque; but it is the lesser of two evils and so it flourishes.

These things clamour for a remedy; and no simpler or more conservative remedy could be devised than that which the Joint Committee recommended. It is intolerable that the Church of England should go on with a Rite, closely akin to the Scottish and American Rites, and yet so abjectly inferior to both of them. Measures of reform and restoration more comprehensive and ideal than this might easily have been proposed, and could easily have been justified. But that this minimum of change should be rejected seems almost incredible. Even with it made, our position would still have been a long way inferior to that of Scotland or America. And those liturgies, even though they are better than the Roman, are still not all that they should be, judged by the standard of the other great and ancient liturgies of Christendom. We can but hope that this decision is not final. The proposal has not yet come before the members of the Lower House of Canterbury; and when it does, we may hope that they will have sufficient courage and faith to stick to their guns. If it were to turn out so, it would not be the first time that the Lower House saved the situation.

If this decision of the Upper House had emanated from a body of extremists on either wing, no one would have been surprised; since for

The Rearrangement of the Canon

widely divergent reasons both wings wish to keep things as they are. If it had come from the opponents of Prayer Book Revision, it would have been intelligible, for it is a good wrecking measure; and no one will rejoice over it so much as the various sections who favour chaos and disorder—doctrinal, liturgical, disciplinary, &c.—and therefore wish to keep things as they are. The warnings and instructions of the Bishop of Oxford (Dr. Gore) seem to have fallen on heedless ears in the Upper House—or were they too deafened for the moment by the impotent thunder of the Protestant extremists to take in what he said?

Anyhow, the immediate result seems to be that some of those who have hitherto been keenest on Revision will have to reconsider their position: and that the whole project, if not wrecked, is gravely endangered.

In November of the same year Frere also expressed his views on the subject in the Lower House of the Convocation of York, to which he had been elected as Proctor for the Archdeaconry of Halifax on 29 January 1914.[1] The House was discussing the Report of the Joint Committee of York on the Royal Letters of Business recommending the provision of a Book supplementary to the Book of Common Prayer with alternative forms of service 'provided that no alternative Service of the order of Holy Communion be included'. He pleaded that the real need of the day was not rigid uniformity, but a frank recognition of diversities. There should be some provision for a modest rearrangement of the existing materials with the insertion of an Epiclesis. The majority of the House was evidently with him, for they finally passed an amendment by Canon Scott and seconded by Frere omitting the proviso on Holy Communion by 23 votes to 12.[2]

At the end of 1915, therefore, the situation was that the Lower Houses of both Canterbury and York were in favour of some rearrangement of the Canon, while both Upper Houses opposed it, the Upper House of York having also rejected it in July by 6 votes to 1.[3] With the passage of time, however, the situation improved. The Lower House of Canterbury remained firm in its decision and eventually the Upper House gave way; on 7 February 1918 it agreed to the Lower House's recommendation 'subject to amendment' by 13 votes to 7.[4] Only the Upper House of York persisted in its opposition. In October a Joint Conference of representatives of the four Houses of Canterbury and York (of whom Frere was one) was held to review the whole of the Revision proposals of both Provinces. On the question of the rearrangement of the Canon, in view of the lack of unanimity, it was agreed

[1] *York Journal of Convocation*, 1915, pp. 4–6. [2] Ibid., 1915–16, pp. 58–72.
[3] Ibid., 1915, pp. 313–16. [4] *Chronicle of Convocation*, 1918, pp. 86, 165.

unanimously, 'That their Graces the Archbishops be respectfully asked to call together a conference of clergy belonging to different schools of thought, in which younger men and liturgical scholars should have full representation, to discuss (after Communion and Prayer) the question of permissive alterations in the structure of Holy Communion, in order to find an agreed settlement in the matter.'[1]

Frere did not wait for such a Conference to be summoned, but immediately invited Dr. Drury, the Evangelical Bishop of Ripon, to explore the possibilities of a solution to the problem. His suggestion met with a ready response; not only was Dr. Drury a keen liturgical scholar, but his attitude to the whole question was much more reasonable than that of his Evangelical Northern brethren.[2] A lengthy and fruitful correspondence ensued.

Frere to the Bishop of Ripon   18 *November* 1918

My dear Bishop,

I hope you will not think me presuming or interfering if I venture to write a word to you on the subject for the proposal of an alternative Order of Communion Service. That proposal is now, I suppose, to come more or less soon before a Conference for consideration and, we hope,

---

[1] *Canterbury Convocation. Royal Letters of Business. Report* 517, 1919, sec. 65, pp. 41–42.

[2] His position is shown in the following extract from a speech in the Upper House of York in July 1915, when the proposal for an alternative Canon was rejected by 6 votes to 1. '... He could not agree with the Bishop of Manchester (Dr. Knox) that these changes altered the doctrine of the Church of England. What was done might possibly be mistaken to mean certain doctrines, but it was quite possible in each case, by making suggestions, to meet the question of the reconstruction of the canon. He was not saying for a moment that he advocated it, but it would be possible to do so without in the slightest degree altering the doctrine. The words of the Prayer of Oblation as they now used it could not be misconstrued. In regard to the Epiclesis it was possible that they might have a prayer such as that in the American Book which he considered was well within the four walls of Holy Scripture, and he would strongly dissent from the Bishop of Manchester saying that the Epiclesis would necessitate alterations of the doctrine of the Church of England. With regard to the Prayer of Humble Access he thought there was a good deal of confusion in what was suggested. He was heartily in favour of putting the Prayer back to its old place and he hoped it might be possible to restore the Sursum Corda to its old position as the introduction to the Prayer of Consecration. He did not think they would be likely to make any change that could in the remotest degree be said to change the doctrine of the Church, even although they might alter the position of the Prayer of Humble Access, introduce a Scriptural form of invoking the help of the Holy Spirit, which was needed in the service, or even by placing the Prayer of Oblation as a part of the Prayer of Consecration....' *York Journal of Convocation*, 1915, pp. 315–16.

a settlement. My point, to put it briefly, is this; that there is not much hope of such a Conference being of value unless some of those who have hitherto opposed the proposal, or at least been anxious and troubled by it, feel able to come to the Conference prepared to offer some alternative.

I venture to write to your Lordship on the subject as holding a mediating position in this matter.

First, as to the justification for having an alternative at all:

(a) I don't suppose anyone would feel that there was no alternative possible for the English Church besides its present Office. The existence of several Anglican Orders, like that of Scotland—and still more of America—is sufficient to show that point.

(b) In Scotland there are two Offices in use; and the joint use of the two works well as a compromise. Some prefer one, some the other. In an increasing number of congregations both are in use.

(c) It may, of course, be said that our circumstances are different, and that the sanctioning of two Offices would accentuate party division, and difference between one type of church and another. I should be the last person to wish to accentuate differences. It seems to me that the opposite might be the result. I mean that all here depends upon the nature of the alternative service which might be provided. If it was one that was really acceptable to those who are now opposing, or regretting, the sanctioning of that alternative, then surely the opposite would be the case? There would be real hope that the alternative would be used in churches of various types; and those who think thus would not be as now in the odious position of not wanting anything themselves and not letting anybody else have it either.

I come therefore to the second part of my plea. Is it not possible to provide an alternative form of service which would not merely be tolerable to the Evangelicals (and of course it must be that), but definitely accepted and welcomed by them? This leads me to say a word or two about the reasons which prompt so many people of different kinds to wish for an alternative.

(a) There is the question of balance. It is felt that our present prayer is too curtailed and insignificant; it has not the dignity required for a central prayer in the Communion Order, and it ends too abruptly.

(b) It ends on Maunday Thursday and has no mention of the Resurrection or Ascension. It anticipates a reference to our Lord's second coming, but does not actually look forward to that. Such features, as your Lordship is well aware, are in more or less degree general features of the old liturgies; and one cannot but feel and wish that they should be included in our Communion Office in some way which all churchmen alike could share.

(c) The present ending of the prayer gives a very uncomfortable sanction to an extreme form of the Western doctrine of consecration. From many points of view, which I need not describe, this seems to be undesirable. We already have too much influence of the West, and it is not according to the wisdom of the English Church to take such a partisan position in the difference between East and West as is implied in the present prayer, ending as it does with the recitation of the Words of Institution.

(d) The original proposal merely to invert the order was made, I think, not because this was merely the best way of providing an alternative; but because it was thought that by confining the proposal to words already in use in the Prayer Book, the best means were taken to assure all who needed assurance, that no alteration in the balance or permissible area of eucharistic doctrine was either intended or effected. If this is felt to be unsuitable, those who wish for some sort of change have, I think, the right to ask what the others would think was suitable. I have no right to speak on their behalf; but I am sure that the great bulk of those who, for example, in the Convocation Committee were prepared to vote for some alternative were not anxious to get any party gain, or get any tactical advantages of a doctrinal kind. I believe the bulk of them would be quite prepared to say, 'Give us our alternative and let the Evangelicals draw it up themselves, and say what they heartily would approve of.'

I have left to the end one further consideration, which I know must be in your mind. It is only of quite a secondary kind in itself, but it has a real importance in the practical working of any discussion. No one can doubt that brevity in our present prayer has led to the widespread habit of using parts of the Latin Service, whether legitimately in the form of private devotion, unobtruded upon the people and brief in character, or in the form of supplement to the deficiency of our present Rite, said silently but in the mind of the celebrant treated with an importance equal to that of the official Rite. There is a widespread, and I had almost said, universal desire that such a state of things should cease. But it will not cease until the cause which has produced it is removed. It is the natural result of the brevity of our present prayer, that for one cause or another, clergy add a good deal privately; most of them with entire loyalty, as I should judge, to the Church in which they minister.

But one cannot conceal from oneself the fact that the present position of our Office is one of the chief causes which makes for a Romanizing tendency, and encourages men who would far prefer to take their directions from the English Church to look elsewhere for them. The English Church fails them, as they feel it does, in this matter of the Consecration Prayer.

I speak only from a limited experience, of course, as to the effect that such a change would have, but I am confident that an alternative Order would be a sovereign preservative against Romanizing. There are certain places now, where, by permission of the Bishop, such a transposition which has been proposed is habitually made. Many of the churches where this is done would probably be ranked as extreme. I think a loyal inquiry into the present position would show that as a result of that permission the long private prayers have ceased, still more the conformable and intentional interpolation of the Latin Canon, and that in fact a root of bitterness and source of disloyalty has been removed. I believe that, given an alternative form, this healing process would be greatly extended so as to include all but an insignificant minority of irreconcilables, such as there always are in any flank.

In venturing to write all this I don't want to add to your Lordship's correspondence. I merely send this letter as a suggestion over which I have been thinking ever since the Conference—not expecting an answer, but merely hoping that, if there is anything in it of profit, it may be in your hands in exercising a mediating influence in the present discussion. . . .

The Bishop of Ripon to Frere   *23 December* 1918

My dear Dr. Frere,

I cannot express how ashamed I am of my silence in reply to your kind and suggestive letter. I once began to write and never finished, and now I write under much pressure. But I have considered the question all round, and while I have not much hope of a *via media* which both sides would tread, yet I could not let your appeal receive anything but careful thought and effort. I propose to see one or two of those who think with even judgement on both sides.

I cannot enter now into the details of your letter but would like to have your opinion of some such proposals as these.

Yours most sincerely,
T. W. Ripon

A

1. Leave the two prayers after the Lord's Prayer where they are, substituting 'and' for 'or' in the Rubric.

2. Add at the close of the present Prayer of Consecration a clause of memorial so worded as to omit phrases which have unfortunately been associated with doctrines to which grave objection has been taken. I feel so unfit even to suggest that I hardly dare send you a modification of the Scottish and American form.

3. The Lord's Prayer to be restored into its old position. And I should like to introduce it by that bold word of faith—*Audemus dicere*.

4. If possible, a prayer for the operation of the Holy Spirit in what I always regard as our 'Epiclesis', but after the manner of the American form.

I add for your private eye something of what I mean.

B

1. Hear us we most humbly beseech thee, O merciful Father, and send thy Holy Spirit upon us and upon these thy gifts of bread and wine, that we receiving them, according to our Saviour Jesus Christ's Holy Institution, in remembrance of his death and passion, may be partakers of his most blessed Body and Blood.

2. Wherefore, O Lord and Heavenly Father, we thy humble servants do commemorate with these thy holy gifts his great oblation (once), offered for us all, having in remembrance his blessed passion and precious death, his mighty resurrection and glorious ascension: rendering unto thee most hearty thanks for the innumerable benefits procured unto us for the same, and looking for his coming again.

3. As our Saviour hath commanded and taught us we are bold to say, Our Father.

C

I quite agree with you in wishing for the restoration of the memory of the resurrection, &c., and surely for the reference to 'his coming again (till he come)'. The phrase 'do commemorate with these thy holy gifts his great oblation once offered for us all' is of course the most crucial point. Personally I have no objection to 'celebrate the memorial' omitting 'and make', but I fear . . . I tried also 'do continue the perpetual memory' from the opening words of the Prayer. I have avoided (perhaps unnecessarily) repetition of 'According . . . holy institution'.

I feel sure it would also ease matters if 'We do not presume' were restored to its original place after the Comfortable Words *where they now stand*, i.e. before the Sursum Corda. This is important in view of Gardiner's charge against Cranmer of having maintained the Mass in 1549. I confess that in view of the state of our Church, I fear the same use of it would be made now. . . .

Frere to the Bishop of Ripon   6 *January* 1919
My dear Bishop,

Many thanks for your letter of 23 December. I am very much encouraged by it, and by a prospect which I hope there is of something coming from your action which will be valuable to the Church.

My main preoccupation was to try and see if something could not be found which would really be welcome to the Evangelicals, and not raise suspicions but allay them. From that point of view I felt, and still feel, rather dubious about attempting anything that would introduce difficulties, or bring out unnecessarily the different shades of view.

1. I don't think 'and' for 'or' really solves the question or gives much relief.

2. The simplest form of the problem as it suggests itself to my mind is this, that the Lord's Prayer should precede communion not follow it (with its prayer for daily bread), and that therefore some link is necessary between it and the present brief consecration prayer; and that link affords the opportunity for the commemoration of our Lord's resurrection, ascension, and return.

What I may perhaps call a more ambitious plan, which would contemplate some invocation of the Holy Spirit, would seem to me more dangerous as likely to produce or reveal differences of opinion; therefore, however I should value that and some other things, I should hesitate to suggest them at the present stage of things. This I think very much agrees with your No. 2.

Of course I cordially agree with your No. 3, restoring the old link of the Lord's Prayer with the Consecration Prayer.

In general I do not want so much to urge things which I or people like me would value, as to ask what would be valued, or at least deemed harmless, by those who hitherto have not seen their way to contemplate an alternative form. At the same time, perhaps I might say in general that I am not myself greatly in love with the Scottish form of memorial, for it seems to make the memorial to consist, not in reproducing our Lord's action in the Upper Room as already has been done, but in doing something further and supplementary to this—'We do here make with these thy gifts'; and though personally I don't object to that as a statement, I can imagine others having much stronger feelings against it than I have myself. My idea would be that it would raise much less objection merely to have some such phrase as 'Wherefore, Lord and Heavenly Father, we thy humble servants having in remembrance ... do render unto Thee ... and shew forth his death until his coming again; entirely desiring thy fatherly goodness, &c.' I am not thinking of what is ideal but of what would be irenic and unquestionable common ground.

I am very thankful to think that the Prayer of Humble Access might be transferred to stand after the Comfortable Words as you suggest. Personally I much prefer to have the whole of that preparation made before the Sursum Corda, rather than after the Consecration.

Most grateful I am for all that you are doing, and hopeful indeed for some good outcome, please God. . . .

The Bishop of Ripon to Frere   18 *January* 1919

My dear Dr. Frere,

Your letter seems to shed a ray of hope on our darkness, and I am sincerely thankful. I am inviting four of those who take reasonable views and long for some way of escape from the present dilemma to spend a night here and talk matters over.

We seem to agree on three points.

1. The removal of 'We do not presume' to a position *after* the Comfortable Words and *before* the Sursum Corda.

2. The position of the Lord's Prayer, and the restoration of the words of introduction to it. I think the petition for 'daily bread' is much more significant just before receiving our spiritual food.

3. The need for some connecting link between the Words of Institution and the Lord's Prayer, beginning with 'Wherefore', and commemorating not only the death, but also the resurrection and the ascension.

Where we seem to differ is in the actual wording of the Commemoration. Your suggestion is to place there, after words of grateful commemoration, the main body of the Prayer of Oblation (the first after Communion). To this I personally have no objection, but unfortunately it raises the real storm-centre of our unhappy divisions. And both sides have pulled so hard and made it so distinctly their battle-cry, that I am almost sure that the knot is drawn too tight for us to unravel. This we

The Rearrangement of the Canon 69

will discuss when I meet the others—i.e. the position of the first Post-communion Prayer.

The only solution I can hope for, if we are to win over the moderate Evangelicals, is to suggest *some such* words as I have suggested in the draft that I sent to you.

I am very much disappointed that a wisely chosen Epiclesis seems impossible to find, both as to words and place.

With sincere regards and thanks,
Yours most sincerely,
T. W. Ripon.

PS. I am putting down a next 'line of approach'.

'Wherefore, O Lord and Heavenly Father, we thy humble servants, having in remembrance thy Son's blessed passion and precious death, his mighty resurrection and glorious ascension, do render unto thee most hearty thanks for the innumerable benefits procured unto us by the same, and do look for his coming again . . . to whom with thee O Father Almighty, in the unity of the Holy Ghost, be all *honour and glory* (world without end—omit?).

As our Saviour . . . Our Father'.

The repeated 'Honor et Gloria' is I think not objectionable. Was it not the point (generally) of the Western 'Elevation' of the Consecrated Elements? I should like to retain the words in our Prayer of Consecration.

I see the difficulty of making the ascription at the end of the Consecration Prayer too identical with the end of the Prayer of Oblation. It is, of course, almost verbatim from the end of the old Canon.

Frere to the Bishop of Ripon   20 *January* 1919

My dear Bishop,

Thank you very much for your letter, which makes me feel that the hopes are on the increase. The three points that you note as points of agreement are I think really important, and I trust they may form the basis of a real advance to be made with hearty agreement.

I quite see the point about the Prayer of Oblation. I suppose it is true that at least since 1552 there has been a body of people who objected to having a Prayer of Oblation at all. When it was made an alternative to the Thanksgiving, the situation became a possible one for them, for they never need use it. The same would, of course, be true now in any restoration of the Prayer of Oblation to follow immediately after Consecration, for such an arrangement would, of course, only be for optional use. The ancient compromise would in that way still be preserved.

But what I am anxious to see is not any compromise so much (though there is a good deal to be said for them) as a continuation of the Consecration Prayer which all can heartily accept and use. Your draft seems to me certainly of that sort. I don't suppose it will be welcomed with enthusiasm by most of the High Church people, but at least they could have no objection to it, and they would recognize that it was an improvement on what we have. For myself I should be thankful to have it, if it represents the largest amount of common ground that is possible at the present time.

But I wonder whether the historic objection to the Prayer of Oblation concerns the whole prayer equally, and makes all of it equally unsuitable to be incorporated in your draft? Does it, for example, concern 'And here we offer and present unto thee' and the rest? If not, could not that be incorporated in your draft? One might even go further and ask, does it concern 'Humbly beseeching thee to grant' and the rest?

It seems to me highly desirable to get the Thanksgiving Prayer into more general use than it has at present in many quarters. This will most easily be effected if the new conclusion of the Consecration Prayer contains at any rate the bulk of the elements contained in the Prayer of Oblation. I do not think we can expect people to use both after Communion. The Post-communion of our rite is already more heavily weighted than is the case I think in any other rite, and to have the two prayers said would upset the centre of gravity still more. But I am drifting off again to expressing my own views, which is not really what I intend. What I am really interested in is eliciting the views of others, and particularly those which are likely to be different from mine.

Indeed my suggestion that at any rate the latter part of the Prayer of Oblation might be incorporated is merely put as a suggestion in order to elicit the opinion of those whom you have called in to discuss the matter. If it is felt that none of the Prayer of Oblation can be utilized, then probably there are some further elements which might be added in your draft (after the words 'coming again'), which all would accept and welcome, which would give rather more fullness and distinction to this part of the prayer, and lead quite naturally into the doxology.

Yours sincerely,
W. H. Frere

Frere to the Bishop of Ripon   22 *January* 1919

My dear Bishop,

Forgive me for adding to my letter of yesterday a small point, but of some material interest. If the Prayer of Humble Access is moved back, as is suggested, the opportunity comes then for restoring the link between the Sanctus and the Consecration Prayer, and two or three words there seem valuable. To myself the restoration of the Vere Sanctus seems the best link, thus linking the Consecration Prayer to the essence of the Sanctus and not merely as the Scottish do, the rather mistranslated end of it—'All glory'. If words such as 'Holy indeed art thou, for truly thou art holy' were prefixed, the whole would run on without change, except a change of stop before 'Hear us'.

Yours sincerely,
W. H. Frere

Shortly afterwards Dr. Drury sent the following undated draft to Frere:

Wherefore, O heavenly Father, according to his divine (holy) institution and solemn dying command, we, (thus) breaking and eating the Holy Bread, and drinking of the sacred Cup of Blessing, which is the communion of his blood, do here shew forth his lifegiving death, commemorating also his mighty resurrection and glorious ascension, and looking for his dread coming again.

Grant, O Lord, that the spiritual sacrifices which we thine unworthy servants offer (up), assembled before thee as an holy priesthood, may through his prevailing mediation be found acceptable unto thee.

Grant also that these our humble prayers may be brought by the ministry of thy holy angel and offered upon the golden altar that is before thy heavenly throne.

And grant, we beseech thee, O merciful God, that we ourselves who receive these inestimable gifts, bequeathed unto us by thy Son Jesus Christ, may be accepted of thee in him the beloved; and so, according to his great and precious promises, may escape the corruption that is in the world and be made partakers of thy divine nature and of the blessed inheritance of all thy saints in light and glory everlasting; where all blessing, honour, glory, and power are ascribed unto thee with him and with the Holy Ghost by every creature in earth and heaven now, henceforth, and for evermore. Amen.

Frere returned this with certain amendments:

> Wherefore, O Father, according to his holy institution and express command, we thus breaking and eating the Holy Bread which is the communion of the Body of Christ and drinking of the Cup of Blessing which is the communion of his blood, do shew forth his life-giving death; commemorating also his mighty resurrection and glorious ascension and looking for his dread coming again.
> Grant that the spiritual sacrifices which we now offer up, assembled before thee as an holy priesthood, may by (through) his mediation be found acceptable unto thee.
> Grant also that these our humble prayers may be brought by the ministry of thy holy angel and offered upon the golden altar that is before thy heavenly throne.
> Yet further we beseech thee, O merciful Father, that we ourselves who receive these pure and holy gifts according to the institution of thy Son, our Saviour Jesus Christ, may be accepted in him the beloved; and so, according to his great and gracious promises, may escape the corruption that is in the world and be made partakers of thy divine nature and of the blessed inheritance of thy saints in light everlasting, where all blessing, honour, glory, and power are ascribed unto thee with him and with the Holy Ghost by every creature in earth and heaven (world without end) (for ever and evermore). Amen.

Frere then added this form of Epiclesis:

> And we most humbly beseech thee, O merciful Father, to hear us and of thy almighty goodness vouchsafe to bless and sanctify with thy Word and Holy Spirit this Holy Bread of Eternal Life and this Cup of Everlasting Salvation, that we may receive this mystery of the Body and Blood of thy Son to our everlasting welfare.

Some little time elapsed before the Bishop of Ripon replied, for he was occupied in discussing with others what he called 'our common lines of approach'. Meanwhile, on 24 March the Archbishop of Canterbury issued invitations to some fifty people, among whom were the Bishop of Ripon and Frere, to attend the proposed conference on 2 May. Opposition to the plan was considerable: a weighty Memorial was presented to the Archbishops, signed by nine bishops, 3,000 clergy, and 100,000 laymen protesting against any changes in the Communion Service. Nevertheless, this was not quite so serious as it appeared: Dr.

Drury discovered that 'not a few who signed the Memorial are not averse to *some* modification of the Canon, if it helps to meet reasonable wishes for improvement, without altering the present balance of doctrine'.

The Bishop of Ripon to Frere   12 *April* 1919

My dear Dr. Frere,

I enclose a letter written some days ago but never dated or sent. I am ashamed of my silence, but it has been quite unavoidable. I have, however, been sounding others on what I hope I may call our common lines of approach.

I think the first clause of your amended draft is very good and worth while considering; though I venture to doubt if it would be accepted. As a whole I think the draft too long. My own idea (for what it is worth) is that we should fix attention on the three or four points in my earlier letter and try to cull words to express the addition which we seek after the Words of Institution from the 1549 or Scottish books. This would also bring us *somewhere* into line with the American words. I wonder if you have at all sounded those who are eager for a change, as to their acceding to what we have tried to map out. I am hopeful as to a good few of those who have opposed all change.

Let us 'agree together' to pray till 2 May for the *recta sapere* which we shall so much need.

Yours sincerely,
T. W. Ripon

PS. I still wish it were possible to introduce the mention of the Holy Spirit as the efficient agent in the consecration, but . . .

Rough Draft of a Suggestion

'Hear us, we most humbly beseech thee, O Merciful Father, and send thy Holy Spirit upon us, thy humble servants, that we receiving these thy gifts of Bread and Wine . . . may be partakers. . . . Wherefore, O Lord and Heavenly Father, we thy humble servants, having in remembrance thy Son's blessed passion and precious death, his *mighty resurrection and glorious ascension* . . . *do render unto thee most hearty thanks* for the innumerable benefits procured unto us by the same (? and will ever be showing forth thy praises from one generation to another). Amen.

As our Saviour Christ hath taught us we are bold to say, Our Father. . . .'

The previous letter not sent was as follows:

My dear Dr. Frere,

I was sorry not to get a word with you at Convocation, and to be unable to get to R.C.C. when we might have met.

I have had a good many conversations since we last corresponded, and at any rate they encourage further attempts to produce a more healthy atmosphere, even if no definite results at present can be reached.

It is something to find that not a few who signed the Memorial are not averse to *some* modification of the Canon, if it helps to meet reasonable wishes for improvement, without altering the present balance of doctrine.

In view of the proposed Conference on the Canon, I think, so far as you and I are concerned, we are agreed on these points. . . .

1. The removal of 'We do not presume' to its old position immediately after the Comfortable Words, but before the Sursum Corda.

2. The removal of the Lord's Prayer (with the ancient words of introduction) to its ancient position following the Canon and before Communion, where the prayer for 'daily bread' is very suitable.

3. The insertion of some connecting link between the Words of Institution and the Lord's Prayer, commencing with 'Wherefore' and including

   (a) Words of thanksgiving—our Lord 'gave thanks' over both the bread and the wine.

   (b) A commemoration not only of the passion and death, but also of the 'mighty resurrection and glorious ascension'.

I am afraid that any attempt to move the Prayer of Oblation in whole or in part will at once raise opposition. The suggestion that the omission of the words 'accept this our sacrifice of praise and thanksgiving' might solve the difficulty, but would to my mind involve a loss which *all of us* would feel very deeply. The words represent so fully our Eucharistia—the oldest post-apostolic name, and one which we can claim as ours through the Latin version of our Articles. I would therefore suggest that we leave that prayer where it is, but seek to enrich the present Prayer of Consecration as above.

I see no objection to your proposed addition from the Greek Liturgies in itself—'Holy art Thou', but the *less change we suggest the greater the prospect of acceptance*. If you would come and spend a night here before 2 May I will gladly try to find a vacant day. In any case we shall pray together, though apart, at the same Throne of Grace.

It has at any rate been a pleasure to have had this act of fellowship with you.

Yours very sincerely,
T. W. Ripon

PS. I have been told by a correspondent that in the Liturgy of St. Mark the Prayer of Oblation comes before Consecration. I have not had time to verify this, but I suppose it refers to the 'First Oblation of the Offerings'.

Shortly afterwards the Bishop wrote to Frere again, revealing that he had informed the Archbishop of Canterbury of their correspondence and had suggested submitting their findings to the Conference.

The Bishop of Ripon to Frere   25 *April* 1919

My dear Dr. Frere,

... I like *your* first clause which I have gone over several times, and I hope you will bring it forward. ... I venture to think *the whole* rather long. ... Still, if the general line indicated by our four points were accepted, the details would have to be worked out in Committee.

I have told the Archbishop of Canterbury of the result of your first letter to me and our subsequent correspondence, and said that if he thought it wise to bring it forward, you and I were in *general* agreement.

May I send him a copy of your alternative suggestion? Or will you write yourself?

With every good wish for the season of hope,

Yours most truly,
T. W. Ripon

The Conference met on 2 May and was attended by thirty-eight representatives of different schools of thought and including a number of liturgical experts. It soon became evident that the Evangelicals were unwilling to agree to moving the Prayer of Oblation, although they were not averse to considering other proposals involving a rearrangement of the existing wording or an addition of fresh material to the Canon. Finally the Bishop of Ripon, seconded by Frere, made the following proposals, which were carried by 33 votes to 5.

1. That the Prayer of Oblation be not moved from its present position.

2. That the Prayer of Humble Access be moved so as to follow immediately after the Comfortable Words.

3. That the Lord's Prayer be placed after the Prayer of Consecration, and immediately before the Communion.

4. That the Words of Institution be followed by
   (*a*) An Act of Remembrance.
   (*b*) An Act of Thanksgiving.
   (*c*) A Prayer for the Holy Spirit.[1]

The preliminary work of the two men had therefore borne much fruit. Not only were their 'agreed points' accepted, but also their doubts as to the acceptance of any mention of the Holy Spirit were not realized. Only in the case of the Prayer of Oblation were their previous misgivings justified.

A small committee was then appointed by the Conference to draft the wording of the three additions to the Prayer of Consecration in preparation for the next meeting: the Bishop of Ripon was appointed Chairman and, as might be expected, Frere was included. Before the end of the month Dr. Drury was asking for comments on the suggested wording.

The Bishop of Ripon to Frere   31 *May* 1919

My dear Dr. Frere,

I enclose a draft of the Report of the recent meeting and shall be glad of comments on it from you. I cannot but feel that the first clause still needs revision as to the balance of its wording; possibly something might be done by correspondence.

If the Invocation paragraph is not accepted, the words 'in the unity of the same Spirit' would have to be altered to 'in the unity of the Holy Spirit'.

Yours very sincerely,
T. W. Ripon

Draft of the Report

The Committee appointed by those whom Your Grace invited to Lambeth on 2 May to draft the suggested changes in the Prayer of Consecration met at the Church House on Saturday 24 May.

They did not feel it their duty to consider the proposed change in the position of the Prayer of Humble Access, the Lord's Prayer, or the Prayer of Oblation, as these changes were accepted at the Lambeth

---

[1] *Chronicle of Convocation*, 1920, pp. 66–69. *Convocation of Canterbury. Royal Letters of Business*, Report 529, pp. 2–3.

The Rearrangement of the Canon

meeting, but confined themselves to an endeavour to draft the proposed additions to the Prayer of Consecration.

After full consideration of several suggested forms, they recommend that the present Prayer of Consecration remain unaltered, but that the following words should be added at its close, embodying

1. An Act of Remembrance.
2. An Act of Thanksgiving.
3. An Act of Invocation of the Holy Ghost:

'Wherefore, O Lord, we thy humble servants do show the death of thy Son our Saviour Jesus Christ, having also in remembrance his mighty resurrection, and his glorious ascension into heaven, and looking for his coming again, do render unto thee most hearty thanks for the innumerable benefits which he hath procured unto us.

And, we most humbly beseech thee, O merciful Father, to hear us, and of thy almighty goodness vouchsafe to send upon us and upon these thy gifts thy Holy Spirit, that the Bread which we break may be the Communion of the Body of thy Son, and the Cup which we bless the Communion of his Blood—Who liveth and reigneth with thee in the unity of the same Spirit, one God world without end, Amen.

As our Saviour Christ hath commanded and taught us we are bold to say, Our Father.'

Frere's reply is unfortunately missing, but the next two letters indicate that he was reluctant to hurry the matter and preferred to discuss problems personally rather than deal with them by letter.

The Bishop of Ripon to Frere 10 *June* 1919

My dear Dr. Frere,

In response to my letter to the Bishop of Gloucester,[1] I find that he agrees with me that the first clause is still lacking in rhythm and balance; and he further suggests what is, I think, an admirable change—that for the word 'show' we should substitute 'here proclaim'—'We thy humble servants do here proclaim the death'. The insertion of 'here', I think, would satisfy all parties and avoids what will, I fear, be a difficulty—namely, the use of the word 'show', which is patient of varied colouring.

[1] Dr. Gibson was also a member of the Committee.

He also suggests that the clause should begin, 'Wherefore, O Lord our God, we thy humble servants'.

I am sending this letter to all members of the sub-committee, as the Archbishop is anxious for us to get on, and if we agree on this alteration, it could then be accepted as, I hope, our unanimous resolution. I am suggesting to the Archbishop of Canterbury a meeting about 29 July.

This only modifies very slightly your suggestion to wait till the meeting of Conference. But it would be better if we could agree on this, as the Bishop of Gloucester has suggested it.

Yours very sincerely,
T. W. Ripon

Frere to the Bishop of Ripon 27 *June* 1919

My dear Bishop,

... I am not one of those who are impatient about the revision. I think that in many respects besides the present one we shall be wise to spend a good deal more time and trouble over the amendments and improvements before approaching Parliament, or taking any such steps.

I note the points that you think need reconsideration, and will think them over again in view of our having a further meeting of the Committee if you are able to arrange it. ...

The sub-committee finally met again on 29 October. The Bishop of Ripon was unfortunately prevented from attending by a severe cold, and in his absence the Bishop of Gloucester took charge. The wording of the Acts of Remembrance and Thanksgiving was agreed upon, but two forms of Epiclesis were submitted for the consideration of the Conference.

The Bishop of Ripon to Frere 10 *November* 1919

My dear Dr. Frere,

I am sorry that very busy days have prevented my acknowledging the receipt of your letter. But you will forgive me. ...

I quite hope that the Acts of Remembrance and Thanksgiving will be accepted by the majority; but I am not yet happy about the Epiclesis, and I am afraid that the prayer for the coming of the Holy Spirit upon the Elements will be strongly opposed, though I have tried to modify the views of several prominent Evangelicals upon it. My own objection is that I think either form is practically a duplication of the prayer which now precedes the Words of Institution.

With every good wish,
Yours very sincerely,
T. W. Ripon

Appended to this letter was a copy of the sub-committee's Report.

The Committee appointed by the Conference on changes in the Prayer of Consecration will recommend to the Conference an addition to the existing Prayer, containing

1. An Act of Remembrance.
2. An Act of Thanksgiving—of which a copy is enclosed.

They have not agreed as to the wording of

3. A Prayer for the Holy Spirit, but have under consideration the two forms also enclosed.

The Conference is to meet at the Church House on Thursday, 27 November, at 11 a.m.

T. W. Ripon, 15 November 1919

The enclosed suggestions

'Wherefore, O Father, we thy humble servants, having in remembrance before thee the precious death of thy dear Son, his mighty resurrection and glorious ascension, looking also for his coming again, do render unto thee most hearty thanks for the innumerable benefits which he hath procured unto us.

And we most humbly beseech thee, O merciful Father, to hear us, and of thy Almighty goodness vouchsafe to send upon us and upon these thy gifts thy Holy Spirit that the Bread which we break may be the Communion of the Body of thy Son, and the Cup which we bless the Communion of his Blood. Who liveth and reigneth with thee in the unity of the same Spirit, one God, world without end, Amen.

And we pray thee of thine almighty goodness to send upon us and upon these thy gifts thy most blessed Spirit (or Holy and Blessed Spirit) the Sanctifier and the Life Giver, to whom with thee and with thy Son Jesus Christ our Saviour, be all honour and glory, world without end. Amen.

As our Saviour Christ hath commanded and taught us we are bold to say, Our Father.'

The Conference reassembled on 27 November and by a large majority agreed to these proposals. The second Epiclesis was accepted with a few small alterations:

'And we pray thee of thine almighty goodness to send upon us and upon these thy gifts thy Holy and Blessed Spirit, who is the Sanctifier and the Giver of Life, to whom with thee and thy Son Jesus Christ be ascribed by every creature in earth and heaven all blessing, honour, glory, and power, now henceforth and for evermore. Amen.'[1]

Before the results of the Conference were submitted to the several Houses of Convocation, a further short correspondence passed between Dr. Drury and Frere dealing with the problem of a second consecration. They agreed that the whole of the new addition should be said in addition to what was before ordered; but Frere's letter is interesting, not only for his suggestion for a return to primitive custom in the matter, but also for his views on the way Convocation had undertaken the whole work of revision.

The Bishop of Ripon to Frere   15 *January* 1920

My dear Dr. Frere,

There is a point on which we ought to be agreed before the matter of the Prayer of Consecration is brought up in Convocation, namely the words to be used when additional bread and wine have to be consecrated.

If the present rubric stands it will seem to point definitely to the Words of Institution as constituting the act of consecration, which I gather from your speech would be undesirable in view of our relations with the Eastern Church. I suppose the obvious course is that the words for further consecration should include the Invocation, with or without the closing ascription. I am sorry that we did not think of this when we were in Committee.

With every best wish and kindest regards,

Yours very sincerely,

T. W. Ripon.

Frere to the Bishop of Ripon   16 *January* 1920

My dear Bishop,

I did not know that we were in any way empowered to deal with this matter, but it seems to be among the many which the Convocations'

---

[1] *Chronicle of Convocation*, 1920, pp. 66–69; *Convocation of Canterbury*, Report 529, pp. 3–4.

The Rearrangement of the Canon

Committees have either neglected or been unaware of in their schemes of Revision. The South Africans have, as their new Liturgy shows, dealt with the matter, not altogether satisfactorily I think, but at any rate they were alive to the difficulty, and saw that our present plan when there is an additional consecration is unsatisfactory. Whether the Convocations will allow us to do anything I don't know. In the last four years they seem to me to have been in the position of saying, 'You must not raise any new questions.' And even if the new question is absolutely involved in the old, as it is in the present case, I wonder if they will at all see the point, or will not say if they do, 'This new proposal if it passes is merely incomplete and we don't propose to alter the Prayer Book in view of it.'

The minimum that could be done I suppose would be to put some rubric at the end to direct the saying of the whole of the new addition as well as what was before ordered. This will I think be satisfactory so far as it goes, but it will leave the main difficulty untouched.

I have come increasingly to think that the real solution is a return to the custom of earlier days, so far as the consecration of the chalice is concerned (which is the main one to be considered), of adding unconsecrated wine to the consecrated wine, provided it be a small amount added to a large amount—the old plan which they called *augere calicem*. But before propounding such a solution I should have to feel much more secure of the ground, and it would require a great deal of discussion; for to revive such an idea may be a right way of profiting by the customs of the past, or it may be regarded as a piece of mere antiquarianism, or as a practice of the past which was rightly superseded. As to all that, I don't know where I or we in general should be likely to stand.

There is, I think, a very valid objection to our present custom of consecrating in one species only, for it is not in accordance with the Gospel precedents or with usual Church order. But my doubt is whether Convocation itself will get out of their habit of being bored by the whole concern and really take the trouble to think about it and find a solution for the trouble as a whole.

Forgive me if I am pessimistic as to these Committees of Convocation. I am intensely dissatisfied both with the way in which the revision has been carried on and with the results. I exclude from this entirely the last bit of effort with regard to the Canon. That seems to me the only piece of the revision which we have stirred ourselves to try and do on the right lines. . . .

The Bishop of Ripon to Frere 19 *January* 1920

My dear Dr. Frere,

 Thank you for your letter. I quite agree that the alteration of rubric does not lie within our terms of reference, but I think that we are bound to consider how the additions we propose affect any rubric, and that we might at least be able to meet objections.

 I am sorry we did not consider what recommendation to make on the matter I named. I will speak to the Bishops of Ely [Dr. Chase] and Gloucester [Dr. Gibson] on the subject, and at any rate it would be well for those who introduce the subject into our Northern Convocation to agree as to what we recommend. If I understand your letter aright, we are at one in suggesting that the rubric affecting further consecration of the Elements should direct the use of the whole of the new addition as well as that before ordered. . . .

With every good wish,
Yours most sincerely,
T. W. Ripon.

 The Conference's proposals were submitted to all four Houses of Convocation on 11 February 1920. Canterbury accepted them, but at York they were rejected, although not without a struggle. In the Upper House of York a number of amendments were proposed; that of the Bishop of Manchester (Dr. Knox) to reject the proposals was only defeated by Archbishop Lang's casting vote, while two others were successful. The first, proposed by the Bishop of Liverpool (Dr. Chavasse), was to delete the Invocation of the Holy Spirit upon the Elements: the second, by the Bishop of Newcastle (Dr. Wild), altered the terms of ascription at the end of the prayer.[1] The Lower House accepted the proposals by 34 votes to 29.[2] At a meeting of the full Synod, however, on 29 April, the Bishop of Manchester returned to the attack and his resolution of 'No change' was passed by 28 votes to 25.[3] On this point, therefore, the Southern and Northern Convocations failed to achieve unanimity: but the struggle had not ended. It entered its next phase in the deliberations of the newly created Church Assembly.

[1] *Journal of Convocation*, 1920, pp. 56–57.
[2] Ibid., p. 75.
[3] Ibid., pp. 211–16.

IV

INITIAL WORK IN THE CHURCH ASSEMBLY

ON 19 November 1920 the newly constituted National Assembly appointed a committee of twenty members of the three Houses of Bishops, Clergy, and Laity to consider the answers of the Convocations to the Royal Letters of Business. Those appointed were as follows: the Bishops of Gloucester (Chairman), Chichester, Ripon, and Truro; the Dean of Westminster; the Archdeacons of Sheffield, Surrey, and Wisbech; Dr. Frere; Canon A. W. Robinson; Colonel Ames; Sir Montague Barlow; Lord Hugh Cecil; Sir Edward Clarke; Dr. Eugene Stock; the Hon. Edward Wood; and Messrs. G. A. Bryson, G. A. King, A. Mitchell, and Athelstan Riley. Later Canon Robinson ceased to be a member, no longer having a seat in the Assembly, and Major Wood, Colonel Ames, and Sir Montague Barlow resigned. They were replaced by the Dean of Gloucester, Sir F. Holiday (who also subsequently resigned), Lt.-Col. H. L. Oldham, and Mr. H. C. Hogan. During the early stages of its work Frere was absent in Canada, but he was back in time to take part in the meetings of summer 1921. His absence had evidently been felt, for the Bishop of Gloucester wrote, 'I very much hope you will be able to be with us . . . as we need your help badly.'

The Bishop of Gloucester to Frere   9 *June* 1921

My dear Frere,

I hear that you are now back from Canada where I trust you have had a good time, and I hope that we may now have your help on the Prayer Book Revision Committee of the National Assembly. You have probably already had notice of the next meeting at the Church House on 30 June and 1 July, and of the meeting here on 2, 3, 4, 5 August, and I very much hope that you will be able to be with us on both occasions —as we need your help badly. Meanwhile we have been through the Calendar; there are a few questions on it reserved for further consideration at the next meeting. . . .

Ever yours affectionately,
Edgar C. S. Gloucestr.

Shortly afterwards Dr. Gibson invited Frere to serve on a sub-committee with the Bishop of Truro (Dr. Warman), the Archdeacon of

Wisbech (the Ven. J. H. Srawley), and Mr. G. Mitchell to 'build a bridge' in the troublesome question of the Canon. Each member was asked to make suggestions as to the form the bridge should take, and these were to be discussed at a meeting on 28 October.

The Bishop of Gloucester to Frere   10 *August* 1921

My dear Frere,

Will you kindly serve on the sub-committee of the P.B. Revision Committee to 'build the bridge' in No. 65? I am also asking the Bishop of Truro, Archdeacon Srawley, and Mr. Mitchell, and propose to act as Chairman myself, if agreeable to the others.

It is very difficult to find a time for meeting, but as most of us are going to be in town for C.A.C.T.M. on 27 October, and that is not likely to last for more than one day, we might perhaps meet on Friday, 28 October; and if you could make any suggestions as to the form the 'bridge' should take, perhaps you would kindly let me have it at least a fortnight before, so that I might circulate it with other suggestions before we meet. . . .

Ever yours affectionately,
Edgar C. S. Gloucestr.

The Bishop of Gloucester to Frere   18 *August* 1921

My dear Frere,

Thanks for your letter. I have now heard from all the suggested members of our sub-committee, accepting nomination and agreeing to Friday, 28 October, and I am therefore summoning it for that day at the Church House at 10.30 a.m. . . . I have asked every member to let me know beforehand if he has any design for the 'bridge', so that it may be circulated beforehand, and I hope that Truro will give us something.

Ever yours affectionately,
Edgar C. S. Gloucestr.

The Ven. J. H. Srawley to Frere   5 *October* 1921

My dear Frere,

I have been trying to think out some suggestions for the proposed 'bridge' in the Canon of the Prayer Book for our Revision Committee.

I had in mind something quite simple—a form of Anamnesis,

Initial Work in the Church Assembly

introducing the words 'entirely desire thy fatherly goodness, &c.', which would then become the form of oblation. I find that a somewhat similar suggestion is made by one of the Cowley Fathers in the August number of the journal *Theology*. I have not got a copy by me, so I cannot quote it. But the same idea had previously occurred to me after working through some of the Mozarabic Post-pridie prayers. . . . The result would be in the simplest terms without further elaborations which might, or might not, be found desirable—something of this sort:

'Wherefore, O Lord and Heavenly Father, we thy humble servants, having in remembrance his blessed passion, mighty resurrection, and glorious ascension, and rendering unto thee most hearty thanks for the innumerable benefits which he hath procured unto us (by the same), entirely desire thy fatherly goodness mercifully to accept this our sacrifice of praise and thanksgiving.'

This omits all the contentious phraseology contained in 'do celebrate and make . . . with these thy holy gifts, the memorial which thy Son hath willed us to make'; which, innocent as it is, arouses so much hostility.

The words in Edward VI's 1st Prayer Book, 'according to the institution of thy dearly beloved Son, our Saviour Jesus Christ', which follow the 'Wherefore, O Lord and Heavenly Father' have in the 1552 Book been transposed and slightly altered, so that they stand in connexion with 'Hear us, O Heavenly Father'. It would not be easy to repeat them here, and it would be perhaps rather bathos not to do so, if the words 'celebrate and create . . . the memorial' are omitted. I think it will save us criticism if we use as little as possible of unfamiliar language, and that a quite short Anamnesis (without even the reference to the Second Coming) will be the safer course, at this stage.

But I should be glad to know how your mind is moving, as it will save much time and trouble if we can form some sort of common mind before our meeting and could agree on a course of action. Another form that had occurred to me, though perhaps slightly more open to criticism is: 'Wherefore, O Lord and Heavenly Father, we thy humble servants, commemorating the blessed passion, mighty resurrection, and glorious ascension of thy dearly beloved Son, our Saviour Jesus Christ, and rendering . . . thanks . . . benefits . . . entirely desire. . . .'

I shall be glad to hear what you think about the matter. . . .

Yours ever,
J. H. Srawley.

On 12 October a proposed form of Anamnesis by the Bishop of Truro was circulated among members of the sub-committee, which found favour with both Srawley and Frere.

'Wherefore, O Father, we thy humble servants, having in remembrance the precious death of thy dear Son, his mighty resurrection and glorious ascension, looking also for his coming again, render unto thee most hearty thanks for the innumerable benefits which he hath procured unto us; entirely desiring thy fatherly goodness, &c.'

Frere inserted in his copy two additions: 'Lord and Heavenly' between 'O' and 'Father', and 'do' before 'render', and it was this amended form which finally appeared in the Report of the Revision Committee, N.A. 60. He reported this agreement of opinion to the Bishop of Gloucester on 14 October, at the same time making a valuable suggestion about Reservation.

Frere to the Bishop of Gloucester   14 *October* 1921

My dear Bishop,

I am very glad to see the Bishop of Truro's suggestion and can vote for it either with or without a meeting on the subject. Srawley seems to have arrived at the same view independently of either of us, so there appears to be a remarkable agreement: and this is hopeful. I hope also your own judgement goes with it.

As to Reservation I cannot help feeling that we ought to make provision that no one should die without the Sacrament; and I believe the solution in the matter, based on principle as well as on policy, is that we should frankly encourage this ideal; so that it would become a normal incident in a well-worked parish of whatever ecclesiastical outlook that the Reserved Sacrament should be at any time available for a dying communicant. The fatal thing is that at present Reservation is in the hands of a few, comparatively speaking; and some of them not very trustworthy. If it becomes the custom in countless parishes it would lose this invidious and unpleasant and possibly dangerous connexion. The bulk of the clergy would gladly accept the Bishops' direction about it. There would be no demand for uses of the Sacrament other than Communion in the larger percentage of parishes, and the people who now agitate for such things would be a small minority and no longer in the limelight. I believe a bold policy of this kind might save the situation; and I believe it is the right policy, because it recovers for our people the viaticum. The longer we go on putting off something of this kind, the worse the difficulty gets, and the more insatiable are the extremists. It is rather like the dealings with South Africa and Ireland—the longer we put off, the worse things get; and generosity in the early stages would solve the difficulty: but if the quarrel is allowed to go on there is less and less chance of any concession or settlement bringing peace. I do wish we could take the bold step now and I am venturing to draft a small addition to the rubric already in our scheme, which I am inclined to send round with one or two suggestions on the later part of our work. . . .

I shall be up in London and at the Church House anyhow on the 28th, as I think I mentioned before, so it is immaterial to me whether there is a meeting or not of the sub-committee; but it seems quite possible now that there may be such general agreement with the Bishop of Truro's proposal that a preliminary sub-committee meeting might be given up.

Yours sincerely,
W. H. Frere.

The Bishop of Gloucester felt that a meeting was still necessary in order to hear the views of Mr. Mitchell, who, as it happened, raised no objections to the Bishop of Truro's proposal. On the question of Reservation Dr. Gibson considered Frere's suggestion most helpful and worthy of further discussion.

The Bishop of Gloucester to Frere 15 October 1921

My dear Frere,

Thank you so much for your important letter received this morning.

1. As to the 'Bridge' Committee, I think we must have our meeting on the 28th. Mitchell would, I think, feel hurt if we reached agreement without giving him his say. He has made a suggestion which is now being typed, and which you will receive in a day or two—but I quite hope we shall find ourselves in agreement without much difficulty; and if we carry him with us it ought to help matters greatly in the full Committee.

2. And now for the still more difficult matter of Reservation, about which I am very unhappy: but I think it is possible that your suggestion may help to provide a way out of the difficulty. I should greatly welcome it, if it would be accepted by the bulk of the High Church party, and if we could feel that it would end the controversy, and be regarded generally as adequate by those who are now pressing forward. Anyhow it ought to be fully considered. May I add privately that I have already consulted the Archbishop as to what is best to be done; and he wants to

have a talk with me and a few others on the subject, for he is much disturbed and perplexed. May I therefore read your letter to him and others? I think it would be a real help if I might use it with other Bishops—confidentially, of course—but I cannot do this without your permission.

Ever yours affectionately,
Edgar C. S. Gloucestr.

Frere's proposal for Reservation finally met with approval and the Committee embodied it in an additional rubric for the Order for the Communion of the Sick in N.A. 60. 'When the aforesaid provision is not sufficient to secure that any Communicant at his last hour should be able to receive the Holy Communion (i.e. from elements consecrated previously at a public celebration and conveyed to the sick person in a "simple and reverent manner"), the Curate, with the permission of the Ordinary, given in accordance with Canon, or such rules as may be from time to time made by the Archbishops and Bishops in their Convocations, may make further provision to meet the needs of the sick and dying.'[1]

Two other matters of interest directly concerned Frere in N.A. 60—a second consecration at Holy Communion, and an Order for the Burial of an Unbaptized Child. On the former he drew up an interesting Memorandum for the consideration of the Committee.

A Second Consecration at Holy Communion

1. The rubric for a second consecration is drawn from the Cautelae in the Missal of Sarum (col. 651) and other uses. These and the corresponding *rubricae generales* in the present Roman Missal depend in the main upon the Summa of St. Thomas (pars. III, quaest. lxxxiii, art. vi). But on one point a rival opinion to that of St. Thomas is also cited. If there is a defect of wine and the host is already consumed, St. Thomas argues that the priest must consecrate in both kinds, beginning at *qui pridie*, because otherwise he cannot carry out the orders of the rite. He therefore allows a separate consecration of wine only if the host is there. Innocent (*De mysterio altaris*, iv. 24) had taken the view that in any case, even after the host had been consumed, a separate consecration was allowable; but directed that it should be done by intinction. Thence some held that a separate consecration, beginning at *simili modo* could be allowed, in order to minimize the scandal of having such a second consecration. These two views are therefore set side by side both in the Sarum cautels and the modern Roman rubrics.

[1] N.A. 60. *Second Report of the Prayer Book Revision Committee*, 1922, p. 93.

In the case contemplated by our rubric (1) there is no scandal; (2) the fresh consecration of wine alone is only needed (as a rule) when there is sufficient of the other species; and (3) our rite does not bring the two together at consecration as the Latin rite does, in commixture, &c.

We conclude that there is no reason against a separate consecration of wine.

2. The Latin rules take for granted that the words repeated will end presumably at *in mei memoriam facietis*; and with our present prayer no question arises on this point. But it is questionable whether with the new prayer this narrow conception of the words of consecration should be maintained.

'The Order of Communion' put the end at the words *in remissionem peccatorum*, in case a second consecration of wine was needed. This rubric was dropped in 1549 and no provision for a second consecration was made till Canon XXI of 1604, prescribing that 'the Words of Institution should be rehearsed'. This led to our second Rubric of 1661.

The Scottish Book of 1637 said, 'The words of consecration may be repeated again over more, either bread or wine . . . beginning at . . . Our Saviour in the night in which . . . &c.', without mentioning any end. In 1755 the Invocation was placed again in its historical position after the Oblation; and the above direction is absent, having been omitted in 1735. In 1764 a second consecration is mentioned which is to begin at the beginning with 'All glory be to thee' and end after the Invocation: and this is still the Scottish rule.

The American Book also requires the Oblation and the Invocation as well as the Institution.

We recommend now that in the case of the new prayer the Oblation should be required at any second consecration, ending with the words 'benefits of his passion'.

This Memorandum drew comments from Archdeacon Srawley and Athelstan Riley, who, with Frere, formed a sub-committee to deal with the question.

Athelstan Riley to Frere   24 *January* 1922

My dear Frere,

Many thanks for your interesting paper on a second consecration. I gather that you and Srawley recommend

    1. a separate consecration of the wine;

2. a form beginning 'likewise after supper' and ending 'death and passion'. Is this so?

My difficulty is that this proceeding is founded upon Cautelae dealing with the offering of the sacrifice in the case of grave accident, when something *must* be done. We apply it to the question of communicating the faithful—quite a different matter. Have you got any evidence that the Church ever reconsecrated at Mass for the purpose of the communicants?

I have been inquiring into the practice of the Easterns, through the Russians. Their clergy tell me that even at Easter, with throngs of communicants, they never have any difficulty, because as all communicants have to make their preliminary confession, they can consecrate to a nicety. And with them 'what is left over' cannot be given to communicants but must be consumed by the deacon.

There is, however, a specific direction, in the case of failure, in P. Nichaef's *Practical Manual for the Clergy* (2nd ed., St. Petersburg, 1887) as follows: 'If on any day the numbers of the communicants is so great that they cannot all participate in the Holy Eucharist owing to an insufficient quantity of the Holy Gifts in the chalice, the priest can either postpone the Sacrament for a certain number of communicants until the following day or he can put into the chalice an additional quantity of the unused gifts (if the amount is adequate); but in no case may he add to the contents of the chalice any unconsecrated wine or ordinary bread, nor may he administer the Sacrament with particles taken from the prosphora during the proscomidia, in memory of the Saints or for the health of the living or the resting of the souls of the dead.'

This is interesting. You see a fresh consecration is not even considered.

I wonder whether the committee realize that by modification of the 'Notice' Rubric they have deprived themselves of an opportunity of restoring the discipline on which any well-ordered Church would rely for preventing their Communion difficulties?

Yours ever,
Athelstan Riley.

Archdeacon Srawley to Frere   25 *January* 1922

My dear Frere,

Many thanks for sending me your Memorandum on a Second Consecration at Holy Communion. I had put together some rough notes on the question, but have not been able to get access to the University Library to look up the text of the Cautelae of the Sarum Missal. I am glad to have the passage of St. Thomas Aquinas on which the directions rest. On a question of detail, as a matter of fact, I was rather pulled up by what you say as to Innocent (*De mysterio altaris*, iv. 24). Is this the Innocent referred to in the Cautelae of the Sarum Missal, and is it Innocent III? If so, the words 'directed that it should be done by intinction' are rather startling. Freestone (*Sacrament Reserved*, p. 164, n. 2) quotes Innocent III (*De sacro mysterio altaris*, vi. 13) as forbidding the use of Eucharistia Intincta. If you have access to a text, could you kindly verify and see if your statement is correct?

I quite agree with your practical conclusions. Perhaps if we draw up a joint memorandum, it might be well to add a reference to the earlier practices of (1) consecrating wine by placing a fragment of consecrated host into the chalice; (2) consecrating wine by pouring contents of a consecrated chalice into it (as in *Ordo Rom.*); and also the practice of the Eastern Church of communion by intinction. This would round off the historical résumé.

Riley was the third member of the sub-committee. He told me that he had been making inquiries from his 'Orthodox' friends, and that they told him that the difficulty would not arise, as their people would have made their confessions before Communion, and they would know what provision to make. But that if it *did* arise by accident, they would probably tell the communicants to 'come another day'!! That was my impression of his conversation, but I may have misapprehended it. It sounds delightfully Oriental. . . .

Yours ever,
J. H. Srawley.

A rubric on the lines of Frere's proposals was inserted in N.A. 60.

'If the Consecrated Bread or Wine be all spent before all have communicated, the Priest is to consecrate more according to the Form before prescribed. Beginning at the second paragraph with the words (Hear us, O merciful Father, &c.), he shall say for the blessing of the Bread (who, in the same night that he was betrayed, took Bread, &c.), or for the blessing of the Cup, if that alone be required, (who, in the same night that he was betrayed, took the Cup, &c.), and shall continue the prayer with (Wherefore, O Lord and heavenly Father, &c.) down to the end of the third paragraph. And after the words (benefits of his Passion) the people shall say Amen.'[1]

The Order for the Burial of an Unbaptized Child was the joint work of the Dean of Westminster, Bishop H. E. Ryle, and Frere. Although accepted in N.A. 60 it failed to survive the committee stages of the Church Assembly and did not appear in the Revised Prayer Book. It read as follows.

On the way to the grave the following sentences may be said,

God made not death: neither delighteth he when the living perish. He created man for incorruption: and made him an image of his own proper being. (Wisdom i. 13, ii. 23.)

Despair not then, seeing that thou art far from being able to love his creature more than he. For as his majesty is, so also is his mercy. (Ecclus. ii. 18.)

He shall feed his flock like a shepherd, he shall gather the lambs with his arm, and carry them in his bosom. (Isa. xl. ii.)

The Lord gave, and the Lord hath taken away; blessed be the name of the Lord. (Job i. 21.)

When they come to the grave shall be said,

Dominus regit me. Psalm xxiii.

Then may be read one of the following

St. Matt. xviii. 10–14 or Baruch iv. 19–23.

As the body is being laid in the grave shall be said,

Unto God's loving mercy we commit this child, that he may grant *him* a share in the unsearchable riches of the redemption wrought by his Son, our Lord and Saviour Jesus Christ. Amen.

Then shall the Priest say,

Lord have mercy, &c.

Our Father . . . evil. Amen.

Let us pray.

O God, whose ways are hidden and thy works most wonderful, who makest nothing in vain and lovest all that thou hast made; Comfort thou thy servants, whose hearts are sore smitten and oppressed; and grant that they may so love and serve thee in this life, that together with this thy child, they may obtain the fulness of thy promises in the world to come; through Jesus Christ our Lord.

[1] N.A. 60. *Second Report of the Prayer Book Revision Committee,* 1922, p. 64.

Initial Work in the Church Assembly

The grace of our Lord Jesus Christ, and the love of God, and the fellowship of the Holy Ghost, be with us all evermore. Amen.[1]

There are only two short letters dealing with this Order, but they give some indication as to the way in which it reached its final form. Frere was responsible for the original draft.

The Dean of Westminster to Frere   25 *March* 1922

My dear Frere,

I have been looking at your draft, and am quite well pleased myself with the selection of passages.

There will be a shriek raised against the use of the Apocrypha in so free a measure. I think we had better drop 2 Esdras viii. 46, as the English construction ('comest far short that') is difficult for the people.

Re Psalm lxii. 5–end, the laity are much prejudiced against omitting verses. Perhaps two alternatives will suffice.

As an alternative to Baruch iv. 19–23, what do you think of Micah vii. 7–9?

Will you send it on to the Secretary? Or to me, if you suggest emendations?

                                         Yours very sincerely,
                                         Herbert E. Ryle, Bishop.

Frere to the Dean of Westminster   28 *March* 1922

My dear Bishop,

Thank you for your letter and suggestions.

I don't know that we need give our biblical references. I should be a little inclined to make them also not exact quotations. For example, in Sentence 1 to substitute 'He' for 'God'; and similarly to amend No. 2 into a more modern shape. I think something of the sort is wanted here, otherwise I would gladly drop it; because 'Despair not' seems to be the note it is desired to strike. If we could get that in any other way I should of course quite agree to the excision of that passage.

I think two alternatives are enough for the Psalms as you say, and it is certainly better to have canonical Old Testament than Baruch if we can; or perhaps to give the two as alternatives.

---

[1] N.A. 60. *Second Report of the Prayer Book Revision Committee,* 1922, pp. 100–1.

You will see that I am largely in agreement, and hope that you will put this into its final form and send it on to the Secretary. I am sure I shall accept anything that you may make of it.

Yours sincerely,
W. H. Frere.

The Order for the Visitation of the Sick was entirely Frere's work. This was destined to meet with the approval of all three Houses and finally was embodied in the Revised Prayer Book virtually without amendment.

N.A. 60 was presented to the Assembly in June 1922. It contained the greater part of the Convocations' proposals unchanged, but hints of future controversy were given in a Note and a Memorandum. The former, opposing the rubrics permitting Reservation, was signed by five lay members of the Committee, all of whom were Evangelicals—Sir Edward Clarke, Dr. Stock, and Messrs. Hogan, King, and Mitchell. The latter, which appeared as a separate document, N.A. 60a, was a critical survey of the proposals by Athelstan Riley, with special mention of the New Calendar, the Athanasian Creed, the expurgation of the Psalter and of the Scriptures, the Eucharistic Office, the method of Reservation, and the Anointing of the Sick.

In October 1922 the House of Bishops introduced into the Assembly the Revised Prayer Book (Permissive Use) Measure N.A. 84, to which general approval was given by all three Houses, sitting separately, in January and April 1923. The Houses of Clergy and Laity then began the lengthy task of considering the Measure in detail. Frere, together with the Archdeacons of Surrey and Wisbech was appointed Member in Charge in the House of Clergy, and he took a leading part in the initial debates in the July session. By this time the spate of literature on the revision of the Prayer Book had started, and the House of Clergy found itself faced, not with one set of proposals, but with at least three. The proposals of the English Church Union were published in the 'Green Book'[1] in October 1922, while those of the Life and Liberty Movement appeared in the 'Grey Book'[2] between April and June 1923, being largely the work of the Revds. Percy Dearmer, F. R. Barry, and R. G. Parsons. Frere distinguished himself in the House, not only by his liturgical knowledge, but also by his willingness to accommodate a considerable range of variations. This was, however, the only session in which he took part, for before the end of the year he had been appointed to the see of Truro.

[1] *The Prayer Book as revised by the English Church Union, 1923.*
[2] *A New Prayer Book (Proposals for the Revision of the Book of Common Prayer and for Additional Services and Prayers, drawn up by a Group of Clergy), 1923.*

V

THE HOUSE OF BISHOPS. CANON AND RESERVATION

BY 1923 it was obvious that Frere's contribution to the revision of the Prayer Book had been considerable. Nor had his contribution been solely one of scholarship: his tact, sound common sense, and ability to work with men of outlook vastly different from his own had been impressive. Of this his collaboration with the Bishop of Ripon on the proposed reconstruction of the Canon had been a shining example. Archbishop Davidson had long been conscious that the Church was 'suffering from the fact that there was no one who could speak with responsibility on behalf of what is called, however inadequately, Anglo-Catholicism, and yet be able to regard these questions largely, sanely, and with the equipment of scholarly knowledge. . . . We need someone . . . who carries the confidence of Churchmen generally, whether they are of his school or not.'[1] When, therefore, Dr. Warman was translated from Truro to Chelmsford, Frere was prevailed upon, after much pleading, to accept the vacant see.

The next two years were taken up by the consideration of N.A. 84 by the Houses of Clergy and Laity—a task in which Frere played no part except during the first session. Nevertheless he made a notable contribution to the revision movement during this period by his work on the 'Orange Book', the Alcuin Club's *Survey of the Proposals for the Alternative Prayer Book*. The work appeared in three sections: the first, in 1923, dealt with the Order of Holy Communion; the second, in 1924, the Occasional Offices; and the third, in the same year, the Calendar, the Collects, Epistles, and Gospels, and the Ordinal. Their issue was Frere's own idea, and in each instance he was responsible for the drafting, although other members of the Club gave him valuable assistance. They exemplified the views which he had expressed in his first publications on liturgical reform as long ago as 1911–12, and which he had reiterated in the House of Clergy in July 1923, namely that alternatives and variations should be permitted, and ordered experiment should be on a broad rather than a narrow basis. This was a necessary provisional step until greater unity of mind on these matters was possible. His object, therefore, in this work was not to produce yet another set of revision proposals, but to bring together as far as possible

[1] G. K. A. Bell, *Randall Davidson*, 2nd ed., 1938, p. 1251.

all that was worth considering in the various suggestions of N.A. 84, the *Green Book*, and the *Grey Book*. It was an attempt to survey all three, 'in order to explain the proposals rather than criticize them'.

His method is best shown by quoting from the Introduction to the Order for Holy Communion.

'We find that it is perfectly possible to combine O [N.A. 84] and E.C.U. [*Green Book*] into one Order, comprising within itself some alternatives. A number of the proposals of E.C.U. involve only the making of a change where O proposes none: these are then easily combinable: e.g. as the Prayer for the Church we print, not the Prayer Book form, which O left unchanged, but an alternative as proposed in E.C.U. (with some additions from M [*Grey Book*]).[1] Another group of proposals of E.C.U., on the contrary, are directly opposed to those of O: so a decision must be made between them, and whichever wins will be the one alternative to the present Prayer Book. In other cases where E.C.U. and O differ it would be possible to have both proposals and to incorporate them both in one Alternative Order. The Canon is here the crucial instance.... There is no real difficulty in having two options in the one Order: we have it already. We choose not only in a relatively small matter such as the Prayer for the King; but in regard to the Canon itself we have, as it is, to choose between the Prayer of Oblation and the Thanksgiving.... It is at (the point of structure and sequence) that we reach the chief difficulties that stand in the way of combining the various proposals within the course of one Alternative Order. We must admit that we have found this to be impossible with M; but the task is not impossible in regard to O and E.C.U. They differ in structure mainly in three points—the position of (1) the *Gloria in Excelsis*, (2) the Ablutions, and (3) the Preparation of the Communicants. The first two differences are easily combined by rubrics directing that the position desired by E.C.U. is an allowable alternative to the position in O. No such simple expedient will meet the third difficulty.

We venture, therefore, to suggest that E.C.U. should be followed in placing the Prayer of Humble Access after the Consecration Prayer, there to serve as an immediate preparation for the communion of priest and people alike. This leaves the Short Exhortation, Confession, Absolution, and Comfortable Words in their present position. It is the South African plan. But we suggest that the Preparation, which E.C.U. places at the beginning of the service, should be adopted to serve for

---

[1] M refers to the Bishop of Manchester (Dr. Temple), closely associated with the *Grey Book*.

The House of Bishops. Canon and Reservation

the priest and congregation, and be a permissible alternative to the other Preparation, provided that that other be said at least once on every Sunday and Holy-Day.

In this way we suggest that (except in the clash of certain rival details) O and E.C.U. may be combined in one Alternative Order containing a choice between two Anaphoras or Canons. . . .

This leaves M outside the scheme.... But there is something attractive in its individuality and independence; and if it commands a considerable body of support it must stand apart as a Second Alternative Order. . . .'[1]

On the subject of Reservation, destined to be another focal point of controversy, a synthesis of the other proposals was again suggested. The general lines of O and M were followed, in that Communion from the Reserved Sacrament was recognized, but some accommodation was made for the different views of E.C.U. E.C.U. took Reservation for granted, and permanently too, for the relevant rubric began, 'When the consecrated gifts are taken from the Church to the Sick Person' and ended with the instruction that 'immediately thereafter any of the consecrated elements that remain over shall reverently be taken back to the Church'.[2] Here in the *Orange Book* continuous Reservation was authorized by replacing the injunction to the minister to go to the sick person 'on the same day and with as little delay as may be' after the open Communion in O, with the injunction to go 'thereafter at a convenient season'.[3] The provision of O and M that none of the elements should be taken back to Church, but whatever remained over should be consumed, was retained, however. The safeguard as in M was also inserted that Reservation was not to be used for any other purpose than the communion of the faithful, while a further regulation enjoined that where the Sacrament was reserved continually, it should be renewed at least once every seven days.[3]

In March 1925 the House of Clergy produced their amendments to N.A. 84 in the document C.A. 158. Their resolutions on the Canon and Reservation were by far the most important and controversial. The proposed Canon in N.A. 84 was omitted and was replaced by two alternative canons, which were the result of an unofficial conference in the Jerusalem Chamber on 13 and 14 November 1923 between the Members in Charge and representatives of the *Green Book*, the *Grey Book*, the *Orange Book*, and the Evangelical 'No Change' Group. The

---

[1] *A Survey of the Proposals for the Alternative Prayer Book* (the Alcuin Club), 1923–4, Part 1, pp. 3–5.
[2] *The Prayer Book as revised by the English Church Union*, p. 442.
[3] *A Survey . . . Alternative Prayer Book* (the Alcuin Club), 1923–4, Part 2, p. 85.

two Canons were in effect modified forms of the second Orange Canon (itself an amended recension of the Green Canon) and the Grey Canon: in the words of the Chairman of the House, 'they had drafted a form of Canon which would be acceptable to those who represented the *Green Book*, and which representatives of the *Grey Book* felt in no way trespassed upon the doctrinal principles of the Church of England. They were also submitting another form which was accepted by those who represented the *Grey Book*, and to which the representatives of the *Green Book* would not wish to raise objection.'[1] The first form followed the lines of the Latin Canon: the Invocation came before the Words of Institution, and contained no explicit reference to the Holy Spirit: like the Scottish Rite it followed the words of the 1549 Prayer Book in the Prayer of Oblation, of which it included the whole. The second form was modelled on the Eastern Canon: the Invocation came after the Words of Institution and had special reference to the work of the Holy Spirit: while self-offering was mentioned in the actual Prayer of Consecration, the actual words of self-offering (from the Prayer of Oblation) were postponed until after the Communion, where they were added to the Prayer of Thanksgiving: the elements were also referred to as Bread and Wine after the Words of Institution.[2]

On the subject of Reservation a rubric was inserted at the end of the Order for Holy Communion permitting it not only for the Communion of the Sick but also for others who could not be present at the celebration in Church, although this proposal had only been adopted by 103 votes to 98. A further rubric also took the control of Reservation out of the hands of the individual bishop: henceforth it was to be 'in accordance with such rules as shall be framed from time to time by the Archbishop and Bishops of the Province or with Canons lawfully passed by the Convocations of the Province, and (subject to such Rules and Canons) with the directions of the Bishop'.[3]

The amendments proposed by the House of Laity were published in July in the document C.A. 169. On the Canon and Reservation there was little comment: their views were embodied in Resolution 6: 'That while this House believes that the great majority of the laity are satisfied with the present Service of Holy Communion, the House will nevertheless agree to the insertion by the Bishops in the Prayer Book of one alternative form containing provision for Vestments and Reservation for the Sick only, if in their opinion this will promote peace and order in the Church.'[4]

[1] *Church Assembly. Reports*, vol. 4, pp. 360–1.
[2] *Amendments made by the House of Clergy in the Revised P.B. Measure 1923*, C.A. 158, March 1925, pp. 77–82.   [3] Ibid., p. 87.
[4] *Amendments made by the House of Laity in the Revised P.B. Measure 1923*, C.A. 169, July 1925, p. 26.

The House of Bishops. Canon and Reservation

On 20 October 1925 the House of Bishops began its own task of revision, confronted with N.A. 84, the Clergy and Laity amendments, the *Green, Grey,* and *Orange Books,* and a whole host of pamphlets. On the questions of the Canon and Reservation feelings ran particularly high, and a considerable body of opinion, including nine diocesan bishops, was opposed to any change in or alternative to the 1662 Canon at all.[1] It was in connexion with these two problems that Frere was invited to attend two conferences at Farnham Castle, summoned by the Bishop of Winchester, Dr. Woods. The first, dealing with Reservation, was held on 24–27 October 1925, immediately after the first session of the House of Bishops. Seventeen representatives, lay and clerical of different schools of thought, attended, not, in the words of the convener, 'to reach an agreed statement or to formulate definite judgements', but 'to clear our minds in regard to the theological implications of the use of the Reserved Sacrament as a focus of "devotions" in the hope of stimulating students of the Church of England to unprejudiced inquiry'.[2] Frere attended but spoke little; some of his views are stated, however, in a letter to the Bishop of Southwark, Dr. Garbett, who was chairman of a small committee of bishops appointed to draft regulations for Reservation.

Frere to the Bishop of Southwark   8 *November* 1926

My dear Bishop,

I want to send you a few considerations upon two points for the consideration of the Committee about Rules for Reservation.

First: I want primarily to advocate the method of the hanging pyx. This is our English tradition universally, and on that account alone I think it is desirable to keep to it. With very few exceptions this is the method of Reservation which prevails from the tenth to the sixteenth century in England: the tabernacle is Italian in its origin; the aumbry or sacrament house we find in Scotland, is common in Germany, and is found in France, roughly speaking, equally with the hanging pyx. We should, I think, make it quite clear that we are reverting to English custom and not adopting a foreign one.

Secondly: it is better in its effect; it does not locate the Sacramental Presence in the same way; the church is filled with it, so to speak, and not merely a corner or chapel. There is much less of the instinct to genuflect or do things in a particular direction. In that sense it minimizes

[1] Bell, *Randall Davidson,* p. 1330.
[2] *Reservation. Report of a Conference at Farnham Castle,* 24–27 October 1925, Introduction, p. iii..

the tendency to bring Christ down and to look at the prisoner of the tabernacle on the worshipper's own level. The psychological difference is, I think, enormous.

Thirdly: it does not hamper the course of services in the same way. The celebrant at the altar, the people in choir or congregation do not feel the same way constrained to pay respect and reverence; because all is on a higher plane, and the Presence is pervaded rather than localized.

It might, of course, be said that it is inconvenient, and the people who want us to copy Rome will press that hard. In practice I do not think it is found so. It may be said that it is unsafe, but that is not true; for with a chain hung well to the roof, it is perfectly safe. Then again, it is quite possible to make this method of Reservation convenient and safe if the hanging pyx with its chains is properly adjusted and the end of the chains shut up in a locked cupboard; there is no difficulty about the raising or lowering of it even when the Sacrament is reserved in both kinds, nor is there any real risk of profanation. It may be said that the Reserved Sacrament is not so accessible. That in a sense is true: but I do not wish to see it accessible in that sense, so that the celebrant keeps it as a reserve to draw upon on ordinary occasions and for ordinary communicants, instead of communicating them from what is consecrated in the service itself. It is all consonant with reserving for the purpose of the sick that it should not be too handy; there should be some sort of little trouble involved in taking the Blessed Sacrament from the place where it is reserved.

This leads me to my second point, which is this; that there should be a single regulation saying that the Sacrament may not be moved for any other purpose except the giving of Communion; that is to say in whatever form we authorize it for the giving of Communion. I mean this: it is no good trying to restrict things that we can't restrict. People will come into church, and we can't prevent them going to the church by preference where the Sacrament is reserved; nor can we prevent them from saying their prayers with the Sacrament in the forefront of their minds. We can only get that attitude of mind right by teaching and explanation, not by regulation. Similarly, we can't regulate the services in any complete sort of way, or prescribe what may be said or what may not. Someone reciting the ordinary Prayer Book Litany to the Sacrament may be doing exactly what we should not wish, but we can't prevent it; still less can we prevent the singing of such a hymn as 'Jesu, my Lord, my God, my All' with that intention. So it is no good trying to prescribe what may be said. What I think can be prescribed is, that the Sacrament should not be removed for any purpose except Communion, and that the door or opening of the receptacle should not be set open for any other purpose except for taking the Sacrament out for Communion. This is the only way of stopping Exposition and Benediction. If we content ourselves with that, I think it will be a thing that can be enforced; but if we attempt other things they will not be manageable. Besides, honest people will know then exactly what they can do and what they can't do. This second consideration reinforces in a way the first consideration that I have put forward, urging the hanging pyx; there is much more temptation to open the door of the tabernacle or to take the Sacrament out for other purposes in that case, than there is when it is hanging above in a pyx.

One more word: I hope we shall quite definitely advocate Reservation in all churches where there is a real pastoral care for the sick; the pity of it hitherto has been that Reservation for the purposes of communicating the sick has been taken up by certain people who have gone into excesses. Now the remedy for all this is to have Reservation as widely as possible, and to have it, as far as may be, irrespective of party views. The moment it becomes a general requisite of any well-worked parish in order that the sick may have their Communion at their deathbed, then it loses a great part of its danger. So on that ground besides wishing not to seem grudging in the matter I urge that once the custom becomes lawful it will be urged as one that will be readily adopted wherever there is the need, and by all sorts of churchmen. . . .

The Bishop of Southwark to Frere   *9 November 1926*

My dear Bishop,

Thank you very much for your most important letter about the rules for Reservation. Personally I am in favour of the aumbry, but I have always felt that it was very difficult, if we desired to follow the English tradition, to refuse the use of the hanging pyx. I entirely agree with what you say in the second part of your letter, namely, that the Sacrament should not be removed for any purpose except Communion. . . .

You might be interested to glance at the regulations we have in this diocese, so I enclose a copy.

Yours sincerely,
Cyril Southwark.

Diocese of Southwark

Regulations for the Reservation of the Blessed Sacrament issued by the Bishop after taking counsel with his clergy in the Synod held on 12 and 13 May 1925.

1. Application must be made to the Bishop if it is desired to Reserve the Consecrated Elements. He will then instruct the Archdeacon to inspect the proposed place and report to him as to its suitability.

2. The normal place for the Reservation of the Blessed Sacrament is an aumbry, constructed in the north wall of the Sanctuary or Chapel of the Parish Church.

3. The aumbry should consist of a steel safe, firmly fixed into the wall and provided with an adequate lock, the key of which should be deposited in a secure place, accessible only to those who have the right to move the Blessed Sacrament.

4. The Blessed Sacrament should be reserved and administered in both kinds. When wafer bread is used, the Blessed Sacrament may be administered to the sick by the method of intinction, if circumstances make this advisable.

5. The Blessed Sacrament reserved should be changed not less often than once a week.

6. In cases where the Blessed Sacrament is not reserved perpetually, but only occasionally, and where no aumbry is provided, it is necessary that the Bishop should be satisfied that adequate care is taken to secure reverence and safety.

7. Organized devotions before the Blessed Sacrament reserved, whether or not they involve the moving of the Consecrated Elements, or any form of Exposition or Benediction are not permitted in the Diocese of Southwark.

9 June 1925.   Cyril Southwark.

As will be seen later, these Rules formed the basis of the Episcopal Regulations which were settled in March 1927.

The second Farnham Conference to which Frere was invited was held on 28–30 April 1926. This was the outcome of a meeting on Thursday, 14 January, between the House of Bishops and a committee of the House of Clergy, who attended to answer questions on a number of their amendments, the most important being the two alternative Canons. Notes of this meeting among Frere's papers provide some interesting details. It seems that although two alternative Canons had been submitted, it had only been lack of time that had prevented the Jerusalem Chamber Conference from reaching agreement on one form. Since then certain people had still been at work and it was most likely that their efforts to produce a single acceptable Canon would be successful. Their work would have no authority from the House of Clergy, but it was hoped that the results of their labours might be communicated privately to the House of Bishops. The Bishop of Winchester, therefore, summoned a small conference of interested parties to attempt to reach agreement and asked Frere and the three other episcopal Members in Charge to attend as well.[1]

The Bishop of Winchester to Frere   22 *April* 1926

My dear Bishop,

It will, I am sure, interest you to know that a small conference is to meet here next week, in order if possible to find an agreed alternative Canon to the Canon in our Communion Service.

It will be within your recollection that we were given to understand by the representatives of the House of Clergy who attended at our last session that there was a certain dissatisfaction with the result of the two alternative canons which have now been submitted by their House, and it was further understood that if more time had been available at the Conference between representatives of various schools of thought which took place in the Jerusalem Chamber, an agreement on one alternative might have been arrived at.

It is my hope that the conference which meets here may come to an agreement on one alternative, and, if so, I could (of course privately and unofficially) bring it to the notice of our House when the matter comes up for discussion. The men who are coming are, I think, representative of the main sections of opinion on the subject.

I write this not only to bespeak your sympathy and indeed your intercession for the guidance of the Holy Spirit in this endeavour, but to say that if it were possible for you to be present on any or all of the days concerned you would be warmly welcomed. It would, I think, be singularly fortunate if at least one of the Members in Charge were to be present at these discussions, for it would, I hope, assist in some degree to the determination of the line which they may be led to take in bringing the subject before the House.

                                       Yours very sincerely,
                                             Theodor Winton.

PS. I am sending this to the four bishops concerned.

[1] Dr. Burrows, Bishop of Chichester; Dr. Warman, Bishop of Chelmsford; and Dr. Strong, Bishop of Oxford.

Names of Conference

Revd. H. M. Dale; Canon Dwelly; Canon Hepher (if health permits); Revd. R. G. Parsons; Revd. H. L. Pass; Canon A. G. Robinson; Revd. E. G. Selwyn; Canon Srawley; Canon Storr.

Provisional Programme.

Wed. April 28. 5.30 p.m. 'The Eucharistic Sacrifice.' Two papers of 30 mins. each. Revd. E. G. Selwyn and Revd. H. M. Dale.

8.30 p.m. 'The Theory of Consecration.' Two papers of 30 mins. each. Revd. R. G. Parsons and Revd. H. L. Pass.

Thurs. April 29. 10–11 a.m. Opening discussion on outline Draft Canon submitted, followed by further discussion of the Draft in regard to its doctrinal principles, its liturgical structure, and its actual wording. . . . Canon Srawley has agreed to open the discussion on Thursday morning on the Draft Canon.

Frere did not attend this conference, for its purpose was not in accordance with his own views on variations and alternatives. His reply to the Bishop of Winchester is unfortunately missing. Dr. Srawley has, however, very kindly commented on the situation:

'I think the really moving spirit in the Conference was Parsons. Bishop Frere did not attend it, and from what I remember of conversations with him, he thought it inexpedient to attempt to reconcile the difficulty of the two Canons, and preferred that both should be submitted to the Bishops. . . . The Canon itself was really the work of Parsons. I had no hand in its composition, and personally had little hope that it would secure acceptance, but was willing that it should go forward to see if it would have a chance of resolving the difficulty: but in view of Frere's opinions and the great influence which he would have in the Bishops' Councils I thought it unlikely.'

The result of the Conference was what came to be called 'The Farnham Canon', a copy of which exists among Frere's papers. The influence of the *Grey Book* is evident, particularly in the post-communion prayers, and it dealt with the invocation of the Holy Spirit in a way which it was undoubtedly hoped would win more general acceptance:

All glory and thanksgiving be to thee, Almighty God, our heavenly Father, for that thou of thy tender mercy didst give thine only Son Jesus Christ to take our nature upon him and to suffer death upon the Cross for our redemption; who made there (by his one oblation of himself once offered) a full, perfect, and sufficient sacrifice and propitiation for the sins of the whole world; and did institute, and in his Holy Gospel command us to continue, a perpetual memory of that his precious death until his coming again:

Hear us, O merciful Father, we most humbly beseech thee, and vouchsafe to bless and sanctify these thy creatures of bread and wine, that they may be unto us the Body and Blood of thy Son our Saviour Jesus Christ, to the end that all who shall receive the same may be made partakers of his life:

Who in the same night that he was betrayed . . . in remembrance of me.

Wherefore, O Lord and heavenly Father, we thy humble servants, having in remembrance the precious death and passion of thy dear Son, his mighty resurrection and glorious ascension, according to his holy institution do celebrate before thy divine Majesty with these thy holy gifts, the memorial which he hath willed us to make, rendering unto thee most hearty thanks for the innumerable benefits which he hath procured unto us.

And we entirely desire thy Fatherly goodness mercifully to accept this our sacrifice of praise and thanksgiving: most humbly beseeching thee to grant, that by the merits and death of thy Son Jesus Christ, and through faith in his blood, we and all thy whole Church may obtain remission of our sins, and all other benefits of his passion.

And humbly offering ourselves unto thee, O Father Almighty, we pray thee to accept this oblation of thy Church, through the ministry of our great High Priest, that in the power of thy life-giving Spirit all we who are partakers of this Holy Communion may be fulfilled with thy grace and heavenly benediction.

Through Jesus Christ our Lord, by whom, and with whom in the unity of the Holy Ghost, all honour and glory be unto thee, O Father Almighty, world without end. Amen.

As our Saviour Christ hath commanded and taught us, we are bold to say—Our Father . . . Amen.

Priest. O give thanks unto the Lord, for he is gracious.
Answer. And his mercy endureth for ever.

Almighty and everliving God, we most heartily thank thee, for that thou dost vouchsafe . . . prepared for us to walk in. And here we offer and present unto thee, O Lord, ourselves, our souls and bodies, to be a reasonable, holy and living sacrifice unto thee; and although we be unworthy, through our manifold sins, to offer unto thee any sacrifice, yet we beseech thee to accept this our bounden duty and service; not weighing our merits, but pardoning our offences, through Jesus Christ our Lord; to whom, with thee and the Holy Spirit, be all honour and glory, world without end. Amen.

In June 1926 the House of Bishops agreed that there should be an alternative Canon by 29 votes to 5. The Members in Charge then moved the adoption of a Canon, which was that of N.A. 84 with certain amendments. The most significant of these, which was partly if not wholly Frere's idea, was the provision of alternative Invocations. The first immediately preceded the recitation of the Institution—'Hear us, O merciful Father, we most humbly beseech thee, and vouchsafe to bless and sanctify these gifts and creatures of bread and wine, that they may be unto us the Body and Blood of thy most dearly beloved Son Jesus Christ.' The second, which followed the recitation, made specific reference to the Holy Spirit—'Hear us, O merciful Father, we most humbly beseech thee, and with thy Holy Spirit bless and sanctify both us and these thy gifts of bread and wine; that we receiving them according to thy Son our Saviour Jesus Christ's holy institution may be worthy partakers of his most blessed Body and Blood.' A note was placed at the end of the Prayer, saying that only one of the two clauses was to be said. The Bishop of Winchester then moved the adoption of the Farnham Canon, while the Draft Canons of the House of Clergy were not brought forward. After considerable discussion one alternative canon was produced. It was fundamentally that proposed by the Members in Charge, with an Anamnesis taken from the Farnham Canon and an Epiclesis proposed by Dr. Lang, Archbishop of York, inserted after the Words of Institution. The proposal for alternative Invocations was not adopted.

By the beginning of 1927 the Bishops had completed their work of revision and on 7 February submitted a Draft Book to the Convocations. It aroused considerable feeling among all parties. New material—the most important being the Accession Service and the Ordering of Deaconesses—had been added without consultation with the other Houses, a proceeding contrary to the constitution of the Church Assembly. References to the doctrine of Original Sin in the alternative Order for Baptism, and to the obedience of a woman to her husband in the alternative Order for Marriage, had been removed. The new Canon was unpopular with many Anglo-Catholics, who disliked the Epiclesis, while the rubrics dealing with Reservation were severely criticized. The principle of continuous Reservation was recognized, but the rubric permitting it was unfortunately worded; the priest could reserve continuously 'if the Bishop shall so permit'. This, at its face value, placed the priest completely at the mercy of his bishop who could, if he felt so inclined, act in an arbitrary manner. The idea that it was intended to convey was quite different, however: it meant that the bishop was to choose the churches in which Reservation was to be permitted to serve a particular locality. Another rubric permitted

Reservation for the communion of sick people only. These rubrics set out the purpose of Reservation, but the method was to be settled by Regulations framed by the Archbishops and Bishops. These Regulations, which had not the permanent character of rubrics and could be rescinded or modified with little difficulty, aimed at preventing the use of Reservation for 'Devotions'. Unfortunately, they were not published with the Draft Book, and the fears of many people that continuous Reservation made 'Devotions' inevitable were not allayed.

Frere had many misgivings about the Book, as the following memorandum and letters show. He felt strongly about the insertion of new material without consulting the other Houses, and he considered the modifications in the alternative Baptism and Marriage Services to be contrary to the teaching of Scripture and the Catholic Church. He felt, too, that it had been unwise to reject the proposal for alternative Invocations in the Canon—it would have been practical, simple, and peacemaking. On the question of Reservation he not only agreed that the phrase 'if the Bishop shall so permit' needed modification, but also deplored the limitation of communion to sick people only.

Memorandum

The House of Bishops and the Prayer Book Measure.

It seems necessary to bring to the notice of the Archbishops of Canterbury and York certain considerations in respect of the amendments made by the House of Bishops in the Prayer Book Measure. These considerations fall under three headings.

1. The unconstitutional character of some additions to the Annexed Book.
2. The breach of comity in the relation between the House of Bishops and the other two Houses.
3. The tendency to doctrinal error and injury to the Catholic character of the Church of England involved in permitting the alternative services for Marriage and Baptism.

1. Article 14 of the Constitution directs that a Measure of this kind 'shall be debated and voted upon by each of the three Houses sitting separately and shall then be either accepted or rejected by the Assembly in the terms in which it is finally proposed by the House of Bishops'.

Standing Order XXXII sets out the elaborate procedure by which this direction is carried out. The Article and the Standing Order both clearly assume that a defined proposal is to be considered by the three Houses sitting separately, and when it has been approved or revised by the Houses of Clergy and Laity, it is to be finally shaped by the House of Bishops. The Measure is still to be, like all Measures, the work of the collaboration of all three Houses; but the Houses are to deliberate separately and therefore free from each other's influence and the House of Bishops is to have the final, and because the final, the decisive word. The Measure all the time is to be the Measure as introduced with whatever amendments the Houses may make. It follows that the House of Bishops is precluded from adding anything which is new matter and is more than can fairly be called an amendment, unless it can be said that the new matter really arises out of the deliberations of the other two Houses and is relevant to those deliberations. For if the Bishops do this they are adding something distinct from the Measure, which does not belong to it and has not been 'debated and voted upon' by the other two Houses. The collaboration of the Houses, which is the essence of all the procedure of the Assembly, has not taken place. The collaboration is meant to be modified in form and method in respect to liturgical Measures, but it is not meant to be abolished or neglected. All three Houses ought to have generally approved and revised the whole Measure when it comes on for final approval, though its shape as amended the Bishops alone have determined. For the Bishops to add now distinct additions to the Measure, which have never been debated and voted upon by the other two Houses, must be called unconstitutional.

This objection appears to apply to the addition of the Accession Service and the Service for the Ordering of Deaconesses to the Annexed Book. The Accession Service has never been part of the Prayer Book nor has it ever had the consent of Parliament or statutory authority. It has always rested on the Royal Prerogative. The Ordering of Deaconesses is a novelty. It is distinct, absolutely new, and hitherto unknown to the Church of England. It has never been considered by the Houses of Clergy and Laity. The Clergy have indeed considered it in the Convocations: but if the Convocations be different from the House of Clergy, the House of Clergy must be different from the Convocations. And the House of Clergy has never debated and voted upon the Service. To the House of Laity it is wholly unknown. To add these Services to the Annexed Book is therefore in Parliamentary language to 'tack' them and to seek to obtain for them the final approval of the Houses of Clergy and Laity and so statutory authority under the unconstitutional pressure of 'tacking'.

It is hardly necessary to add that the point is important not only in itself but as a precedent. The share of the Houses of Clergy and Laity in legislation of this character might be most seriously diminished by the House of Bishops. Very grave changes in the Creed, for example, might be added by the Bishops to a Measure about the Psalms; and the other two Houses would only have the debate and vote, aye or no, on Final Approval of the whole Measure in respect of these changes. It may be said that the Clergy and Laity may (and the Clergy, I think, in fact did) make large additions to a Measure; and it may be asked: Can not the Bishops do as much? But the answer is twofold. The Bishops had a full opportunity of settling the scope of the Measure when they introduced it: they could have put into it whatever they pleased. And secondly, the additions made by the Houses of Clergy and Laity can be communicated to each other. (This was in fact done in respect to all the amendments made in the first revision stages in the Houses of Clergy and Laity.) And the Bishops, of course, have all the work of the other two Houses before them. Collaboration is therefore not superseded: all three Houses work together. It is otherwise with new additions inserted by the Bishops: there can be no collaboration about them by the Clergy and Laity. The enormous power of the final word has this slight corresponding drawback, that in the last House novelties ought not to be added; a drawback, which as has been pointed out, is no hardship to the House which introduced the Measure and determined its scope.

2. The Accession Service and the Ordering of Deaconesses seem the only two additions so new and distinct as fairly to be said to be against the Constitution. But the permission of free personal prayer and the insertion of the word 'Holy' in the Nicene Creed in the Alternative Communion Service come near the line—especially the first. They are novelties of very great importance, added to the Measure and not debated and voted upon by the Houses of Clergy and Laity; but they are saved from actual violation of the Constitution by their form, which may fairly be called that of amendment. And they are, I doubt not, perfectly acceptable to the Houses of Clergy and Laity. But it must frankly be said that from a technical standpoint, they are added by an abuse of procedure; and they constitute a dangerous precedent. The amendment to the Creed would in form have been just the same, if important words had been struck out. It may be called a breach of propriety for the Bishops to use their last word in order to carry important novelties, originating not out of the proceedings of the other Houses, but purely from the wishes of the House of Bishops.

The orderly time for the Bishops to deal with novelties, in respect to a liturgical Measure, is at its introduction, unless the proceedings of one or both of the other Houses give occasion for the insertion of novelties in the revision stage. If this rule be not observed, the House of Bishops is guilty of irregularity; and this irregularity may easily become oppressive to the other Houses. It is tainted with the vice of 'tacking'.

An innovation thus irregularly made may become oppressive to the other Houses or to one of them, or may at the least be a breach of that comity of relation which should exist between the Houses, if the innovation is well known to be unacceptable to one of the other Houses. This seems to be a fair objection to the alternative Marriage Vow which has been sanctioned by the Bishops. This is, of course, in form an amendment, and thus not unconstitutional. But it is in substance a startling and highly contentious innovation; and while it goes far beyond anything suggested by the House of Clergy, it is directly contrary to a decision of the House of Laity. This seems to be an irregular use of the Bishops' last word, for the new vow is a grave innovation beyond the original Measure, beyond the proposals of the House of Clergy, and in contradiction of a decision of the House of Laity. It is the more harsh to the Laity because the subject-matter closely concerns them, and is one about which they are clearly entitled to be heard. The Bishops are using the machinery of the Enabling Act, which was only passed because there was a House of Laity in the Church Assembly, to carry an innovation in the Marriage Service which the Laity have rejected; and the Bishops have seen no impropriety in inserting this innovation at the last stage, leaving to the House of Laity only the desperate remedy of rejecting the whole Measure. It is not strong language to call this a breach of comity.

I hope it will not be thought disrespectful to say that the House of Bishops throughout its work seems hardly to have borne in mind that the principle of collaboration between the three Houses, which is essential to the action of the Assembly, is broken if the House of Bishops uses its last word to propose innovations. It is submitted that it ought to have felt itself limited to the proposals of the original Measure except in so far as the proceedings of the other Houses made it expedient to go beyond them. These last-word innovations seem the less defensible, because the Convocations deliberated for fifteen years, when the Bishops in the Upper Houses might have made any proposals they chose; because four Bishops sat in the Assembly Committee which framed N.A. 84; and because the House of Bishops, when it introduced the Measure might have made any further changes it thought fit.

It is important to press this point not only for its bearings on this present Measure, but because the procedure on this Measure is a precedent for the future.

3. The third part of this Memorandum is altogether of a different kind from the rest; and in strict propriety it ought to form a separate document. It is only included in the same paper for purposes of convenience. Hitherto the Memorandum has dealt with questions of procedure and of the machinery of the Constitution of the Church Assembly and kindred topics, in which I have always been interested and may pretend to some slight degree of authority. In this part of the Memorandum I write altogether without the slightest authority, as an ordinary individual Christian, distressed by some of the decisions of the House of Bishops. But the subject-matter of this part is much more important than that of the earlier part. For I am here concerned with the supposed dangers to the catholic and scriptural character of the Church of England, whereas earlier the subject was only the procedure and machinery of the Church Assembly.

My anxiety arises in respect to the changes in the marriage vow in the Service of Holy Matrimony and the changes made in the alternative form of Baptism as framed in N.A. 84. I take the least important subject first.

The changes in the Marriage Service appear to constitute a complete departure from the teaching of St. Paul about the subordination of women in the family. Subordination, it need hardly be said, is something utterly different from inferiority. St. Paul (and the whole of the New Testament) seems to teach the absolute equality of the sexes in spiritual status; and it may be recognized as a matter of experience that women are in character not merely equal but generally superior to men. But subordination does not relate either to status or character, but to the order of the family. According to St. Paul, marriage is a mystery analogous to the relation between Christ and his Church, and in that mystical order the woman is subordinate to the man. That this is St. Paul's teaching will, I think, not be disputed. The question then follows, 'What authority has St. Paul over the Church of England today?' It may at once be conceded that there may be, and are, things in his Epistles that were only relevant to the circumstances existing at the time. But the main principles of his teaching about the sexes relate to human nature and the family in all ages. And it has hitherto been the accepted tenet of the Church of England, as of the whole Catholic Church, that St. Paul writes by the inspiration of the Holy Ghost. That does not mean that every word has been dictated by God; but it surely does mean that St. Paul was used as an instrument and was controlled by the Holy Spirit, in order that he might give true teaching about the Christian Faith to the Church. I accept, therefore, St. Paul's teaching about the subordination of woman in the family as being, in its main substance and purport, the teaching of the Holy Spirit. How then can it be right in an alternative service allowed by the Church of England, to set this teaching altogether on one side, or rather to reject it? The Church of England claims to be Scriptural and Catholic; but in permitting the rejection of St. Paul's teaching about the subordination of woman, it can neither appeal to the authority of Scripture nor of the Catholic Church. This seems very grave. What becomes (for instance, in the Roman controversy) of our talk about the appeal to the Holy Scriptures? What becomes of the maxim that we accept what has been held *semper, ubique, ab omnibus*? For if there be any propositions that have behind them the authority of Scripture and of the whole Catholic Church in all ages and in all places, one is the subordination of the woman in the family.

I pass to the Baptismal Service. Here the departure from Catholic and Scriptural doctrine is less in degree; but on the other hand the subject-matter is greatly more important. The alternative Service for Baptism as framed by the House of Bishops is a second revision of the Service in the Book of Common Prayer. In N.A. 84 an alternative Service was set out in which expressions open to criticism on the ground of archaism or of harshness were omitted. But in that form care was taken to avoid any appearance of change in the doctrinal basis of the Prayer Book Service. In the opening exhortation of the Service, which is of special importance as expressing the main purport of the rite which is to follow, the form of N.A. 84 began: 'Seeing that all men are by nature born in a state of sinfulness.' In the new form these words are omitted, nor are any equivalent words inserted. It is not too much to say that the opening exhortation by itself is Pelagian in doctrine. Doubtless it may be urged that by such expressions as 'washing away all sin' and 'remission of sin' in the prayers which follow, the orthodox doctrine is preserved. But it is surely very difficult to understand why a clear expression of the true doctrine should be omitted from the opening exhortation, unless it be that it is desired to make the Service acceptable to those who in fact reject that true doctrine. This impression is increased by an alteration made in the Service for the Reception of a Child after Private Baptism. The declaration of the minister beginning 'I certify you' had originally these words: 'Born in original sin and in the wrath of God.' In N.A. 84 the words 'and in the wrath of God' were left out in deference to the sentiment of kind-hearted people; but the vital words 'born in original sin' were retained. They are now omitted by the House of Bishops. It seems quite impossible to imagine any reason, except the desire to please persons of heretical opinion, why these words should have been cut out. They are not harsh, and they are not archaic; no one who is not of Pelagian opinion could be offended by them.

These changes seem seriously alarming and distressing. In dealing with this matter we are not dealing with a bygone controversy, nor with one which is becoming less anxious or less powerful to divide men's minds. The opinion that human nature is naturally good and ought to be treated as naturally good both in the region of theology and of morality is widespread and most mischievous. Scientific materialism and humanitarian pantheism accept the natural goodness of man as the basis of a rejection either of the whole of Christianity or of all Christian belief relating to redemption and atonement. The influence of the opinion that human nature is naturally good and not bad may be traced far and wide in all sorts of discussions, social and ethical. It is in such an atmosphere that the Bishops have made these changes. The changes also raise afresh the anxious question of what is the relation of the Church of England to the teaching of St. Paul, already discussed in respect to the Marriage Service. It is not too much to say that the whole fabric of St. Paul's teaching depends on the belief that man is born in sin; and clearly, though it may be still possible to hold some doctrine of redemption, the orthodox doctrine that we have known and accepted is fundamentally modified if we discard the belief that the Incarnation was necessary to rescue human nature from hereditary ruin. The changes sanctioned by the Bishops therefore cut into the very vitals of our faith; and though doubtless there remain phrases in the Service which are reassuring and which may save it as a whole from the imputation of heresy, it is surely of great gravity that the Bishops should appear willing to tolerate Pelagianism as an opinion recognized as permissible within the Church of England, and to be conciliated in the choice of liturgical language.

It must be said in conclusion that if the changes in the Marriage Service and the Baptismal Service indicate that the Church of England is moving in the direction of rejecting the authority and teaching of St. Paul, then its essential character will be changed, it will cease to deserve to be called either Scriptural or Catholic, it will depart utterly from the position of the Reformers, and to many people the idea of secession and schism will begin to appear upon the horizon. The authority of St. Paul is an issue if ever there was one: *stantis aut cadentis ecclesiae*.

On a number of fundamental issues, therefore, Frere was not in agreement with his episcopal brethren, nor was he alone in his opposition; and ultimately on a number of points they made important concessions. The Canon and Reservation still continued to be stumbling-blocks, however.

Dr. J. H. Srawley to Frere   12 February 1927
My dear Lord Bishop,

... I have had many talks while in London with various types of people in the Assembly about the Prayer Book. The 'Grey' people are very pleased and whole-hearted in acceptance. Guy Rogers, while not easy about Reservation, accepts it as inevitable, and thinks the book shows real 'statesmanship'. Canon Wilson of Cheltenham asked me several questions and seemed eased in mind when I explained the practical effect of the new Canon. Darwell Stone was, of course, unhappy about the new Canon, as making difficult the position of those who consecrate on a Western basis, and still more about Reservation and its restrictions. I gathered from Dr. Harris that there might be a move to get the Epiclesis put back in the 1549 position. This would be disastrous; besides alienating all the better Evangelicals to please a section only of Anglo-Catholics, many of whom, like Dr. Harris and Sparrow Simpson, I believe, are willing to accept the Canon as it stands. But the one difficulty which all feel, that I have spoken to, is the actual wording of the rubric on perpetual Reservation—'if the Bishop shall so permit'. This, as it stands, certainly lends colour to the idea that we may be back in the old days of 'local' or 'diocesan' option in the matter. I know that is not what is meant, but only that the Bishop may choose in what churches he is prepared to allow Reservation for the needs of a locality. But I think some revision of this rubric, to make the matter clear, would help enormously and narrow down the opposition. Perhaps you may be able to suggest something privately to me, which the Convocation of the Lower House might embody in an amendment. Several Anglo-Catholic priests to whom I have spoken would be willing to accept a rule which left the Bishop to determine in which churches of a town or district there might be Reservation, while at the same time making it clear that Reservation in any diocese could no longer be prohibited in toto in any church.

Canon Wilson asked me what I thought of dividing the proposals and taking in one Measure all except the case of Reservation. I think I shewed him the futility of this convincingly. . . .

Yours very sincerely,
J. H. Srawley.

Frere to Dr. J. H. Srawley   15 *February* 1927

My dear Srawley,

. . . Your talks and your reports of them are interesting. I have no doubt that there are some modifications which the House of Clergy would be wise not only to consider but to formulate, and of course the points you mention are among the most important.

I have never been a believer in getting all to rally to one Canon. If they are not to be allowed to have two of them, and I expect public opinion is too strong against that to be resisted, then I think the best way is to have a Canon like what is suggested in the new book, but to put as a second paragraph in the prayer a clause 'Hear us, O merciful Father' like the one in our present Prayer Book, and to treat this as the alternative to the other clause lower down, putting a footnote at the bottom of the prayer to say, 'Only one of the clauses beginning Hear us, O merciful Father is to be said'. In that way both views would be satisfied; and I think there is a great deal to be said for doing it that way. I don't think any attempt to make us all agree on one will ever succeed. The differences of view are too ancient and too deep, and after all most people will be content to use either provided they are both there.

As regards perpetual Reservation, certainly the phrase 'if the Bishop so permits' needs modification. I think the best way is to establish a definite licence which should be required in case of perpetual Reservation; the Bishop could issue it, and if he declines there could be an appeal from him to the Archbishop; then some phrase in the rubric such as 'having obtained the necessary licence from the Bishop' would do; it assumes that the licence is to be had. The right of appeal, I think, should not be put in the rubric, but safeguarded in the Regulations.

Another point which is much in my mind is the restriction of Communion from the Reserved Sacrament to the sick. I doubt whether this can be maintained; in any case I do not think it ought to be prohibited by rubric. If it is to be prohibited, it should be merely prohibited in a temporary measure by regulation. I think there is a legitimate grievance which may be maintained against the rubric in its present form. . . .

These views were given more fully in a letter which Frere wrote two days later to the Bishop of Winchester. Dr. Woods had invited him to attend another Conference between a few Bishops and leading Anglo-Catholics to try to find a solution to the vexed questions of the Canon and Reservation.

The Bishop of Winchester to Frere   11 *February* 1927

My dear Bishop,

. . . The day before yesterday Underhill of Liddon House came to see me and represented strongly that much good would accrue if a small and private conference could be got together between a few Bishops and some of the leading Anglo-Catholics both in London and in the provinces. He thought that a great many questions might thereby be answered and possibly susceptibilities soothed. He was particularly anxious that such a conference, if held, should take place in the very near future before any definite hardening of opinion could take place. I consulted Manchester and Lichfield, who happened to be with me, and they agreed, as also did the Archbishop of York, that it was well worth while to attempt such a conclave. Accordingly I have asked the following bishops to come to the Church House, Westminster at 10.45 a.m. on Friday the 18th: Lichfield [Dr. Kempthorne], Manchester [Dr. Temple], Salisbury [Dr. St. Clair Donaldson], St. Albans [Dr. Furse], Southwark [Dr. Garbett], Chelmsford [Dr. Warman], and yourself, and possibly Oxford [Dr. Strong]: all of whom have promised to come with the exception of St. Albans, from whom I have not yet heard.

Further, I am asking the people whose names are on the enclosed list, most of whom, I dare say, will endeavour to come. The whole thing, of course—both the fact of the conference and what transpires therein—is and will be strictly private and confidential. It would, of course, be of *peculiar helpfulness* if you could come, but I fully realize that it is much to ask; that is, if you have retired again into your West Country.

                                      Yours very sincerely,
                                            Theodor Winton.

The House of Bishops. Canon and Reservation

Frere fully approved of the idea, but begged to be excused: he was faced with a heavy list of engagements in his diocese. As an alternative, however, he sent a lengthy statement for the Conference to discuss.

Frere to the Bishop of Winchester   14 *February* 1927

My dear Bishop,

Thank you for your letter.... I am glad that you are getting together with these people. For many reasons I should like to be there with you, but I feel it can't be managed: I have engagements thick down here and can't well transfer them, as there is no time to transfer them to. I think the Conference ought to do a great deal of good.

As far as I can see, the main places at which we are vulnerable and in which I think we must make some change from that point of view are these.

First, with regard to the Canon. There have always been, at any rate since the fourth century or so, two theories with regard to the time and exact method of Consecration in the Eucharist. They have lived comfortably side by side with one another, but they are not in a sense reconcilable. No formulation of doctrine has ever pronounced either the one or the other to be the right one. My view therefore is, that we should recognize both. The Prayer Book in its present form recognizes the Roman view, namely, Consecration by certain words. Our new Canon recognizes the other, which, without wishing to be too precise, treats the Invocation of the Holy Spirit at any rate as an important part of the Consecration. So far, so good. Our position in England is on the whole in favour of the Roman point of view, and our present Prayer Book has encouraged and, in a way in the minds of many people, overemphasized it. We cannot, therefore, expect a large block of our church people to give that up. It isn't only the extreme Anglo-Catholics; it is a very large part of the old Tractarian body too which has regarded the Words of Institution as the time of Consecration, has made obeisances and rung bells and so on then. It is not enough, I think, to say that while the new Canon recognizes one point of view, people who don't like that must use the present Prayer Book. We must give them something better than the present Prayer Book which is consonant with that theory. Otherwise we shall have those who dislike the Invocation going on with their old plan of saying our old prayer but sticking pieces on at the end of it, or else (worse still) we shall have people adopting simply the Latin Canon as they have in some quarters at present. If we don't provide them with any adequate equivalent, the tendency will then be for there to be more rebellion and less conformity on that side. I think, therefore, that we must provide in some way for a better prayer than the present Prayer Book one, and one which does not alter its line. I have always therefore held on these grounds that it is not possible to be content with a single alternative. However much in theory that may be desirable (I am not sure myself that it is), in practice that is impossible. How then are the two needs to be met, and the two theories to be allowed and satisfied, if there are not to be two Canons, as the House of Clergy report, though not liking it? I think the only way is what was suggested by the Members in Charge but rejected by the House; namely, that there should be two alternative clauses, beginning 'Hear us, O merciful Father': one would be the second clause in the prayer, as it is now more or less; the other would be our new clause with the Invocation. These should be alternative—only one should be said. Those who like the Roman theory would, of course, take the first and not the second; others would take the second and not the first. We should thus have only one Canon but two alternatives in it. I still think that is very much the best way in dealing with the situation; unless, indeed, we are to have frankly two fresh alternatives to the Prayer Book. What will not do is to transfer the Invocation to a point earlier than the recitation of the Institution; *of that I am quite clear.* The proposal made by the Members in Charge is practicable, simple, and peacemaking; I hope we shall come back to it.

Secondly, with regard to Reservation. There are two things which I think we must revise.

1. We must be clear that the parish priest is protected against an arbitrary Bishop refusing him leave to reserve when it is really necessary. Of course, such precaution ought not to be needful, but in present circumstances it obviously is so. We must keep the substance but alter the phrase, I think. I should be inclined myself to suggest instead of the words 'if the Bishop shall so permit' substituting the words 'having received the necessary licence from the Bishop'. We ought to have a definite written licence for the purpose I think, and in the Regulations it would be well to add 'In any case of the refusal of a licence there should be an appeal to the Archbishop'. This, of course, would not go into the rubric, though I think it might well be in the Regulations; this would save any arbitrariness.

2. With regard to Reservation, I have never felt that we were justified in saying that Communion from the Reserved Sacrament is to be only

The House of Bishops. Canon and Reservation 119

for the sick. Certainly this ought not to be in the rubric; there is really no justification in theory for this. If it is a practical matter it should be regulated by the Regulations, and not included in the rubric as if it was a doctrinal or necessary matter. In fact we shall find we are quite unable to resist the plea of Communion from the Reserved Sacrament for people other than the sick—especially farm hands, milk boys, market porters, and the like, to say nothing of some classes of women. I hope therefore we shall take out this restriction from the rubric. We must make what restrictions are necessary in the Regulations, and not in the rubric at all: they can then be modified as experience shows necessary. I think myself the best plan will be in these cases again to say that the communicant must have a definite licence from the Bishop to receive outside the service. That at any rate would be a wise restriction to make until we see more of how the matter works.

These three things would go a long way, I think, to meet the pressure we are likely to have from the Lower House for having turned down what they had approved on these particular points. They are three out of the four things about which I am very anxious and unsatisfied, the fourth being a matter in which we are not overriding the House of Clergy, namely, the proper provision for all the Black Letter Days. That is another matter; but I feel that it is going to do an immense deal of harm, because as it is everyone who keeps those sort of days will have to have another book beside the Prayer Book upon the Altar and amateur, unauthorized liturgiologizing will continue. . . .

The Bishop of Winchester sent Frere a report of the Conference, from which it is clear that his only point which did not find acceptance was the provision of alternative Invocations in the Canon.

The Bishop of Winchester to Frere   18 *February* 1927

My dear Bishop,

I enclose a copy of an account of our Conference this morning which I have sent to the Archbishop. The main points which you mention were fully discussed. I gathered, however, that on the whole they did not feel the difficulty about the Epiclesis and the alleged departure from Western tradition as keenly as you do. No one thought of suggesting the 'alternatives in the alternative' which you put forward, and I cannot think myself that that would be a very happy solution. Though I am not an expert like you, I have given some attention to the ancient liturgies and it seems to me to be at least arguable that there was some kind of Epiclesis in the Western forms, though, of course, in the case of Justin and Irenaeus it was more connected with the Logos than specifically with the Holy Spirit. It seems to me that the prayer we have constructed, though it does in marked degree depart from the present Western tradition, includes all that is most precious in the ancient liturgies, and that people will grow accustomed to it more quickly perhaps than they think at present is likely. More of this, however, when we meet.

Yours very sincerely,
Theodore Winton.

Report of the Conference

Clergy present. Preb. H. F. B. Mackay, Revd. A. Pinchard, Dr. Darwell Stone, Revd. C. P. Shaw, Canon Long, Revd. W. E. Kemp, Revd. E. G. Selwyn, Revd. H. P. Bull SSJE, Revd. E. D. Merritt, Revd. J. F. Briscoe, Revd. V. S. Ellis, Revd. E. Milner-White, Revd. D. Rawlinson, Revd. F. Underhill, Dr. Kidd, Revd. A. S. Duncan-Jones.

Laymen present. The Earl of Shaftesbury, Sidney Dark, Rt. Hon. Sir H. Slesser, Sir Robert Newman, Bart., W. Spens.

The main points raised were:

1. *The Question of the Third Rubric in the Communion of the Sick*

Strong hopes were expressed that this might be reworded so as to give any individual bishop the power of regulation but not of absolute veto. It was urged that in its present form it will perpetuate the undesirable state of affairs with which we are already familiar. For instance, in the adjoining dioceses of London and Southwark, what is permitted in one is forbidden in the other.

If, on the other hand, it is found impossible to alter the rubric, the wish was expressed that there might be some appeal to the Archbishop or some higher authority.

Further, many questions were asked in regard to where it was proposed to draw the line in regard to Devotions. Whether, for example, informal gatherings of a few people with no set service or officiating minister would be held to be forbidden under the rubric. I said I thought that the rubric forbade anything like official and set services with notice given and forms used, but that beyond that we could not attempt the total prohibition either of individuals or groups in the presence of the Blessed Sacrament.

2. It was strongly urged that the use of the Reserved Sacrament should not be limited to the sick. Instances were given in which it was

alleged that 'cattle-men, paper-boys, milk-boys', and many others whose employment is often continuous on Sunday and who cannot attend services at the usual times, need to be provided for. It was agreed that this should only be done under licence from the Bishop, but the hope was expressed that the rubric would not entirely close the door to any such provision. Rawlinson, Pinchard, Kidd, and others were strong about this.

Will Spens said some sensible things about the difficulty of tying up the future in rubrics as contrasted with regulations which, however stringent, can be revised if need be from time to time.

3. There was a long discussion mainly over the Epiclesis in the Prayer of Consecration. It was agreed that this was entirely orthodox, and I gather that there are some represented, for example by Kidd and Duncan-Jones, who do not really feel any serious difficulty about it.

On the other hand, regret was expressed that we should here depart (as it is said) from the tradition of the West, and evidently the fact that, so to speak, the act of consecration is spread over the whole prayer rather than limited to one formula is a matter of difficulty and regret to some of them. Personally I think this is one of its chief glories. Spens was eloquent about the awkwardness involved for people who had been used to gather their devotional life round the old Prayer with its moment of Consecration, being suddenly required to adjust themselves to quite a new use, and, in some respects, a new point of view. Duncan-Jones, however, said that in a visit to America, where the Consecration Prayer is much akin to our new proposal, he felt a great sense of liberation into a larger and truer atmosphere of devotion.

Some difficulty was expressed in regard to the use of the words 'these thy gifts of Bread and Wine' in the fourth paragraph of the Prayer as describing the elements after the Words of Institution. Preference was expressed for the form in use in South Africa in this connexion: but I did not gather that this would be a serious difficulty.

4. Lord Shaftesbury raised Lord Hugh Cecil's point about the doctrine of original sin in the new service of Holy Baptism; but it was evident that there was no very strong feeling about this. One point was raised which I think escaped our notice in the revision; namely, that in Prayer No. 3 in the new form of Marriage Service, the allusion to the institution of Matrimony is omitted as compared with the prayer in the old form. It was thought that any such omission would seem to detract from the Church's teaching about the solemnity of marriage at a time when lax views are all too prevalent. I think, as a matter of fact, that, so far from being intentional, this was a point which somehow escaped us when we were at work upon the Service.

Signed. Theodor Winton.

On 22 February the Lower Houses of both Convocations met to consider the Draft Book and submitted a number of amendments to the Bishops. The following were the most important.

The Rubrics

The revision of the rubrics, so that, where the new were intended to supersede the old, two contradictory sets did not exist side by side. (Canterbury proposal.)

The Calendar

The restoration of St. Denys, St. Crispin, St. Catherine, and St. Nicholas, all of whom had been omitted by mistake. (Canterbury.)

Holy Communion

1. Permission to omit the Gloria in Excelsis on any day not being a Sunday or Holy-day. (Canterbury and York.)

2. The provision of a Proper Preface for optional use on Sundays when no Proper Preface was appointed. (Canterbury and York.)

3. The consideration of a Memorandum on the Epiclesis by the Revd. E. G. Selwyn. (Canterbury.) He drew attention to two points in the Epiclesis as it stood in the proposed alternative Canon.

   (a) 'With thy Holy and Life-giving Spirit.' The 'with' was clearly an ablative of the instrument. It should be changed to 'by' or 'through' or 'through the power of' or 'by the grace of', which would not obscure the witness of the prayer to the personal agency and God-head of the Holy Spirit. In the ancient Greek liturgies there was no case of a word being used implying an instrument and not an agent.

   (b) 'Vouchsafe to bless and sanctify both us and these thy gifts of Bread and Wine.' This implied that the operation of the Holy Spirit in the consecration of things was identical with his operation in the consecration of persons. It would be valuable if the wording could be slightly altered to show, as the ancient liturgies did, that the consecration of persons and things by the Holy Spirit were not entirely of the same kind.

Baptism

The restoration of the allusions to original sin. (Canterbury and York.)

Visitation of the Sick

The restoration of Unction. (Canterbury and York.)

Reservation

1. The modification of the rubric dealing with continuous Reservation to safeguard against arbitrary action by the Bishop. (Canterbury and York.)

2. The reservation of the Sacrament not only for the sick, but also for those who could not be present at the celebration in church. (Canterbury.)

3. The publication of the Regulations, if possible, before final sanction of the Composite Book. (Canterbury.)

Before the Bishops considered these amendments, Frere received a letter from another of the Members in Charge, the Bishop of Chichester (Dr. Burrows), warning him of the Memorandum on the Epiclesis by the Revd. E. G. Selwyn. He was evidently not impressed by its arguments, and subsequent events proved the Bishops to be of a like mind.

The Bishop of Chichester to Frere   23 *February* 1927

My dear Truro,

The Archbishop and I have received strong pleas from one who knows the inner life of the Greek Church, that . . . the words 'both us and' should be omitted as likely to raise difficulty with the Orthodox. He says: 'The phrase "to bless and sanctify both us and these thy gifts" is liable to misunderstanding as implying that the operation of the Holy Spirit is the same in the case of the persons as in the case of the oblations. This is avoided in the Eastern liturgies. There is no objection whatever to the inclusion of "ourselves" in the petition, provided that it is made clear by the wording that the operation of the Divine Spirit is different in relation to the persons and the oblations. This distinction appears to be safeguarded both in the Eastern and in the present form of the Scottish rite.'

I should have thought that the words that follow—'that *they* may be unto *us*' would serve to make this distinction quite sufficiently clear. Moreover, I am not anxious to emphasize it; for in Holy Communion we are made one with Christ and Christ with us, as our bodily food becomes one with us. Mystically and spiritually the elements are made to us the Body and Blood of Christ for this purpose. So it is surely not amiss to ask that the Spirit may consecrate us, somewhat as He consecrates the elements, when He uses them to unite us to our Lord's human nature.

It is most unadvisable that we should reopen discussion of the new Canon; but Convocation may compel it, and if my Hellenizing friend is right in accusing us of admitting false theology, we must.

It is also urged that 'the phrase "Hear us, O merciful Father, and with thy Holy Spirit vouchsafe to bless and sanctify" could be misunderstood as implying that the Holy Spirit is the *instrument* rather than the *agent* in the Divine operation. The possibility of such a misunderstanding is clearly avoided in the Eastern and Scottish uses, where we have something like "Send down thy Holy Spirit upon us, and upon these gifts, *in order that he may* sanctify", &c.'

This does not appeal to me at all in view of Luke xi. 20 and Matthew xii. 28. I am not sure that the objection does not betray a tendency to Tritheism, but probably that is to be over-critical.

These are deep matters, and should therefore be considered by us before we meet, so I write now.

Yours affectionately,
Winfrid Cicestr.

The House of Bishops undertook its final revision of the Book in the light of the Convocations' proposals on 2–4 March. They conceded all the points mentioned except the following—the revision of the Epiclesis in the light of the Selwyn Memorandum, the restoration of Unction, Reservation for people other than the sick, and the publication of the Regulations for Reservation before the final presentation of the Book. In addition to these concessions, they also agreed to delete the Ordering of Deaconesses, Lord Hugh Cecil having raised the technical objection mentioned by Frere in his Memorandum that it was new material and had not been before the rest of the Assembly. Frere again tried to secure approval for the introduction of alternative Invocations into the Canon, but the motion was decisively rejected by 31 votes to 3.[1]

At the same time the Bishops drafted their Regulations for Reservation. These were five in number together with a footnote:

'To the end that due reverence may be observed in all arrangements concerning the reservation of the Consecrated Bread and Wine for the Communion of the Sick, the Archbishops and Bishops have agreed, in the event of the Prayer Book Measure becoming law, to put forth the Rules following, as to the manner of carrying into effect the Rubrics of the Alternative Order of the Communion of the Sick.

1. The Consecrated Bread and Wine set apart under the Rubrics of the Alternative Order of the Communion of the Sick shall be reserved

---

[1] Dr. Srawley also failed with a similar motion in the Lower House of Canterbury Convocation.

in an Aumbry set in the north wall of the Sanctuary or of the Chapel; or, if need be, shall be reserved in some other place approved by the Bishop.

2. The Aumbry shall consist of a safe firmly fixed into the wall and provided with an adequate lock, the key of which shall be deposited in a secure place accessible only to those who have the right to move the Consecrated Bread and Wine.

3. The receptacle in which the Consecrated Bread and Wine are reserved shall be kept locked, and the door shall only be opened when it is necessary to move or replace the Consecrated Elements for the purpose of Communion or renewal.

4. The Consecrated Bread and Wine shall be renewed at least once a week.

5. The manner in which the Reserved Sacrament is to be conveyed to the sick is to be subject to the direction of the Bishop.

N.B. The licence issued under the second rubric shall have effect only within the church (or churches) named in the licence. The authority given by such licence shall be exercised by the priest to whom the licence is given or by his deputy.

In order to secure unity of procedure, a common form of licence will be used in all the Dioceses of the Provinces of Canterbury and York.'

These rules were obviously based on the Southwark Regulations. The influence of Frere's Memorandum is nevertheless there. Provision for the hanging pyx is allowed by the last part of Rule 1—'some other place approved by the Bishop', while his suggested safeguard against 'Devotions' is embodied in Rule 3. The Note at the end also gave further welcome assurance that continuous Reservation was not to be subject to the arbitrary action of a Bishop.

VI

THE FINAL STAGES

FRERE supported the Book, but not without some misgivings. The most important point which still troubled him was the Epiclesis: he felt that less than justice had been done to those who objected to any reference to the activity of the Holy Spirit in the Canon.

Frere to the Archbishop of Canterbury   11 *March* 1927

My dear Archbishop,

    May I be excused from coming up for the meeting on the 15th and 16th? The whole of the week is very fully occupied with engagements which I hadn't foreseen would fall upon us, and I should find it very difficult to get three days clear, which at the least would be necessary in order to get up. Besides, I think anything I can contribute to the framing of the Book is now practically done; there will be a little more proof correcting which I can do here.

    I have done my best to help in the preparation, but now that I look at the result, I confess that I am greatly puzzled to know what I am to do —in the way of supporting the great bulk of things which I can support, and not supporting the one or two vital things which I cannot support, on the ground that I do not think them either just or wise. I won't enlarge upon all the turmoil that is in my mind, but I thought I ought in honesty to say so much to your Grace, and in loyal gratitude for your unfailing kindness and sympathy. . . .

The Archbishop was most sympathetic; but he hoped that it would not mean Frere's voting for its rejection.

The Archbishop of Canterbury to Frere   12 *March* 1927

My dear Truron,

    I shall be very sorry indeed not to see your face at the meeting on the 15th and 16th, but I quite understand the difficulty of your being absent again from the Diocese so soon. I do not at all think that you cannot materially help us in what we are now trying to do. On the contrary, I think we are at a stage where your help would be particularly useful: but I realize too the difficulty you are in as regards recommendations which we have made and with which you do not sympathize. I can honestly say that it is a real distress to me to be recommending things that you do not like. I have tried my best to look at everything fairly, but I cannot help still hoping that, notwithstanding your objection on particular points, you will shrink from voting for the rejection of the whole Book. . . .

All good be with you. We owe you a great deal for what you have done in these anxious and difficult months.

I am,
Yours very truly,
Randall Cantaur.

Frere assured the Archbishop, however, that his misgivings would not prevent him from voting in favour of the Book. In fact, the prospect of voting against it had never occurred to him.

Frere to the Archbishop of Canterbury   14 *March* 1927

My dear Archbishop,

Thank you very much for your very kind letter. . . . .

The prospect of voting against the result of our labours has never occurred to me; my mind is merely disturbed as to the measure of support that I could honestly give. There are so many things which one dislikes and even disapproves, but yet can quite well recommend as being the best to be had under the circumstances. The thing that troubles me most is, that we have failed to do any justice, as I think, to the grievance represented by the Dean of Wells and his following, combined as they are with a considerable section of the Anglo-Catholics. I can't help hoping that even at the eleventh hour we may meet this, to me, legitimate grievance; and so clear away what I fear will otherwise be a perpetual trouble and destroyer of peace and order. . . .

In another letter to his old friend the Bishop of Moray and Ross, Frere briefly reviewed the final amendments made to the Book.

Frere to the Bishop of Moray and Ross   15 *March* 1927

My dear Arthur,

I have at last got time to write to you and report a little bit to your private ear what has been done.

We had very strenuous sittings, mainly going through the suggestions of the York and Canterbury Lower Houses. There is still a lot of clearing up to be done in order to get the final state of things into the hands of Convocation early next week. Here are one or two papers you would like to see. I am afraid I haven't got a York one to send you; their points are very much the same as the Canterbury one, and we were much less fully documented with regard to their proceedings. You will note with interest Selwyn's Memorandum; but it didn't move us to make any change, as there seemed hardly sufficient reason for doing so, having got so far as we had.

The chief points to be noted, I think, are these:

1. In the Calendar, Sts. Denys, Crispin, Catherine, and Nicholas, omitted by mistake, have been put back.

2. We have simplified the rubrics a good deal by deciding not to print the old rubrics where they are legally superseded by the new ones.

3. We have altered some more of the details in the Epistles and Gospels.

4. We authorized the omission, except on Sundays and Holy-Days, of the Gloria in Excelsis, and provided a Proper Preface for every Sunday, for optional use.

5. We put back the bits taken out that were supposed to weaken the Baptismal doctrine.

6. We refused, I am sorry to say, to make any definite provision for the Unction of the Sick, but we very much altered the rubric about Reservation, so as to secure that the Bishops should not arbitrarily refuse, where there was a real need. But we were obdurate, again I regret it, in regard to confining the method for the sick.

7. A certain amount of the new modifications and language in some of the Occasional Offices.

8. One of the most important things we owe to you; namely the amendment of the Ordination Prayer for the Priest. We put in some words in order to bring in the direct prayer for those being ordained—'And we humbly beseech thee by the same thy Blessed Son to endue them with all grace needful for their calling and to grant' &c. I am very grateful for your calling attention to this defect.

The Final Stages

9. We drafted some of the Rules for regulating Reservation under the rubric; these will appear shortly, and be before the Convocations when they vote. There is much to be said against this plan, and much for it; so we finally decided that it was better to err on the side of openness than otherwise.

This will give you, I think, the main things; you see they do not amount to very much. . . .

The Book in its final form was presented to the Convocations on 29 and 30 March and was agreed to by large majorities.

Canterbury. Upper House: 21 for, 4 against.
              Lower House: 168 for, 22 against.

York.   Upper House: unanimous.
              Lower House: 68 for, 10 against.

It was then finally debated in the Church Assembly on 5 and 6 July. Here again, in spite of strong opposition from the extreme Anglo-Catholics and the Evangelicals, it secured large majorities in all three Houses.

              House of Bishops: 34 for, 4 against.
              House of Clergy: 253 for, 37 against.
              House of Laity: 230 for, 92 against.

Five months then elapsed before the Measure was submitted to Parliament, during which period controversy raged unabated, members of all parties striving hard to secure support both in the Lords and in the Commons. The opponents of the new Prayer Book derived no little benefit from certain utterances of Dr. Barnes, Bishop of Birmingham. On 25 September in Westminster Abbey he preached on the irreconcilability of the theological with the biological doctrine of the origin of man, while on 6 October at Birmingham he repudiated in derisive terms the doctrine of the Real Presence. This was followed by a scene in St. Paul's Cathedral on 16 October when Canon Bullock Webster and a large body of supporters appeared in the Cathedral and publicly denounced his teaching on the Sacraments.

Frere appreciated the damaging effect all this would have on the Book, and urged the Archbishop of Canterbury to issue an authoritative repudiation of these 'crude views'. If this were not done, not only would it create further opposition, but also it would set a precedent for acts of defiance and lawlessness in matters of worship.

Frere to the Archbishop of Canterbury   18 *October* 1927

My dear Archbishop,

    You are probably inundated with protests against the Bishop of Birmingham's latest utterances, and I very reluctantly add to the number; but I am anxious to say that I hope something will be arranged in the way of definite repudiation by the authorities of the Church of England of the crude views that he has put forward. It will not do for us to be supposed to sit still while we are told that Eucharistic practice or doctrine is like Hindu idol worship, while we are asked to investigate the consecrated elements to see whether they are consecrated or not. The responsibility of the moment seems to me to belong to the House of Bishops, if for no other reason than that the passing of the Prayer Book at the present moment is being much hindered by these utterances and will be much more hindered if they are not repudiated. Already the Bishop's earlier utterances had caused (to my knowledge) a certain number of clergy in Convocation to vote against the Book; and that attitude of mind has been multiplied indefinitely the last week or two, I believe. We had some little evidence of it here when our clergy expressed their desire that the Book should pass by only a majority of two to one, the minority being mainly I think of the Anglo-Catholic type. There are two very serious things in view unless something is done. First, that we shall have fresh opposition to the Book on the whole, on the ground that these views of Bishop Barnes unless they are repudiated are to be taken as governing the action of the Bishops and underlying the policy of the Book. The argument, we all know, is not a sound one, but I am thinking not of its worth but of its effects on the voter; there I think it will be powerful.

    But further there is the question of the administration of the Book. Here still more we are brought face to face with danger unless his whole attitude of mind is repudiated; for it is quite obvious that it is being openly said on all sides that if Bishop Barnes may take this line unrebuked, the only way for individuals to protest is to take up an attitude of defiance towards the restrictions upon the adoration of the Reserved Sacrament as a protest against Bishop Barnes. Further there is the disciplinary point of view. If he is allowed to go on unrebuked like this, more opponents of all sorts will say, 'Though I do things that are prohibited, I am at any rate not such a culprit as Bishop Barnes, who has repudiated the whole of the doctrine of the Church, and not merely in small things but by gross insults'. I fear, therefore, that our future task of administration will be made infinitely more difficult unless something is done. Perhaps already something is planned so that some notice of it should be taken in the House of Bishops; that seems to me the place so far as I have any power to judge at this moment, because of the burning controversy on the Eucharistic doctrine in connexion with the Prayer Book. I dare say others far more competent than myself will raise the matter in the House of Bishops. If no one else wishes to do so I should ask to be allowed to raise it myself. But I hope very much that task will fall to someone else.

Your Grace may very naturally say, 'What exactly do you propose?' I therefore subjoin a proposition, though very tentatively and reluctantly: 'That in view of statements made with regard to the doctrine of Holy Communion by the Bishop of Birmingham, this House desires to declare that in the new forms and rules proposed for the Celebration and Administration of Holy Communion it does not intend any change of the sacramental doctrine of the Church, such as would seem to be implied in the statements mentioned.' . . .

The Archbishop, however, not only considered this Resolution insufficiently clear in meaning, but also doubted the wisdom of a published Resolution in any form by the Bishops. Nevertheless, if there was a general desire for such action to be taken and the Resolution was a well-considered and a wise one, he would not oppose it.

The Archbishop of Canterbury to Frere   19 *October* 1927
My dear Bishop of Truro,

I have your important letter suggesting action which might be taken by the House of Bishops in connexion with Barnes's sermons. The position is not a simple one, for as a matter of fact Barnes did not, *I think*, base his original sermon, where he talked about magic, &c., on Prayer Book changes, though naturally the fact of Prayer Book changes, and especially Reservation, was imported by readers and possibly implied by the Bishop.

On reading the words of your suggested Resolution, I am not quite clear what it means—i.e. what you would expect the public to learn from it if it were published. It would not, of course, be published unless we definitely directed that it should be: but I imagine that publication is what you want. As the words stand I should take them (coming from yourself) as meaning—we are simply adhering to the broad Catholic doctrine which has always been ours, one element of which Dr. Barnes has snatched from its context and denounced as superstitious. But your words are also capable of being interpreted as meaning—Bishop Barnes supposes that under the new Rules we have done something which makes easy an exaggerated view of what is meant by the Real Presence. We have done nothing of the kind. Of these impressions the former would seem likely to please one section of the Church and the latter to please the other.

It may be that you do not intend either of the interpretations to be markedly given to your words, but that you are simply getting the Bishops to say that Dr. Barnes has been frightening people quite unnecessarily. I do not know whether you would like to tell me anything further about your meaning and intention, or possibly to modify the words in some way, though I do not want to be urging this.

Personally I would greatly doubt the wisdom of our publishing a Resolution of the House of Bishops unaccompanied by any report of a debate and liable therefore to be very crudely and ignorantly criticized. Perhaps you simply feel that you resent the suggestion, undoubtedly current, that the Bishops are timid about dealing with a great doctrinal question. I am quite prepared myself to submit to that attack with which I have been familiar for twenty years; but I certainly do not want to run against any general wish on the part of the Bishops for a Resolution, supposing the Resolution to be a well-considered and wise one.

I am,
Yours very truly,
Randall Cantuar.

PS. I rather think something from Bishop Barnes is going to be published tomorrow, though I have not seen it.

On the following day there appeared an Open Letter from Dr. Barnes to the Archbishop. It was not pacific in tone. The apparent refusal of the Church to accept the discoveries of science on the evolution of man and its increasing adherence to erroneous sacramental doctrines were both condemned: Dr. Barnes himself claimed to represent the traditional sacramental doctrine of the Church of England and had no intention of retracting anything he had said. Frere considered the letter to be 'as good a climb down as perhaps we could expect from him', and thought it best to delay further action until its effect on the public mind could be estimated.

The Final Stages

Frere to the Archbishop of Canterbury   20 October 1927

My dear Archbishop,

Thank you very much for your very kind letter in answer to mine and your consideration of the bearing of my suggestion upon the present position.

Clearly, however, the Open Letter to yourself published this morning puts the matter upon a different footing. How far it will allay the agitation of mind I don't know, though no doubt it is calculated to do so in certain respects; the language is less violent and the statements less crude. It still remains, as I read it, a curiously nineteenth-century document of old-fashioned theology and still more old-fashioned natural science; but after all that is not our affair. It is as good a climb down as perhaps we could expect from him; and I suppose the only thing is to see what effect it has on the public mind before considering the matter that troubles at any rate my mind, namely, the effect of it on a large number of our people and on our prospects of regaining our lost leadership by the united action of the Bishops with regard to the Prayer Book and other things. These altered circumstances, of course, mean that I do not wish to go further with the Resolution that I sent to your Grace. The whole matter needs reconsideration, I think, in the new light. . . .

Frere undoubtedly tried to read far more in the Open Letter than it contained. Far from being anything in the nature of a 'climb down', Bishop Henson described it as being expressed in 'the sharpest and most inflammatory terms', and 'designed to destroy in advance all chance of pacification',[1] while it drew from the Archbishop a courteous but statesmanlike letter of rebuke. He suggested that, after further consideration, Bishop Barnes might 'find further cause to modify the width and scope of [his] negative and destructive statements', and reminded him that the larger tasks which lay beyond the recent Prayer Book discussions demanded a lead from the Bishops imbued with a spirit of restraint and consideration for others.[2] The Bishop of Birmingham remained unconvinced and uncooperative, however: on 26 October he addressed a second Open Letter to Dr. Davidson in similar terms, but this time it went unanswered. Whatever advantages the opponents of the Prayer Book Measure may have derived from these incidents, they were more than offset by the effect of the Archbishop's reply. It carried weight and influence, and undoubtedly strengthened the Bishops' hands.

On 18 November the members of Convocation were notified that,

[1] H. Henson, *Retrospect of an Unimportant Life* (Oxford, 1942), vol. 2, p. 159.
[2] G. K. A. Bell, *Randall Davidson*, p. 1324.

if the Measure was passed by Parliament, it might be necessary to summon the Houses of both Provinces to give Synodical approval to the Revised Prayer Book. Frere immediately wrote to Lord Hugh Cecil expressing a doubt as to whether the old Letters of Business were sufficient to authorize them taking such action. Lord Hugh Cecil thereupon showed his letter (of which unfortunately there is no copy among Frere's papers) to the Archbishop, who sent to Frere for an explanation.

The Archbishop of Canterbury to Frere 22 *November* 1927
My dear Truron,

I have just seen your letter to Hugh Cecil written on 19 November, and am puzzled by one part of it. With regard to the accomplishment of the Convocation business when we give Synodical sanction you write as follows: 'The Royal Letter must authorize the Canonical Sanction. Have the Convocations got this authorization sufficiently? We must make sure of that. There is no doubt about this.'

What is your authority for thinking that some Royal Letter is needed for our giving Synodical sanction to the Book which has gone through all these processes based originally on our Reply to the Royal Letters of Business? These Letters of Business were issued in the early stages and complied with, and our Answer appears in our present handwork. What further Letter can the King be asked for, or issue? I find nothing about such a letter in Joyce's account of what happened in 1661–2 as set forth in his *Acts of the Church*. That book gives the full story including the Form of Subscription and the signatures.

... As soon as ever you get this, will you send me a telegram stating either that I have misunderstood you or that you have authority which was not given in your letter for the statement that Royal Letters are needed? ...

I am,
Yours very truly,
Randall Cantuar.

Frere then reiterated his doubts to the Archbishop emphasizing the necessity of being quite sure of their position in case of 'objections on the part of the most tiresome'.

Frere to the Archbishop of Canterbury 24 *November* 1927
My dear Archbishop,

I came in to find your letter, and I have sent off a telegram, which I hope may be a little intelligible; but it wants further explanation. I have no clear view as to whether all that is needed has been done or not, but in order to make assurance doubly sure I think some further inquiry seems needed. First as regards the old Letters of Business—they may be adequate for the present purpose; I do not say they are not; but I confess to a certain feeling of insecurity on the point up to the present. For one thing, I think it was said that our reply to the Letters of Business finished them off, and that chapter in the matter had been closed. That was certainly said—whether truly or not I do not quite know. Secondly, I think that people used that argument to justify the revision going a good way beyond what was mentioned in the Commission and presumably in the Letters emanating from it. When it was objected that the revision went too far and outran its authority, it was said that the original Letters of Business had had their reply and the revision was not a direct but an indirect consequence of them, the direct Reply being what we sent some good time ago. Again I do not know how far any of that argument was sound, but it was used I think. Like Hugh Cecil, I am anxious to try and anticipate any possible objections on the part of the most tiresome of critics and opponents, so forgive me for being tiresome in self-defence. When I looked up the matter again the other day at Hugh Cecil's suggestion, I did so mainly with one idea in hand, namely trying to come to a decision whether it was better to proceed by Canon or by Canonical Subscription; and I came to the conclusion that to follow the old way was the stronger way. But when I looked in detail into the procedure, I tried to follow up what exactly was meant by the Royal Letters in the formula of subscription. I could not find in the Canterbury Records any note of such a special letter having been received, but in the York Records it was stated that the Letter for Licence to the Convocation of York to review the Prayer Book was sent down and received on 22 November: that is quite the last stage of the work of preparation, and less than a month before signature. I couldn't help feeling, therefore, that probably there had been a similar Letter sent to Canterbury and that these Letters so sent were the ones referred to in the Formula of Subscription. If so, they were presumably different from the Letters summoning the Convocation and they seem certainly different from the Letters licensing the proceedings of revising the Canons. In other words they seem to be licence given *ad hoc*. If that is so, it seemed all the more necessary to my mind to make sure that we have got for the coming Convocation all and every authority that the most meticulous person could require of us. If the authorities of the Crown are satisfied with what we have got, nothing can be better; and if they encourage us to go forward on what we have, obviously nothing more is needed. But it seems to me to be at least arguable that it would be well to ascertain whether we have in fact got all that the most exacting criticism could require.

I am not sure whether the York Records are given in that book of Joyce's which your Grace quotes, namely the *Acts of the Church*. They are summarized in his book called *English Sacred Synods*, or some such name, which is the one I was using. The authority that lies behind Joyce so far as the York Convocation is concerned is, I think, Trevor's *History of the York Convocation*: but it is quite likely also that the documents are given, perhaps even more fully, in the *Collection of Acts in the Convocation of York*, published about ten years ago by the Surtees Society. I just mention this in case your Grace may think it worth while to have the point about the Licence addressed to York looked up further. I didn't notice any corresponding mention in the statutory records, but I did not look up exhaustively with that point of view expressly before me.

I quite hope that it is all right as your Grace says, namely that the old Letters of Business are adequate for authority to go straight ahead until we deal finally with the completed Prayer Book: but in view of the lapse of time that has occurred in our case, and the apparent proximity of the issue of the Letters in 1661 to the acceptance of the Prayer Book, I can't help feeling that it would be well for us to clear up the point and to have our answer ready in case anyone objects. . . .

The Archbishop assured him, however, that he considered no further Letters necessary to proceed to Synodical approval.

The Archbishop of Canterbury to Frere 25 November 1927

My dear Truron,

I am grateful to you for your letter following your telegram. You are quite right in thinking that we need to be very careful at this time. . . .

You suggest that we should ask from the State whether they are satisfied with what we are doing. . . . As I believe there is really nothing that needs doing, I am not prepared, as at present advised, to bring our proceedings virtually to an end—to the consternation of the whole country—by invoking what would probably be a statement that the matter is so complicated that it must be fully considered, and that meantime the objections to our proceedings seem insuperable! I should regard such an opinion as altogether wrong, but I think we should have brought it on our heads if we applied to the Home Secretary now.

Letters of Business started the Convocations on their work years ago. The work has now been completed and has passed through phases which were wholly unknown at the time to which we look for precedents. We cannot ignore the Assembly and the submission of its Measure to Parliament. With regard to the Letters of Business, no one I think will say that *these* are what we now need to justify canonical sanction to the now completed Book. Joyce in his *Handbook of the Convocations* (p. 142) says clearly what I believe to be absolutely true, that no Letters of Business are needed for the ordinary deliberations of Convocation. Had there never been any Letters of Business bidding us consider the Report of the Royal Commission and so on, we might say now that there had been a terrible lacuna in the Church's proceedings at this time, but no one will say that who looks fairly at the matter; and my present belief is that our wise course is to go forward, following, as regards phrasing the Form of Subscription, &c., the precedent of 1661 so far as it is reasonably applicable.

Surely Letters of Business issued now to bid the Convocations consider a matter which already has passed first through Convocation and then through the Assembly and then Parliament, would be altogether an anachronism and impossible of application. I think the less the matter is talked about the better. If it is raised when the Convocation meets I shall be prepared to give an answer, and shall probably be glad to get your help about it beforehand. I do not think you substantially differ from what I have here said.

I am,
Yours very truly,
Randall Cantuar.

Frere was reassured and was prepared to let the matter drop. His reply to the Archbishop is not among his papers, but the notes of his proposed reply were written on the top of the foregoing letter and dated 26 November. 'Very sorry to have caused you trouble unintentionally for my letter was mere answer to Lord H. C. I am last person to wish to ask more permission of Crown than need: glad you take firm line and rule what has been done to be sufficient—after this very full consideration of all the circumstances. Presidents have final authority in such matters at any rate over members of their Houses when they see their way clear to exercise it. So all I hope is well.'

His final public action in support of the Deposited Book was a commendation of the new Canon in the November issue of the *Truro Diocesan Gazette* which was subsequently reprinted in the *Church Times*. He pointed out that the earliest consecration prayers had followed the model of the Baptismal formula and had been Trinitarian in character. This threefold type of prayer, consisting of Praise to the Father, Commemoration of the Son, and Invocation of the Holy Spirit had once prevailed throughout the Church, and it was a mistake to regard it as merely Eastern. The Roman Canon, which had obtained such prominence in the West, was an exception rather than the rule. The attempt of the 1549 Prayer Book to remedy the defect in the Roman Canon had been unsuccessful, as was manifest in the action taken by Scotland, America, and South Africa. The new Canon therefore represented a return to Catholic precedent and an avoidance of the mistakes of past years. Not only did it safeguard Catholic theology but it afforded 'a peaceful reconciliation to the two opposite camps, who in the West and East have been landed in disputes, which are not only regrettable, but unnecessary. Modern theological thought and liturgical research have justified a new and peaceful policy; it will be the wisdom of the Church of England to pursue it.'[1]

The fate of the Prayer Book Measure is well known. The Archbishop of Canterbury presented it to the House of Lords on 12 December and after a three-day debate it was passed by 241 votes to 88. On the following day, when it was debated in the House of Commons, the opposition led by Sir W. Joynson Hicks was successful, and it was rejected by 238 votes to 205. The Bishops then met to consider the situation and on 22 December the two Archbishops issued a long statement on their behalf. They were determined that the labours of the last twenty years should not be so lightly cast away without a struggle. Admittedly it was within the right of the House of Commons to reject the Measure, but mere acquiescence in its decisions would be inconsistent with the responsibilities of the Church as a spiritual society. In any case they considered that the decision had been influenced by 'certain avoidable misunderstandings as to the character of the proposals'. Consequently the Measure would be reintroduced into the Church Assembly as soon as possible with changes which would tend to remove apprehensions and clarify its intentions and limitations.

As may be expected Reservation and the alternative Order of Communion were the main stumbling-blocks, and on the day after the issue

---

[1] *Walter Howard Frere* (Alcuin Club Collections No. XXXV), London, 1940, p. 178.

of the Archbishops' Message, the Bishop of Gloucester, Dr. Headlam, wrote to Frere suggesting that one difficulty might be overcome by inserting two Epicleses in the alternative Canon.

The Bishop of Gloucester to Frere 23 *December* 1927

My dear Bishop,

I have thought many times about the new Canon and wondered whether anything could be done to adjust matters. You will remember that the original proposal before us was that we would have a Canon with an alternative Epiclesis, allowing it to be placed either before the Words of Institution, or in its place in the present alternative Canon. That was turned down, and you will remember I amongst others opposed it quite definitely. It seems to me that to allow people to pick and choose and that sort of thing would not be quite right in any way. But another solution has occurred to me, and that is this: that we might follow the Alexandrian rite and have an Epiclesis in both places. That is to say, just something quite simple before the Words of Institution, and the rest as we have arranged it. I cannot conceive that those who were strong advocates of the present Canon could have any objection to that, and it occurs to me that it may get over all the difficulties which the Anglo-Catholics feel on the subject. Nor would it make it any worse, as I imagine, for our Protestant friends, though one can never say.

Now if we could get the whole Anglo-Catholic party behind a revised Canon, don't you think that it would make matters very much easier? Then I think they will accept the new Book *con amore*, especially if we put it before them as something that the House of Commons has turned down. As far as I can see, the ultimate result of the vote of the House of Commons may be very good indeed. So far as I can judge from the testimony of this place, every one is on our side that counts; all the clergy seem to me to be so, except, of course, a few; every one I met at my Club; and, I am told here, the men in the street. And the Archbishops' letter has made a very good impression. What we shall have to do is to make it quite clear that whether the Church is Established or not Established, it is not a department of the State—and that is a very important thing.

Yours very sincerely,
A. C. Gloucestr.

Frere did not consider the proposal a happy one. It would play into the hands of those people who accused them of following Eastern tradition, whereas the position they wished to maintain was non-Roman

Western. Furthermore, while it would not satisfy those who did not want an Epiclesis at all, those who did want an Epiclesis would be already satisfied with the alternative Canon. Once again he urged the adoption of the optional use of alternative Invocations in the one Canon: it would be a temporary expedient, providing opportunity for the gradual growth of a permanent solution. Frere then revealed a view of the new Prayer Book which, if given greater publicity, would probably have secured for it a greater measure of support: it was to be a temporary Book, lasting for five or ten years, during which time the Church would be able, by means of increased knowledge and ordered experiment, to move gradually towards settled forms of worship.

Frere to the Bishop of Gloucester   27 December 1927

My dear Bishop,

    I have read and pondered much your letter; we are all, of course, trying to think in preparation for our next meeting. We have no doubt not only to consider Parliament but also the Assembly; I expect opinion has shifted a little bit since the Measure went through the last time. Probably in two directions I think there is an increase of Anglo-Catholic objection to the things they don't like; on the other hand there is among them, and possibly at the other end also, a considerable indignation at the thought of the Church being turned down by the State. So far as the Assembly is concerned, I expect it would be a good thing to make some modification that will reconcile the Anglo-Catholics; though I am anxious, as I expect we most are, to make as few changes as possible consistently with offering something to Parliament which they can accept next time with self-respect. Also I am inclined to include, if we can, some quasi-explanatory change which may conciliate the right wing of the Anglo-Catholics. It will be a good thing that what we present to Parliament should not merely have Parliament in view, or merely consider the prejudices reached and manifested there.

    On the other hand I do not think we should gain anything by taking an Alexandrian type of Canon; we should just be surrendering to people who call us Easternizers, while I maintain that what we have adopted is the custom of the Western Church everywhere apart from Rome. I do not think anybody would be very comfortable with an Invocation of the Holy Spirit in both places; the people who don't want it at all won't like it, and the people who want it at all actively are the people who are satisfied with our new Canon. I still think, however, that there is a good deal to be said for allowing the option of putting the 'Hear us, O merciful Father' clause in either position, or rather choosing one or other of those clauses. I shouldn't expect this option to continue for ever; I think it would give an opportunity for a settlement gradually and slowly to grow up. After all, what we are planning is not a permanent Book, but something to last five or ten years, especially in the matter such as this question of the theory of consecration. Nothing I think would really conciliate people who have committed themselves to the Roman theory of consecration except the omission of the clause of Invocation. These people are not by any means the extreme people; a great many quite unritualistic clergy who would indignantly repudiate the F.C.P. are of this view. While they want to conform they are really quite distressed at what they regard as an upsetting of all their traditions and plans, and (in a sense) a denial of the teaching which they have been accustomed to give. The only way to conciliate them, either to bring them over to vote for, or else make them more comfortable in voting against, is in some way or another to let them omit it: and I think the best way is by the form of option which the Members in Charge proposed last time, that one or other of the 'Hear us' clauses should be said. The difference really would not be very marked; the 'Hear us, O merciful Father' in its present position is familiar enough; to say that there and have no 'corresponding clause after the Anamnesis would have come quite natural to people—more natural in fact than the Canon now as set forth; it would merely add an Anamnesis to the existing form, and so be a form which was altered from the familiar words rather less than the present new form. It didn't occur to me till your letter came that it was worth while to reopen this question, but I think it probably is, now that I have read your argument; only I hope the change may be as I suggest here, rather than the Alexandrian plan which you put up. I quite agree that there is very good hope now for a more satisfactory result after this outburst than we should have had if we had secured the vote the other day. The Protestant explosion is now over and it won't return again, at any rate in the same sort of form, nor, I expect, in any form for some time. It will be a great gain if all goes well to have had our little tussle with the Commons; they will feel the better for having made their protest and we shall feel the better for having gained a delayed and dignified victory for our side. . . .

At the same time Frere informed the former episcopal Members in

Charge of Dr. Headlam's proposal, in case they were asked to act in the same capacity with the new Measure, and they all agreed that it was not a happy one.

Frere to the Bishops of Chelmsford (Dr. Warman),   28 December 1927
   Chichester (Dr. Burrows), and Oxford (Dr. Strong)

My dear Bishop,

   I am not sure whether we shall be still 'Mice'[1] under the new conditions: in case we are, I am sending a copy of a letter which I have written in reply to one from the Bishop of Gloucester. It has to do with the revival of a plan which we proposed for the revision of the Canon and which the House of Bishops did not accept. I am inclined to think that it should come up again and I argue that in this present letter. The Bishop of Gloucester has proposed that we should have an Alexandrian form of the Canon with an Invocation of the Holy Spirit both before and after the biblical quotation: but I do not think that it is likely to be acceptable to anybody.

                                  Yours sincerely,
                                    Walterus Truron.

The Bishop of Chelmsford to Frere   29 December 1927

My dear Bishop,

   I am afraid that the 'Mice' were put to death like the city pigeons with the death of the Measure, though I expect we shall be revived in due course. The two Archbishops felt that some small committee should be asked to prepare the agenda for the January meeting and invited the Bishop of Winchester, who happened to be in London, the Bishop of Southwark, and myself to form a small subcommittee for that purpose. We met last Friday and have set down some rough proposals which will at any rate form matter for argument. We have made no suggestion about the alternative Communion Office save that we suggest the consideration of a rubric which should prevent it being foisted upon an unwilling parish.

   Speaking quite for myself, I am inclined to hope that it will not be touched. I have grave fears that in dealing with it we might all too easily tend to break the unity which existed so largely amongst the Bishops and which the House of Commons has increased for us throughout the whole Church.

[1] 'Mice' = M(embers) I(n) C(harg)E.

I do not at all think the Bishop of Gloucester's proposal would please anyone. Very clearly the matter of the Canon will have to be considered when the House of Bishops meets, and it may be the general mind that there should be some change. You will probably remember that I only acquiesced in the M-i-Ce proposal in order that it might be discussed and decided by the House.

With every good wish for the New Year,
Yours sincerely,
Guy Chelmsford.

The Bishop of Chichester to Frere   29 *December* 1927

My dear Frere,

I believe that all the 'Mice' were killed as such by the rejection of the Prayer Book Measure. But I also think that when we meet on 11 January, the others will expect the assassinated mice to lift their heads and chirrup again: only not this mouse, for he is ordered to put all these things out of his head for three weeks. I had a spasm yesterday, however, and wrote to Chelmsford on some minor points which occurred to me, but not on the Canon.

Would it be wise to add Gloucester to the mice and drop me out?...

PS. Letter this morning from Chelmsford saying the Archbishops have invited Winchester, Southwark, and Chelmsford to provide agenda for 11 January. I gather they met on the 23rd. The Archbishops seem to think the fewer changes the better.

The Bishop of Oxford to Frere   29 *December* 1927

My dear Bishop,

I have read your letter with care. I have not seen Gloucester's proposal. I confess that I am extremely nervous about making any change which may be taken to have doctrinal significance; and in the present state of opinion in Parliament it would surely seal the fate of our next effort, if it could be said that we had made further concessions to the Anglo-Catholics. I think it is impolitic to talk about, or make *concessions* to, this or that party. We have presented the Book as containing in our judgement a form of worship consistent with Church of England teaching. It will be very difficult to maintain this position if we make concessions that can be represented as having doctrinal value. I hope we shall limit ourselves within the language of the Archbishop for 'making those changes, and only those which may clear up misunderstandings'. I should not so much mind a quasi-explanatory note somewhere else than in the Canon. But we must, of course, discuss the matter. How horrid it all is.

Yours ever,
Thomas Oxon.

The Bishop of Gloucester too, after further consideration, felt that it would be best to make the minimum of change in the Book and proceeded no further with his suggestion.

The Bishop of Gloucester to Frere   30 *December* 1927

My dear Bishop,

Thank you very much for your letter. I have been thinking about things since I wrote and also talking to people, and I am certain now that we had better give up the idea of doing anything to improve the new Prayer Book. If we send it back to the Commons, it must be with a minimum of alterations, and we must not distract people with subordinate issues. The question is one now of spiritual independence of the Church, and the more we confine people's attention to the one issue the better. After all, any improvement which we made in one direction would be considered harmful in another direction, and so I think we had better quite clearly make up our minds not to attempt alteration, and our general policy should be the minimum change possible. Of course, there are many things which many of us would like, one in one direction and one in another, but to raise them for action would be disastrous.

Yours very sincerely,
A. C. Gloucestr.

The House of Bishops met on 11, 12, and 13 January 1928 to consider what changes they should make in the Book. Frere and the Bishops of Chelmsford (Dr. Warman), Coventry (Dr. Carr), Oxford (Dr. Strong), and Southwark (Dr. Garbett) were appointed Members in Charge. The results of their deliberations were published in the Report C.A. 252, the most important being as follows:

1. One of the Prayers for the King should always be said at Morning and Evening Prayer, or at Holy Communion if it followed.
2. The 'Black Rubric' was to be inserted at the end of the alternative Order for Holy Communion.
3. Clause 4 of the 1927 Measure, permitting the Bishops to make or rescind rules to have the force of rubrics in the Deposited Book was omitted.

The Final Stages

4. The arrangements with regard to Reservation were incorporated in the rubrics instead of being issued in a list of Regulations. This involved the insertion of the following three rubrics.

(a) 'If further provision be needed in order to secure that any sick person may not lack the benefit of the most comfortable Sacrament of the Body and Blood of Christ, the Priest, if licensed by the Bishop so to do, may to that end when the Holy Communion is celebrated in the church, reserve so much of the consecrated Bread and Wine as is needed for the purpose. And the Bishop shall grant such licence if satisfied of the need, unless in any particular case he see good reason to the contrary.'

(b) 'The consecrated Bread and Wine set apart under either of the two preceding rubrics shall be reserved only for the Communion of the Sick, shall be administered in both kinds, and shall be used for no other purpose whatever. There shall be no service or ceremony in connexion with the Sacrament so reserved, nor shall it be exposed or removed except in order to be received in Communion, or otherwise reverently consumed.'

(c) 'The consecrated Bread and Wine thus set apart shall (according as the Bishop shall direct) be reserved in an Aumbry or safe set in the North or South wall of the Church or of any chapel thereof, or, if need be, in the wall of the vestry. The door of such Aumbry shall be kept locked, and opened only when it is necessary to move or replace the consecrated Elements for the purposes of Communion or renewal. The consecrated Bread and Wine shall be renewed at least once a week.'

These proposals were considered by the Houses of Clergy and Laity at the February session of the Church Assembly and in the main were accepted. They also made certain amendments themselves, some of which proved to be extremely contentious. These appeared in the Report C.A. 257.

1. If the Parochial Church Council desired it, or if the Bishop was satisfied that there was a sufficient desire in the parish, the 1662 Order for Holy Communion should be celebrated at least one Sunday a month, or by arrangement to suit those concerned. (Clergy and Laity.)

2. When the Litany was said, the suffrages for the King, provided they were used in full, should suffice instead of the Prayers for the King. (Clergy.)

3. The Minister or the Parochial Church Council should have the right of appeal to the Archbishop and Bishops of the Province in the case of objections to the granting of a licence or the giving of directions by a Bishop in the case of Reservation. (Clergy and Laity.)

4. The form of Invocation should be changed in the alternative Canon. (Clergy.)

5. A rubric should be inserted declaring that the fast before Communion was both optional and unessential. (Clergy and Laity.)

6. Some form of declaration on Eucharistic Doctrine should be inserted in the alternative Order for the Communion of the Sick. (Clergy and Laity.)

When the Bishops made their final proposals in the light of these amendments in Report C.A. 252 A, they agreed to Nos. 1, 2, 3, and 5, and rejected Nos. 4 and 6. Further changes were also made in the first and third new Rubrics on Reservations in order to make the conditions of Continuous Reservation more definite. In their new form they read:

(*a*) 'If the Bishop is satisfied that in connexion with hospitals, or in time of common sickness, or in the special circumstances of any particular parish, the provisions of the preceding rubric are not sufficient, and that there is need of further provision in order that sick and dying persons may not lack the benefit of the most comfortable Sacrament of the Body and Blood of Christ, he may to that end give his licence to the Priest, to reserve at the open Communion so much of the consecrated Bread and Wine as is needed for the purpose. Whenever such licence is granted or refused, the Minister or the people as represented in the Parochial Church Council, may refer the question to the Archbishop and Bishops of the Province.'

(*b*) 'The consecrated Bread and Wine thus set apart shall be reserved in an aumbry or safe. The aumbry shall (according as the Bishop shall direct) be set in the North or South wall of the sanctuary of the church or of any chapel thereof, or, if need be, in the wall of some other part of the church approved by the Bishop, provided that it shall not be immediately behind or above a Holy Table. The door of the aumbry shall be kept locked and opened only when it is necessary to move or replace the consecrated Elements for the purposes of Communion or renewal. The consecrated Bread and Wine shall be renewed at least once a week.'

VII

IN OPPOSITION

FOR Frere these final amendments were critical. In 1927 although he had not been happy about many points, he had continued to support the Measure. With the changes now proposed, however, he felt that he could go no further. The Book, far from offering a hope of settlement, seemed to him to be an inevitable cause of further trouble. He disliked the power given to Parochial Church Councils to decide what form of service should be used—it was an insult to the Clergy and a snub to the Bishop: he disliked the handling of the question of fasting and regarded the rubric as outrageous: he considered the restrictions involved in the Reservation rubrics to be excessive: and he still deplored the fact that no form of Canon had been provided for those who did not like an Epiclesis. Although he was a Member in Charge he did not attend a meeting of the House of Bishops for the conclusion of their deliberations on 8 March, and he took immediate steps to publish a statement on his position. For this purpose he secured the co-operation of Canon Cooper, Chancellor of Truro Cathedral. Having acquainted him with his reasons for withdrawing his support from the Prayer Book Measure, he asked him to draw up a letter asking for advice on how to act in Convocation; this, together with his reply, could then be published. At the same time he wrote to the Archbishop of Canterbury and the Superior at Mirfield, Father E. K. Talbot, telling them of his line of action and enclosing a copy of the letter he proposed to publish.

Chancellor S. Cooper to Frere   10 *March* 1928

My dear Bishop,

Will this do? I am afraid it is rather long, but I had thought it better (*a*) to say what was really bothering us, and that (*b*) before I had read your letter so that the latter might be really an answer. I hope my query will fit in with what you have written and will not necessitate your redrafting it. But if it won't, do let me know.

Yours affectionately and obediently,
Sydney Cooper.

With this was enclosed the official letter.

Chancellor Cooper to Frere   10 March 1928

My dear Lord Bishop,

    I am sure you will not mind my writing to ask you for your advice in this time of grievous perplexity, and in view of the vote we shall have to give in Convocation on the 29th. There must be many like myself who have so far loyally supported the Bishops in their policy with regard to the New Prayer Book, as they in their turn have, on the whole, responded to the suggestions of the Lower Houses of Convocation. We have not liked all the alterations proposed; we have desired improvements which have not been carried; we have objected strongly to the cumbersome form of the new book and to the timidity which refused to supersede the old, as has always been done at former revisions: but we have recognized that the book marked an advance in many ways on its predecessors and corresponded better to modern needs. And when the Bishops decided to put it a second time before Parliament, we agreed that they were the best judges of the situation, and we voted accordingly for general approval in the House of Clergy on 7 February, trusting that certain amendments which appeared in the agenda paper would be rejected, if not on their merits, at least as being contrary to the proposals of the Bishops to reintroduce the Book *with only explanatory alterations*. It was a vain hope. The proposers of the motions were, of course, technically within their rights in bringing them forward as the Measure was technically a new one: but constitutionally they were wrong to spring upon the Assembly, at a few hours' notice, resolutions concerning matters of doctrine and principle which either had not been raised at all, or had been defeated in the course of twenty years' debates, and had left no mark upon the Book which had been so laboriously completed and which was in fact before us. It was not fair that a much hustled House, for the approach of Lent as well as an inevitable adjournment interfered sadly with both the attendance of members and the sufficiency of debate, should be called upon to decide off-hand on such weighty and difficult questions as the rule of Fasting Communion and the modes of our Blessed Lord's Presence with his Church. It should have been enough to have maintained the silence which the Book of Common Prayer has hitherto maintained concerning the former and to have been satisfied with what it already says about the latter. But now that the Bishop of Middleton's [Dr. Parsons] and Mr. Douglas's motions have been carried and a motion similar to the latter has passed the House of Laity, and their endorsement by the Bishops is generally anticipated, many of us feel that the whole situation has been altered, and that we cannot conscientiously support a Measure which, under the guise of making better provision for public worship, by the gratuitous insertion of rubrics, which are not strictly rubrics at all but statements of doctrine, commit us to positions which, to say the least, are extremely doubtful, and one of which would raise yet another barrier between us and our brethren both of the Eastern and Roman Communions at a time when, if we are loyal to the spirit and injunctions of the last Lambeth Conference, we should rather be seeking for points of agreement.

We should be grateful for your counsel.

Yours sincerely and obediently,

Sydney Cooper.

Frere's draft reply to this letter was as follows.

Frere to Chancellor Cooper   10 *March* 1928

My dear Chancellor,

Your letter asks me to comment on the present situation of Prayer Book revision: and I do so with a strong sense of responsibility because I think, as you do, that the position has been worsened by recent events.

I supported the Deposited Book which the Assembly approved but the House of Commons rejected. It contained besides a number of things which I merely disliked, one or two things which seemed to me not only unwise but unjust. However, in the hope that it might serve, at any rate for the time, as a basis of peaceful and orderly administration in matters of worship, I supported it. The Deposited Book has now been amended by all three Houses of the Assembly; and in this new form I now cannot support it, for it seems to me to offer now no sufficient hope of settlement, but on the contrary, to lead up to acute trouble.

You will not expect me to go into so voluminous a subject at any length: but I will try to indicate very briefly some of the chief points of my indictment.

1. In the General Rubrics governing the Book the Houses of Clergy and Laity have demanded an insertion which I think revolutionary. Hitherto the initiative and first responsibility about services has rested on the shoulders of the Parish Priest: the Parochial Church Council has been given a formal right of protest; and in case of discord the Bishop

is to arbitrate and decide. The new demand is that the Council should be able to issue a certain command to the Priest, apart from the Bishop, which he must thereupon carry out.

That some provision should be made for communicants who desire the rite of 1662 is of course desirable: but the already existing method of securing this by joint action of Priest and People (and Bishop if needed) was adequate. This new provision is an insult to the Clergy and a snub to the Bishop.

2. I am personally well satisfied with the new Canon: but, being so, I am the more concerned for the large body of those who are not, both Evangelicals and Anglo-Catholics. The Roman type of liturgy has prevailed in the English Church from St. Augustine's time till now; and I think it is unfair that no form of Canon should be provided for those who wish to keep it, or who for other reasons dislike an Epiclesis. Peace and contented worship can hardly be secured while the desire of so large a class of worshippers is ignored or refused.

3. The subject of fasting in general and of the fast before Communion in particular is a large one. It calls for fresh investigation, so far as the relation of past custom to present conditions is concerned, and probably for some reconstruction and restatement. But such needed handling of the matter will only be hindered by the adoption, in the form of a rubric, of any such brief statement as is desired by the Houses of Clergy and Laity. Besides this, the seriousness and adequacy of preparation for Communion (difficult enough to secure in any case) would necessarily be impaired by any such rubric, even if it did not take the outrageous form suggested, of saying in effect that it is as good to break with Catholic custom as to observe it. Such an Antinomian line is contrary to the tradition of the English Church.

4. Lastly with regard to the Reservation of the Blessed Sacrament, there has been during the closing stages of the revision a steady deterioration of outlook and statesmanship. Unworthy influences such as suspicion and intolerance have led to excessive restriction. The Parish Priest in his pastoral office is tied up too tight, the Bishop as administrator is fettered, and the Laity have their privileges unfairly curtailed.

(a) There is no justification for rigidly confining the benefit to the sick. Administration to the whole would no doubt need regulation: but it is unfair to make it impossible for persons who are debarred from coming regularly at the times of service. Besides, it is surely very undesirable that the Sacrament Reserved should be isolated from all

Communion given in the church, and so from the idea of Communion.

(*b*) For the purpose of Reservation is Communion. This primary purpose, however, does not preclude advantages secondary and incidental.

These should be recognized and even taken to some extent into account in determining the places where Reservation is licensed. The restrictions in the Deposited Book were too narrow; but those which are now put forward are worse and will soon be found impracticable.

Reflecting, therefore, on the present situation and passing over many minor matters I reluctantly realize that we tend to hinder Communion, to discourage prayer, to decry fasting, to subjugate the Parish Priest to the Council, to hamper episcopal administration, besides ignoring the legitimate claim for another form of Canon.

Unless, therefore, in the Convocations some modifications are made, with great regret I find myself unable to vote for sending the Measure on to the Assembly.

Yours affectionately,
Walterus Truron.

Frere to Fr. E. K. Talbot, C.R.   10 *March* 1928

My dear Keble,

I am sending along to you a copy of a letter that I have written to our Chancellor by way of publication in the Diocese as to the position to which I have now come with regard to the Prayer Book. I report to you officially as Superior, but please not for publication until the 16th. I have sent a copy of it to the Archbishop in case he wishes to raise any protest, which I do not think he will. I wonder if the Lower House in Convocation will regret it if they take steps to try and recover the position which they betrayed so badly the other day in the House of Clergy?

This doesn't want a reply of course; it is only in the nature of a report. You may imagine it's rather reluctant, but it can't be helped. I can't honestly regard the present proposals as likely to effect the needed reform and order.

Yours affectionately,
Walterus Truron.

Fr. Talbot replied most sympathetically. He supported the line Frere had taken, and hoped that it might stimulate the Convocations to take action at the last minute and retrieve the situation.

Fr. Talbot to Frere   *12 March 1928*

My dear Walter,

    Thank you very much for your letter and enclosure which certainly lacks nothing in high explosive quality.

    I presume that you have written it in the light of the Bishops' decisions, though you refer in the main to the amendments proposed by Clergy and Laity. I infer that the Bishops have included in their revision these amendments (or something like them) on the points you enumerate. If that is so I certainly share your strong objections. Certainly that last day of the Clergy's session was a 'Black Wednesday', including as it did the proposals about the P.C.C. and the use of the 1662 Book, the monstrous fasting rubric, the rubric about the 'area of ceremonial observances' in regard to the Reserved Sacrament, and the declaration about the doctrine implied in Reservation (to my mind a very inadequate and misleading one). On the three other matters you mention, I had hoped that the Clergy's amendment about the place of Reservation—though not entirely satisfactory—would at any rate rule out the hasty proposal of the Bishops and allow considerable latitude (e.g. as to tabernacles). I still hope the Bishops have not narrowed this. Communion for the 'whole' from the Reserved Sacrament was lost by only one vote—though in a tiny house—and I had hoped that this might have provided an opportunity for the Bishops to make some allowance for it. Evidently they have not. Likewise I had hoped that the—not very satisfactory—motion about the Epiclesis, carried again in a small house, would at any rate enable the Bishops to make provision for another alternative. Again I infer from you they have not.

    In view then of all this, I cannot help applauding the line you are taking. It will at any rate stimulate the Convocations to try and retrieve the situation—though I greatly fear it is too late to do so; and it is as well that the world should know what is likely to occur if it is not retrieved. Moreover, I welcome a strong word from the Catholic side, other than Darwell's [Stone]. We have been a ragged army.

    It must be beastly for you—and I sympathize very much with you in having to undertake a very unpleasant duty. But I entirely agree that the moment has come for strong action. And who better to take it than you?

    I'm not sure whether you wished the brethren to see your letter. I have shown it only to Gerard [Fr. Sampson]—who is writing to you (I think in an opposite sense to mine). But I suppose it will be public when the Bishops' proposals appear. I don't really think I could wish anything altered in your letter.

The only thing which clouds my mind is the prospect of the Book being rejected in the ecclesiastical bodies. What is to happen then? But perhaps it is enough to take one step at a time....

Yours affectionately,
Keble.

Frere to the Archbishop of Canterbury   10 *March* 1928

My dear Archbishop,

I am sending you a draft of a letter which I have written to the Chancellor of the Cathedral here by way of explanation to him and other Proctors and the Diocese generally as to the position in which I now find myself. I hope I do not do wrong in sending it to you. Let me, of course, make clear that I do not think it needs an answer; only I thought that I should let you have timely notice of what is going forward. I propose that the letter should be published on the 16th. You will perhaps note that it doesn't go beyond the immediate issue in the Convocations. Beyond that point I haven't tried to see my way clearly as yet....

The Archbishop was distressed at Frere's decision but, like Fr. Talbot, most sympathetic. He made it quite clear, however, that there would be no chance of last-minute changes when the Measure came before the Convocations; they were merely being consulted as to whether or no the Measure should go forward to the Assembly. As an act of courtesy, the Bishops wished to acquaint the Convocations with their decisions before making them public, and they hoped to do this on 17 March: it would therefore be helpful if Frere could postpone the publication of his correspondence until this was done.

The Archbishop of Canterbury to Frere   12 *March* 1928

My dear Bishop,

I thank you for sending me a copy of your exceedingly important letter to your Chancellor. I need not say that it distresses me intensely to find that you regard as you do what we have been endeavouring to effect; but I perfectly understand your position, and no one could possibly state the matter more frankly and considerately.

But are you not under a misapprehension when you speak of Convocation now making alterations? I do not understand that Convocation will have any further opportunity of altering what we propose. We did on the former occasion, just a year ago, as a matter of grace consult the Convocations before reaching the final conclusion of the House of Bishops. Many people thought we were wrong in so doing, but I believe that in the then circumstances it was right. We have not, however, done so on this occasion, but are, according to present arrangements, simply consulting Convocation as to whether or no the Measure is to go forward to the Assembly. This is, as I read our Standing Orders, in full accord with what is intended; and the stricter people thought we were unwise in what we did on 7 February of last year. I mention this because your letter seems to indicate that you think the Convocations can reopen the question. Surely this is not so.

When we meet on Thursday next the House of Bishops is simply to check in its final form the decisions we reached last week and to authorize the Measure being in those terms printed off for submission to the Convocations and for publicity. We discussed last Thursday how soon it would be possible to make our decisions public, and it was felt that it would be more courteous that the members of Convocation should receive it first. It was arranged accordingly that the final form reached on Thursday should, if possible, be printed and circulated so as to reach members of Convocation on Saturday and that it might be made public in the Press on Monday the 19th.

I think you will agree that it would be undesirable that your letter commenting on what we have now done should be made public prior to the publication of the Measure itself.

I am,
Yours very truly,
Randall Cantuar.

After writing to the Archbishop on the 10th, Frere discovered that on the last day of the session, when he was absent, the Bishops had agreed to the sixth of the Clergy and Laity's proposals—the issue of a Declaration on Eucharistic Doctrine. A Draft Declaration was drawn up by the Archbishop of York (Dr. Lang) and the Bishops of Winchester (Dr. Woods) and Gloucester (Dr. Headlam) for the consideration of the Bishops at their final meeting on Thursday the 15th:

'Lest the provisions made in this Alternative Order for the Communion of the Sick should be misconstrued it is hereby declared that there is intended thereby no use of this Holy Sacrament other than that which our Saviour himself commanded. Moreover, while his presence in the Lord's Supper is to be ever most reverently and thankfully acknowledged it is likewise to be remembered that as we are taught in the Holy Scriptures he dwelleth by faith in the hearts of his people; that where two or three are gathered together in his name there is he in the midst of them; and that he himself hath said "Lo I am with you alway, even unto the end of the world".'

This too was a change of which Frere disapproved and he immediately informed the Archbishop that he was arranging with Canon Cooper to add a further section on the subject to his letter.

Frere to the Archbishop of Canterbury 12 *March* 1928

My dear Archbishop,

Since writing you on Saturday I see with great regret that the House is contemplating the issue of a declaration on the lines of those adopted by the other Houses. In view of this in the reply to Canon Cooper I am adding a brief section on the subject. I had hopes from what I heard in Convocation with other Bishops that at any rate that project would be rejected. I therefore said nothing about it in my previous draft....

Frere to Canon Cooper 12 *March* 1928

My dear Cooper,

... I am putting down a further bit of the letter to you—an extra piece to be put in—with regard to the proposed Declaration on Eucharistic Doctrine. I meant to leave this out if I thought it could be omitted, but I don't now believe that it can: so here it goes into your letter as No. 4, and the present No. 4 becomes No. 5.

I have heard now from the Archbishop: it rather upsets plans and the letter will have to be modified. He is to settle whether it is to be published this week or next; if next week it will be deferred till then so that the Bishops' final decisions may be published. They will come out on Monday the 19th. If publication is to be deferred till then, I shall have to rewrite the whole letter in view of that publication. I am asking the Archbishop to telegraph which he decides will be the right thing to do, leaving the matter in his hands. But it occurs to me that if the thing is deferred in this way, your own letter may want modification as well as my own; you will probably have the Lower House less in view and the Upper House more in view in writing. Will you consider that point? I will let you know tomorrow what the Archbishop decides as to the date....

Yours affectionately,
Walterus Truron.

Section 4 to be inserted. 'The proposed Declaration about the Holy Eucharist is inadvisable. The first part is only a repetition of what is better and more appropriately said in the Preface. The second part, if it is anything more than platitudinous, is, in my judgement, ill-balanced and therefore provocative.'

On the following day Frere wrote to the Archbishop again, this time in answer to his letter of the 12th. He accepted the decision that the Convocations should not be allowed to make any further alterations to the Book, although he did so regretfully. It meant that the Lower House would have no opportunity of expressing a mind on the proposals of the House of Bishops. As the letter to Canon Cooper notes, the decision as to the date of publication of the correspondence was left to the Archbishop, but Frere still preferred a date before the Bishops' proposals were made known.

Frere to the Archbishop of Canterbury   13 March 1928

My dear Archbishop,

Thank you for your very kind and generous letter. I am sorry to have to bother your further, but there is one point still outstanding. First let me thank you for making it clear about Convocation. Of course, as you say, it must make alterations formally; but I understand you to say that it will not be possible for any House of the Convocations to attach any conditions to this assent to the sending forward of the proposals for revision; and that any attempt to attach such a condition would be out of order; and this in spite of the fact that the Lower House has had no opportunity of expressing a mind upon the proposals as now made by the House of Bishops. I will not say more but that, of course, I accept that decision very regretfully.

The other is quite a small matter of immediate and personal interest only. I shall, of course, act with regard to publication according to your wish; but let me first explain. Canon Cooper's letter to me had in view only the things that were known to the public after the meetings of the Houses of Clergy and Laity. I confined myself to that same area, and did not disclose what had taken place in the House of Bishops.

On every ground it seemed to me better, that, if I had to dissent, I should dissent preferably from the proposals put forward by the other Houses, or from those decisions of the Bishops that were previously clear. In the latter case I only utilized material that was already public property; in the former case I confined myself to differing with the other Houses and not with the House of Bishops. In every way this seemed to me less offensive. I was anxious, therefore, to keep to this area. This ought to imply publishing before the Bishops' results were known. By that method I should avoid a direct clash. It seemed more polite to say, 'If so and so happens I shall have to do so and so', than to wait till it did happen and then rebel. You may think this too subtle; or perhaps worse; but my intention was to mitigate the wrench. If, however, your Grace decides that it is better that I should wait until the Bishops' decisions are published and I issue our little correspondence then, I will of course do so; but that means an acute form of frontal attack, such as I had wished to avoid. May I ask your Grace to be so very kind as to send me a telegram conveying your decision as to whether it should be on the 16th or the 19th? If you decide for the latter I shall have to recast a good deal of the present form, which has last week in view, into a new form which has next week in view. In any case I shall strike out some hard words in the section originally numbered 4....

The Archbishop appreciated his considerateness, but still insisted on publication on the 19th, first by telegram and then by a short letter of explanation.

The Archbishop of Canterbury to Frere   14 *March* 1928
My dear Bishop,

I read very carefully your letter this morning and had an opportunity of discussing it with the Archbishop of York. I entirely see your point. You have behaved with great considerateness to us in the matter, and I realize that in some ways the publication of your letter before general attention has been concentrated on the actual words of our proposed new rubrics might have advantages; and I appreciate the thoughtfulness of your desire not to make what you call a 'frontal attack'. But on the whole I came to the conclusion, and the Archbishop of York was stronger than myself, that we should confuse matters by the publication of a document not yet in the hands of the Church, and although I think your criticism of our wording will be more adverse to *us* if delayed till Monday, I think it fairer all round that it should appear then rather than earlier.

I am,
Yours very truly,
Randall Cantuar.

The Bishops met on 15 March for the final consideration of their proposals. After considerable debate they decided against inserting any Declaration on Eucharistic Doctrine, and the Archbishop immediately telegraphed the news to Frere. The telegram and the above letter were therefore received on the same day. As a result Frere not only decided to delete Section 4 of his letter, but also agreed to wait until the 19th before publishing the correspondence, although it would be dated for the 14th as he had originally proposed.

Frere to the Archbishop of Canterbury   16 March 1928

My dear Archbishop,

I am very sorry that I have been giving you so much trouble. Best thanks for your telegram and for your kind letter just received this morning.

I was very much rejoiced to get your telegram. I can now suppress one of the paragraphs, and that will be all to the good. But I am much more rejoiced that we are free from having committed ourselves by any statement of the kind.

When the telegram came, I came to the conclusion that the best plan would be to keep our correspondence at the date to which it properly belongs, only making it clear that it took place while the matter was still before the House of Bishops and was not released for publication until the later date. This will save any rewriting in a more directly hostile form, and I think will be intelligible, as I have now put it, to anybody who wants to understand. Some slight modification has been introduced in order to make this position stand out clear. . . .

In its amended form, Frere's letter to Chancellor Cooper therefore ran:

Frere to Chancellor Cooper   14 March 1928

My dear Chancellor,

Your letter asks me to comment on the present position of Prayer Book revision and especially of the changes recently recommended by the Houses of Clergy and Laity. Frankly I think it improper to introduce any changes of substance at this last stage: and I think, as you do, that these new recommendations are likely (if adopted by the Bishops) to make things worse and not better.

I supported the Deposited Book which the Assembly approved but the House of Commons rejected. It contained, besides a number of things which I merely disliked, one or two things which seemed to me not only unwise but unjust. However, in the hope that it might serve, at any rate for the time, as a basis of peaceful and orderly administration in matters of worship, I supported it.

The Deposited Book has now been altered by all three Houses of the Church Assembly and these alterations have cut away the ground of my support. I see now no sufficient hope of settlement, but on the contrary the prospect of acute trouble.

You will not expect me to go into so voluminous a subject at any length: but I will try to indicate very briefly some of the chief points of my indictment.

1. In the directions concerning the Holy Communion the Houses of Clergy and Laity have demanded an insertion which I think revolutionary . . . snub to the Bishops.
2. I am personally well satisfied with the new Canon . . . is refused.
3. The subject of fasting in general . . . tradition of the English Church.
4. Lastly, with regard to the Reservation of the Blessed Sacrament, there has been during the closing stages of the revision a sad faltering in the spirit of generosity and trust which once prevailed; this has led, step after step, to the accumulation of a mass of rigid restrictions . . . be found impracticable.

Reflecting, therefore, on the present position, and passing over many minor matters, I reluctantly realize that we tend to hinder Communion, to discourage a valued form of prayer, to decry fasting, to subjugate the parish priests to their councils, to hamper episcopal administration, besides ignoring a legitimate claim for another form of Canon.

I regret to say that I have little hope that the final decision of the Bishops will be found, when they appear, to remedy these defects: and in this case I shall be unable to vote in Convocation for sending the measure on to the Assembly.

Yours affectionately,
Walterus Truron.

Frere still felt that, as a last hope, something might be done to save the situation in the Lower Houses of Convocation, and in this he was not alone. Two interesting letters which passed between the Bishop of St. Albans (Dr. Furse) and himself indicate this and also reveal that Dr. Furse was partly instrumental in securing the rejection of the Declaration on Eucharistic Doctrine.

The Bishop of St. Albans to Frere 16 *March* 1928

My dear Truro,

...I am terribly sorry that you have felt that you must come to this decision. I have had a rotten time myself lately and I think if the Bishops had passed the doctrinal statement yesterday I should have had to take the same line as you in Convocation, but fortunately they didn't. I managed to see and talk with some of the Bishops before the meeting, which I think made a bit of difference, and fortunately York came down on the right side and we managed to defeat the suggestion, which was an enormous relief to me.

I hate the fasting rubric and all these beastly efforts to tie up everybody. I made an attempt to get them to reconsider the question of the appeal from the Parochial Church Council; but the Archbishop of Canterbury, perhaps rightly, took the line that the meeting yesterday had been definitely summoned for the Bishops to consider the doctrinal statement and the report of the Printing Committee, though I think he himself would probably have voted against this Church Council appeal.

What I wish the Lower House of Convocation would do would be to send up resolutions asking the Bishops to reconsider these points before giving their final approval; and I cannot see that they would not be justified in doing so, as we have really changed things other than those referred to in the Resolutions of the Lower House.

Now that the doctrinal statement is out I don't feel that I can vote against the Book in Convocation, though I shall certainly take an opportunity sometime or other of expressing my grave objection to some of the things that we have done. I shouldn't be a bit surprised if the Lower House refused to send the Book on to the Church Assembly. However, we must see what happens.

Thank you for sending me your letter,

Yours affectionately,

Michael S. Albans.

In Opposition

Frere to the Bishop of St. Albans   17 *March* 1928.

My dear Brother Michael,

Indeed it is a great relief that you have managed to get rid of the doctrinal statement. That, I think, would have done more harm than anything, not merely in this country but all over the world; so it's a great cause of thankfulness that that's done.

I supposed from the terms of the Notice that there would be no business taken at that meeting except what was specially referred to; but it didn't seem to me that it was any use for me to come up, or that there was anything to be done about any other point until we get to Convocation itself. As you say, it now remains to be seen what line the Lower Houses will take. It's the House of Clergy that is largely responsible for these last bricks, so it is up to them I think to try and remedy them; but whether they will do so or not I don't know. I don't mean to be in the position of stimulating underground a revolt on their part. All that I need do, I think, is to say my say with such publicity as is decent and take no further action; though, of course, to one's own friends and others, individually, one must explain a little more fully. I am very anxious though not to make more rifts than are inevitable in our ranks, and as you may suppose, I shan't at all relish the company in which I find myself when the vote comes on in Convocation. Necessity makes strange bed-fellows.

                                 Yours affectionately,
                                        Walterus Truron.

Further evidence of a hope of last-minute action in Convocation was also given in correspondence with Canon A. G. Robinson of Winchester, in which Frere again claimed that the plan of optional alternative Invocations would have solved the difficulties of the Canon.

Canon A. G. Robinson to Frere   19 *March* 1928

My dear Bishop,

Thank you for sending me a copy of your letter to Canon Cooper.

The Bishops seem to me to have made their final revision mainly with a view to satisfying the House of Commons. Mixing religious questions with political ones has so often been the undoing of the Church, and nowhere more so than here in England.

I am most grateful to you for what you tried to do in regard to the Prayer of Consecration. Those of us who feel strongly about the new form of Epiclesis have, I think, some ground for complaint.

It is just nineteen years since I was placed on the Convocation Prayer Book Revision Committee, and I was for twelve years its secretary. It is sad that the work should end in such a muddle. But the blame does not rest entirely with the Bishops. The House of Clergy has much to answer for. The Anglo-Catholics were often badly led; the Grey people were mostly cranks; and the Evangelicals had no policy at all beyond mere opposition.

I think I shall vote for final approval. Further revision will then be absolutely necessary within the next fifteen years, because the confusion produced will soon become intolerable. If after twenty years' work we decide to do nothing, the doing nothing policy is likely to become permanent. At present I am not satisfied that there are any mistakes which we are now asked to make which cannot afterwards be rectified. It seems to me that we must at once get rid of the idea that in 1662 the worship of the Church became fixed for all time.

Yours gratefully,
A. G. Robinson.

Frere to Canon A. G. Robinson   22 *March* 1928

My dear Canon Robinson,

Thank you for your letter.

You know, I think, what my view of the case is. I am quite anxious to see another alternative. I do not think it need necessarily mean a whole alternative printed out in full. There are two or three possibilities, I think, of dealing with the matter on the lines that I should wish. The first but not the best I think, would be simply to give leave to celebrants to omit the Invocation Prayer. A much better way proposed by the House of Clergy, but not listened to unfortunately, and proposed and considerably discussed in the House of Bishops, was to print both the clauses beginning 'Hear us, O merciful Father'—the present Prayer Book one in its present position, and the new one as at present in the new Prayer Book—and to put a footnote to say that only one or other of those clauses is to be used. That, I think, on the whole is the best plan. A third way, not so satisfactory, would be merely to say that those who use the old Prayer Book Canon may, if they so desire, add to it the Anamnesis, the Prayer of Oblation, and the Lord's Prayer. I think the second of those will be much the best. It would only mean four or five lines of alterations, and it would not be a cold, bald alternative but another option within the second alternative. Would such satisfy the

In Opposition

people of whom you are thinking who want a new Canon, but who do not want an Invocation of the Holy Spirit as at present suggested? I believe if there was a very strong representation in this matter from the Lower Houses, the Bishops would be bound and would not be unwilling to listen to it. I regard some meeting of this need as really essential if there is to be peace and harmony in the future. The only alternative is to go on with the present most undesirable plan of farcing. . . .

Canon A. G. Robinson to Frere   23 *March* 1928

My dear Bishop,

    Thank you very much for your letter.

    Those of us who object to the new Epiclesis would be satisfied if the Bishops allowed either (1) the option to use in the revised Prayer of Consecration the old Invocation, omitting the Epiclesis, or (2) the use of the old Canon followed by the Anamnesis, Prayer of Oblation, and Lord's Prayer. We should prefer the former. As you say, it would be another option within the second alternative. But the Bishops have refused to listen, and in the Memorandum offer no explanation.

    If their policy was to make clear the meaning of the earlier Deposited Book and nothing more, why did they deal with fasting? When the question of fasting came up in the Lower House a year ago, I moved the Previous Question, in order to avoid fresh controversy when we already had more controversies than we could settle.

    I am miserable about the whole thing. But all the clergy can do rightly is to leave to their Fathers in God the responsibility of saying the last word as to what the new Prayer Book shall contain. I suppose that when we meet next week no amendments will be allowed in the Lower House. We have to say Yea or Nay. I shall say Yea with a sad heart, because I don't want to make things more difficult for the Bishops than they already are. The responsibility is theirs, and we inferior clergy must be content with the Bishops whom God has given us.

                                                         Yours very truly,
                                                          A. G. ROBINSON.

Frere's withdrawal of support for the new Book was regarded with no little satisfaction by many of its opponents, and he received a number of offers to join forces with them. He felt very unhappy about the whole affair, however, and refused to co-operate. Having stated his objections, he preferred to maintain a dignified silence.

Frere to the Bishop of Moray　　　　　　　　　　　　19 March 1928

My dear Arthur,

... We have forced things a good deal, I think, since the Commons rejected the proposals. There has been rather a wave of Protestantism which has led to changes being made which I think were quite unnecessary and are really undesirable, particularly in the direction of further restrictions for Reservation; there were already too many in my opinion. I don't see my way, therefore, now to vote in Convocation for sending on the scheme as it is to the Assembly. It isn't at all a pleasant position—this falling out of line and finding myself in the company that I do. But still at any rate at this stage, I fear I must do that because I can't honestly say that I think the scheme as now altered affords a prospect of a working basis in peace and order. These outbreaks of Protestantism are very trying, but perhaps we were too sanguine in thinking we were going to get through without that. And after all, it is by rows of this sort that the public is gradually educated and the crude Protestantism discredited. ...

The Bishop of Norwich (Dr. Pollock) to Frere　　　　19 March 1928

My dear Walter,

I see that from different angles we—you and I—have arrived at the same conclusion that this Prayer Book is not going to bring peace to the Church. I wonder if you are now generally willing to support me in any effort that could be made to concentrate on those parts of the New Book which command general assent, as bringing the Book up to date with modern habits and needs, excluding the Holy Communion? I believe this plan, officially derided, would have large support as an alternative to the 'All or nothing policy'.

　　　　　　　　　　　　　　　　　Yours affectionately,

　　　　　　　　　　　　　　　　　　　　　Bertram.

Frere to the Bishop of Norwich　　　　　　　　　　　20 March 1928

My dear Bertram,

Thank you much for your letter. It was nice of you to write, and any co-operation would be pleasant and welcome. However, I don't quite see that there is much possibility of it over this affair. I am afraid we start backwards again. I think the present revision doesn't go far enough, and I think you think it goes too far. I want another alternative for the Consecration Prayer as well as the one we provide; you want to have no alternative at all, I expect; and so on throughout. So I am afraid I am no use to you, though it would be pleasant going at it hand in hand if we could, and if things were other than they are. Let me add it was a pleasure to get your letter and have even a tantalizing prospect dangling before me for the moment.

Yours affectionately,
Walterus Truron.

The Revd. C. P. Shaw (Superior General of the Confraternity of the Blessed Sacrament and a leading member of the Central Council of Catholic Societies) to Frere   19 *March* 1928

My dear Lord Bishop,

... The knowledge that you have decided that you cannot vote for the Book as it stands, has certainly put new life into many of us.

Is it at all possible that you might find time to meet a few of us who are seriously disturbed by the present events? We should so very much like to be allowed to talk to you freely about our present difficulties.

With very many thanks,
Believe me,
Yours obediently,
C. P. Shaw

Frere to the Revd. C. P. Shaw   22 *March* 1928

Dear Father Shaw,

Thank you for your letter.

I can't be up in London till the meeting of the Convocation and then we shall be all at it hard. I shall only just get up in time for the afternoon meeting, but in any case I think it is better if I do not go beyond the registering of my own view as at present. It is for the Lower Houses of Convocation now I think to repudiate the harm that the House of Clergy did last February and in other ways to make its own objections felt. I hope it may do so effectively: but it would be quite wrong I think for me to take any direct share in its plans. Later on, if a conference was desirable, I would of course try and arrange it, but at this critical moment, I think it would be rather unwise. We must see what happens next week. We shall know our way a little clearer after that....

The English Church Union also tried to gain his support, but without success. On 20 March the Secretary, the Revd. A. Pinchard, sent Frere the following telegram: 'Can you possibly be at Council tomorrow. Resolution will be moved supporting your Lordship and calling upon Anglo-Catholic Bishops and Proctors to vote with you against sending Book and Measure forward to Church Assembly.' Frere replied: 'Sorry. Cannot be absent from here.' The Resolution, which was moved from the Chair by the Earl of Shaftesbury and carried unanimously, read as follows: 'The alterations and additions which the Bishops have made in the Deposited Book as amended, notably in the rubrics governing Reservation and the question of the Fast before Communion, must profoundly affect those Anglo-Catholics who have hitherto given some support to the Prayer Book Measure. The President and Council earnestly hope that all Anglo-Catholic members of Convocation will support the Bishop of Truro against consent being given to sending the Measure on to the Church Assembly.'

On the following day Frere explained his refusal to the Earl of Shaftesbury and again expressed the hope that some effective action might be taken in the Lower Houses of Convocation.

Frere to the Earl of Shaftesbury 22 *March* 1928

My dear Lord Shaftesbury,

... I was grateful for the invitation to come up for the meeting, but in any case I couldn't come. I should have felt, moreover, that I should have been out of place there on such an occasion. The moment demands now that the clergy should take their own action, either repudiating what was done in their name by the House of Clergy a month or six weeks ago, or making their protest against what the House of Bishops has decided in contradiction to the Clergy or apart from them. It remains now to be seen I think, whether the Lower Houses of Convocation can do anything effective. I myself hope indeed that that may be the case, and that we have not yet seen the final form of the Measure....

The Archbishop was most considerate. Although it had been agreed that there should be no debate on the amended Measure in Convocation, he nevertheless gave Frere the opportunity of stating his case in the Upper House if he so desired. Frere declined, however: beyond attending to register his vote, there was nothing further he desired to do.

Archbishop of Canterbury to Frere   22 *March* 1928

My dear Truron,

    The Convocation Upper Houses meet, as you know, on Wednesday next. We are summoned for business at 2.30. That hour was fixed because we came to agreement that this time there would be no need of general debate. Birmingham [Dr. Barnes], Worcester [Dr. Pearce], and Norwich [Dr. Pollock] have all agreed to this, and I have no reason to suppose you to wish otherwise. If by any chance you feel it incumbent upon you to initiate a further discussion I ought to know forthwith; as I should, I suppose, have to telegraph to all the Bishops asking them to attend at 2 p.m. instead of 2.30. I should wish to do just what you would like. The Lower House will expect us at 3 p.m.

                I am,
                        Yours affectionately,
                              Randall Cantuar.

Frere to the Archbishop of Canterbury   24 *March* 1928

My dear Archbishop,

    I sent off a telegram in reply to your very kind letter of 22 March on the subject of our gathering on Wednesday next. I am anxious to avoid speaking, more as everything is already so well known. Though at the most all I would have to say would be repetition; but I would rather find that unnecessary if possible. Very many thanks for all your kind consideration. . . .

Nevertheless, he still did not abandon hope that some last-minute action would be possible in Convocation, and he was much encouraged by an assurance from Lord Phillimore that a way might be found of avoiding the problem of either totally accepting or rejecting the Book.

Lord Phillimore to Frere   23 *March* 1928

My dear Lord,

    In the trouble created by these last unfortunate amendments made by your colleagues, I should be glad if you would allow me to compare ideas with you; and if you could, tell me what you think should be done. I do not know what exactly there is to lay hold on, for the declaration about fasting was asked for (I think) by both Houses, and the provision about consulting the Parish Council, though foolish and likely in some cases to lead to hardship, cannot be said to be doctrinally wrong. But the totality of the changes may be described and will be accounted a mass of pin-pricks for those whom I must call (under protest) the Anglo-Catholics, and the grave fear is that they will so alienate them that they will not obey and we shall be back in the old state of anarchy and disorder.

Is it possible to think of some alteration which Convocation might suggest and which might improve? I know it is said that Convocation must accept or reject in block. But there is no real difficulty in that—'*I* can't amend your plan so I reject it; but if *you* amend it in such and such a respect, I will accept it'.

Yours with all respect sincerely,
Phillimore.

Frere to Lord Phillimore 24 *March* 1928

My dear Lord Phillimore,

Thank you very much for writing. I am greatly interested by your letter, also to talk over the present trouble. It seems to me that the Lower Houses of Convocation now have to consider:

a. Whether they can repair the harm done by the Clergy.
b. Whether they can induce the Bishops to modify the things for which the Bishops are responsible.
c. Whether they should protest in general against these modifications of the Deposited Book as being too much of the nature of a concession to the House of Commons.

Whatever action the Lower House can take now must be regarded either as (*a*) an attempt to get changes even at the eleventh hour, or (*b*) a form of protest against what is now inevitable, but a protest worth making in view of the future. So far as I can see, it doesn't matter which of these two objectives is considered, for I think the procedure would be the same in either case: I expect though, personally, that the latter is now the only one which is likely to come to anything; but I haven't quite given up hope that there might be negotiations even now.

As to the procedure in Convocation I am glad that you reassure us as to the possibility of getting round this 'Yes' or 'No' alternative. At the same time, before we get to that I hope the Lower House will make a protest against being treated in this way. I have suggested to some friends in the Lower Houses that what they had better do in my judgement is to arrange a series of speeches, each of which should end up by saying, 'In the present form I should vote against the Measure, but if so and so could be altered it would be different'.

In regard to the particular points that might thus be raised, the position seems to me rather an easy one. The actual form of the proposals lends itself to such treatment, for we have scheduled the number of differences between the present proposals and the Deposited Book; it is therefore easy to say, 'Give up such and such a one of the modifications and let us get back to the Deposited Book'. This would not be fully satisfactory. I think some protest might still be made again now as to some points in the Deposited Book itself, but the strongest line would be that of a change back to the Deposited Book. . . . It would be more difficult to get any reconsideration of the Alternative Order for the Communion of the Sick. What is raised under that issue is a series of minute points difficult to handle; therefore my hope of getting a readiness on the part of the Upper Houses to negotiate with the Lower ones would depend a good deal upon the efficiency of the impact made on the previous part of the document.

The Lower Houses have a good deal of right to discuss further the question of the Canon, inasmuch as the House of Bishops took no account of the protest that was made on that point. On the other hand, it is always to be remembered that two or three of the worst things which were carried by the House of Clergy were repudiated by the Bishops, especially the very undesirable statement about the Reserved Sacrament being considered outside the area of worship; and again, the very crude attempt at a definition of Eucharistic Doctrine. The refusal of these must be put down for righteousness in favour of the House of Bishops.

I wonder whether it would be a sound proposal to say boldly, 'We want to go back for the directions for Reservation to the Deposited Book. It wasn't all that we wanted or desired, but it was much better than this.' As a means of forcing negotiations, I think it would possibly be quite a good move, especially if the previous attempts to upset the position had nearly succeeded but not quite. After all there is a great difference between the two. The former did leave to the Bishops a certain discretion as to the place of Reservation, but this discretion has now been taken away—with the result that there is sure to be a row over the number of tabernacles which exist. According to the Deposited Book these could have been accepted by the Bishop and continued. As things are now, in theory the Bishop will have to order these tabernacles to be taken down, though in practice I don't suppose they can do anything of the sort: this is in some ways the most sensitive point of the whole position.

I wonder how much of all this long talk of mine you will approve? I have written freely in response to your letter, but of course you will see as much as I do the necessity that I should in common decency not be making public appearances in any form to upset the decisions of the House of Bishops. I am therefore confining myself rigidly to private conversations and letters with individuals, and rejecting—at present at any rate—any proposal to co-operate or confer with groups in the Houses of Clergy or outside. After all, in the present stage it is clearly the business of the Lower Houses in the Convocations; and I think they have a strong case if they can put it up wisely and well. I have no doubt you will be giving them the best possible advice, and I hope what I have said will not be found too contrariant to what your wisdom and experience show. . . .

The Convocations of Canterbury and York met on 28 March. Contrary to his previous decision Frere made a short statement in the Upper House of Canterbury on his inability to give the Measure his support. It was not due to his disapproval of particular things in the new Book in its revised form, but because he felt that it would fail to help them out of their troubles: in fact the new proposals were in more or less degree apples of discord which would cause even more trouble. The Book was too narrow to allow for the growth and development of the Church and they would soon be in the same difficulty as they had been in before the Royal Commission of 1906. Furthermore, the balance they had tried to achieve in the 1927 Book had seemingly now been sacrificed in deference to the House of Commons. This destruction of balance involved the loss of the goodwill of all sorts of people; and without that goodwill the restoration of discipline and order was impossible.[1]

The Archbishop received his statement with sympathy but it failed to move the House, which approved of the Measure by 20 votes to 6. The Upper House of York likewise expressed its approval by 9 votes to none. In the Lower Houses, however, debate was lengthy and vigorous, strong opposition being led by Dr. Kidd in the Southern Province and Fr. E. K. Talbot in the Northern. The measure of disapproval was evident in the reduced majorities in favour of the Measure—at Canterbury 126 votes to 48 and at York 50 votes to 19.[2]

[1] *Chronicle of Canterbury Convocation 1928*, pp. 2-4.
[2] Ibid., pp. 122-6. *Journal of York Convocation*, 1928, pp. 2-6, 63.

In Opposition

A few days later Frere wrote to Fr. Talbot on future action in the Church Assembly. He felt that the best method of registering their disapproval was to abstain from voting. It would be wise to proceed quietly until such time as events demanded a strong line of action again.

Frere to Fr. E. K. Talbot   *7 April* 1928

My dear Keble,

. . . I agree with you entirely about having recorded a protest at Convocation. We need not do any more; indeed I don't think we ought to do so. I don't propose to vote against the Measure in the Assembly, nor do I advise anybody of the Clergy to vote against it there. The Laity I think have their opportunity of protest in the Assembly, and they may just as well vote against it there if they feel so disposed. As to any intention to influence Parliament not to pass what the Church has passed, I repudiate it most vigorously. I hope all our lot will take this line; and it would be a good thing to try and canvass them to do so. I doubt whether a letter to the *Church Times* is the best way of doing it: if it is only a handful of twenty or so of Clergy in the two Houses, I believe the best thing would be for somebody to write to each of them and say, 'Don't let's vote any more; rather let us walk out'. Wouldn't it be rather a good plan if you did that to all the people in the Northern Convocation, and Kidd did it in the Southern? That seems to me the best thing. If you agree, will you write to Kidd and suggest that he do it for his group? You could easily both excuse yourself for taking this step by saying you were the people who had made the first speech. I think everybody would understand it. Far better I think to arrange it quietly like that than to put it out in the *Church Times*. The protest having been made, the more quietly we proceed the better until the time comes when it may be necessary to take a strong line again. . . .

Frere's view of the situation is admirably summed up in a letter which he wrote to Fr. Talbot's brother, the Bishop of Pretoria, three days later.

Frere to the Bishop of Pretoria   10 *April* 1928

My dear Brother Neville,

. . . As for the Prayer Book, things have gone from bad to worse since January. I think the strong declension in the Protestant direction really began earlier. The last six months of last year saw a great fading of the spirit of generosity and was replaced by a general desire to tie up everybody who was supposed to be tiresome—that is to say, of course, the Anglo-Catholics. But, of course, the House of Commons decision made things much worse. Since then I think all have gone in one direction; that did it at last, and the last straw broke the camel's back and the worm turned, if I can combine two proverbs. As it is, we shall have much more trouble when we have got to administer the Book. The Bishops have left themselves no room for discussion with regard to the Reservation rules, and I don't think they can enforce what is there now; nor can they amend it, since it is all put in the form of rubrics. We shall have trouble again about the Canon, because there is no provision made for people who want to keep the Latin theory of Consecration. This is mainly the fault of the House of Clergy not the House of Bishops, as indeed for a good deal of the rest. The House of Bishops declined to follow the lead in some of the worst directions as the House of Clergy set them; but in other respects the House of Clergy presented temptations to the Episcopate which they were not equal to resisting. A disastrous change in the wording of the General Rubric governing continuous Reservation is really due to the pressure of Canterbury himself—pressure that couldn't be resisted. As it is, the advocates of the Book will have to show the Houses of Parliament that the changes have been made in order to pacify them and enable the House of Commons to pass the Measure this time; while in the Assembly they will say there are no real changes made—it is only explanations—in order to pacify the clergy and non-erastian laity.

I can't but think it is a nasty position altogether. I am thankful to be out of it and can't take the responsibility for a good number of things now in the Book. So much personally; but from the general point of view I do not think the defection of the renegades will wreck the prospect of the Measure either in the Assembly or in the House of Commons. The latter I think may even be a little bit reassured by its becoming more clear that the Book doesn't suit those extreme fellows. So I don't think we have hurt the prospects of the Book as a whole, though we have failed to get the sort of amendment which is needed or to negative the amendment which has been incorporated. Happily our Jubilee Week coincides with the week of the Assembly, so I have a good excuse for not being there to vote. . . .

On the same day he expressed his regret to the Dean of Wells, Dr. Armitage Robinson, that it had been impossible to obtain an alternative revised Canon, for the 1662 form was in itself insufficient. Once again he pleaded for a variety of uses, such as the Roman Catholics had.

Frere to the Dean of Wells　　　　　　　　　　　　　　10 *April* 1928
My dear Dean,

　　... I am afraid my little effort to get some consideration for another form of Canon for those who dislike the present one came to nothing, much to my regret. I believe if in the beginning the effort had been made to get an additional form or modified form side by side with what the Bishops had proposed instead of in place of it, it could have been done. But somehow every time that line was taken up, the clergy who are of your point of view, with Robinson, the Archdeacon of Hampstead, and the rest did not seem to rise to the situation. They were always wanting to get what they wanted by depriving someone else of what they wanted; it was a great pity. We might have done so much better if we had boldly said that two alternatives were wanted to the present insufficient prayer. Well, it can't be helped now. We shall have to make the best of a situation which, in this matter as in a good many others, is unsatisfactory but also I expect temporary in its character. I confess I don't regard as the ideal for the future one single form of the Consecration Prayer to which all would be agreed, but just the opposite—a number of forms which all agree in holding to be adequate but which cater for the different groups and temperaments. Why should we Anglicans be more Roman than the Romans themselves on this matter? They are allowed two or three different forms. Why can't we? ...

The Measure was due to come before the Church Assembly on 26 April, and shortly before that date two important letters passed between Frere and Lord Phillimore. They show that although Frere had voted against the 1928 Book in Convocation, he underwent no volte-face in later supporting its use. He felt that the Book had come to stay, no matter what Parliament did: and despite its many imperfections, its gains were so enormous 'that many a burden will be lifted from the minds of the clergy and people even though some will remain and seem more burdensome than ever'. His vote in Convocation had expressed, not his condemnation of the Book as a whole, but his regret that despite all its many good points, it failed to achieve the purpose for which it was intended. Nevertheless, its gains outweighed its imperfections, and this, together with the Church's endorsement of the Book, was sufficient cause to justify its use.

Lord Phillimore to Frere   19 *April* 1928

My dear Lord,

As I troubled you with one letter, I think I should tell you that after reflection, and now that the Book has been approved by the Convocations, I have made up my mind to vote for the Measure. If I speak, I shall express regret for the alterations, not so much for themselves as because they will be offensive to others and hinder (or perhaps postpone is a better word) a return to harmony and order. I am not sure that this may not be your underlying motive, but perhaps in saying this I am presuming too far.

You may have seen the Agenda for the meeting of the Council of the English Church Union which took place yesterday, and have noticed the proposal that E.C.U. should address all its friends in the House of Laity to vote against the Measure. This was passed with three dissentients after Clifton Kelway and I had spoken against it. I took two points:

1. That even with these alterations the new book was a gain, especially in the eyes of one who was a lawyer and knew that all Reservation was at the moment deemed to be illegal.
2. That if the Bishops and Clergy wished for the new book, it did not become *us* to urge the Laity to vote against and veto it.

This especially, as one of our objections to the Measure as amended was that it gave the individual Parochial Church Council some power of preventing its Priest from using the new book, and here were we to adjure the whole body of the Laity to prevent every priest from using it. . . .

I should add that I told the Council plainly that whatever they sent out to the Laity in the House, I should tell them at our usual party gathering on the Thursday evening what my view was.

                         Ever with all respect,
                               Yours sincerely,
                                     Phillimore.

Frere to Lord Phillimore   21 *April* 1928

My dear Lord Phillimore,

Thank you very much for your letter. It was very kind of you to write and I am greatly interested to know how the matter has been working in your own mind and to what conclusion. For myself, I was expecting when I went round to vote in Convocation against the Measure in its existing form, that when the Convocation passed it—even if they did so without alteration—I should then submit and say to myself, 'As Convocation has passed it, I should resist no longer'. That which was then a dim forecast is now I think a clear policy in my mind. I don't intend to oppose any further.

On the other hand I am thankful not to be responsible for the Measure in its present form. I have been in contact with some of the leaders of those in the House of Clergy who voted against the Measure for the first time on the last occasion. They are most of them I think going to take the line that it is better not to vote when the matter comes up in the Assembly. This seems to me to be a reasonable way for the Clergy to behave who recognize all that you say about the need for the Book in some form or another, but wish to vote against and even protest against certain things which have been included in it, whether before or after January last.

Having got a certain popularity myself with the out-and-out opponents, I fear I shall lose it again very soon upon this line. That doesn't much matter. What does, however, matter is that I fear the unanimity represented in the E.C.U. will also disappear. However that can't be helped now. I think before the summer comes the Measure will be practically accepted whether it receives Parliamentary sanction or whether it does not. There will then be a rearrangement of views, though not according to the theory of the Measure, but according to the actual process of its administration. That will take some time to work out, and it is that that will have to be looked to next. Not altogether a very pleasing prospect; and yet, at the same time, I feel as you do that the gains of the Book are so enormous that many a burden will be lifted from the minds of clergy and people, even though some will remain and perhaps seem more burdensome than ever. Forgive this long disquisition. I have put it down on paper because you will see from it how much I am in sympathy with your determination to accept the decision as made by Convocation, and vote in favour of the Book in the Assembly. . . .

On 26 and 27 April the Measure was considered by the Church Assembly and final approval was sought. The motion was carried by substantial majorities in all three Houses, but the voting made it very clear that a considerable number of the Houses of Clergy and Laity had followed Frere's example and had abstained. Here are the figures for both 1927 and 1928.

	1927		1928	
	For	Against	For	Against
House of Bishops	34	4	32	2
House of Clergy	253	37	183	59
House of Laity	230	92	181	92
Total votes cast	517	133	396	153
Grand total	650		549	

The opposition vote increased therefore by only twenty, while those supporting the motion decreased by 121. Allowing for unavoidable absentees, the abstentions probably number over 100.

Shortly afterwards Frere sent his comments on the situation to the Bishop of Nassau, Dr. Shedden, in which he reiterated the views he had expressed to Lord Phillimore.

Frere to the Bishop of Nassau   *29 May 1928*

My dear Bishop,

... It has been a very muddled time, and very difficult to know what is the right thing to do. But I have been much happier since I felt that I was not responsible for this Book in its present form. The House of Clergy really wrecked it at their meeting in January, and as Father Waggett said when the Book came back to them from the Bishops, 'We put complications in the way of the House of Bishops which they were not able to resist'. What will happen now in Parliament nobody quite knows. The Bishops who put forward the case in the House of Lords and who have defended it since have so often had a great part of their field based upon the lawlessness of the clergy—an exceedingly foolish thing to do and not altogether ingenuous. The result of it is, of course, that they get it turned back upon themselves and people say, 'If the clergy are as much lawless as you say, why haven't you stopped them, or why do you promote the people who have broken the laws?' That foolish and false policy is really recoiling upon our worthy leaders now, and it is entirely our own fault; because they have delivered themselves into the hands of the lawyers by their refusal to stand up for their clergy. If they had taken the other line and said, 'There have no doubt been technical breaches of the law, but the law is obsolete and the men were quite justified in what they have done', broadly speaking these people would have followed them. No doubt the lawyer would have objected, but he would not have a popular following such as he has now.

The vote in the House of Commons will in the long run, I expect, be influenced by the question of how they are going to face their constituents. They don't want to see this formal business—still less the question of Establishment—raised to complicate the issues of politics which are complicated enough as it is; and I imagine that is really what will tell in the House of Commons and not any ecclesiastical consideration. This time it will probably go through, but whether it does or it doesn't, I think we shall use the greater part of it probably without much difficulty. There will be rows over some of the things, of course, and especially some of the most recently introduced things. But myself, having voted against it once in the House of Bishops, I am not going to vote against it any more. I don't really stand on the same side as Birmingham in general, and besides that, I don't think it decent to ask Parliament or wish Parliament to turn down something which the Church wisely or foolishly has concluded is the best thing. The Measure of 1928 will not get us as good a settlement as the one of 1927 would have done, but it is infinitely preferable in having that after all the large number of things settled by it and the large number of permissions which we shall be very glad to have. The number of things that would be troublesome and apples of discord are surprisingly small, though some of them are important and the dangers will be considerable.

I don't think there is anything to be said for revision by instalments. We should only fight over each form as it came over again, and in the long run the Bishop of Norwich and the rest would be wanting to reform Morning Prayer by leaving out 'Dearly Beloved' or things of that sort which are perfectly useless. What they want is a kind of Irish revision; and having got that through, there would be more difficulties, as far as I see it all at present. . . .

On 13 June the Measure was presented to the House of Commons and a lively two-day debate ensued. The result is well known. Despite a last-minute effort by the Prime Minister, it was rejected by an even larger majority than in 1927—266 votes to 220. The House of Bishops then met at the end of the month to consider the situation and unanimously agreed to a statement drawn up by the Archbishop of Canterbury: 'It is a fundamental principle that the Church—that is, the Bishops together with the Clergy and Laity—must in the last resort, when its mind has been fully ascertained, retain its inalienable right, in loyalty to our Lord and Saviour Jesus Christ, to formulate its Faith in him and to arrange the expression of that Holy Faith in its forms of worship.' This was commended to the Church Assembly on 30 June. At the end of the year it was arranged for the privileged presses to publish the 1928 Prayer Book bearing the proviso: 'The publication of this Book does not directly or indirectly imply that it can be regarded as authorized for use in churches.'

VIII

EPILOGUE

ALTHOUGH the number of letters dealing with the period subsequent to the defeat of the Measure is small, sufficient remain to show what Frere felt about the problem. At the outset his reaction was one of cautious optimism. On the whole the Bishops seemed to have their dioceses behind them, and provided they displayed unanimity there was no need for despair. The rejection by Parliament might well be a blessing in disguise, for they now had peace and freedom for further experiment with a temporary Book. In effect the Church had now in large measure acquired that long period of authorized experiment which he had advocated in October 1912.

Frere to Fr. Bertram Barnes, C.R.   22 *November* 1928

My dear Bertram,

. . . I am wondering what the result of all these votings in Synods and Assemblies of Laymen will be, and its effect especially upon the meeting of Bishops in January. I hope it will reassure them as to the general support of the Church people in the country; though of course the fact that the two extremes unite in voting against the proposals to a certain extent makes the opposition look more serious than it really is. I have been surprised to find not more hostility in the Northern Province than there is. But as a whole what one seems to see is that the Synod and lay people follow in the main the line of the Bishop of the diocese—to an extent that you wouldn't have thought possible when you consider how much the Bishops are said to be out of touch with the rest of things. In point of fact, however, what generally happens is that the dioceses say, 'Of course, if we all had people like our Bishop it would be all right, but it is those other ones that are dreadful.' Similarly the Bishops say, 'Of course, all my fellows are all right, but it is these dreadful people outside of which we hear such awful things.' Meanwhile Nonconformity is doing its best to make things as difficult as possible and to reap whatever nefarious advantage it can from the situation. . . .

Frere to the Bishop of North China (Dr. Norris)   27 December 1928

My dear Frank,

... Our ecclesiastical situation is straightening out here, I think, and time is all on the side of the Bishops' proposals. On the whole the dioceses have supported them, and when we come to the Bishops' meeting in the middle of next month I expect we shall find that that is the general feeling. We should move on unitedly on the existing lines as laid down for 1928. They aren't good but they are better than nothing, and they will be perhaps all the more easy to administer because they have not got the rigidity of statutory authority. I think we are beginning to see where the hand of Providence was in the rejection; and that it did not mean that the Book was in itself undesirable, but that it was undesirable that it should be authorized. In other words, we have now got peace and freedom for further experiment with a temporary Book.

Of course the Protestant view is the exact opposite of this, but how much they will put that view into practice I don't know. If they wanted to make themselves troublesome by prosecution they could of course do so, but I do not think they will. At all events if the Bishops keep together (that is the anxious thing) I do not think the opposition will come to much. If there is a little Protestant outbreak it will only tend to consolidate the rest and bring over in active support those people who are at present rather indifferent. Technically the outstanding problem is whether the Bishops should get any further sanction for their proposals than this rather sporadic sanction which they have got in their dioceses, or whether they should leave it there. This is I think the most difficult question of the moment. I do not think it would be well to get a formal and official sanction from Convocation; indeed I don't think anybody would desire that. It would be too much like flying in the face of Parliament. But a general approval of a non-formal and a non-canonical kind from Convocation and the Assembly would, of course, strengthen the hands of the Bishops in the line they are proposing to take: and I think this may very likely be asked for. I don't suppose that there is much doubt that it would be given by a very large and possibly even an overwhelming majority ...

Meanwhile Dr. Davidson resigned as Archbishop of Canterbury on 12 November and was succeeded by Dr. Lang. Immediately after his enthronement the new Archbishop became seriously ill and did not return to active work until the following May. Nevertheless the problem of the Prayer Book was very much in his mind during these winter months of inactivity, and in March 1929 he wrote to Frere and other members of the House of Bishops asking for their comments on his suggestions for further action.

The Archbishop of Canterbury to Frere   28 *March* 1929

My dear Bishop,

It may be within your recollection that at the last Bishops' meeting, the Archbishop of York [Dr. Temple] on my behalf indicated certain proposals which it was in my mind to make at the next Bishops' meeting in June—namely, that any statement which might be made public on behalf of the Bishops should not ignore the current Prayer Book discussions but should endeavour to put them in a right proportion; and that our main desire should be in a rather solemn way to call the Church to a deeper and more constructive line of life and thought. It has seemed to many of us from many converging lines that the time is propitious for calling the Church, both clergy and laity, to a serious, sustained, and prayerful effort to revitalize its hold upon the Gospel of God's revelation in Christ. Obviously, this is a matter of the deepest importance and will require much careful thought. I am very anxious to have the counsel of some of my brethren when I return to public work in May as to:

First, whether this proposal is likely to commend itself to the Bishops generally:

Secondly, what form it ought to take and particularly in what form it ought to be presented, if at all, to the Bishops in June.

Accordingly, the Archbishop of York and I would be very grateful if you could make it convenient to come to a confidential and informal conference with us on these matters at Lambeth Palace on Tuesday, 7 May. We suggest that the Bishops who may be willing to assist us with their counsel should come in the afternoon and meet after a cup of tea at five and sit till dinner at eight, and if necessary after dinner.

I know that it may be difficult for you to rearrange your existing arrangements, but this is an *occasion of very real importance* and I earnestly hope that you may be able to be present. If so, I trust that you will give me the pleasure of having you as my guest at Lambeth for the night.

                                             Yours very sincerely,
                                                   Cosmo Cantuar.

Frere apologized for being unable to come, but expressed his views on the matter. He felt that there had already been too much delay and if they waited until June they would have lost all chance of guiding the Church on any important issue, whether liturgical or otherwise. Their only hope lay in immediate action and he announced his intention of writing to the Archbishop of York to see whether something could not be done.

Frere to the Archbishop of Canterbury   30 *March* 1929

My dear Archbishop,

    Thank you for your letter of 28 March which I have received. I am afraid I must ask to be excused from coming on May 7. I shall be leaving Scilly that morning after my annual visit there, which can't be put at any other time very well; and I shall be returning home for a gathering of Women's Messengers in the house here. That means, I fear, that from both points of view I could hardly hope to be at the preliminary gathering at Lambeth on 7 May.

    Meanwhile, I am sorry to be aware that the opportunity of calling the clergy and people to order in liturgical matters is gradually slipping through our fingers. We had a chance in January; now we are in April and practically nothing done; in another month we shall be back in the old chaos and nobody will listen to us any more on the subject. By June we shall have forfeited our leadership in the matter of liturgical reform and anything else too that anybody cares about. If we make a conspicuous failure over that, who will want to credit us with other things? So I am venturing to write meanwhile to the Archbishop of York to see if something cannot be done still to save the situation. . . .

The letter to Dr. Temple suggested that the Archbishop of Canterbury's proposal for June was both too late and too vague. The Prayer Book question had to be solved, but with a proper solution, not by negligence and lapse. Something might be possible in the way of getting accessible Bishops to meet and issue some directions to their dioceses.

Frere to the Archbishop of York   30 *March* 1929

My dear Archbishop,

    I have had the letter from the Archbishop of Canterbury asking me to come to a preliminary meeting at Lambeth on 7 May with a view to planning a call to the Church to a sustained and prayerful effort to revitalize its hold upon the Gospel of God's revelation in Christ. I am venturing to send to you a copy of the letter that I have written to his Grace on the subject, more especially as I suppose it won't reach his Grace until he returns to work again.

I am rather seriously concerned about what happens long before June. The Church has been looking to the Bishops for a lead ever since they promised one last October, but they have never given one; and an irrevocable opportunity is rapidly slipping away. If no general call to order by the Bishops is issued, I suppose a corporate one is out of the question. We have lost altogether the bit of lead that we had in October, and who will listen to us again on any such subject? We shall be back in the old chaos again and worse than ever. People will say, 'We trusted the Bishops to lead us and they have let us down again.' Clergy who were beginning to come round will say, 'We never thought the Bishops were going to give us any directions; and as they haven't, we shall look to Rome for them again in the future.'

I don't want to be a croaking prophet; but really, do you not think the situation is serious? If we are going to have a private meeting, I think it would be better sometime long before May and something much more concrete than what is put forward in the Archbishop of Canterbury's proposal. Would it not be possible at any rate to get the more accessible of the Bishops together, and for them to agree to issue some directions to their several dioceses? As far as I see, very few of them have done any such thing at present. I quite agree that we want to get the Prayer Book question out of the way; but it must be got out of the way with a proper settlement and not merely by negligence and lapse. As it is, Birmingham and Exeter are the people who have come into the public eye with a policy, and even the Church Association is gaining an importance which it hasn't had for a long time because no saner voices are heard. This is not a grumble so much as a proposal. Can't we do something at any rate in a quiet way with a group of people now that Lent is over, so as to get said what we want said before the opportunity is gone? I feel rather like Brown, the head of the Brownists, and his tract, 'On reformation without tarrying for any man'. . . .

Dr. Temple was not convinced, however. Nothing was being lost by taking time; an interval free from controversy provided an opportunity for minds to settle down, while it was important to get the impending

General Election out of the way before making any declaration on policy.

The Archbishop of York to Frere   2 April 1929

My dear Bishop,

I know that you are in closer touch with many of the features of the situation than I am, and this makes me suspect that you are likely to be right and not I. None the less, my own reading of the situation is different. As far as I have any contact, I do not think there is any harm being done by the present delay. Everyone understands the cause of it and many people of the loyal sort are glad of this interval from controversy, during which many minds are settling down. Moreover, it is to my mind important to get the General Election out of the way before anything is issued either by the Bishops as a body or any particular group. On the other hand, I think it is most important that when our statement does come out it should give a very clear lead on the question of order, however carefully we put this in the context of the spiritual demands of the Church. I am very anxious in writing to you in this way. But my own judgement is perfectly clear and I am bound to act upon it.

Yours affectionately,
William Ebor.

Frere did not change his point of view. His reply to the Archbishop of York is not available, but on the top of the above letter he pencilled the following notes, which were obviously the substance of his answer:

'Thank—won't bother you further. Our opportunity then not going but gone. Conflagration already beyond our control. How sad.'

In July the promised Declaration was drawn up and accepted by the Convocations. In view of the fact that the Revised Prayer Book had been accepted both by the Convocations and the Church Assembly, the Bishops agreed that 'during the present emergency and until further order be taken', they would not 'regard as inconsistent with loyalty to the principles of the Church of England the use of such additions or deviations as fall within the limit of these proposals'. On the other hand, they regarded 'as inconsistent with Church Order the use of any other deviations from or additions to the Forms and Orders contained in the Book of 1662'. The use of the Forms and Orders of 1928 was therefore permitted, provided that the goodwill of the Parochial Church Council or the parties concerned was secured.

Epilogue

Despite his former misgivings Frere was satisfied with this Declaration. It permitted his desire for ordered liturgical experiment and he encouraged the use of the 1928 Book with some energy. In his own diocese of Truro he was most happy to see it gain ground with the passage of time, and he had no room for arguments suggesting that it should not be used because it had not been legally authorized.

Frere to Dr. J. H. Arnold   *9 October 1933*

My dear Arnold,

... We use the 1928 a good deal here and I think it is going in these parts. The Cathedral has substituted copies of the New Prayer Book for the Old and they are bound up with Hymns Ancient and Modern.

It would be amusing if it wasn't sad to see from the newspapers how people flounder about because they won't accept what they have been given and spend their time trying to prove that it has got no authority, or in some way or another propose something of their own. This is the real crux of the trouble—every man wants his own plan. I told a group of them the other day, when they talked of being 'advanced', that they were well behind the times, and that is the fact. . . .

The final letters epitomize Frere's views on the Eucharistic Canon. In spite of his enthusiasm for the 1928 Rite, he still felt that less than justice had been done to those who found the Epiclesis a stumbling-block. Could not this difficulty be overcome by making the clause of the Invocation in the 1928 Canon optional? This was certainly better than trying to reassemble the pieces of the Canon which the Prayer Book of 1662 happened to possess.

Frere to the Chairman of the Liturgical Committee
of the E.C.U.   *17 February 1931*

My dear Chairman,

I believe the Union has referred to you the proposal made by Bishop Chandler with regard to the gathering together of our discordant views and practices. . . . I do not believe that Bishop Chandler's proposals will do what he desires, and I will shortly state my reasons.

(*a*) The reassembling of the Canon, as it is sometimes called, that is the gathering of the different bits in the Prayer Book and putting them together, is never anything else but a makeshift. It was quite tolerable when there was nothing better to be had, but it would never do as a rallying-point now.

(b) The first reason is that in reassembling the different bits there is one left out, and one of the most important of all, which was not in the 1662 Prayer Book. That is the *unde et memores*; it is in itself the hinge upon which all else depends. The earlier part of the prayer is preliminary to the latter part, and the point of junction is in the word *unde*. Besides, a prayer without this is not really a Christian prayer, as omitting the recitation of the main features of our Lord's life—i.e. alluding to the Death but leaving severely alone the Resurrection and the Ascension.

(c) Without this prayer the definite offering of the Sacrifice is not included, and it would be quite intolerable to think that we can be content with a prayer that evades offering the Sacrifice. It is true, of course, that the Prayer of Oblation is included in the Prayer Book after the acceptance of the offering. That is a different matter, though it will not do to have a prayer which asks for the acceptance of the Offering which we have evaded.

(d) There is a *non sequitur* if the *unde* or 'wherefore' is the only link between the first half of the prayer and the second. There is a logical sequence in saying, 'Our Lord told us to do this, wherefore we do it': but there is no logical sequence in saying 'Our Lord told us to do this, wherefore we ask thee to accept.'

(e) Another point altogether is in regard to the Invocation. No doubt the proper way to deal with that is to ask that the use of the clause of the Invocation in the 1928 Canon may be optional, recognizing that there are those who will never accept the 1928 Prayer as long as that is in, and others will not be content to do without it. Our real policy, therefore, is to ask for the use of the 1928 Canon, authority being given for the omission of that clause.

(f) That introduces a still further consideration. If that plan were to be adopted it would involve our leaving out the 'Hear us, O merciful Father' clause as well, at any rate when the Invocation was used. Otherwise you would get an unsatisfactory repetition.

I beg, therefore, that the Committee will not easily be led away in thinking that common ground can be provided on the lines of Bishop Chandler with regard to the Liturgy. I suggest that it can be upon what I suggest here. The use of the 1928 Canon seems to be increasing and spreading, so far as my experience goes; but of course the hindrance is the Invocation, and if that were made no hindrance, there would be some hope of reaching unity on this great subject. . . .

Epilogue

Frere's plea for the optional use of the Epiclesis in the 1928 Canon was reiterated by the Dean of Chichester, the Very Revd. A. S. Duncan-Jones, in a paper read to the Alcuin Club in December 1934, entitled 'Why Change the Communion Service?' This drew a severe retort from the *Church Times*, in which it condemned (wrongly)[1] the 1928 Canon for effecting the consecration of the Elements by means of an Invocation of the Holy Spirit instead of the traditional Western method of the dominical Words of Institution. Frere was then surprisingly quoted in support of this thesis: 'As the Bishop of Truro has pointed out, the English Church retained the Western theory of Consecration, and retained it in the most uncompromising form, for it closed the Consecration Prayer with the recital of our Lord's own words, and, if further elements are required, they are consecrated by those words, and by those words only.'[2] To those who had any knowledge of Frere's views, it was perfectly obvious that these words were not of approval, but of the reverse, and Frere immediately wrote an indignant letter of protest to the Editor at this misrepresentation.

Frere to the Editor of the Church Times   14 *December* 1934

Sir,

    I am entirely in agreement with the Dean of Chichester, and disagree with the campaign of suppression and misrepresentation which is being carried on in your columns against the Prayer Book of 1928.

    I have kept an indignant silence until now; but finding myself quoted at length on your Summary page, as if I favoured the campaign, whereas I resent it, I reluctantly write this protest.

    No; I agree with Dr. Duncan-Jones, that '1928' is steadily gaining ground, and that our wisdom is to go as far as we can to rally round it.

                                                                 Walterus Truron.

Unfortunately the *Church Times* neither apologized nor let the matter drop, but took quotations from Frere's *Some Principles of Liturgical Reform* out of their context and distorted his argument in a sorry attempt to justify their original statement.

'In the letter which we print elsewhere, the Bishop of Truro charges us with suggesting that he favours "a campaign of suppression and misrepresentation" against the Revised Prayer Book of 1928. We quoted him simply as maintaining that the English Church retained the

---

[1] The aim of the 1928 Canon was assuredly to avoid pointing to any one element in the Prayer as effecting the Consecration.

[2] The *Church Times*, 7 Dec. 1934.

Western theory of consecration, and retained it in the most uncompromising form. Speaking of our own present Prayer of Consecration, the Bishop said that "it ties the act of consecration more narrowly to the Words of the original administration than any other Christian liturgy has ever done; and it encourages, therefore, inevitably the habit of looking upon the consecration in the narrowest and most partisan way". Well, if so, to insert before Christ's words a definite appeal to the Spirit to consecrate is plainly to react entirely from the very definite position which the Church of England has held for centuries. In his *Principles of Liturgical Reform*, Dr. Frere deprecated any attempt to insert an Invocation in the Consecration Prayer. After emphasizing the difference in this matter between East and West, the Bishop said that "in view of such a situation, it is incumbent on us to move only with great caution. Until this doctrinal point is nearer a settlement, it would be inopportune to take any steps towards the reinsertion of the Invocation of the Holy Spirit in either of the positions which it has come to occupy." That is exactly what we have pleaded all along. Dr. Frere's insistence on great caution was expressed in 1911. But in our opinion, at least, it is not less impressive or less needed at the present day.'[1]

As though sensing the weakness of its argument, the next issue of the paper decided that further correspondence on the subject must cease.

Taken as a whole, however, Frere's book was clearly in favour of an Epiclesis, and it showed how remarkably consistent he had been in maintaining the same position for over twenty years:

'At some future revision there will be, no doubt, a complete reconsideration of the whole matter, and a reconstruction on more primitive lines. But we are hardly ready for this at present. Much further liturgical study and much more agreement as to eucharistic doctrine will be needed before any large change can be seriously considered. There is a wide divergence at present between the Latin West and the more primitive East as to the doctrine of Consecration; ... Until this doctrinal point is nearer a settlement, it would be inopportune to take any steps towards the reinsertion of the Invocation of the Holy Spirit in either of the positions which it has come to occupy. When our own mind is clearer, we may be able to go forward; but not until then. ...
A more satisfactory position is that which has both (Eastern and Western elements), and recognizes the place of each in the act of consecration.

This, then, is the conclusion to which the English Church must be

[1] The *Church Times*, 14 Dec. 1934.

advancing; and in due course it will be able to restore the Invocation and give it its right place, and thus, in this respect as in others, stand as a mediator between the East and Rome, comprehending the parts of truth for which each is contending.

But the present state of our Order is doing harm, and hindering worship. Standing in its isolation as little more than a recital of the Institution, our present Consecration Prayer is more Roman than Rome. It ties the act of consecration more narrowly to the Words of the original administration than any other Christian liturgy has ever done; and it encourages, therefore, inevitably the habit of looking upon the consecration in the narrowest and most partisan way. The betterment of our doctrinal sympathies and the due appreciation of all that side of the truth, for which the East is standing out against Rome, can hardly go on so long as our Order remains in its present form.'[1]

In the light of these words, it is therefore not difficult to understand Frere's enthusiasm for the 1928 Canon. It fulfilled his early hopes; and with its return to the primitive Catholic threefold form of prayer, he considered it to represent of the best mind of the Church of England of the day. It was the form which he himself used regularly. In its details he would have undoubtedly preferred alterations—that is evident from his remarks on the South African Rite, dealt with later in this volume: but it was something which marked a great improvement on anything which the Church of England had possessed hitherto. It was therefore fitting that his last major contribution to liturgical scholarship should be a defence of this Canon, to which he had given so much time and thought. *The Anaphora*, which he called 'an eirenical study in liturgical history', appeared in 1938. Here was a detailed statement of his case. It was, to quote his own words, 'a revaluation of the principles that govern the form and structure of the Eucharistic Anaphora, so far as they are based upon liturgical history.' The Trinitarian form of Eucharistic Prayer was defended and was shown to be both primitive and catholic. The Roman Canon was an exception to the general rule and was the result of mistaken interpretations of the teaching of the Fathers—St. Austin, St. Ambrose, St. Chrysostom. The new Canon summed up the results of the evidence accumulated over the past fifty years.

Frere wrote under pressure; and the impatience of old age sometimes betrayed itself. So then, he spoke of those advanced supporters of the Western tradition as members of a 'determined obscurantist and retrograde movement which poses noisily as catholic, but is really anarchist in method though medieval in outlook; for it aims at

[1] *Some Principles of Liturgical Reform*, pp. 188–90.

re-establishing, often in defiance of law, a position which is historically untenable, and a eucharistic theology which was not truly that of SS. Chrysostom, Ambrose, and Austin, but only that of their decadent successors'.[1] We can understand his disappointment at the limited results of the enterprise on which he had set such store and to which he had given so much. But history may well prove that his labours were not in vain.

[1] W. H. Frere, *The Anaphora* (London, 1938), p. vi.

Part Two

LITURGICAL REVISION
IN OTHER PARTS OF THE
ANGLICAN COMMUNION

MEMORANDUM FOR THE LITURGICAL COMMITTEE OF THE LAMBETH CONFERENCE
JULY 1920

12 *July* 1920

The Bishop of Calcutta, Dr. Westcott (Metropolitan of India) to Frere

My Dear Dr. Frere,

I have been charged with the duty of presiding over the committee dealing with the general subject of missionary problems. Five sub-committees have been appointed which are dealing with the various questions this week. One sub-committee is charged with the discussion of 'The Liturgical Variations permissible to a Province or Diocese'. Two subjects have been submitted from my own province of India and Ceylon upon which expert advice is essential. They are:

1. A request that the Lambeth Conference should affirm the right of the Bishops of a province acting together to give provincial sanction to a service of Holy Communion different from that contained in the Book of Common Prayer, and

2. To suggest any conditions which in the opinion of the Conference should always be observed in regard to the construction or component parts of a service of Holy Communion which is to be used within the Anglican Communion.

Thursday morning, 11 o'clock, has been fixed for the consideration of these subjects in the hope that we could secure the attendance of experts. Would it be possible for you to give us help at that time? We meet in the Great Hall of the Church House.

Yours sincerely,
F. Calcutta

P.S. If you are unable to be present would it be possible for you to let us have a written expression of your opinion.

Frere was unable to attend, so he sent the following important Memorandum.

Liturgical Revision in Other Parts

Memorandum for the Liturgical Sub-committee of the Committee of the Lambeth Conference on Missionary Problems.

1. Should the Lambeth Conference affirm the right of the Bishops of a province acting together to give provincial sanction to a service of Holy Communion different from that contained in the Book of Common Prayer?

(*a*) Formally speaking the province as a legislative assembly has a right, and a consultative body such as the Lambeth Conference cannot either grant or take it away. But it may advise provinces to adopt a self-denying ordinance in this respect: and in past sessions it has gone far in the direction of doing so; and they have gone far in the direction of following this advice.

This being so, if the policy is to be changed, and provinces are to be encouraged or at least not discouraged, in regard to exercising their right of prescribing the services to be used, it would seem desirable that the Lambeth Conference should definitely take such action as will make its former suggestion or advice inoperative for the future. Any province will then feel reassured as to its liberty to proceed in the exercise of this right without hesitation or misgiving.

(*b*) Practically speaking I regard it as highly desirable that the policy should be changed, and that liturgical uniformity should not be the ideal of Anglican Provinces so long as an essential and catholic unity is preserved. This seems to be especially the case in missionary dioceses and provinces. The case for India has been admirably stated in the Preface to the first essay of the book *The Eucharist in India*. I think I am in entire agreement with the first half of the book and in general agreement with the rest.

Mutatis mutandis the same line of argument applies to mission fields other than India: but the Indian case seems for many reasons the ripest at the present moment and the one where experimental steps may first and most easily be taken.

But apart from the mission field the same plea for a measure of liturgical variety justifies itself in more or in less degree. If we argue the point on first principles, there is much to be said both for and against uniformity. But it seems to me more profitable to argue it on historical lines, because what we are concerned with is not the ideal best but the best for a particular place and at a particular time. Historically I think it is true to say that variety and uniformity have alternated. At some periods the one has been prominent, and at other times the other.

Variety of treatment of a certain outline scheme characterizes the early Christian centuries as regards the Holy Eucharist as a whole. Then came a tendency to standardize; extemporization ceased, and big central churches began to set fashions which other churches were glad to adopt. Thenceforward the two principles were both operative in more or less degree. At one time Rome markedly breaks the existing similarity of use by the adoption of the Latin Canon, the suppression of the great prayers of intercession, &c. At another time the Byzantine rite starts on a career of development which others either do or do not copy. In the eighth century France conforms to Roman customs, but in doing so profoundly modifies them and Rome admits many of the modifications. In the divine service of the West, the monastic rite severs itself from the secular rite and the two are sharply distinguished even till today. In the Gallican church of the seventeenth and eighteenth centuries France rejects the Roman Breviary and creates a large number of local diocesan rites, only to give them up again and return to Roman uniformity in the nineteenth century.

These are but a few instances quoted to illustrate the point. I doubt if uniformity (as distinct from unity) was ever adopted as an ideal for any large area until the sixteenth century, under stress of the Reformation changes. The ideal of uniformity which has prevailed in Anglicanism since is a survival of this, and in large measure is an anachronism.

For this oscillation of movement towards variety or uniformity corresponds with the practical needs and impulses and spirit of the time and place. The ventures of variety belong to periods of spiritual awakening with their protests against unreality and their demands that even corporate worship should be 'up to date' and 'real'. When, however, such a movement is consolidated, the need arises for standardizing the rites, and a policy of 'coming into line' follows, which either deliberately or instinctively leads to uniformity.

Our own age belongs to the former class, not the latter. This was apparent even before the War; and since then it is far more clear. So throughout the Anglican Communion there is a great desire for variety, freedom, enrichment, and the like.

The situation in the mission field, already discussed, is but a special instance of this general rule. The early days of a mission are necessarily times of uniformity: the missionaries bring and impose their own customs. But as the awakening of the native church manifests itself, it demands at least a period of venture of variety and experiment. My conclusion is that all provinces should be encouraged to meet the occasion by venture and by cautious, regulated, and developing experiment.

2. What conditions should be observed in regard to the construction or component parts of a service of Holy Communion which is to be used within the Anglican Communion?

A greater measure of similarity of rite is desirable for Holy Baptism and Holy Communion than for other services. At present there is no proper service for Baptism of Adults: that in the Book of Common Prayer is a poor adaptation of the Service for Infants, which in turn is an adaptation of an original Service for Adults. The mission field should be encouraged to go direct to the precedents of the Early Church and frame a new service based upon them.

In the case of Holy Communion it is the primitive scheme underlying all the ancient and the modern historical liturgies which it is advisable to require, i.e.—

(a) the Mass of catechumens;
(b) the Prayers and Confession of Faith of the faithful;
(c) the Anaphora, which should at least include the recital of the events of the Institution;
(d) Thanksgiving.

There is no need to avoid a combination of elements from different sources in one rite provided it is carefully done and stands the test of use. Borrowing has always been the policy pursued. The Sursum Corda is as characteristically Latin as the Gloria in Excelsis or the Kyrie is Greek. But for English-speaking people it may well be recognized that there has grown up an Anglican type of language and rite which has the first claim to their affection and allegiance. There is no need to lay down any provision as to doctrine. It must be presumed that the doctrine implied in any forms accepted by the province would be that of the Catholic Church in all its width and fullness. It would be impossible even if it were desirable to lay this down beforehand. It would be suicidal to set up the English rite as the standard. The Lambeth Conference would go entirely beyond its book if it were to attempt to impose any standard upon the provinces. If ever a disputed case arose, it would be the duty of the other provinces to remonstrate with the province whose decision had raised a dispute.

The Report of the Lambeth Committee on Missionary Problems made it clear that Frere's suggestions on liturgical variations were acceptable. Its recommendations were as follows:

1. Rigid liturgical uniformity is not to be regarded as a necessity throughout the Churches of the Anglican Communion in the mission field.

2. It should be recognized that full liberty belongs to diocesan Bishops not only for the adaptations and additions alluded to but also for the adoption of other uses.

3. In the exercise of this liberty care should always be taken:
   (a) To maintain a Scriptural and Catholic balance of Truth.
   (b) To give due consideration to the precedents of the early Church.
   (c) To observe such limitations as may be imposed by higher synodical authority.
   (d) To remember with brotherly consideration the possible effect their action may have on other provinces and branches of the Anglican Communion.

4. The preparation of forms of service, and especially of an Order for the celebration of the Holy Communion, calls for the highest liturgical skill and knowledge, such as is not always available in every province, and the best interests of the Church would be served by the appointment of a permanent committee of experts in liturgical studies to which, when engaged in such tasks, the various dioceses and provinces might turn for advice.[1]

---

[1] R. T. Davidson, *The Six Lambeth Conferences*, 1929, appendix, p. 88.

THE LITURGY IN JAPAN

The Bishop in South Tokyo, Dr. Boutflower, to Frere   13 *June* 1912

My dear Fr. Frere,

 For the consideration of English friends, and especially yourself and Mr. Rackham, I have drawn out the two enclosures from their (fuller) Japanese originals. Our Prayer Book Committee (and the six Bishops in particular) have to consider them further: and then, if blessed by authority, I shall spend my energies in trying to get them approved by individual voters before the next general Synod—one or other. It is No. 1 with which you have already helped me. That, as less radical, has more chance: especially with a non-liturgical but suspicious 'C.M.S.' element of votes. Do not be hard on certain obvious un-liturgical points inherited in the existing Seikokwai Rubrics from the American Prayer Book. At the same time by all means mention them. What do you think of No. 2? One or other I am most keen to get through. I think the occasion justifies troubling you. Only in this way can we here (and possibly *you* in England) survive at a general eventual substitution of a Eucharistic Service for the dominant 'Sunday Matins'. . . .

The first enclosure was an Order for a Combined Sunday Morning Service, as reported by Sub-committee to the General Synod in 1911. Sections 1 to 16 represented what was already prescribed by the 'Shortened Service Rubrics' and was in constant use where Mattins and Holy Communion were used consecutively. The new part began at Section 17, and was based mainly on recommendations made by Frere for the proper liturgical combination without tautology of the Litany and Ante-communion.

 1. Sentences. Hab. ii. 20. Mal. i. 11. Ps. xix. 14.
 2. Lord's Prayer.
 3. Versicles and Responds.
 4. Gloria.
 5. Praise ye: The Lord's Name.
 6. Venite vv. 1–7.
 7. Rubric ordering Psalm or Psalms.
 8. Rubric ordering O.T. Lesson.
 9. Te Deum.
 10. Rubric permitting Benedicite alternative.

The Liturgy in Japan

11. Rubric ordering 2nd Lesson when Proper of a Holy-Day, to be followed by Benedictus or Jubilate.
12. The Lord be with you, &c.
13. The Versicles.
14. The Collect for Peace.
15. The Collect for Grace.
16. Rubric permitting Anthem or Hymn.
17. The Litany, omitting petitions for the Emperor, Royal Family, Ministers of State, Magistrates, Clergy, 'All thy people', 'An heart to love and dread thee', 'All that are in danger, necessity' &c., and omitting all that follows 'O Lamb of God. . . . Have mercy upon us', to the end of General Thanksgiving; closing with
18. Prayer of St. Chrysostom.
19. The Grace.
20. Rubric ordering celebrant to proceed to Lord's Table.
21. And permitting singing of a Hymn.
22. Let us pray.
23. Lesser Litany.
24. Rubric ordering Office for Holy Communion to begin with Collect, Epistle, and Gospel for the Day, and proceed as usual from this point.

The second enclosure was a freer Form, with the title, 'A Revised Service. Holy Communion: with Enlarged Ante-Communion' presented in 1912 by the Ven. A. F. King and the Revd.-Yoshizawa.

1. Sentence. Mal. i. 11.
2. Versicles and Responds.
3. Gloria.
4. Venite vv. 1–7.
5. Psalms appointed.
6. O.T. Lesson.
7. Te Deum (or Benedicite: or in Advent Benedictus).
8. N.T. Lesson on Sundays and Holy Days.
9. With Benedictus (or Jubilate).
10. Mutual Salutation.
11. 'Let us prostrate ourselves, and beseech the Lord.'
12. Shortened Litany, beginning 'We sinners do beseech Thee to hear us, O Lord Christ' with twelve petitions only, followed by 'O Lamb of God', &c., 'O Christ hear us', Prayer of St. Chrysostom, and the Grace.
13. Introit Anthem.
14. Lesser Litany.
15. Let us pray.

16. Collect, Epistle, and Gospel for the Day.
17. Rubric ordering the Gospel Ascription.
18. Nicene Creed.
19. The Sermon.
20. Offertory Sentences. Matt. v. 16, vi. 19–20, vii. 12.
21. Rubric permitting other Offertory Sentences.
22. Rubric permitting Prayer for Missions and for Catechumens from the 'Occasional Prayers'.
23. Prayer for the Church Militant.
    Preparation of Communicants—unbroken.
24. The Longer Exhortation.
25. The Short Exhortation.
26. The Confession and Absolution.
27. Comfortable Words.
28. Prayer of Humble Access.
    The Anaphora—unbroken.
29. Sursum Corda, &c.
30. Proper Prefaces and Sanctus.
31. The American Prayer of Consecration.
32. The Lord's Prayer.
    Communion.
33. Administration.
    Post-communion.
34. The Prayer of Thanksgiving.
35. Gloria in Excelsis.
36. Pax and Blessing.
37. Reference to the Post-Communion Collects, &c., as in Prayer Book.

Frere to Bishop Boutflower   11 *July* 1912

My dear Bishop,

    Thank you for the two drafts that you sent. I am very much interested to see the way in which you are travelling, but it is a little difficult to get to understand the position from isolated drafts. I don't know, for example, what you are doing about the recitation of the Psalter and the Lessons. That seems to me to be more important than anything. Nor again do you say what alternative you are providing to the Te Deum: the present position of the Benedicite seems to me very unsatisfactory.

    The thing I should first quarrel with in the Combined Sunday Morning Service is the entirely false position of the Lord's Prayer, following the unintelligent precedent of America. It is entirely un-

The Liturgy in Japan

necessary at the beginning of the service; in fact it is only the remains of a piece of private devotion there: whereas it is entirely necessary after the canticles and before the versicles, for that is the place to which according to all liturgical precedent it mainly belongs. America has thrown over the custom of the Church from primitive times to work up to the Lord's Prayer in favour of some foolish late medieval custom of privately beginning with it. I hope you won't do the same.

Next, I hope you will have only one collect following the versicles. There is everything to be said for versicles leading up to a collect; the collect then becomes the fixed collect of the office (if it is not the varying collect of the day) and so the service ends with its proper collect; other collects if added afterwards are of the nature of memorials. This is the perfectly uniform structure: our Prayer Book in its present form conforms to this: it uses the collect of the week as the collect of the service, and then is followed by two memorial collects. But it is meaningless to take that away and leave you the two memorial collects. What is wanted after the versicles is THE collect, which thus becomes the proper collect of the office, and if you don't use the variable one of the week it ought to be a permanent one. Choose whichever you like, the Collect for Peace or the Collect for Grace, but do not give both: the Collect for Grace is, of course, the old collect belonging to Prime; and if your Sunday Morning Service is to be said early there is every reason for treating that as the fixed collect of the office. If you want to keep the little Collect for Peace it must either form one of a little group of memorial collects at this point (but that is one of the things you can easily get rid of), or else it can be made part of a group of occasional prayers such as you have at the end of the Litany. But in neither case is it one such as you want at a shortened form of service.

I do not like so well the completion of the Litany with the Prayer of St. Chrysostom and the Grace, as I like the treating of the Lesser Litany at the end of the Litany as the equivalent of the Lesser Litany at the beginning of the Eucharist: but if you insist on thus duplicating the Lesser Litany it should at any rate be treated as the beginning of the Communion Service: the rubric should not assume that it begins with the collect. Collects are always closing things, and what it closes in this particular instance properly speaking is the Litany, or more specifically the Lesser Litany. In this sense the Prayer of St. Chrysostom is really a duplicate of our collect of the day, though the former is unchangeable and the latter varies. Some precedent may be found for the use of the words of the Grace, but the whole object for their insertion here and their connotation is that they form the close of a service. The use of them therefore is undesirable when you are wanting not to disjoin but to link together services.

I am much interested to see your revised service No. 2. It is a bolder but a very well-justified handling of the problem so far as the Litany is concerned; though I would say the same as before about the Prayer of St. Chrysostom and the Grace. I should be inclined to think too that there ought to be some use of the Lord's Prayer before you get it at the end of the Communion Office; two repetitions are not too many. If you do not have it after the Benedictus it might be regarded as the close of the Litany, the summing up of all those previous petitions in place of the Prayer of St. Chrysostom and the Grace; and this is specially the case if you are going to have an introit anthem, which in any case will divide the one Lesser Litany from the other.

I presume provision will be made for the notices together with the sermon. There is a tendency to get this out of place or to take away requests for prayer out of this category where they really belong, and put them as a sort of amplification of the invitation before the Prayer for the Church Militant. This I don't think wise. After the Creed is the right place for the bidding of prayer, the giving of notices, and the sermon if there is one. And we should do well to use this opportunity for informal prayer of all sorts, and for requests for prayer. Further there is the practical difficulty in keeping these things in their right places, that after giving out the request for prayer there is a certain interval, and generally a little bit of quiet in which the congregation can pray for the subjects recommended, whereas if you don't give out the requests for prayer till exactly before the Prayer for the Church Militant there is no such opportunity.

I am delighted, of course, to see the restoration which is proposed in the right order of the Communion Office. I hope very much you will secure this. From the point of view of the communicant there is nothing that is more important, and if you do it you will perhaps also be able to introduce the Lord's Prayer with its little formula, and finish it up with the amplification of the last clause, working into it some of the special form of doxology. You may find it valuable I think to add some sentences to be said as notice of the administration. It is a practical convenience and I hope you will be able to carry this. The recovery of the arrangement at Communion seems to be accepted here even by the Evangelicals; indeed Dr. Wace has professed himself in favour of it with certain safeguards or compensations I believe. . . .

THE SOUTH AFRICAN LITURGY (I)

The work of drawing up a South African Liturgy began in 1911, when a schedule of permitted modifications to the 1662 Prayer Book was published. The Episcopal Synod made themselves responsible for this undertaking, and availed themselves of the help of liturgical scholars in England. In July 1918 Frere drew up the following masterly Memorandum, which he called 'Rough Notes on the Proposed Form of the South African Liturgy'.

1. It is desirable that the Anaphora should begin with the mutual salutation, 'The Lord be with you' 'And with thy spirit'. This is used to introduce with solemnity a fresh division in any service, and nowhere is it more needed than here to introduce the Anaphora.

2. In the General Preface the blunder should be corrected by which the adjectives are wrongly distributed among the nouns. This need not involve more than one transposition—'O Holy Lord, Father Almighty, Everlasting God'—but perhaps a double transposition would be more symmetrical and more rhythmical—'O Holy Lord, Almighty Father, Everlasting God'.

3. The mishandling of the Sanctus should also be corrected. Its form is as follows both in Latin and in Greek,

> Sanctus Sanctus Sanctus dominus deus sabaoth
> Pleni sunt celi et terra gloria tua.
> > Hosanna in excelsis.
> Benedictus qui venit in nomine domini.
> > Hosanna in excelsis.

It has been barbarously mutilated by the excision of the last two lines. If a return was desired to the older form of the Sanctus the last three lines, not two, should have been amputated. The Hosanna Benedictus and Hosanna Repeat seem originally to have been taken from Ps. cxviii through the account of the Triumphal Entry to a place immediately before Communion: and thence to have been transferred and brought into conjunction with the Sanctus. Thus they hold this position not only in the Roman rite but also in the Gallican, the Syrian, and the Byzantine. This being so, it seems highly desirable that they should be restored in our Order to that position. The only alternative is to end the Sanctus as it ended before this addition, viz. at the words 'Full of Thy Glory'.

The present translation is unfortunate; for the Hosanna is at its first occurrence translated (or rather mistranslated) as 'Glory be to Thee O Lord most high': while in the second place the Hebrew term is preserved, 'Hosanna in the Highest'. The latter form should be adopted in both places, and the connexion of the Benedictus with the Sanctus would then be properly restored, thus—'Holy . . . full of Thy Glory. Hosanna in the highest. Blessed is he . . . Lord, Hosanna in the Highest.'

4. Next the link to the ensuing prayer is to be considered. Such a link forms an important feature of the Liturgy except in the Roman rite where the chief links have been destroyed or ignored. In the other Latin liturgies the link appears normally in the form 'Vere sanctus', or more fully 'Vere sanctus et vere benedictus'. In the bulk of the Gallican post-sanctus prayers it is our Lord who is spoken of as 'Vere sanctus', and in the third person, since, of course, the prayer is addressed to the Father. This no doubt is the natural use of the quotation. It must be regarded as a momentary turning aside to give a spontaneous expression of homage to our Lord. If the precedent of the majority of the post-sanctus prayers is followed, the return to addressing the Father will be made by some such phrase as this, 'Vere sanctus vere benedictus Dominus noster Jesus Christus tuus qui (or quem)', &c. But there is a good number of cases in which the words 'Vere sanctus', and even 'Vere benedictus', are used of the Father and to the Father; and among these are some of the most important, e.g. at Easter in the Mozarabic Rite. (*Liber Mozarabicus Sacramentorum*, Ferotin, 626.)

'Vere sanctus et benedictus es, Deus Pater omnipotens, qui dominum nostrum Jesum Christum Filium tuum in assumptione humanitatis mortem fecisti subire, ut', &c.

Again in the *Missae quotidianae* which often represent the earlier and more normal forms we find:

'Vere sanctus et vere benedictus in excelsis omnipotens tu Deus Pater, cuius munere cunctis hominibus imaginis tuae dignitas conceditur in natura', &c.

Or again in the Advent mass of the *Missale Gallicanum* (Neale and Forbes, *Gallican Liturgies*, p. 157).

'Vere sanctus vere benedictus Domine Deus Pater omnipotens, salus credentium et omnium Redemptor in Christo: per quem te deprecamur et quaesumus ut hanc oblationem', &c. This form of link therefore seems the more desirable one. The 'proposed form' links on the consecration prayer to the mistranslation of the Hosanna, which ought to go. This link is a firmer and sounder one, for it connects with Sanctus and Benedictus and pulls all together. Some such form as this seems therefore advisable:— 'Holy in truth art thou (and blessed in truth) O Almighty God, our heavenly Father, for that thou of thy tender mercy', &c.—which, it will be observed, agrees closely with the Easter prayer cited above.

5. The link of the Prayer of Oblation is satisfactory; but the mention of the Holy Spirit should (as in the creed) follow close upon the mention of the Second Coming, otherwise the whole order of events is thrown into confusion. The 'proposed form' is entirely unsuitable and reprehensible in deferring thus the mention of the Holy Spirit.

The thought that should connect the 'remembrance' of our Lord's mighty acts very closely with the descent of the Holy Spirit is that of the offering of the gifts. The order is as follows:—When the offering has been made, the invocation follows at once, the effect of the invocation is described, and then comes the prayer for acceptance.

6. The offering of the gifts is one of the undisplaced features of the Roman Canon: and if the model of that prayer is used for the 'remembrance', it may well be carried on to this clause also. 'Offerimus praeclare maiestati tuae de tuis donis et datis hostiam puram, hostiam sanctam, hostiam immaculatam, panem sanctum vitae aeternae et calicem salutis perpetuae.'

This procedure is also common in the non-Roman Latin liturgies, e.g. in the *Missale Gothicum* (N. and F. 148): 'Memores gloriosissimi domini passionis, et ab inferis resurrectionis, offerimus tibi Domine hanc immaculatam hostiam, rationalem hostiam, incruentam hostiam, hunc panem sanctum et calicem salutarem.' Or this in the Mozarabic Rite (*L.M.S.* 1288): 'Commemorantes ergo redemptoris nostri precepta, simulque passionem et in coelum ascensionem, offerimus tibi, Deus Pater omnipotens, haec dona et munera, et fidelium tuorum sacrificia illibata.'

Considering that this section leads on to the Invocation, it is desirable to approach that part of the prayer, round which dogmatic difficulties cluster, by a type of phrase which is common to both Roman and Gallican rites. The following is therefore suggested:

'Wherefore O Lord ... glory, do offer unto thy divine majesty these sacred gifts and creatures of thine own, this holy bread of eternal life and this cup of everlasting salvation.'

7. The form which the mention of the Holy Spirit should take is to be called in some sense an 'Invocation': but the intervention of the Holy Spirit, where it is expressly mentioned, has been described in a great variety of ways. Any restoration of this feature should follow one or

other of the many shapes that this section has taken in Western Latin liturgy rather than be modelled on Eastern precedents.

(*a*) A direct Invocation addressed to the Holy Spirit is rare, and these precedents should not be followed.

(*b*) Usually the appeal is made to the Father to bless what is being offered by the outpouring of the Holy Spirit (N. and F. 4, 8, 15): 'uti hoc sacrificium tua benedictione benedicas, et Sancti Spiritus tui rore perfundas'.

(*c*) Sometimes the prayer is that the Holy Spirit may descend (ibid. 59, 153, 157): 'Descendat, Domine, in his sacrificiis tuae benedictionis coeternus et cooperator Paraclitus Spiritus.' 'Descendat precamur, omnipotens Deus, super haec, quae tibi offerimus, verbum tuum sanctum, descendat inestimabilis gloriae tuae Spiritus. . . .'

(*d*) or more generally that the *divine power* may descend and consecrate (ibid. ii): 'Descendat, Domine, plenitudo maiestatis, divinitatis, pietatis, virtutis, benedictionis et gloriae tuae super hunc panem et super hunc calicem. . . .'

(*e*) or a combination of the two (ibid. 135): 'Ut descendat hic benedictio tua super hunc panem et calicem, in transformatione Spiritus tui Sancti.'

(*f*) Another type speaks of the *sending* of the Holy Spirit (ibid. 74): 'Ut immittere digneris Spiritum tuum Sanctum super haec sollemnia.'

(*g*) Sometimes a mention of all the persons of the Trinity is made (ibid. 146). 'Per quem te, Deus omnipotens, deprecamur, ut supraposita altario tuo munera laetus aspicias, atque haec omnia obumbres Sancti Filii tui Spiritus.'

8. It is hardly possible to decide which should be the type of Invocation to be adopted, without first considering also the ensuing clause, descriptive of the effect of the coming of the Holy Spirit. In some instances the description is brief and general; in others it is more detailed, and expresses more explicitly the 'change' involved in consecration, usually by some such word as 'transfusio' or 'transformatio'. The latter type is less likely to be thought suitable now, in view of the controversies that have arisen since these various formulas were penned; to restore such terms would only reopen controversy. The following examples of the former type may serve, therefore, better as guides. The simplest form and a common one is this (ibid. 4, 15, 99):

'Ut (sacrificium) accipientibus universis legitima sit eucharistia (*or* eucharistia pura vera legitima) per Jesum', &c.

Another follows the phrase (ibid. 11, 47, 74): 'Ut fiat nobis legitima eucharistia'; but this is often followed by a description of the 'transformation'. Moreover, 'fiat nobis' anticipates the effect *on the communicant*—a point which is provided for in our prayer at a later stage: and formulas which speak at this point of the effect of reception on the communicant are not, therefore, the best for us to follow.

Another type speaks of the effect of the Holy Spirit's work in terms of sanctification. For example (*L.M.S.* 360, 627):

'Emitte Spiritum tuum de sanctis caelis tuis, quo sanctificentur oblata, suscipiantur vota, expientur delicta.'

or 'Deferatur in ista sollemnia Spiritus tuus Sanctus, qui tam adstantis quam offerentis populi et oblata pariter et vota sanctificet.'

Again there are other general descriptions of the eucharistic significance of the Holy Spirit's work which clash neither with the Eastern nor with the Western theories of consecration (*L.M.S.* 70, 617, 1191):

'Fac quaesumus hoc *tui Corporis sanguinisque mysterium*, spiritus tui rore sanctificatum, ad nostrarum remedium sumere animarum.'

or 'Ut hic tibi panis cum hoc calice oblatus in filii tui corpus et sanguinem te benedicente ditescat: ac, largo oris tui perfusus Spiritu, indulgentiam nobis omnium peccatorum largiatur et gratiam.'

or 'Sic hoc sacrificium respicere et sanctificare digneris quod est verum corpus et sanguis dom. nos. J.C.'

What is required at this critical point is something which fulfils two conditions;

(*a*) that it should be explicit as to the reality of the consecration, and should therefore contrast the 'bread' and 'wine' with the consecrated Body and Blood, and

(*b*) that it should do so in a way that avoids the controversy between East and West as to the moment, or operative words of the consecration.

To follow Greek terms is therefore inadvisable. It is very doubtful whether these terms are early, for the 'primitive' character of the living Greek liturgies has been greatly overstated. While in general form they are perhaps more primitive than the Latin rites, or at any rate than the Roman rite, they have undergone much more modification in detail during the early medieval period. And how far they are from the early form of Invocation will be seen by comparing the third-century formula in the Hippolytean Church Order. Such passages as those cited seem to provide us with terms sufficiently definite and also sufficiently indefinite; their adoption would point to some such formula as this:

'Entreating thee to send from high heaven thy Holy Spirit to sanctify our offerings and to hallow these our vows; that by the dew of his grace this mystery of the Body and Blood of thy Son may be available for the healing of our souls.'

Or this:

'May thy Holy Spirit descend upon these offerings, and hallow this oblation of the Body and Blood of thy Son Jesus Christ our Lord.'

Then the prayer would be continued, 'Thus we entirely desire thy fatherly goodness', &c.; and the words 'that thy Holy Spirit may be poured upon us, and' would be omitted.

9. The Lord's Prayer needs some special eucharistic ending. If the familiar doxology is *removed* from it in all *other* places when the prayer occurs it might serve *here* in that capacity. But there is a better precedent for a fresh piece of prayer linked on to the end of the Lord's Prayer, introduced by a repetition of the word 'Libera'. The briefest type is exhibited thus in one of the *Missae Dominicales* (N. and F. 144): 'Libera nos a malo omnipotens Deus et custodi in bono, qui vivis', &c., and some such incorporating prayer for the celebrant seems all the more necessary if, as now, the Lord's Prayer is sung by the congregation, and not, as once was the case, by the celebrant alone, the people replying at 'Sed libera nos a malo'.

10. The suggestion has been made that the Prayer of Humble Access should be made a *Libera* prayer thus: 'Deliver us from all evil and preserve us in all good, for we do not presume to come to this thy table O merciful Lord', &c. There seems much to be said for this; for the words are familiar, are suitable to the place, and would come much better there than in their present position. But a brief one has many points in its favour. There are plenty of precedents and the Gallican formulas are very similar to the Roman formula.

11. This also raises the question of the position to be occupied by the preparatory prayers for communicants. Granted that the set are kept together, or at least that the Prayer of Humble Access is no longer intruded into the Canon (1) should the preparation be made before the Anaphora or after? (2) Should the celebrant make his preparation with the communicants, or make a separate preparation before beginning the service? These questions are open ones and I would only record

a preference for the preparation being made jointly by celebrant and communicants and being made before the Anaphora. The group of Exhortation, Absolution, Comfortable Words, and Prayer of Humble Access is too long to intercalate between consecration and communion. If such prayers are to be put in that place they must be briefer. As it is, they place the celebrant in an undesirable position having to go through so much movement and turning with the Holy Sacrament lying on the altar.

12. The opportunity should be taken for the amendment of the Gloria in Excelsis. The Scottish form is not satisfactory, nor is the present English form. See *Church Quarterly Review* (lxxxii. 299).

13. Provision might well be made expressly for the saying of a Post-communion collect before the Blessing, as is implied in the Ordination Service.

Frere's advice was followed at almost every point. In 1919 a new 'Alternative Form of the Order for the Administration of the Holy Communion' was published, containing all his suggestions except those on the Preface, Sanctus, and the Post-communion collects, while the latter was ultimately adopted in the final Order in 1929. The suggested Anaphora was as follows:

Priest. The Lord be with you.
Answer. And with thy spirit.
Priest. Lift up your hearts. . . .
Answer. It is meet and right so to do
Priest. It is very meet, right, and our bounden duty, that we should at all times, and in all places, give thanks unto thee, O Lord, Holy Father, Almighty, Everlasting God.
(Proper Preface if appointed.)
Therefore with Angels and Archangels and with all the company of heaven, we laud and magnify thy glorious Name; evermore praising thee, and saying:
Holy, holy, holy, Lord God of hosts, heaven and earth are full of thy glory: Glory be to thee, O Lord most high. Amen.

All glory and thanksgiving be to thee Almighty God our heavenly Father for that thou of thy tender mercy didst give thine only Son Jesus Christ to take our nature upon him and to suffer death upon the Cross for our redemption. . . . Do this, as oft as ye shall drink it, in remembrance of me.

Wherefore, O Lord and heavenly Father, according to the institution of thy dearly beloved Son, our Saviour Jesus Christ, we thy humble servants, having in remembrance his blessed passion and precious death, his mighty resurrection and glorious ascension, do render unto thee most hearty thanks for the innumerable benefits procured unto us by the same; and, looking for his coming again with power and great glory, we offer here unto thy divine majesty these sacred gifts and creatures of thine own, this holy Bread of eternal life and this Cup of everlasting salvation; and we humbly beseech thee to pour thy Holy Spirit upon us and upon these thy gifts, that he may hallow this oblation, and that all we who are partakers of this Holy Communion may worthily receive the most precious Body and Blood of thy Son, and be fulfilled with thy grace and heavenly benediction.

And we earnestly desire thy fatherly goodness mercifully to grant, that by the merits and death of thy Son Jesus Christ, and through faith in his blood, we and all thy whole Church may obtain remission of our sins, and all other benefits of his passion.

And here we offer and present unto thee, O Lord, ourselves, our souls and bodies, to be a reasonable, holy, and living sacrifice unto thee:

And although we be unworthy, through our manifold sins, to offer unto thee any sacrifice, yet we beseech thee to accept this our bounden duty and service; not weighing our merits, but pardoning our offences, through Jesus Christ our Lord; by whom, and with whom, in the unity of the Holy Ghost, all honour and glory be unto thee, O Father Almighty, world without end. Amen.

And now as our Saviour Jesus Christ hath commanded and taught us, we are bold to say:

Then shall the Priest say the Lord's Prayer, the people repeating after him every petition.

Our Father . . .

Then shall follow immediately this prayer, said by the Priest kneeling, in the name of all them that shall receive the Communion.

Deliver us from all evil, for we do not presume to come to this thy Table, O merciful Lord, trusting in our own righteousness, but in thy manifold and great mercies, &c.

Frere reviewed this Alternative Order in the July 1920 issue of the *Church Quarterly Review*. He considered it to be a great improvement on the Proposed Form issued in 1918; it 'bids fair to provide the Province of South Africa with a worthy Liturgy, and the Anglican Com-

munion in general with a very valuable model'.[1] The main threefold aim of the Proposed Form was now more fully carried out
1. to recover the unity of the Anaphora or Canon;
2. to enrich the commemoration there made of our Lord's work, first by introducing a definite reference to the Incarnation ('to take our nature upon him and to suffer death', &c.) before coming on to the events of Holy Week, secondly by the recovery of the Anamnesis of his Passion, Death, Resurrection, and Ascension, and by making mention of his coming again;
3. to bring in some form of Invocation of the Holy Spirit.

His attitude towards the Epiclesis was most favourable. 'The sequence of thought and devotion is now clear. . . . The Holy Spirit's grace is invoked upon the communicants as well as upon the gift: a worthy reception of the most precious Body and Blood is looked for as the outcome of this, and thereupon a fullness of grace and blessing'.[2] He was aware that the Epiclesis had been a centre of controversy, but he considered the compilers wise in following Gallican rather than Greek precedents, for there not only was the method of invocation varied, but the effect was described in general terms. 'The compilers, therefore, have good precedent behind them when they describe the effect of the Holy Spirit's outpouring upon the gifts in such a simple, reticent, and non-controversial phrase as "that he may hallow this oblation".'[3] Indeed he only had two important criticisms of the Anaphora. The first, as may be expected from his Memorandum, was the failure to give satisfactory treatment to the Preface and Sanctus. The second dealt with the rubric for a Second Consecration: this ordered a Consecration of elements of both kinds, with the Prayer of Consecration from 'Hear us, O merciful Father' down to 'Do this as oft as ye shall drink it in remembrance of me'. Frere considered a Second Consecration an expedient which should be avoided if possible. If needed, however, the ideal was a repetition of the whole Consecration Prayer, while the irreducible minimum should begin at 'Hear us', and contain at least the Anamnesis and the Invocation.[4]

The Epiclesis met with opposition in South Africa, and a group of clergy from the Diocese of Natal submitted to the Episcopal Synod a Petition, accompanied by lengthy considerations, asking them to 'reconsider the wording of both Invocations, the old and the new, in the Alternative Form of Holy Communion, and especially to clear up the ambiguity of the new Invocation'. They had three main objections:
1. The second Epiclesis ignored and obscured the existing Epiclesis in the Prayer of Consecration: 'Hear us, O merciful Father, and grant', &c.

[1] *Walter Howard Frere*, Alcuin Club Collections No. 35, 1940, p. 123.
[2] Ibid., p. 125.   [3] Ibid., p. 127.   [4] Ibid.

2. It followed neither Eastern nor Western types of Epiclesis.
3. The verbal defect of the Prayer Book Epiclesis was left unamended. It was rightly addressed to the Father, but did not mention the Holy Spirit as the agent. A return to the 1549 or the Scottish 1637 form was desirable.

Canon Darragh of Durban, who was responsible for drawing up this Petition, wrote to Frere on the matter.

Canon J. T. Darragh to Frere   5 *January* 1921

Dear Father Frere,

You may care to run your eye through the enclosed pamphlet dealing with features in the Alternative Form of Holy Communion recently put forth in this Province. You have yourself dealt with it in a masterly article, in which as a true friend of the South African Church you make as good an apology for it as is possible. I do not know, however, how you came to consider it as a 'South African Liturgy', duly accepted and agreed upon. It is most certainly not so accepted and agreed upon, and is no more than a tentative and experimental document. There is not the least likelihood of its being generally received in the Province without some amendment of the language of the second Epiclesis. This Diocese has taken the matter up, and the example is, we know, likely to be followed in the other Dioceses. I enclose our Petition and the pamphlet in justification of the Petition which the Committee asked me, as a person fairly conversant with liturgical literature, to draw up. The Committee adopted my draft with a few immaterial amendments. Unfortunately the work had to be done against time as a meeting of the Episcopal Synod was imminent. You will notice faults of printing and of arrangement, but the facts on which the argument are based are, I think, indisputable. Your encyclopaedic knowledge of the subject could add much more to the same effect, but I trust there is enough clear liturgical principle set forth to secure a reconsideration of the wording of the second Epiclesis.

I should be very grateful indeed if you would kindly give a thorough review of the second Epiclesis in the light of the considerations contained in this pamphlet. We are not very strong, even on the Bench, in liturgical knowledge, and it would be a serious thing for a small Province such as ours to depart lightly from the usage of the mother Church in the central part of the Eucharistic Office. In subsidiary portions of the Service it is a different matter altogether, and provincial churches might quite legitimately modify or enrich in the matter of additional Saints Days, Epistles, Gospels, and Collects, Prefaces, and additional devotions and so on, but not in the method of Consecration in a manner to depart from historical precedent. . . .

This was followed by another letter, stating the case presented in the Petition in greater detail.

Canon J. T. Darragh to Frere 18 *February* 1921

Dear Father Frere,

 . . . It is to certain features in the 1920 edition that our criticism is addressed in the 'Petition and Considerations' which I recently forwarded to you with an earnest request for your considered opinion on the main contention of the latter. Controversial matters of debatable points in respect of liturgical origins are of quite secondary importance.

We take our stand on the consent of the Catholic Church and its promised guidance of the Holy Spirit. We see no call for the Church of today to go behind that consent, which both Eastern and Western types of Consecration can claim without question during the centuries of the undivided Church. From the end of the fourth century there are three great things clearly accepted as the adequate expression of the Church's faith and practice: (1) The Canon of Scripture. (2) the Constantinopolitan Creed. (3) the Consecration of the Holy Eucharist in either of two ways. Of these three accepted things, the last is the least subjected to controversy until recent times, and, as far as literary records go, not at all from the fourth to the sixteenth century. As to what exactly was done before, we have clear evidence in the fourth century. Any amount of learned investigation is legitimate in the case of the Consecration, as indeed in the cases of the Canon of Scripture and of the Creed. But we should not forget that the Church of the fourth century not only had all the fragments of liturgical lore which have survived and more also, but with regard to the Consecration had the minute, intimate knowledge which we can only tentatively arrive at from casual, fragmentary scraps which have come down to us. Is there any more reason for considering the decisions of the fourth century on the Canon of Scripture and the Creed to be binding on us than for holding to her practice with regard to the Consecration? Does not the desire to go behind her consent in one case inevitably open the way for departing from her consent in the other two cases mentioned? Could the whole Anglican Communion on its professed principles legitimately abandon Catholic consent in either of the three cases? If not, surely a small, young, and unlearned Province is precluded from making the attempt to go behind Catholic consent in the case of the Consecration of the Body and Blood of Christ.

If our young bloods were proposing that the Province should adopt a genuine Greek Liturgy, it would be glorious if—per impossible—they were to succeed. What they talk of is an amalgamation of Eastern and Western methods of Consecration in one rite, an absolutely impossible proceeding. The only result is to stultify both methods and throw the whole into inextricable confusion.

We hope for a clear lead from you on the main question, leaving debatable points and side-issues severely alone. . . .

At the same time Frere received a letter from the Rt. Revd. James Nash, C.R., Coadjutor Bishop of Cape Town, in defence of the line taken by the Episcopal Synod.

Bishop Nash to Frere   16 *February* 1921

My dear Superior,

I do not know when you will be back from the West, but when you get back, would you look at Darragh's onslaught and let me know what you think?

The motive is really I think dislike of any movement away from Roman tradition. Play is made with the rubric about Supplementary Consecration—rather for embarrassment—for clearly it is open for us to claim that the short formula allowed is intended to be covered by the whole Prayer of Consecration. Still, as you advise in the *C.Q.R.*— for which kind notice many thanks—it would be better to alter to the Scottish or American model. But to claim that a scarcely necessary rubric aimed at an accidental occurrence is to govern the whole scheme of Consecration is monstrous.

The main attack, however, is on the formula of the Invocation. No doubt the petitioners want to tie us down to what we have desired to avoid, i.e. the statement of the moment, and the exact words which consecrate. But would you say that in themselves the words used are too ambiguous and need to be made more explicit? I should have thought they pray definitely for hallowing. Is the word 'sacred' too strong for gifts solemnly selected and presented on the altar?

Darragh has written to F. E. Brightman and got him to curse us. But the same F. E. B. said to me—for I sent him a copy—'It's all right'. But he seems to have been impressed by the Supplementary Consecration argument.

However, a few words would be gratefully accepted. I think myself the form is adequate, but we should be prepared to try to improve. Though I think nothing short of a return to Consecration by the Words of Institution will appease Darragh and his friends. . . . .

Frere replied to both Bishop Nash and Canon Darragh, supporting the line taken by the Bishops. At the same time, however, he reiterated his criticism in the *Church Quarterly Review* that the arrangements for a Second Consecration were defective and needed revision.

Frere to Bishop Nash   8 *July* 1921

My dear James,

Your letter of 16 February awaited me on my return from Canada after Easter. I did not want to reply hastily, and was anxious to go over the whole matter again before sending you a considered opinion on the Office, looking at it afresh; also upon the attacks by Darragh and others.

I have now been able to go over the whole ground afresh, and find myself a convinced supporter of the line which the South African bishops have taken. Let me sketch out the main points which bring me afresh to this conclusion.

1. We have now before us a primitive form of the Consecration dating to the end of the second or beginning of the third century, carrying us 150 years behind anything previously known. This has cleared up the dark places, and we now can see the history of the divergence between East and West in this matter. It is clear that the Invocation of the Holy Spirit following the Anamnesis is a primitive and universal feature, and not as Westernizers used to say, a late importation.

2. This primitive Canon shows us the Invocation in a very simple form, which does not as yet insist that it is through the coming of the Holy Spirit that the elements are consecrated.

3. We can now observe Rome adopting the view that Consecration was by the word, and in course of time getting rid therefore from its

Canon of the Invocation of the Holy Spirit in this position. The Invocation of the Holy Spirit, however, seems to have survived at any rate in the memories, if not actually in the formula of the Roman Church down to the end of the fifth century, for Pope Gelasius alludes to it twice.

4. The Western view begins to influence the non-Roman rites, and make them indifferent as to whether they have or have not an Invocation of the Holy Spirit in the post-pridie, i.e. after the Words of Institution. This implies that they took no side in the matter; i.e. they did not insist that the Words of Institution were the Consecration; for had they done so they would like Rome have struck out the Invocation of the Holy Spirit. Nor on the other hand did they insist that it was that Invocation that was consecratory, otherwise they would have had it in every Mass. Their view presumably was still the primitive one, that it is the prayer as a whole and not particular words in it which are consecratory.

5. We observe in the East from the middle of the fourth century, if not earlier, the insistence upon the Eastern view, and the consequent enlargement of the Invocation by additional clauses, making it clear that it is through the Holy Spirit that the Consecration takes place. This we see in Cyril of Jerusalem. It also probably has something to do with the Macedonian controversy which was then current in the East, and has its bearing also upon the Arian controversy. From the end of the fifth century onwards this unfortunate quarrel between East and West goes on with increasing bitterness. Rome apparently persuades Alexandria for a period to come over to its side, for the recently discovered papyrus shows us an Alexandrian service in which the Invocation of the Holy Spirit is retained, but put out of its position to precede the Institution. Alexandria's second thoughts were wiser. They must have seen that this was an entire blunder, both in liturgical structure and in theology, and they returned to take the same line as the whole of the rest of the world, except Rome, i.e. not only the Easterns but the Non-Roman West, replacing their Invocation of the Holy Spirit in its logical and historical position after the Anamnesis.

6. Cranmer, if it was he who made the Canon of 1549, had a mind that was sufficiently anti-Roman to wish to adopt the Invocation, but fundamentally Roman in that he still considered that the Words of Institution were the consecrating force. He therefore made the same half-hearted blunder as Alexandria fell into for a brief space; hence the Invocation of 1549 placed in the wrong position. The Scotch were

wise and learned men when they restored it to its right position in the eighteenth century. It is not worth while considering any proposition to go back to Cranmer's blunder and put in an Invocation in the wrong position. It would upset the whole of the historical order of the Consecration Prayer, and have none but bad precedents behind it.

7. If an Invocation of the Holy Spirit is to be inserted, it is highly desirable that it should not be made an additional bone of contention between East and West, and that the Anglican influence which has hitherto stood out of this controversy should not come in on one side and against the other. We are wise if we take the same line as the non-Roman liturgies, namely, maintain that the whole prayer and not any particular words of it are the Consecration, and therefore retain the power either to have the Invocation or not to have it.

8. In order to adopt this line, which has every primitive justification, and every irenic consideration in its favour now, it is essential that such an Invocation should not be accepted in the sense in which the present Eastern Invocations are accepted. The South African Church is therefore well advised in going back to Western and primitive models rather than to the Eastern models subsequent to the time of Cyril of Jerusalem. I conclude, therefore, its present form of Invocation is right in character, right in position, right in charity, for it does not join in the quarrel between East and West; wise in regard to our own people for it leaves them at liberty to take whatever theory of Consecration they please. If they wish to tie it rigidly down to a form of words, they may do so: but the Church does not encourage this because it places the two side by side, and defers its Amen, which is the official ending of the prayer, till both have been said.

9. This, however, implies that I cannot for the moment defend the present rubric for a Second Consecration. It is that that is really the cause of all the trouble. It is that that enables Darragh to start with the assumption that the liturgy assumes that the Consecration is effected by the Words of Institution. As long as that rubric stands there is no adequate reply possible to Darragh. I hope it will not stand any longer. The liturgy must in all consistency direct that for a Second Consecration the prayer is said, if not in its entirety, at least down to 'heavenly benediction'. I would much prefer that it should be said in its entirety, for it will then emphasize the main point, namely that the wise plan is not to tie the Consecration to particular words of the prayer but to the prayer as a whole.

As to the rest of Darragh's argument, there is nothing in it at all. He seems not to have any knowledge of the recent developments of the last ten years, which have made the whole subject clear. At least I prefer to think this, and not to think that he has the knowledge but has suppressed it. It is unpleasant, however, that he should quote one of the Gelasian passages—the weaker one, and not the stronger one. He can hardly have been aware of one and not the other. His quotations from Fortescue are laughable. There is nothing in Fortescue but what other people have said before. The only original part of Fortescue is his mistakes; and besides that book is out of date, so rapid has been the growth of knowledge in the last ten years.

His statement in Note 16 is contrary to the facts.[1] Both Houses of Canterbury Convocation have agreed to an Invocation in the right place, and the general resolution in that direction was carried at the most representative meeting which has been had, namely the Conference between the two Convocations. The matter is still *sub judice*, and is not likely to be settled for some time, because the Low Church object to any change at all. Darragh in private letters to me talks of the theory of Consecration as one of the things about which there is no controversy between East and West—that we are each agreed to go our own way. This is pure moonshine, I think. The trouble is in fact acute, and all the recent evidence show that Rome is on the wrong side of the matter. He muddles up everything by using the word 'Invocation' in several senses. That is a characteristic thing to do; he is not the inventor of that particular method of obscuring the facts, but he has adopted it. I hope, therefore, the South African bishops will stick to their guns and make their position an unassailable one by altering the rubric about a second consecration. But as long as they have that in its present form the position is an exceedingly vulnerable one. Even when that is amended there will be some fighting, but I think the stronghold will be secure, and the victory will be clearly with the South African liturgy....

Frere to Canon Darragh   9 *July* 1921

My dear Brother,

Thank you for your two letters of 5 January and 18 February, and a copy of your pamphlet and petition. I was away in Canada till after

---

[1] Note 16 in Darragh's Petition read as follows: 'It is significant that, though Fr. Frere is a member of York Convocation and though both Archbishops are Scotsmen, no suggestion to tamper with the Prayer Book method of Consecration, or to conform it to the Scottish model, has been proposed, much less carried in the Convocations of the Mother Church.'

The South African Liturgy (1)

Easter, and on my return I was anxious to go carefully into the whole matter again before replying; so please forgive the delay; I can now at last write something more of a considered opinion.

I confess I read your pamphlet with surprise, and with regret that it does not seem to be awake to the new light which has recently been thrown upon the whole of this subject. It therefore, I think, misrepresents the most important things in the case, and contains a great deal for which I see no justification at all. The general line of argument proceeds upon the assumption, which I think is not true, though I admit that the unfortunate rubric about the Second Consecration gives a certain handle for it; namely the supposition that the liturgy binds you to accept the Roman belief that Consecration is effected simply and solely by the recital of the Words of Institution. The whole liturgy as I read it speaks to the contrary, and even that particular rubric, which I don't for a moment defend, is interpreted by the framers of it as not involving the Roman view.

Your letter seems to speak of an agreement between East and West on this subject. I rub my eyes again and again, and ask where is the agreement. What I know is a quarrel, which we can now trace back to about the middle of the third century, or not much later; a quarrel which has become embittered more and more since. I think the South African Church is much wiser if it declines to take sides in this quarrel as it does, rather than if it throws itself into the Roman scale as your policy seems to suggest. It will certainly throw itself into the wrong side if it does so, though I don't wholly defend the East.

I think it is quite clear now that the early Consecration Prayer contained an Invocation of the Holy Spirit in the only logical and historical position, that is to say after the Anamnesis. Rome got rid of this, and in so doing put itself in the wrong. It gradually persuaded non-Roman liturgies also to withdraw from the Catholic precedent and accordingly disuse or disregard the Invocation of the Holy Spirit at that point which they once had shared with the rest of Christendom. I regret, therefore, that the tendency of your argument seems to be to ask us to take sides in this controversy, rather than to try to heal it; and to take what seems to me the side that is most in the wrong. The Greeks are I think to a certain extent to be blamed for having altered the primitive form of Invocation by adding clauses to it which emphasize their own controversial side. But that again is only another argument why the English Church should mediate between the two instead of taking sides, and it does so by having an Invocation of the Holy Spirit in the place to which it belongs, and in a form which does not run any particular theory of Consecration. The Primitive Church regarded the prayer as consecrating, not any particular words of it. The non-Roman Western Churches must have done the same until Rome caught them in its net; for they were, at any rate in the later days, indifferent as to whether they had an Invocation of the Holy Spirit or not. We are wise, therefore, on all grounds to follow them in the matter, for they have kept closer to the original than anybody. This is not merely a matter of archaeology; it is a matter of ecclesiastical statesmanship of the highest order. If we are to mediate between the quarrelling parts of Christendom, this is one of the points on which we must most of all mediate.

I regret your way of using Invocation to mean several different things. I know people have used 'Invocation' and even 'Epiclesis' when they did not mean the Invocation of the Holy Spirit; but it only seems to me to cast dust in the eyes of people who don't understand. Of course every prayer is *an* invocation.

There are many other things in your pamphlet which seem to me not only misleading but actually wrong. I won't go through it all. The quotations from Fortescue are the opposite of impressive. It is a book of no particular value, with nothing original in it but its mistakes. Besides, it was written before a great part of the modern discoveries, and is therefore quite out of date.

I cannot understand your description of the Scots on page 7.[1] The real Invocation of the Holy Spirit has never been anywhere except after the Anamnesis, except for a short time—so far as we know—in Alexandria which afterwards came to a better mind, and in 1549 where it also did not survive long. The liturgical scholars of the eighteenth century knew quite well what a blunder had been made, and were quite right in rectifying it. To import the Invocation of the Holy Spirit into the midst of the recital of our Lord's life is to throw the whole prayer into confusion. It follows the same line of development as the Creed, and the Invocation of the Holy Spirit comes accordingly after the recital of our Lord's acts and return is concluded. You cannot suddenly insert Pentecost into the middle of Holy Week without making confusion. I am amazed, therefore, at your trying to justify such a proceeding.

Your Note 16 is not the case. The most authoritative meeting of the

---

[1] 'What the men of 1755 did was to take the Epiclesis of the Scottish Liturgy of 1637 from its right place in the Prayer of Consecration and transfer it to an alien position in the Prayer of Oblation.'

Convocation which has ever been held endorsed a proposal to include the Invocation of the Holy Spirit in the reform of the Canon. The prospects of getting that done were not very immediate because the Low Church people oppose any change. Your end of additional Note A also surprises me.[1] Why do you omit the more direct and illuminating passage of Gelasius? Why did you not explain that St. Isidore deals with the matter in his description of the post-pridie prayer, indicating that he only knew of the Invocation as being in that position? I just give these as specimens of what seems to me serious blots upon your argument of a detailed kind. My main objection to the argument is of a much more fundamental nature, for it seems to me to rest upon wrong presuppositions, and to tend to war and not to peace or progress. It is too late in the day nowadays to say that Rome must be right, especially in such a matter as this, and after the revelations which have come to us on this matter in the last ten years.

Forgive me for writing in this brusque manner. I do it for brevity's sake, not because I want to be quarrelsome or overbearing. . . .

Canon Darragh, however, remained unconvinced.

Canon Darragh to Frere 8 *August* 1921

My dear Father Frere,

Thank you very much for your letter. It is very good of you at a time when you must have been overwhelmed with business on your return from your Canadian visit to have written so fully. I wish I could say that I find your forcibly expressed opinions convincing. But I cannot honestly say I do. Will you permit me to deal in order with what you write?

---

[1] 'Gelasius I (492–496) ascribes the sanctification of the Eucharist to the agency of the Holy Spirit: *In hanc, silicet, in divinam transeunt spiritu sancto perficiente substantiam, permanente tamen in sua proprietate natura* (*Thiel. Ep. Rom. Pont.* i. 542): but he gives no indication as to whether the agency of the Holy Spirit was expressed verbally in the Office used; or, if expressed, in what words or in what position with regard to the Narrative of Institution the words stood. Nor are these points indicated in Optatus (writing about 370) nor in St. Isidore (646), who both speak of the Holy Spirit as the agent in the Consecration of the Eucharist. There may have been verbal mention of the operation of the Holy Spirit in the Liturgies used by these holy men, but there is no evidence as to the wording, if there was wording, nor of its position in the service. No existing Liturgy contains a direct address to the Holy Spirit, praying him to effect the Consecration. The Prayer is invariably addressed to the Father, asking him to send the Holy Spirit for that purpose.'

In the first place, it is probably owing to my clumsy and too condensed method of writing that I seem to have given you the impression that we commit ourselves to the 'Roman belief that Consecration is effected simply and solely by the recital of the Words of Institution'. I do not feel called on to discuss the question whether that is a correct description of Roman belief. It is not a correct description of the practice of the Book of Common Prayer, to which alone we in South Africa owe allegiance by our Constitution. Consecration is effected there by a composite prayer, which ends with the Words of Institution, following on an Anamnesis and an Invocation. I deprecate the tendency to be so over-curious as to tie down the moment of Consecration to any particular words of the Consecration Prayer. I believe that God hears the prayer of the Church, and that is enough.

Again it must have been my faulty phrasing which led you to infer that I maintain there is 'an agreement between East and West on this subject'. Surely it is so far common knowledge that they differ in their method. What I do maintain is that both methods existed in the undivided Church and that prior to the Great Schism there is not a word in any extant author which reflects on the validity of either method. In all the controversies at the time of the Schism, no question is raised on either side of the validity of the other's method of Consecration. And in the divided Catholic Church of today the English and the Roman portions alike do not question the validity of the Eastern Eucharist. The Roman, for example, allows both methods within her jurisdiction, with this provision, that priests and congregations must stick to one or the other, and this not on theological but on psychological grounds. Nor is there any synodical act of the Eastern Church which questions the validity of the Western Eucharist on the ground of its method of Consecration. Both Eucharist and Baptism are conferred differently in East and West—indeed all the sacraments. The East claims that her method is better than that of the West—that of Baptism in particular, but the real question at issue is not methods so much as authority. I have been in correspondence with the Phanar regarding my Baptisms of Greek children and no difficulty was raised as to their acceptance by the Orthodox authorities κατ' οἰκονομίαν. This was before a Greek priest was sent to Johannesburg on my urgent request. Joachim III sent an autograph rescript of thanks for what I had done for Orthodox residents. I have been in close touch with the Orthodox authorities and have discussed these questions over and over again with Greek priests and educated laymen. The Greek archimandrite at Johannesburg kept the Reserved Sacrament in the Tabernacle on the High Altar of St. Mary's of which we both had keys. He called me to be present when he took out the sacrament for private communions and invited me to be within the Iconostasis when he said Mass. So I can honestly claim to know a good deal about Orthodox ways and feelings, and not alone from books; though I have been a close student of the best that has been written in English and in Greek for the last fifty years on the subject of Irenics.

Then as to 'my asking us to take sides in this controversy' I respectfully demur to that charge. It is not a question of taking sides. The English Church has taken the Western side all through her history, as is only natural from her origin and her geographical position. And we of the South African Church are pledged by our Constitution to the standards of Faith and Worship of the English Church. Thus, so far as the following of different methods of Consecration can be called a 'controversy' we have already taken our side. You speak of both the English and Eastern Churches as being in the wrong in this controversy. I should prefer to describe it as both being in the right, for both act as they acted in this matter whilst the Church was undivided. Twofold action which existed without controversy and without rebuke in the undivided Church can fairly, I think, be considered to have Catholic consent in the absence of unquestioned Scripture authority.

It is common ground, is it not, that the exact method of the first Consecration is unrecorded. It is left, therefore, to the Church to determine. If for centuries she permitted both methods, is it not clear that no one of these methods can claim to supersede the other? The important thing is not so much this method or that, as that the Church's intention to consecrate should be undoubted and should be declared by word and act. If the Church when reunited were to be guided by the Holy Ghost to readjust these consensual methods, that would be another matter. But for a Province like this to depart from her Mother Church and adopt a novel method, which is neither Eastern nor Western, would be a monstrous act of presumption. You will say perhaps that it would not be novel, but a revival of a primitive form anterior to those of both East and West. I know that some scholars think they can reconstruct a form of that sort, but it is so problematical that no tiny fragment of the English Church would be justified in acting on it. We are on comparatively firm ground, as far as extant documents are concerned, when we come to the fourth century, and can reasonably infer that what the Church accepted then was the natural development of her practice in earlier times. But there is no sufficient extant evidence to prove by itself what was the Apostolic and sub-Apostolic practice. I venture to say that positively, though I know every scrap of extant evidence including all that has been unearthed during the 'last ten years'.

On the negative side, there is a high degree of improbability that the Holy Spirit was mentioned in Apostolic or sub-Apostolic times as the agent of the Father in the Consecration. He is nowhere brought into connexion with the Eucharist in the Apostolic writings, and as late as Irenaeus he is not generally set forth even as the agent of the Incarnation itself. The working out of the doctrine of the Holy Spirit is a later development, as we have learnt from Dr. Swete, and more recently in Dr. J. Armitage Robinson's preface to his translation of the *Demonstration of Apostolic Preaching*. It is much more probable that the explicit mention of the Holy Spirit in connexion with the Consecration arose when the doctrine of the Pneuma was more developed than it was in the times of Justin or Irenaeus.

You speak positively when you say that 'the Primitive Church regarded the Prayer of Consecration as consecrating, not any particular words of it'. That may be true for all we know, but where is there any explicit statement to that effect in any Primitive writer? And where is there any explicit statement that any of the 'non-Roman Western Churches' did the same? Ambrose was non-Roman, and yet we find him connecting the Consecration with the Words of Institution. Earlier still Tertullian was non-Roman, and yet he connects our Lord's own Consecration with *Hoc est corpum meum*.

You 'regret (my) way of using Invocation to mean several different things'. I thought I had taken special pains to explain myself, but evidently I have once more failed and for this I am sorry. I called attention to the often forgotten fact that in the most developed Epiclesis τοῦ πνεύματος it is the Father who is directly invoked to effect the Consecration. Nowhere is the Holy Spirit by himself invoked to fulfil that function. You refer in your edition of Proctor to some such instance, but I think that must have been a slip. Everywhere it is the Father who is the prime agent in the Consecration. This was emphasized in defence of the 'Hear us, O Merciful Father' as a true effective Invocation, even though there is no explicit mention of the Holy Spirit. Of course, I do not forget Serapion's direct appeal for the descent of the Logos on the elements, but this is not an Invocation to the Father or of the Father to send the Spirit to consecrate.

The South African Liturgy (1)   225

You find 'the quotations' from Fortescue the opposite of impressive and express a low opinion of the book. I am not concerned to enter into that, beyond assuring you that the extensive use of Fortescue was for purely topical reasons. The local apologists for the 'Alternative Form' kept on saying: 'Oh, you have only to read Fortescue and you will be convinced that it is all right!' Hence the large use of Fortescue. The facts quoted from him could quite easily have been proved by other references. In a similar way Dr. Gummey's book has been appealed to as clinching the matter. It was not felt necessary to go into that. The really useful appendix to that volume, though not quite up to date, contains a sufficient antidote to the text. Dr. Gummey's pamphlet on the Eucharist and Seabury's prefatory letter to the book itself show them to be pure virtualists, i.e. holders of the banknote theory of the Presence. But believers in the Catholic doctrine of the Real Presence cannot accept as final the judgement of men, who do not believe in it, on questions of the Consecration.

'The real Invocation of the Holy Spirit has never been anywhere except after the Anamnesis.' You give one ancient exception to this dictum and might have added certain Mozarabic and allied Masses. But you leave out of account that the explicit Invocation in 1549 as well as the implicit Invocation of our present Prayer Book do follow the Anamnesis in the Prayer of Consecration. True, the Pauline usage is followed, and the Death of Christ is taken to include the Resurrection and Ascension which followed and without which the Death could not have been the atoning Death that is commemorated—'Ye do shew the Lord's Death till he come'. The Prayer Book's compendious use of the Lord's 'Death' to include all that made it what it is—a usage derived from St. Paul—neutralizes your complaint that the Credal sequence is violated by the mentioning of the Holy Spirit at this point. There is no need, therefore, to add that no ancient liturgical writer, Greek or Latin, parallels the order of the members of the Eucharistic Service with the sequential order of the Articles of the Creed.

'Your Note 16 is not the case.' It was the case at the time the note was written. I am well aware that afterwards a sort of mention of the Holy Spirit was added to the Prayer of Consecration, and the restoration of the tradition of Overall and other Fathers was withdrawn. Whether this lame and feeble compromise will be finally accepted by the Home Church remains to be seen. But of course if the 'Considerations' were to be printed anew, Note 16 would be brought up to date. Your surprise at 'the end of Note A' surely shows that you are criticizing a brief pamphlet as if it were a volume. There was nothing material omitted for the purpose of misleading the reader, but there is such a thing as space limit.

I am afraid, dear Father, you will think that I have forgotten that very thing. I have written at perhaps wearisome length. But it would not be polite to you to leave your important letter without some attempt at noticing its chief points.

If you will do me the honour of reading *The Resurrection of the Flesh*, which S.P.C.K. publishes immediately, and in recognition of which my University has conferred the D.D. on me, you will see, I think, that I am a diligent student of Christian origins. I may add that I know as well as you do yourself every scrap of 'fresh light' that has been thrown on liturgical problems in these recent years, and yet cannot accept some of your interpretations. . . .

Here the correspondence ends. It is interesting, however, to compare the Alternative Form of 1919 with the final Form as set forth by authority in 1929. There were few changes, but nearly all of them were in line with suggestions made by Frere, either in his 'Rough Notes' or in his article in the *Church Quarterly Review*.

1. The Ten Commandments were set out in shortened form.
2. 'Holy' was restored to the Creed—'One Holy, Catholic, and Apostolic Church'.
3. 'Impartially' was substituted for 'Faithfully' in the Prayer for the Church Militant—'impartially minister justice'.
4. 'These sacred gifts and creatures of thine own' was omitted from the Prayer of Oblation—'We offer here unto thy divine majesty this holy Bread of eternal life and this Cup of everlasting salvation'.
5. The Epiclesis is retained, but in a shortened and more general form, by the omission of the words, 'That he may hallow this oblation', thus: 'We humbly beseech thee to pour thy Holy Spirit upon us and upon these thy gifts, that all we who are partakers of this holy Communion.'
6. The words 'this our sacrifice of praise and thanksgiving' were restored.
7. 'And now' in the introductory sentence to the Lord's Prayer was omitted—'As our Saviour Jesus Christ'.
8. The last petition in the Lord's Prayer was no longer connected to the Prayer of Humble Access.
9. For a Second Consecration the Prayer of Consecration was to be recited from 'Hear us' down to 'heavenly benediction'.
10. Provision was made for Post-communion collects.

Indeed, the only points where Frere was not followed wholly or in part were:
1. The opening Lord's Prayer, which he had criticized in his *C.Q.R.* article, was retained.
2. The Preface and Sanctus were not revised.
3. In the Prayer of Oblation his suggestion, 'these sacred gifts and creatures of thine own', was omitted.
4. The connexion between the Lord's Prayer and the Prayer of Humble Access was not retained.

THE SOUTH AFRICAN LITURGY (2)

The Bishop of Pretoria, Dr. Neville Talbot, to Frere   29 *April* 1932

Dear Brother Walter,

    I had no sooner written the enclosed to Dr. Brightman and sent it off than I heard that he had departed this life. R.I.P.

    I don't know whether you can read the rather faint carbon. The point is the right translation of 'particeps humanitatis' and 'consortes divinitatis'; and this for the Collect for the 2nd Sunday after Christmas. I am keen on 'Who partook of our humanity, that we might be made partakers of his divinity'.

    But the rest of the P.B. Revising Committee had demurrers, and so I undertook to write to Brightman. And now I ask your verdict. . . .
I wonder how you are. I hope we may meet in Heaven.

                                       Ever affectionately,
                                               Neville Pretor.

The letter to Dr. Brightman.

                                                     15 *April* 1932

Dear Dr. Brightman,

    How long it is since we have met; and I have an idea that in my Balliol time my boisterousness was an affliction to you! Forgive me, even now.

    I have just come away from our Episcopal Liturgical Committee consisting of six bishops, meeting this time at Bloemfontein. You know, I am sure, that the Church of the Province has its own Liturgy (which we long to improve in some quite small respects, but the process of getting things through Provincial Synod is cumbrous and delicate, and the raising of small issues might open the door to Protestant raising of big ones); and I expect you know that we have our Occasional Offices (S.P.C.K.), though they haven't received final sanction. Now we are going on to Collects, Epistles, and Gospels and have been working at them last week. We are decidedly a committee of General Practitioners rather than Liturgical Experts; but we have much to help us and at least your monumental 'English Rite' and all the other 'books'—1928, E.C.U., Scottish, Grey (we find that except in occasional suggestions little to our taste), Alcuin, &c. &c.

    We crave your advice on one point—a point raised in your *Church Quarterly* article, wherein you examined the 1927 Book. It has to do with the Collect for the 2nd Sunday after Christmas and the parallelism between 'particeps humanitatis' and 'consortes divinitatis'. It was suggested that we should translate 'As thy Son our Lord Jesus Christ partook of our humanity, so we may be made partakers of his divinity'. Some (not I included) thought this too bold in the latter half and I was asked to get your advice. I feel the suggested translation is quite right. If you condemn it, have you a suggestion or suggestions?...

With every good remembrance,
Yours sincerely in Christ,
Neville Pretor.

PS. Somebody said 'Brightman never answers letters', but I don't believe it.

Frere to the Bishop of Pretoria   28 *June* 1932

My dear Neville,

I have at last got down to your letter on the subject of a Christmas collect. I wonder what your discussion was about? I should have thought it would have been wise to keep closely to the wording in our English translation. That would justify what may easily seem to be otherwise a too bold expression. Personally I don't like words like 'divinity' and 'humanity', which are really not English and are too slippery for liturgical worship in any case, as we pronounce them now: so I like to keep 'nature' probably in both cases. But perhaps it isn't so much a question of that as of the dogmatic significance of the translation that you have been thinking. I don't remember what Brightman said about this particular thing in his *Church Quarterly* article; so I am afraid I haven't heard his view and indeed I don't remember what was in it; it was probably as learned and as perverse as usual.

How delightful and how naughty the dear man was when it came to practical things. Clearly everybody was wrong and on the whole probably nothing had better be done. That was generally the opinion, I think, and the general formula of his criticism....

Frere's view ultimately prevailed, for the present Collect in the South African Liturgy is the same as that in the 1928 Prayer Book.

THE LITURGY IN NORTHERN RHODESIA

Frere was largely responsible for a projected Diocesan Liturgy for Northern Rhodesia, which was prepared for submission to the Liturgical Committee of the Lambeth Conference in 1922. The suggested outline was as follows.

Mass of the Cathechumens

1. The Preparation.
   (Confession, Absolution, and Lord's Prayer omitted: ends with Prayer Book Collect for Purity.)
2. Introit.
   (Ten Commandments or Kyries.)
3. Proper Collect, Epistle, and Gospel.
4. Dismissal of the Catechumens.

Mass of the Faithful

5. The Creed (inserting 'Holy' before 'Catholic and Apostolic Church').
6. The Offertory.
7. The Prayer for the Church. (A revised form.)
8. Confession and Absolution. (Short forms with very short Invitation.)
9. Comfortable Words.
10. Sursum Corda. Preface and Benedictus.
    ('O Holy Lord, Almighty Father, Everlasting God.'
    'Hosanna' instead of the paraphrase 'Glory be to Thee, O Lord most high.')
11. Prayer of Consecration, including Anamnesis, Epiclesis, and Oblation.
12. Lord's Prayer. The Pax.
13. Prayer of Humble Access (shortened form).
14. Agnus Dei.
15. The Communion.
16. Ablutions?
17. The Prayer of Thanksgiving (shortened form).
18. Gloria.
19. Blessing.
20. Ablutions?

The Liturgy in Northern Rhodesia

The Bishop of N. Rhodesia, Dr. A. May, to Frere 22 *August* 1922

Dear Fr. Frere,

I am enclosing with this two copies of our projected Diocesan Liturgy, which we have now revised in view of the criticisms and suggestions you made to Harold Leeke; and I hope you will not think we are trespassing quite unwarrantably on your kindness if we ask you to help us with it yet again.

The situation is this. Before submitting it to the Liturgical Committee of the Lambeth Conference, we should very much like your judgement on a few outstanding questions. But we are anxious to get it through without unnecessary delay; and as we are all prepared to accept your decision on these points as final, I undertook to ask you to be so kind as to do two things: (1) to settle these points and make necessary changes in the draft, and then (2) to submit it on my behalf to the Liturgical Committee without sending it back here.

The questions we want to submit to you are these:

1. *The position of the Prayer of Humble Access.* Leeke's note of your view on this point is: 'The Prayer of Humble Access to follow immediately on the Comfortable Words', and I think there was something to the same effect in some notes of yours on the S.A. Liturgy which Barnes[1] has got. Some of us, however, feel that the prayer loses point by being said so early on in the Service, and that for the sake of our very simple folk it would be good to have some common act of devotion immediately before the Communion of the people, to be said after the Commixture and before the Agnus Dei, if this were permissible. In the existing draft we put the prayer in this place 'without prejudice'. Will you please put it back after the Comfortable Words, if you think that its present position is liturgically unsound or otherwise seriously undesirable?

2. *Proper Prefaces.* Would you recommend the provision of a Proper Preface for the Feast of the Transfiguration, as in the S.A. Liturgy? If so, please make a note to that effect.

3. *Gloria in Excelsis.* We have retained the P.B. version as it stands, not because we imagine it to be correct, but because there seems to be so much uncertainty as to what the correct form is; and we thought that perhaps the simplest plan was to make no change until the experts have made up their minds about it. Shall we do this, or are there certain

[1] The Revd. Fr. Bertram Barnes, C.R.

changes that ought to be made? If there are, will you please indicate these in the drafts?

4. *The Place of the Ablutions.* Leeke's note of your view is as follows: 'Keep the Ablutions till the end. The Roman method may be right for them, as their Mass ends with Communion; but the Anglican has the Thanksgiving, Gloria in Excelsis, and Blessing afterwards, all of which would be out of place if the Ablutions were taken before. The old Latin rule said, *Defer, ne sit altare sine sacrificio*'. The argument seems to me conclusive, and personally (in the case of the English Liturgy) I have always disliked the 'catholic' practice of departing from what appears to be the clear direction of the P.B. In the course of our discussions, however, a practical consideration was urged which seemed to me possibly to justify the adoption of the Roman use in this country, even though it conflicts with the structure of our Liturgy. Natives being what they are, the chalice is sometimes in a somewhat unpleasant condition when it is returned to the celebrant after the people have communicated. If the Ablutions are taken at the end of the Service, the priest must first (on receiving the chalice) cleanse the lip and the outside of it with his lips, and then subsequently consume what remains of the consecrated wine—neither of which operations is always altogether pleasant. Whereas if the Ablutions are taken immediately after the Communion of the people, there is only one operation, facilitated by the fact that what remains of the unconsecrated wine is consumed at the same time, and water is used in addition. Do you think that this consideration justifies out here the inconsistency of taking the Ablutions immediately after the Communion of the people? If so, will you add a note to the Liturgy either directing that they be taken at this point or permitting it as an alternative use?

5. Arising out of this, we should be glad to have your judgement (and that of the Liturgical Committee, if you should think fit to ask for it) on the question of communicating by intinction. I am bound to say that I think there is a great deal to be said for it in a country like this, where the condition of the chalice is liable to become not only offensive but actually dangerous. As you know, venereal disease is very common, especially in some districts, and it is not at all infrequent for the lips to be affected. Communicant Christians are just as likely as anyone else to be suffering from disease, and it would never occur to them to refrain from communicating on that account. With some diffidence I made the suggestion of the permissive use of intinction (as a general practice, not merely in individual cases) when we last met at

Chipili, and was somewhat surprised to find that it was more than favourably received by all the brethren. If we might have some guidance in the matter, we should be extremely grateful. The question, however, does not affect the actual Liturgy. It would be a matter for episcopal direction. . . .

If any members of the Liturgical Committee should be worried about the phrasing, rhythm, &c., of the Liturgy, will you point out that it is not intended for use in English, and that therefore we have not been at any pains to produce a polished composition? Perhaps I should add in this connexion that in translating it into our various languages we do not propose to adhere at all strictly to the English version, but to aim at an idiomatic native rendering as far as possible. There are obvious dangers in this course, but I am sure it is right, and we can only do our best to secure that the sense of the original is preserved. . . .

In due course Frere reported to the Secretary of the Liturgical Committee of the Lambeth Conference.

Frere to the Revd. C. Jenkins   12 *December* 1922

My dear Jenkins,

Here is a copy of the Liturgy of Northern Rhodesia—a copy in full and an outline. I am sending it exactly as they have drawn it up themselves. The Bishop asked me to decide on four points before sending it in: (1) as to the position of the Prayer of Humble Access; (2) as to a Proper Preface for the Feast of the Transfiguration; (3) as to the version of the Gloria in Excelsis; (4) as to the place of the Ablutions. They also ask for the judgement of the Liturgical Committee on the question of communicating by intinction, in favour of which they see many practical reasons.

There was in any case no reason to alter No. 2 or No. 3. The Prayer of Humble Access is a thing which we shall have to discuss, but personally I rather think I prefer it at the earlier place, but I did not feel strongly enough about it to alter what they had done. And the fourth point, the place of the Ablutions, is with them a practical question, for they would naturally be satisfied with their position at the end, as they are in the English Service; but they know on the other side that in communicating natives a somewhat elaborate and almost immediate cleansing of the chalice is necessary also almost as soon as the Communion is finished; and it is better that it should be done immediately after Communion and finally done at the later stage. Their draft does not settle the point, but leaves it open, and again they send it to me, for I should like to discuss the matter before coming to any conclusion.

In general in regard to our action I am very glad to hear that a memorandum on intinction is being got ready. It is the sort of question that may be settled in its broad outlines once for all, though personally I hope not in an adverse sense. I think we should also settle the question as to whether we can or can not approve an Invocation in the position of that of 1549. Thirdly we also want to come to a conclusion as to the place of the Ablutions and in connexion with this as to the Gloria in Excelsis. These are points which will come up over and over again. We had better get to a clear mind about it if we can, and most of it might be done by circulating correspondence and memoranda rather than by meeting. . . .

At the same time Frere wrote to the Bishop of Northern Rhodesia urging the advantages of liturgical construction on a wider than diocesan basis.

Frere to the Bishop of N. Rhodesia   12 December 1922

My dear Brother,

I was away abroad when your letter and the copies of the Liturgy came. I was only able when I got back a short time ago really to go into it and now I have had the opportunity of consulting with Claude Jenkins, who is the Secretary of the Committee, and have sent in the Liturgy to him as you desire.

I have not felt strongly enough about any of the four points which you left me to settle to feel justified in altering what you have done, therefore I have sent him the draft exactly as you sent it.

Some of the points seem to me to need further discussion, and I hope the Committee will secure that. No doubt the discussions in the Assembly upon our English alterations in the Liturgy will help to bring the points out, and to make the position of the Liturgical Committee as advisors more clear.

Have you had any conference with the Nyasa diocese? It seems to me privately a pity that the three Central African dioceses and the South African province cannot work in harmony in the matter. I quite think it is well that in the present uncertainty individual dioceses should not be discouraged from acting on their own. But it is easy for them to do that if they say, 'This is our private contribution to a result which we are trying to reach in conference with others as circumstances permit it.' The South African province have not, I think consulted the Committee, and probably won't do so; there is no particular reason why they should. You and Nyasaland both consulted the Committee; I am not quite sure whether Zanzibar has; though personally I have had dealings with the Committee about it.

Most of the important questions are, of course, common ground to all three of you. I quite see that it is possible that your lines of discussion may converge in England rather than in Africa. That is to say a Liturgical Committee in England may be the easiest way for all three or four parties including South Africa. Anyhow as I look at it this end I think what the Liturgical Committee can best do is to try and make up its mind on some of these points which concern you all, and then submit the reason for their conclusions to you. That is what I hope we shall try and do now that we have definite material to work upon and definite questions raised. . . .

The Bishop of N. Rhodesia to Frere　　　　　　St. Matthias' Day 1923

Dear Father Frere,

Many thanks for your letter of 12 December. . . .

I entirely agree with all you say as to the desirability of concerted action in such a matter as liturgical revision in the three dioceses of the U.M.C.A. In fact one has always had it in mind, but with our very scanty opportunities for discussion it is very difficult to achieve. However, one result of your letter has been that I have now written to Zanzibar and Nyasaland, and (quoting you) have suggested that we should meet together and with the Zanzibar Liturgy and the Nyasaland drafts before us, together with the Liturgical Committee's comments and recommendations, try (possibly with your help if you could spare the time) to agree upon a U.M.C.A. Liturgy which we could recommend to our several dioceses.

I have no very great hope that the proposal will lead to anything, if only because, though both Zanzibar and Nyasaland are intending to be in England this year, Zanzibar will probably have left before Nyasaland arrives. However, it seemed worth while to make the suggestion.

We have not conferred with the Nyasaland diocese up to now, though they have seen our draft and we theirs. Our original draft was already completed before we knew they were moving in the matter, and it seemed impossible at the time to arrange for any discussion of the points of difference. It has been a tedious business arriving at unanimity amongst ourselves in this diocese, owing to the fact that we cannot meet and all the negotiations between the different stations have had to be carried on by correspondence. If we had complicated matters by trying to work in with Nyasaland at the same time, I think the results would have been fatal! But your letter is most opportune because it seems to me that this is the precise moment at which, as you suggest, our lines of discussion might well converge. I do not know to what extent the Zanzibar diocese is wedded to its Liturgy, which of course has now been in use for some years; but if they could be induced to join us in an effort to achieve a U.M.C.A. Liturgy, I can hardly believe that the thing could not be done.

As to the possibility of joining forces with South Africa I am far more doubtful. Excellent as it is, their Liturgy is obviously intended for Europeans, and in some respects they seem to me to have been hampered in their revision by the necessity of dealing tenderly with prejudices and prepossessions which we need not consider. . . .

Unfortunately these schemes remained at a standstill for some years. As the next letter shows, the efforts at Prayer Book revision in England were a dominant factor in the delay.

The Bishop of N. Rhodesia to Frere   9 *October* 1928

My dear Bishop,

You will remember our diocesan Liturgy for which we are almost entirely indebted to you. You will remember, too, that some years ago I sent a typed copy of it home for submission to the Liturgical Committee of the Lambeth Conference, and that they postponed consideration of it (and presumably of other liturgies) until such time as the revised Prayer Book should have assumed its final form. As we could not wait indefinitely, we decided to render the Liturgy into our various languages and take it into provisional use; with the result that it has now been tested for several years and met with general approval. And hitherto we have not suffered much from having to wait all this time for an expression of opinion from the Lambeth Committee, beyond the inconvenience of being without printed copies except in one language.

Now, however, we are in a difficulty. For some time before he left us, Fr. Barnes was occupied in making a new Chibemba translation of the Collects, Epistles, and Gospels, which he has now completed. Our hope was that S.P.C.K. would publish them for us together with the Liturgy: and the Society had undertaken to do this, subject to the approval of the Archbishop. But I now learn that the Archbishop, while he has 'nothing but approval' for the Collects, Epistles, and Gospels, 'feels that he cannot sanction the publication by S.P.C.K. of a diocesan liturgy not approved by the Consultative Committee of the Lambeth Conference'.

Of course this is only right and reasonable: but it is most unfortunate, because the Collects, Epistles, and Gospels would be of little use to our people without the Liturgy; and it is peculiarly tantalizing, because it is hard to imagine that the latter can be open to objection, as it is very much on the lines of the revised Liturgy accepted by Convocation and has, I believe, your full approval.

It occurs to me that you might perhaps be willing to suggest to the Liturgical Committee that as there is now no immediate prospect of a revised Prayer Book, it is no use waiting for it any longer; in which case it might be possible to obtain their approval of our Liturgy in time for it to be published by S.P.C.K. along with the Collects, Epistles, and Gospels. Or failing this, that a word from you to the effect that you know the Liturgy and are prepared to stand sponsor for it might induce the Archbishop to consent to its publication by S.P.C.K.

I need not say that if you can help us in the matter I shall be extremely grateful. I should add that some slight alterations have been made in the Liturgy since I submitted it to the Liturgical Committee. But these changes are only in matters of detail and arrangement, and in no way affect its tone and character. However, Harold Leeke will be reaching England by the same boat as this letter, and if you should wish to re-assure yourself on this point, he could tell you exactly what the changes are. . . .

Fr. Barnes also wrote to Frere on the same subject, but revealed that the 'slight alterations' in the Liturgy were not quite so unimportant as the Bishop had suggested. At the same time he gave some interesting information about the problem of dialects.

Fr. Bertram Barnes C.R. to Frere   20 October 1928

My dear Walter,

    A hitch has occurred over the Bemba Prayer Book at which I have been so long at work. My job has been to translate (i.e. revise existing translation of) Collects, Epistles, and Gospels, and my manuscript, after waiting for a month or two, went off last week. But, of course, we want these printed and bound up with the rest and it seems that S.P.C.K. are unable to do so because the Liturgy hasn't received the authorization of the Archbishop's Liturgical Committee. The main part of it was all referred to the Committee in 1922 and we had a lot of criticism and help from you. The Bishop's impression is that we acted on your advice on every point of importance and he assumed that this amounted to authorization. Meanwhile—and he seems to have forgotten this—several alterations were made by the first Synod of N. Rhodesia at Broken Hill last year, and one at least of these was clean contrary to your known views. They shifted the Gloria from its English place to the beginning. This was desired and done by people who think it is right because it is Roman, but in point of fact there is more justification for it than that. Where Catechumens are actually dismissed before the Creed, a Mass without Sermon after the Gospel does become rather skimpy for them, and the occasional use of the Gloria in the first part does enrich the service and give it a colour which Catechumens would otherwise miss. I should have opposed the alteration probably by vote as well as speech but I was unable to be present. I didn't find the change in practice so intolerable as I had felt it to be in anticipation.

    The other change was as follows:

> 1922. Short Confession and Absolution. Comfortable Words 1–2–3–4.
>
> 1927. Comfortable Words 2–1. Short Confession and Absolution.

Also our Mass as printed begins with the Asperges for use on Sundays. No other changes have been made from the Liturgy as it was submitted to you in 1922.

    My manuscript has gone on and they are going on with that anyway. The Bishop hopes the Liturgy may be passed in time to join up with the rest before binding. I think I had better send you the corrected copy of the Liturgy as I had it prepared for the printers. If you can get it sanctioned, this copy will serve still if you will be so kind as to send it on to them. We are to use the orthography of the International Institute according to my selection from their recommendations. A very useful bit of work their pamphlet is and I wish it could solve all our problems of orthography. Our dialects contain four or five sounds not yet dealt with by the International Institute, and the case is further complicated by the fact that the various dialects have been reduced to writing by missionaries of at least four nationalities—Dutch, German, English, and American. I'm Chairman of a Committee of three—Dutch R.Ch., English Jesuit, and me a very English Anglican, appointed by the Government to investigate the possibilities of unifying orthography and dialects. My solution, if I can get the others to agree, is to unite orthography as completely as possible, even though different districts go on pronouncing the selected symbols in their own local way; and not to attempt to unify vocabularies, but to pool the lot in a comprehensive 'Shora' Dictionary which I should love to compile. So all dialects would be well represented in the Dictionary, and each district could make its own selection of words for its own local productions; and best of all, each could get familiar with the corresponding words in the other dialects. Gradually some differentiation of senses would probably take place and ultimately a Shora language might evolve, richer than any single dialect, and understandable by all.

If this is the line decided on I should hope to be allowed to concentrate on producing the Dictionary and to make a desperate effort to do it before I go on furlough in 1930. Then I could see it through the press during my furlough and come back waving it in the air as my banner. It is a job I should enjoy immensely. I haven't had such a one since 1900 when I produced a Nyanja vocabulary which is only being revised this year. The new job would be more difficult because of the variety of dialects to be comprehended and the amount of literature in existence in these dialects.

If the Archbishop's Committee jib at the place of the Gloria, do get the Missa printed with the Gloria in its old place. I'm sure N. Rhodesia would rather have that than have the Liturgy left out.

I hope Anglo-Catholics are going to support loyally the policy indicated by the Bishops in regard to the Prayer Book. I think it is a very quiet and dignified snub to Jix and Co. to give out that the Bishops will not regard as illegal anything allowed by the 1928 Book. I wish they'd gone back as far as 1927. We do live in interesting times. I've just been reading your *English Church History* under 'Eliza and our James' and really our days if less perilous are just as interesting....

When Fr. Leeke heard of Fr. Barnes's suggestion that the Liturgy should be printed, even if it involved having the Gloria in its old place, he immediately wrote to Frere in protest.

The Revd. C. H. Leeke, O.G.S., to Frere   20 November 1928

My dear Lord Bishop,

Father Barnes has just written to me to tell me that he has sent you various documents and suggestions relating to our Liturgy. He tells me that he has made a suggestion with regard to the position of the 'Gloria in Excelsis'.

I think it right to tell you at once that the position of the Gloria *cannot* be altered, as the Gloria has been put in its present position by the Bishop in Synod.

Our Bishop has, I believe, written to you about the Liturgy, and if there are any questions which I can answer I shall be only too ready to do so. . . .

Subsequent events indicate that Fr. Barnes's suggestion was not followed. Indeed much deeper issues were involved. On the following day Frere wrote to the Bishop of N. Rhodesia asking for answers to two questions, one of which he had raised in 1922: was it desirable and necessary to have so many diocesan uses? and what was to be done about English congregations?

Frere to the Bishop of N. Rhodesia   21 November 1928

My dear Bishop,

Thank you for your letter about the Liturgy. I have since also had one from Father Barnes with a copy of the latest form of it. I have approached the Secretary of the Archbishop's Liturgical Committee and I am going to try and circulate copies of the English outline for their consideration. This I hope will enable the subject to go forward with a view to securing what you want, namely, the issue of the Liturgy with the Collects, Epistles, and Gospels. I expect there are some preliminary questions which will want answering before the Liturgical Committee comes to its final conclusion. The first is a doubt as to whether it is advisable that there should be so many liturgies in use. The practical question arises, what is the relation of your Liturgy to the others of the U.M.C.A., and why is there not one in common between them? Some of the members of the Committee are very loath to multiply diocesan uses; especially in homogeneous or at least similar dioceses. The second question is, what is the relation of this to services in English? The Committee would I understand be far more ready to accept a native liturgy if they could be assured that it would not be used for English-speaking congregations. They do *not* want to multiply the difficulties for the Englishman; they *do* want to meet as far as possible in any way that concerns them the needs of particular native congregations; you will see the difficulty. I am writing then at once to you to tell you about these two questions, which have been raised informally. I think an answer to each of them would probably facilitate proceedings with the Liturgical Committee. I am trying to get the matter before their consideration, so it will help if we have some answer from you about those two points, I expect. I am sending them therefore in advance without waiting for a gathering of the Committee or any elaborate correspondence between its members. . . .

He also wrote to Father Barnes on similar lines.

Frere to Fr. Barnes, C.R.   *22 November 1928*

My dear Bertram,

    Thank you for your letter and all its contents. . . . I have tried to see how I could get a clear enough view from these various documents to send to the Liturgical Committee, but I found it difficult to work them all together, ignorant of the situation and the tongue. Latterly, however, I heard from Leeke and I am sending your documents to him asking him to prepare for the Committee an outline of the Liturgy which they will be able to understand. I will then get that typed out here and the Secretary will distribute it to the Committee: in that way I hope it will get on.

    I have also written to the Bishop of Northern Rhodesia on the subject and I have put to him two questions which were put to me, quite unofficially, from someone important there, as questions which I expect will be in the mind of the Committee. Therefore it may be well to have an answer from the Bishop ready.

1. Why have so many diocesan uses? Why at least can't one use prevail through the U.M.C.A. dioceses?
2. What is to be done about English congregations? Is an English translation of this to be used if it is printed?

The Committee is likely to say as regards native congregations, 'We should, of course, take strictly to account merely what they needed, and if the book is to be used in English congregations our standard and view would necessarily be different.' You see the point of these two questions; I hope we shall get a satisfactory answer to them from the Bishop for submission to the Committee with the Liturgy itself.

I am very interested to hear of all this work of yours and see it looking forward to fruition. The scheme of the dictionary sounds very enchanting but a tremendous piece of work. Never mind; all your cares and studies have been drawn that way for many a long day, and it is a great work.

Incidentally, it is quite a good thing for our authorities to have to deal with these overseas liturgies. It makes them see how petty and small are a great many of the things which cause a stir here, and helps them to see that the English Liturgy is that of a Communion, and not merely of a couple of provinces tied down by the State. . . .

On 12 December Fr. Leeke sent the following amended form of the Liturgy for submission to the Liturgical Committee and this was soon followed by an important letter from the Bishop, containing the necessary replies to Frere's questions.

Mass of the Catechumens

1. Asperges.
2. The Preparation.
    (The usual, without the Confession and Absolution, but with Collect for Purity.)
3. Introit.
    (No Lord's Prayer. Commandments farced and beginning 'Thou shalt have only One God' or Ninefold Kyrie.)
4. Gloria.
5. Collect, Epistle, and Gospel with usual Salutation and Responses.
6. Dismissal of Catechumens.

Mass of the Faithful

7. The Creed.
8. Offertory.
9. Orate Fratres.
10. Prayer for the Church.
11. Comfortable Words.
    ('God so loved the world . . .'. 'Come unto Me . . .'. The other two are omitted.)

The Liturgy in Northern Rhodesia

12. Confession and Absolution.
    (The Compline form introduced by 'Let us confess our sins to the Lord'.)
13. Sursum Corda.
14. Preface.
15. Prayer of Consecration.
16. Lord's Prayer.
17. Fraction.
18. Pax.
    (Not given in deed.)
19. Prayer of Humble Access.
20. Agnus Dei.
21. Communion of Priest and People.
22. Ablutions.
23. Communion Sentence.
24. Post-communion Collects.
25. Blessing.
26. Last Gospel.

The Bishop of N. Rhodesia to Frere   21 *December* 1928

My dear Bishop,

Thank you very much indeed for your letter, which reached me this week, and for your kind offices on behalf of our Liturgy.

In regard to the three questions you raise:

1. *Relation to other U.M.C.A. Liturgies.*

Broadly speaking, our Liturgy is based on Zanzibar, though we had had the S.A. Liturgy before us and followed it in some respects. As you will remember, we availed ourselves freely of your advice, and (I think) adopted all your suggestions. At a Synod held last year certain changes were made as a result of experience gained during some years' tentative use of the Liturgy. Of these the only one of any importance is the inclusion of the Gloria in Excelsis in the Missa Catechumenorum—chiefly for the benefit of the Catechumens. The Last Gospel is now directed to be said aloud. In both these points we have followed Zanzibar. I think I am right in saying that our Liturgy was drafted before that of Nyasaland was in print. I certainly do not remember that we followed it at any point where it differs from Zanzibar and South Africa.

2. *Multiplication of Liturgies*

I quite agree that this is undesirable, and before embarking on a Liturgy of our own, I wrote to the Bishops of Zanzibar and Nyasaland, making what seemed to me an obvious proposal—that the three U.M.C.A. dioceses should have a common liturgy. I cannot now lay my hands on their replies, and can therefore only give you my recollection of the gist of them. F. Z. (Dr. Weston) entirely agreed with my suggestion, but was doubtful whether his clergy—especially his African priests—would consent to any alteration in their rite. In fact he indicated pretty clearly that if there was to be a common liturgy, it must be that of Zanzibar. Fisher on the other hand said that there were certain features of the Zanzibar Liturgy which he did not like; and that in view of the possibility of a Province he considered that separate diocesan liturgies were to be preferred, as being likely to form a better basis of discussion with the C.M.S. Bishops and Clergy than a fixed and uniform U.M.C.A. use, when the question of a provincial liturgy came up for consideration.

3. *English-speaking Congregations*

There need be no misgivings on this point. Our European congregations are the most conservative in the world; it is unlikely that they will ever willingly consent to anything but 1662 for use on Sundays, and I shall certainly never force a change. At present we use the S.A. Liturgy on weekdays at Livingstone and Broken Hill. When the 1927 Prayer Book is published in convenient form, we shall probably adopt it instead; and if ever a change were made on Sundays, it would almost certainly be to the 1927 Prayer Book. Our own Liturgy is never likely to be printed in English.

I think I have now given you all the information you asked for, and I very much hope that it will satisfy the minds of the members of the Liturgical Committee, and that they will be able to see their way to giving their imprimatur to our Liturgy. It will be very inconvenient if we cannot ask S.P.C.K. to publish it, while on the other hand any substantial alterations will involve retranslation into all our different languages and considerable expense in reprinting.

Lest the Committee should feel that we have asked for trouble by having translated and printed the Liturgy without first obtaining their approval of it, it is perhaps fair that they should be reminded that, as you will doubtless remember, we did submit it to them some five [?] years ago, and were informed that nothing could be done till the revision of the Prayer Book was completed....

In spite of efforts made by Frere no decision had been reached by

April 1929. The Bishop therefore wrote to him again, saying that, in view of the unlikelihood of the matter being settled until after the next Lambeth Conference, he had asked S.P.C.K. to let the publication of the Liturgy alone and proceed only with the Collects, Epistles, and Gospels.

The Bishop of N. Rhodesia to Frere   25 *April* 1929

My dear Bishop,

Harold Leeke, who went through recently on his way out from home, told me that you were kindly proposing to make yet another attempt to obtain a decision from the Lambeth Liturgical Committee, which would permit S.P.C.K. to publish our Diocesan Liturgy.

As 'Liturgical Questions' are to be discussed at the next Conference under the head of 'Missionary Dioceses', it seems to me quite unlikely that the Liturgical Committee will give any decision till after the Conference; and I am therefore asking Dr. Lowther Clarke to let the Liturgy alone, so far as S.P.C.K. is concerned, and proceed with the publication of the Collects, Epistles, and Gospels, which are badly needed.

If by chance you should have reason to think that the Liturgical Committee is going to deal with the question of the authorization of the Liturgy in the near future, would you mind sending a line to Lowther Clarke asking him to hold his hand a little longer?

I am sorry to have given you so much trouble....

The Liturgy has remained 'provisional' but is still the only liturgy used in services in the vernacular, having been translated into the various languages used on the mission stations in the Diocese. For services in English the South African use is always employed.

HEBREW CHRISTIANS

Archbishop Davidson to Frere   25 *May* 1924

My dear Bishop of Truro,

    Mr. Levertoff has, as I think you know, prepared a version of a Communion Office for the use of Hebrew Christians. The S.P.C.K. refers it to me on the basis of its being a translation, as I have to sanction translations of our Prayer Book into unknown tongues, and I do it (odd as it may sound) with great care and on a basis of principle as to particular words the translation of which causes perplexities. But this is not a translation, and it strikes me as a Communion Office of a novel kind which has not been hitherto known in the Church of God: but I am staggered by finding in the statements made that '*the Bishop of Truro approves of it*'. Will you please tell me what this means, for I hardly need say (and I say it with completest honesty) that I should attach very great weight to your opinion in the matter. I doubt its being really a question for me as custodian of translations, and I think it ought possibly to be referred to the Episcopal Referees of S.P.C.K.—for the moment I do not remember who they are—and, of course, something would turn upon that as regards the weight of their judgement in this particular and rather profound matter. I may have real responsibility as to sanctioning a new office if it be new, and this I do not shirk; but I want my basis of knowledge to be as wide as possible.

                                         I am,
                                                 Yours very truly,
                                                     Randall Cantuar.

Frere to Archbishop Davidson   29 *May* 1924

My dear Archbishop,

    I thought some time ago when Levertoff was living with us at Mirfield about all his schemes for the Communion Office for Hebrew Christians. I went through parts of it in brief outline with him, and we talked over plans in general. Since then I have seen much less of him and we have only had a few words of conversation on the matter, not touching the details at all: but I no doubt assured him that I am in sympathy with the plan for having a liturgy which is not that of the Church of England, but is made for the particular purpose of Hebrew Christians and embodies a good deal of their traditional synagogue worship and is based on that, rather than on the Latin liturgical tradition. As I had it in view in fact, it corresponds more with the move for a native liturgy in India on Eastern lines than with any scheme of translation of the Book of Common Prayer. What I had in view was not by any means that, but a Hebrew-Christian liturgy, Oriental and fundamentally Hebrew. Clearly anything of that sort would have to be very narrowly scrutinized, but it is the general idea that I have encouraged so far; the actual Liturgy as finally drawn by him I have never seen and only discussed parts of it in any sort of detail, and that some time ago. But I would like to endorse his plea so far, that it seems to me that it is highly desirable with such an effort as he is making to make Hebrews into Christians without their ceasing to be Hebrews or giving up their own strong piety and liturgical traditions. They should not be tied too closely to English formulas or to the Latin traditions, but should be encouraged to have such a liturgy as is Anglican in its final conception but different from the Anglican traditions in form and detail. In fact I would submit that it is more to be compared with the scheme of a liturgy coming from the mission field than with any question of our own particular Prayer Book or its translations....

Dr. Levertoff finally produced his Liturgy under the title 'The Order of Service of the Meal of the Holy King' and used it at the Church of Holy Trinity, Shoreditch, where he was priest-in-charge. The following interesting comment is quoted from *Liturgy and Worship*:

'It is derived from early Christian and Jewish sources, and represents the kind of rite that might have been evolved by a Hebrew Christian Church of the first centuries that had preserved its national idiosyncrasies without drifting into Ebionitism.... The Ark with the rolls of the Book and a New Testament stands at the right-hand side of the Altar. Haloth (Jewish loaves) are used, except on the Passover, when they give place to Matzoth (unleavened bread). The celebrant wears cassock, Talith (prayer-shawl), skull-cap, and stole. The congregational responses are numerous. Lessons are read from the Law and the Prophets, besides the Epistle and the Gospel. Considerable use is made of the Old Testament, especially the Psalms and Isaiah liii. After communicating himself the priest says: "This is the bread of the Messiah.

All who are hungry, let them come and eat." The beauty and the impressiveness of the rite are beyond praise. Whether so drastic a departure from all other Liturgies past or present can be justified depends upon one's attitude towards the ideal of a Hebrew-Christian Church which Jews should be invited to enter.'[1]

[1] W. K. Lowther Clarke and C. Harris (editors), *Liturgy and Worship*, 1932, pp. 815–16.

THE LITURGY OF
THE SOUTH INDIAN CHURCH

The Bishop of Bombay (Dr. Palmer) to Frere   12 *April* 1928

My dear Bishop,

   The Joint Committee who are negotiating for a union in South India between our Church and the South India United Church and the Wesleyans in those parts are to meet in Bangalore on June 28th.

   One of the subjects we shall be considering is the Liturgy of the United Church. In general the prospect is that at first the Holy Communion will be celebrated as is accustomed at the present by the three separate Churches. But more than that is desired. It appears likely that a liturgy will grow up which will be adopted finally by the whole united Church. There is no wish to hurry this very important work. Consequently, the Churches which have a liturgy will go on using the one they have: that is, our own Communion Service will be used both by the congregations which now belong to us and by the Wesleyan congregations. The customs vary in the South India United Church according to the origin of the different sections of it.

   There is an idea that all would like to take steps towards the eventual formation of a liturgy in regard to the congregations of the South India United Church. This would probably at first take the form of some kind of outline which would correspond with the most important elements in the Liturgy which we use. I am very anxious to obtain the advice of a few highly qualified persons in England in regard to this question of outlines. I remember that at the time of Kikuyu the Bishop of Zanzibar (Frank Weston) said that, so far as the words of the service were concerned, he would regard any Communion Service as valid in which our Lord's Words of Institution were used and also the Elements which he used. I should like to hear your opinion incidentally on that judgement, but I do not think it is likely that we shall be asked to go so far. I conceive that the stage which we could easily reach in the negotiation is to name certain topics which ought to have a place in the Service and perhaps to suggest a scheme for the Order of the Service. It is from this point of view that I ask your advice. Dealing, as we shall be dealing, with persons accustomed to an almost completely *ex tempore* Service, or one at the discretion of the officiating minister, even if he uses written or printed forms, what would you try to persuade them always to include in their Service of Communion? I conceive that the answer to this would be partly in the form, 'There must be certain elements in the Service, such as reading from the works of the Apostles and from the Gospels, Confession and Absolution', &c.; partly in the case of the prayers, you would say, 'The Prayer of Consecration should contain certain ideas', or you would say, 'Certain fixed words should be used, whatever other words were added.' Then there would arise also the question whether we should ask for certain very ancient words to be used, e.g. the Sursum Corda and the Sanctus, or the Kyrie Eleison. These are the classes of questions which would naturally arise; and you would help us most, I think, if you would just write down the sort of outline that you think we ought to try to persuade our friends to adopt; remembering that this will be done as a transitional stage between no directions to the clergyman at all and the adoption of a formal liturgy which appears at present to be the probable final result.

Having drawn up this outline of things which are desirable to recommend or ask for, I would ask you finally to say whether any of the things mentioned are in your opinion indispensable, and if so which. By 'indispensable' I mean that if they were absent you would have serious doubt whether the Service as conducted without them was really a Communion Service. . . .

I am,
Yours very sincerely,
Edwin James Bombay.

Frere to the Bishop of Bombay   16 May 1928

My dear Bishop,

I have answered your questions as best I can, but I don't find it at all an easy thing to do; perhaps I can put a little more discursively what is in my mind.

First: I should deprecate being too precise. I think an outline is the thing to aim at; the outline should be a good bit fuller than is represented by our English Service, which after all is only a contracted form of an earlier and much more completed scheme. I therefore should wish to urge, in putting out a model, a pretty full scheme; leaving people to fill it in with more or less amplitude. I imagine that being Orientals they will want to fill it in much more amply than we do; but that will all come in time. I should make the scheme therefore sugges-

The Liturgy of the South Indian Church

tive and quite full. Secondly: as regards the indispensable minimum, I am not really sure that in theory there is any. In practice I think it would be a scandal if a Communion Service did not contain the recital of the Institution in biblical language, because it would be really unprecedented. That's the only thing, therefore, I should be inclined to stipulate for as indispensable. I should make the stipulation though, not on the ground that I thought a Service which did not contain it would be inefficient or would not accomplish the mysteries, but merely on the ground that it would be an unwarrantable departure from universal custom and tradition. Thirdly: apart from this recital the things that I should suggest and rather urge, though not impose, would be such things as and chiefly, the Sanctus coming in its place; it should be recovered in its proper form, the first part ending with 'full of thy glory', and the second part beginning with the true form 'Hosanna in the Highest'. I should urge the second part much less than the first, for the second part is, I think, a little illogical; it is an interpolation of an appeal to our Lord in the middle of the section which deals with God as Creator. This expression is to my mind no doubt an early instance of the inclusion of Christocentric ideas into a place where they were really alien. Then there is the scheme of the Service as a whole to be considered, and it would be well, I think, to come to some agreement as to the logical sequence of this. What has to be settled is (*a*) the position of the Intercession; personally I should wish it to be where you have placed it according to the Anglican rite and the primitive uses, not according to the present Eastern custom interwoven with the Canon.

(*b*) There is the preparation of the communicants. Should this come between the Offering of the Oblations and the Consecration, or should it come between the Consecration and Communion? There is much to be said for each of these views.

(*c*) There is the relation of the Ablutions (for which I think there ought to be some provision in the outline) to the Thanksgiving and the final Blessing or Dismissal. The settlement of this I think depends largely upon the quality and character of the Thanksgiving; if the Thanksgiving is very small—only a sort of dismissal collect, then I think the Roman rite is quite natural; Ablutions should follow Communion. If on the other hand the Thanksgiving is made considerable, as it is in our rite—and I think with great advantage, then it is desirable that the Ablutions should be postponed and kept till the end of the Service. In making a scheme of this kind it would be well to indicate where hymns could suitably be sung, or at any rate to indicate where not.

You will see that my main occupation is in getting the whole outline right as far as can be, rather than in giving details at any particular point; and I should think that would be the line of least resistance as well as the wisest line. The High Church Presbyterians, for example, have worked much along these lines and thought out their position; and a very Catholic position too it has been in the hands of the best of them. I think the same was the case with the Protestant Church of Spain and Portugal; I remember finding that they had a very good scheme of liturgy provided for them, whence it came I know not, but so it was.

My reasons for confining the attention mainly to the outline are really two. First: that, I think, is the only way to make it right in any union comprising the liturgical and non-liturgical traditions. Secondly: I think in dealing with people with such an entirely different mentality from our own, we want to leave them the fullest liberty to make their own sort of expansion of the sequence of ideas that must be common to all alike. I have always been greatly interested in that scheme for an Indian liturgy put out by Winslow, I think it was;[1] it seemed to me to have got a good deal of the right idea about it; and though as I say, I should not want to put forward liturgical formulas, I fancy—if I remember right—the scheme there implied was a good one. In any case I am sure the scheme should pay more attention to Eastern liturgies than to Anglican ones; not merely because they are Eastern, and therefore presumably rather allied to what you would want in India, but because they have kept much more the devotional logic that is required.

[1] *The Eucharist in India*, by Fr. J. C. Winslow, London, 1920.

THE LITURGY OF CEYLON

The Archbishop of Canterbury asked Frere in March 1932 to comment on the draft of a Liturgy prepared by the Ceylon Liturgy Committee after consultation with some other liturgical expert. Frere asked Dr. Srawley to help him, and the result was the following memorandum.

Considerations with regard to the Liturgy proposed for Ceylon

1. It is assumed that this Liturgy will be used both for those who are accustomed to the English tradition and are attached to its book, as well as for the Church of the place, consisting mainly of worshippers of different languages or traditions. This seems to suggest that the Liturgy for the moment is an interim liturgy, experimental therefore in character, rooted probably in the English Prayer Book, but tending in the direction of some future and perhaps quite different form of liturgy which may be required for the Church of the Diocese.

2. The best way to meet such a situation of a transitional kind, is probably by the method of alternatives. There are always certain points at which the present scheme might well look eastwards as well as westwards, for it is desirable that ultimately a form of liturgy corresponding to the Eastern's own nature and outlook should result. The cases in which such alternatives might be considered are as follows:

   (*a*) The alternative use of the Beatitudes, instead of the Ten Commandments, with some suitable response.

   (*b*) The provision of a General Intercession in litany form to make an alternative to Christ's Church.

   (*c*) In the Consecration Prayer itself some alternative might be produced on a larger scale than is customary now in the West. Not only to have a considerable number of Prefaces, but also some alternatives in other places in the Eucharistic Canon.

It is desirable to consider the proper use of psalmody, which is almost entirely cut out of the English Rite. The Introit is not always the most suitable place for much varied music. A single psalm (Ps. xliii for example) as a permanent Introit would be desirable; it should be made congregational and not merely a duet between the priest and server.

It is desirable to have some variable psalmody between the Epistle and the Gospel. This could be printed together with the Lectionary. It should be selected portions of psalms, not a whole psalm.

It is desirable to recover the ceremony of the Offertory, something like a Great Entry, and to give music accordingly; possibly the Greek alternative might be used here in place of psalmody. Similarly some psalmody at the end might be considered, either preliminary to Communion or Thanksgiving afterwards.

The question of the right place of the penitential elements has to be considered. I suggest that what is wanted is:

(i) the preparation of the worshippers at the beginning of the Service, which applies to all;

(ii) the Preparation of the Communicants coming before their Communion, which applies only to those who are making their Communion. This section would be omissible, if the communicants were few or nil. The prayers on pages 5 or 7 are suitable to the latter and not to the former of these two.[1]

The Gloria in Excelsis should not be put as part of the Introduction but as part of the Thanksgiving. The Offertory Sentences on pages 15 to 19 are more suitable for the Introit than for the Offertory.[2] This is not the point at which to introduce such specializing of particular festivals or fasts. The Prayer for the Church should mostly be kept as it is—the 1928 form; but prayers inserted about the monsoon and the like would come more appropriately in the larger text of the suggested Litany Prayer; the clause is quite unsuitable in the Prayer for the Church as we have it, which is a prayer for groups of people. The last clause but one of this is better however than that of 1928.[3]

(i) On page 25 the Benedictus is not added here (to the Sanctus); that may be quite wise: but whether it is or not, the last clause of the Sanctus should begin Hosanna and not paraphrased as here.[4] On page 31, however, I see the Benedictus is here (between the Commixture and the Pax), but with it Hosanna; but the Hosanna is the connexion between it and the Sanctus.

---

[1] These prayers were (a) the alternative forms of Confession and Absolution in the 1928 Prayer Book with a slight amplification of the Confession, and (b) the Prayer of Humble Access.

[2] In addition to six general Sentences, a special Sentence was provided for festivals and special occasions.

[3] 'And here we give thee most high praise and hearty thanks for the wonderful grace and virtue declared in all thy Saints, and chiefly in the Blessed Virgin Mary, Mother of thy Son Jesus Christ our Lord and God, and in the holy Patriarchs, Prophets, Apostles, and Martyrs; beseeching thee to give us grace that we, rejoicing in the communion of the Saints, and following the good examples of those who have served thee here, may be partakers with them of thy heavenly kingdom.'

[4] The form given is 'Glory be to thee, O Lord most high.'

The Liturgy of Ceylon 255

The Preparation of the Communicants must come here, following the Communion of the Priest.

(ii) I do not like the Ablutions being put into the Service (before the Blessing); it is not part of the Service itself, it is part of the tidying up afterwards.

3. Further I think there is a good deal to be said for systematically restoring the part of the Deacon in the Liturgy. It is probably desirable that the Diaconate should be not merely a brief year preliminary to the Priesthood, but a considerable apprenticeship, to say the least. The Service, therefore, should contemplate a real and effective part given over to the Deacon. In a way it may be said that that belongs to High Mass rather than what is set out here; to which I would reply that though it is entirely illogical to begin from a Low Mass and then add ceremony to make a High Mass, the proper order is to give the Service at its fullest, and then to leave such reductions to be made, as must be made, in practice. In other words there is a great incongruity in making the norm a Low Mass. In this respect at any rate Ceylon should follow the East and not the West; I suggest before anything else that the Order be recast in order to give the full service and not the reduced one.

It is interesting to note that in the Ceylon Liturgy as it appeared in 1938, nearly all the points mentioned in this Memorandum were incorporated. Only two were completely disregarded; the Ninefold Kyrie was inserted instead of the Ten Commandments or the Beatitudes, and the references to the monsoon and the weather were retained in the Prayer for the Church. In the case of three other points a compromise was effected:

(i) The Gloria was inserted as part of the Thanksgiving, but permission was given to use it in the Introduction instead.

(ii) The special Sentences were 'to be sung as Introits or said or sung at the Offertory'.

(iii) The Ablutions were retained between the Communion and the Thanksgiving, but permission was given to the Priest 'at his discretion to take the Ablutions immediately after the Blessing'. The part of the Deacon in the Liturgy was also restored, with the proviso that in the absence of an ordained minister to assist, the Priest should say the portions assigned to the Deacon. So the full Service was given and not the reduced one.

APPENDIXES

APPENDIX I

MEMBRA DISIECTA

1. The *Jus Liturgicum* (a) (*p.* 259).
2. The *Jus Liturgicum* (b) (*p.* 261).
3. On Access to the Blessed Sacrament (*p.* 262).
4. Extra-liturgical Devotions (*p.* 265).
5. Open Communion (*p.* 266).
6. Holy Communion on Good Friday and Easter Eve (*p.* 267).
7. The Rubric regulating the Reception of Communion (*p.* 269).
8. The Collects on the Weekdays following Ash Wednesday (*p.* 270).
9. The Consecration of a Church (*p.* 271).
10. The Bishop's Throne (*p.* 274).
11. The Dedication of Altars (*p.* 276).
12. Episcopal Ceremonial (*p.* 277).
13. The Consecration of Oil (*p.* 279).
14. A Part-time Ministry (*p.* 280).
15. The Indelibility of Orders (*p.* 282).
16. The Ministry (of the proposed United Church of Persia) (*p.* 284).
17. Papal Claims (*p.* 286).
18. The Church of England and Comprehension (*p.* 287).
19. The Transference of Sisters to Different Communities (*p.* 289).
20. The Appointment of Deans (*p.* 292).
21. Episcopal Signatures (*p.* 295).

MEMBRA DISIECTA

1. THE *JUS LITURGICUM* (a)

The Metropolitan of India (Dr. Westcott) to Frere   28 *July* 1925

My dear Bishop,

I am presuming on our acquaintance in early days and also upon your expert knowledge of the subject to ask your help on a matter which is exercising me much in connexion with the drafting of the constitution for the liberated Church in India. It affects the limitations which may justly be imposed upon the exercise of *jus liturgicum* by the individual Bishop.

In the Canon dealing with this subject it is laid down that the Diocesan Bishop must not exercise his *jus liturgicum* to sanction anything which is contrary to a Resolution of the Episcopal Synod which has already been passed, nor should he so exercise it as to threaten the unity and peace of the Province. No doubt this last phrase should be worded in more explicit terms, but I believe that where a Province is organized and the Bishops regularly meet in Synod, the *jus liturgicum* of the individual Bishop must be subject to the control of the Episcopal Synod. I am anxious to know where I can find any account of the historic development of provincial organization and whether the principles which have thus been embodied in our draft constitution are or are not in accordance with historic precedent.

This seems to me a matter of the utmost importance, not only for maintaining the unity of the Church in the Province, but also for exercising due control over the Bishops of the Church who in a new country like India may well have a tendency to become heretical, as in the early days of the Church in other countries. The control of the Episcopal Synod of the Province would naturally be subject to the decisions of the larger Council having authority in such matters. I should be very grateful for any help you can give me, or for any reference to sources whence I can obtain information on this subject.

Yours sincerely,
Foss Calcutta.

Frere to the Metropolitan of India   5 *August* 1925

My dear Brother,

It is very nice getting a letter from you, and sending an answer. I should entirely endorse so far as I have any right to do so, what you say about the relation of the individual Bishops to the Province in regard to liturgical discipline. I think your statement is in the nature of things; that is to say, that in the first instance the Bishop in his Diocese is responsible for the discipline of the services within the borders, but that when the Province takes action, the Bishop has his share in what is done there as the result of what is done by him and his companions. They remain free, however, in matters in which the Provincial Synod has not tied them up. Therefore I imagine that the sort of thing that you have in your Canon merely represents the position, except that perhaps it should be put rather the other way—that where the Province has not legislated the Diocesan should be free to do so, I should hope in consultation with his own Diocesan Synod; but that is another matter.

As to precedent, it is not very easy to know where to look; it is somewhat a new thing in Church History, that on the one hand there should be so much excitement as there is now about uniformity of services, and on the other hand that Bishops should resume their inherent right over the services of their jurisdiction. Till the Reformation time services were not a matter of quarrelling, and it all worked out without very much difficulty. From time to time, no doubt, provincial synods regulated the particular points, especially in Spain, but those did not form as a rule burning topics; when they did so, at the Reformation time, other tendencies were the dominant ones, and, of course, as far as England was concerned the scheme of uniformity seemed in many ways to tie the hands of the Bishop with a sort of secular knot, especially after the eighteenth century, when the theory of parliamentary government over the Church was so strongly emphasized for want of the existence or activity of Convocation. In that sense then, I think the problem is a new one; but I think it really settles itself on those general principles which I have mentioned above, and that those rather than particular precedents would be the things that people would understand and be guided by. For the reasons that I have mentioned, I do not think that anyone has written about these different responsibilities and relationships; at least, I don't know of any place where the matter is handled in a way that would suit our present freedom from the State on the one hand and from a centralized Papacy on the other.

Yours sincerely,
Walterus Truron.

2. THE *JUS LITURGICUM* (b)

Canon C. L. Robinson to Frere   12 *December* 1929

My dear Lord Bishop,

You don't remember me! But we had many talks in your Mirfield days. Please guide us!

We are in friendly discord with our Bishop and others. I want to find out—to what extent 'Extra Liturgical Devotions' came under the control of the bishops in the Middle Ages.

Langford James in the *Church Times* seems to believe that the parochial clergy could 'go their own way' in 'Devotions'. My friend Gilman is of opinion that 'Extra Liturgical' were under episcopal rulings.

Do please 'state the situation'. If you desire—'privately'. But it would greatly help us to have your opinion.

Yours with affectionate regard,
C. L. Robinson.

Frere to Canon C. L. Robinson   14 *December* 1929

My dear Robinson,

It is nice to hear from you again, and I notice that you are signing the letter in the *Church Times* which I suppose deals with the same business. I do not suppose that there is any very good precedent except a negative one, so far as the Middle Ages are concerned. There are, of course, a number of the clergy who have really become Presbyterians in their outlook and imagine that a parish priest does everything that he likes until the Bishop intervenes; and when the Bishop intervenes he maintains that the parish priest is the final authority. I can only say that it is subversive of all Catholic order, and I don't think that there is any precedent for it. The medieval Bishop kept absolute control of the services in his diocese; I don't suppose it was very difficult in most cases, because medieval clergy didn't want to do more services than they had already got, nor did they want to alter the services to another type than what they had in their book, so far as I know. I think if it had occurred to any medieval parish priest to introduce a new form of service on his own, he would very speedily have been snuffed out;

such a thing was inconceivable to them in general I think. But, of course, what was conceivable and what was actually done was the introduction of new saints—local people and so on. It was with regard to them, of course, that the Bishops from time to time had to keep a tight hand and suppress the local custom. A more common thing, of course, was for the Bishops to take the initiative and put in order an extra service. This in fact the Bishops do still; but I should entirely deny so far as I know that any medieval parish priest claimed any initiative at all. Bishop baiting even then was, of course, a popular sport, and more inclined towards the side of dissent than excess. In fact it was the sort that we are more familiar with now in Evangelical circles than in Anglo-Catholic.

These are only surmisings, but I should very much like to see in print a medieval parish priest inventing a new service and maintaining use of it in his church in spite of the Bishop's lack of approval. . . .

3. ON ACCESS TO THE BLESSED SACRAMENT

Frere refused to sign a Memorial opposing the policy proposed in the Draft Rubric to regulate the Reservation of the Blessed Sacrament in the Order for the Communion of the Sick and declaring that compliance with the proposed regulation—refusal of access to the place of Reservation—'cannot rightly be demanded and will not be given'.

Frere to Canon Scott Holland   29 *January* 1917

My dear Holland,

. . . I declined to sign the Memorial. The first two lines were enough for me, as I do not hold that the faithful have any right of access either moral or legal. The access in question, where it is allowed, is allowed as a concession, and not as a right, I believe. But this is technical criticism: the larger question is the important thing. The best thing at this stage is that there should be enough opposition to make the promoters withdraw. It would be a great pity, I think, that this should be published, and still more a pity that it should be followed by a rival expression of opinion; for that would accentuate the divisions, which in this matter are very close and domestic. Cowley is sharply divided on the point; so are we; and I have no doubt elsewhere households will be divided in the same sharp way. I have already declined to take part in getting up a rival memorandum on the ground that what I thought was wanted is not demonstration but instruction in the matter. We want a book on the subject. As you say, it is the theology that really matters; and to my ignorance at any rate it is quite clear that the theology behind this devotion is, as you say, very questionable. The sort of questions that rise in my mind continually when I try to think the matter out, and where I feel I want simply instruction, are these:

(*a*) How far is the Presence of Christ's Body and Blood to be taken as the equivalent of the Presence of Christ?

(*b*) In general what is the relation of the Eucharistic Presence to the general presence of God and of Christ? This is the great topic which the Black Rubric certainly did not settle, but it is very material and very difficult.

(*c*) How far is the Presence vouchsafed to a particular locality? Or how far is it vouchsafed to a particular purpose, i.e. Communion?

(*d*) If it is granted for one purpose, how far can it be counted upon if used for another?

(*e*) Even if presumably the Presence is not withdrawn in such a case, how far have we the right to use it otherwise than according to this ordinance?

And so on.

Further, there are practical and historical questions which seem to me to come in. What is the effect upon the worshipper? I seem to see three dangers:

I. The danger of substituting sentiment for devotion.
II. The danger of materialism in the conception of the Eucharist altogether being forced upon us by such access.
III. The very real danger of losing the sense of God's Presence apart from the Blessed Sacrament.

Such things as these are not guesses. They are known results so far as I can see. Besides, history has its warnings I think:

1. It was 'bread worship' which brought the profanities at the Reformation especially, but also at other times as well.

2. It was also that which spoilt our doctrine and gave us the revulsion of feeling which drove us into anything almost except a balanced eucharistic belief.

3. It is still this which is a stumbling-block to many devout seekers, as one may tell very well from France at the present day.

4. The practice is common in the West no doubt, but many practices in connexion with the Eucharist, which at one time had been tolerable and even encouraged, have since been dropped and condemned, e.g. the use of the Eucharist as an amulet or as an ordeal.

Now I confess what I should hope for is a book which will answer these and many more questions: or failing that at least a well-prepared and thought-out round-table discussion like the Fulham ones of old days, only on the basis of high eucharistic views—a conference, I mean, not between High and Low, but between High Churchmen of different views. If this could be done and papers prepared beforehand and circulated and discussed on some of these topics, the book might ultimately emerge; or at any rate we might come to a better position than we are in at present. Will Oxford provide us such an opportunity as this, if it won't provide the book? Or would it be well to ask the Bishop of London to have another Fulham Conference as soon as the war is over? For myself, I think it had better not be done by a bishop, but by someone who has more time to give to it, and will be less compromised by having it.

Lastly, if there is to be any sort of a reply or counter-memorandum, I hope it may take an independent form and emphasize this point in particular, and perhaps this only, that the Bishops should encourage a much wider use of Reservation for the Communion of the Sick, making such provision as they think fit for guarding the Blessed Sacrament from misuse. I think the true solution lies along this line. If in the vast proportion of parish churches Reservation was now to be authorized the comparatively small little band of people who want it for purposes of devotion would be an inconspicuous minority. As it is, they seem to be the people identified with the restoration of Reservation for the Sick, and I fear that they are really setting back the possibilities of Reservation in general. Possibly a memorial of the kind that I have suggested might be a good thing if it was a purely private memorial to the Bishops. What personally I wish to avoid incidentally is an obvious rent in the catholic minded being published on this subject.

Yours ever sincerely,
W. H. Frere.

Frere's suggestion for a conference and a book was largely met by the Bishop of Winchester's Farnham Conference in 1925, the results of which were published in 1926 in *Reservation. Report of a Conference held at Farnham Castle on October 24–27, 1925.*

4. EXTRA LITURGICAL DEVOTIONS

The Bishop of Lichfield (Dr. Kempthorne) to Frere   14 *August* 1929

My dear Bishop,

   I want your advice. Forgive me for bothering you during the holiday season.

   There are some twenty-seven churches in this diocese where the Blessed Sacrament is reserved. In about four or five of these churches some sort of service of 'Devotions' is in use.

   One of the vicars concerned—a thoroughly good and loyal man—asks if I would permit a service of Devotions according to the enclosed form. What do you think about it?

   Also what about the Angelus with its direct Invocation of the Blessed Virgin Mary?

Ever yours sincerely,
J. A. Lichfield.

Frere to the Bishop of Lichfield   20 *August* 1929

My dear Bishop,

   It seems to me the only thing one can do is to say to oneself, 'Would this service and each bit of it be justifiable in a church where there is no Reservation?' No doubt that is not a very precise test; but I can't get anything more precise than that; and it is more precise than any other way of looking at it that I have devised. Judging myself from that point of view, it seems to me that the little bit that must be disallowed of the ordinary services is the Antiphon 'Let us adore for ever the most Holy Sacrament'. For that *does* seem to me definitely to imply the presence of the Sacrament. In itself that seems to me to be true, and also I think it is true in its history. That is to say that numbers of other things which look almost like in kind were really written for the Office of the Blessed Sacrament or for Corpus Christi Day in the Offices, therefore they are intended to be said when the Sacrament is not reserved. So far as I know this particular Antiphon belongs purely to the Reserved Sacrament; and I should be inclined therefore to say that that is disqualified. Something else might easily be found to take its place in the ordinary services of Corpus Christi Day in the Latin Rite....

5. OPEN COMMUNION

The Bishop of Salisbury (Dr. St. Clair Donaldson) to Frere

17 *January* 1928

My dear Walter,

I want to 'take your reactions' to a certain question, as the Yankees say!

The International Missionary Council meets at Jerusalem at Passiontide; and they are inviting 100 representative Oriental and African Christians, with a view to disarming suspicions as to any desire of ours to dominate the Conference with European Christianity. And the Secretary has approached me in the hope that an invitation might come from the Anglicans to the whole Conference to attend the Anglican Celebration of Holy Communion in the Cathedral during the Conference. He pleads for this in the interests of the Orientals, who are far more impatient of Western divisions than most Westerns know.

Now do you hold that no Conference, however unusual or unique, offers any excuse for such an invitation? Personally I don't think I should go so far as that, though I am glad that no united service was held at Lausanne.

But there is a further point. Supposing such a special United Communion were unobjectionable in ordinary circumstances, would you say that at the present moment, when folk are on edge and our main business is to keep the Church together? Would it merely add to our home difficulties? It is this latter point of view which weighs with me. Do I exaggerate it?

Yours affectionately,
St. Clair Sarum.

Frere to the Bishop of Salisbury 19 *January* 1928

My dear St. Clair,

I am afraid I am rather stiff and stodgy on this subject. As to the rightness in itself, I don't see what authority we have for accepting people who probably in many cases are not confirmed, and that not merely by accident but by deliberate disregard, and possibly in some cases also may not be baptized. That in itself seems to me to be prohibitive. Secondly, there is, as you say, the scandal caused to people who feel strongly on these points: I feel that is very serious especially in view of our relations with Rome and the East. Thirdly, if anybody is to hold an open Communion in Jerusalem, I should have thought it ought to be the Orthodox Church and not we: on their principles and by use of that blessed word 'economy', they could do even more than we could in dispensing with the proper safeguards, if they were so minded: but of course I suppose there is no doubt that they wouldn't be. Lastly, on the general question; I think we do incalculable harm when we don't face up to the facts of disunion. If we are ever to be reunited, the first thing I think essential is to recognize our differences, and then to repent of them. A policy which merely refuses to recognize them or to say they are unimportant, therefore implying that we are not penitent on the subject, seems to me to be a false plan in morals as well as in theology. So you see I am stiff and stodgy on the subject. The Orientals are no doubt impatient about these things: that is really part of their weakness and we ought not to encourage them in that.

Yours affectionately,
Walterus Truron.

The Bishop of Salisbury to Frere 30 *January* 1928
My dear Walter,

Thank you for your letter about the 'open Communion' at Jerusalem. I have come down quite definitely myself on your side of the fence, so far as this matter is concerned; though I think there are reasons for the matter being considered at the Lambeth Conference. But I am not sure of carrying all my colleagues of the Anglican Delegation with me. I hope to. I have written to Manchester, who is the one who matters most, I suppose. I don't know yet what Raven and Quick may say. . . .

Yours affectionately,
St. Clair Sarum.

6. HOLY COMMUNION ON GOOD FRIDAY AND EASTER EVE

The Bishop of North China (Dr. Norris) to Frere 30 *March* 1932
My dear Walter,

Ever since I have been in Peking we have had celebrations of the Holy Communion on Good Friday and Easter Eve. Dear old Bishop Scott felt (*a*) that the Prayer Book was behind him; (*b*) that phrase upon phrase, passage upon passage of the Communion Office made it *natural* to have one on Good Friday; and (*c*) that Easter Eve seemed a no less natural day on which to try to enter into 'the Communion of Saints at rest'.

I entirely agreed with him.

But, of course, some have wondered. And last week one good woman was disposed to ask me for my reasons in justification, and referred me to 'Proctor and Frere'. I'd like to know what you really think, if you can spare a few moments to tell me. I doubt if I shall change my ways—whatever happens—but I hesitate to urge people to change theirs (clear as I am in my own mind); and perhaps there's more to be said than I can see and think for the curious practice of having no Celebration on those days.

Ever yours affectionately,
Frank L. Norris. Bishop.

Frere to the Bishop of North China   29 *April* 1932

My dear Bishop,

In the early days they had a celebration on Good Friday, but never a consecration; the Communion was probably from the Reserved Sacrament. That seems to me what we need to restore. Certainly Good Friday ought to be a day of Communion, and the instinct to desire it is a true one and well authenticated and approved. There is probably more to be said for that side of the matter than there is for the abstaining from consecration on the Friday and Saturday, which some people might think more fanciful than practical; but it is, if fancy, a piece of fancy which has laid a widespread and long-lasting hold of the Christian mind. Besides, there is this effect—that it has its spiritual fast before the great Easter Communion which is, I think, something of the utmost value. It is only since the Reformation that we have come to be critical and controversial about that. We have worked through a bad time on the subject and I hope are getting back to a more reasonable and less prejudiced view that will give us the old liberty of Communion on Good Friday without breaking the old custom of not celebrating. Here there is a tendency which I think bad; we try to recover the Mass of the Pre-sanctified on Good Friday without making any general Communion. That seems to me to be characteristic of unfortunate Romanizing—keeping the husk and missing the kernel. But Good Friday

Membra Disiecta

without either is really badly at fault, and no amount of Three Hours devotion makes up for the lack of the rest—to my thinking at any rate....

7. THE RUBRIC REGULATING THE RECEPTION OF COMMUNION

The Revd. E. Lyttleton to Frere   22 *May* 1932

My dear Frere,

    Our Bishop has just been quoting Gwatkin or Stubbs to show that the rubric about Communion being withheld from all except Confirmees or those desiring Confirmation was originally only directed against members of the Church, and the application to Nonconformists is modern. Bishop Barry in *The Teacher's Prayer Book* says a concession would be an irregularity not an illegality.

    Could you very kindly spare me five minutes to say how it strikes you? I have poked about in Proctor and Frere's *Prayer Book*, but have not yet found anything exactly *ad rem*.

    (I wish we were all in your Diocese.)

    Next Thursday I have to let on to a bevy of Anglo-Catholics—of which I am now an unlabelled member—so I am late in writing, but I should be grateful for a reply however hurried.

                                                      Yours sincerely,
                                                            E. Lyttleton.

Frere to the Revd. E. Lyttleton   24 *May* 1932

My dear Lyttleton,

    I do not know what the quotation from Gwatkin or Stubbs is that he has been making. Of course it is literally true to say that the application of the Confirmation rubric to members of the Church of England is modern because Nonconformity itself is modern. Until the Toleration Act there was nobody that could be said to hold a recognized Nonconformist's position. All were compulsory Church of England, compulsory Communicants and compulsory Confirmed where Confirmation could be had. But the argument is of no value, unless it is stated in its proper historical setting. So it must be put thus: that the Anglo-Church people have no right to come until they have been confirmed or anxious to be confirmed; the Non-Church people have no right to come at all because they have themselves contracted out of that right, if ever there was one from the civil point of view.

But, of course, it is not the legal point of view that really matters; it has no historical value, still less spiritual value. Some people regard Confirmation as a kind of obstacle, like the water-jump, which we expect the Church people to negotiate but which we refuse the outsider. Against that I am sure it is right to say that Confirmation is from the Church point of view a boon or privilege, not to say a sacrament, and therefore it is quite right that we should treat it as above. Further than that, as to the need of it, it is a boon or sacrament which is the natural and necessary final preparation before Communion. It is the sanctifying of the Spirit and it would be presumptuous to come to receive the Holy Communion before neglecting the sanctification of the Holy Spirit as part of the preparation. Here again, looking at it from the other end, Confirmation is the complement of Holy Baptism, and whatever particular theory one holds about the relation between the two forms, a Christian's initiation is not complete without it. Of course this is no argument to a Nonconformist, or to those people who have given up all ideas of the necessity of Baptism. But then, of course, it is no good arguing about anything on these lines, especially with people who have thrown over the old principles not only of the old Catholic Church but that of Nonconformity itself. But the rubric itself in the present form is, I think I am right in saying, a pre-Reformation rubric carried on in 1549.

As you know the whole matter of the history in the Anglican Communion is very fully and competently treated by Ollard in the fourth volume of the S.P.C.K. volumes on Confirmation, published in 1926. . . .

8. THE COLLECTS ON THE WEEKDAYS FOLLOWING ASH WEDNESDAY

The Bishop of Oxford (Dr. Strong) to Frere   *9 November 1927*

My dear Bishop,

I am perplexed again about the Collects for Thursday, Friday, and Saturday after Ash Wednesday. The Cambridge Press is doing a large book with the Collects, Epistles, and Gospels of the Second Series all printed out. What Collects are they to print for these three days? Quinquagesima followed by Ash Wednesday? Ash Wednesday followed by Quinquagesima? or Ash Wednesday alone?

The rubric after the Ash Wednesday Collect leaves this ambiguous: but the statement on an earlier page (p. 56) that Quadragesima begins on Ash Wednesday seems to point to the third, and the rule on p. 58 concerning St. Matthias's Day seems to confirm this. It must somehow be settled. What is your view?

Yours very sincerely,
Thomas Oxon.

Frere to the Bishop of Oxford　　　　　　　　　11 *November* 1927

My dear Bishop,

I don't think I have any real doubt about the matter that on the Thursday, Friday, and Saturday the Collect should be Quinquagesima and followed by the Ash Wednesday one. First because Quinquagesima is a name of a week, which ends on the Saturday and is not superseded by anything, except Ash Wednesday itself, which I take to be a special fasting day superseding the ordinary course, in the same sort of way in which a special feast day does. That occurs quite well on p. 58. I think the remark on p. 56 is unhappy, and I think that I am responsible for it. It would have been better to put the forty days of Lent, and then we should not have had this ambiguity. But I do not think it is serious and I do not think that particular passage should be taken to overrule the question of the Collect. After all, it is true, so far as the fasting days are concerned, that that is the case. . . .

Yours sincerely,
Walterus Truron.

9. THE CONSECRATION OF A CHURCH

Frere had been consulted by a priest who was asking for guidance on the many problems which arise in the consecration of a church. The inquirer was undoubtedly already familiar with the information contained in the essay by Dr. John Wordsworth, Bishop of Salisbury, entitled *On the Rite of Consecration of Churches especially in the Church of England*—a work which had long been regarded as a classic. This covered a whole host of points, including the handing over the site and the building, followed by a solemn celebration of the Eucharist; the alphabet ceremony; the rites of taking possession and of dedication to Christ answering to baptism and confirmation; consecration to special purposes of sacramental acts, analogous to ordination—the practice of

Bishop Andrewes; the burial of relics and the conceptions attaching to it (not properly an English action); together with a note on the foundation-sacrifice of paganism, and a list of seventeenth-century forms.[1]

The circumstances suggested in this query were those of a church which had been built and put into use in stages. First there had been built a small part, such as a single chapel, which had been consecrated many years ago with all the usual ceremonies—procession, knocking on the door, blessing of the font, altar, ornaments, and vestments. Later a second portion of the building had been built and put into use —the chancel, further chapels, and part of the nave. Finally the nave was completed and the tower and other minor works added. What then remained to be done? Would the first consecration suffice, and all that would follow be just dedication? What would be necessary? Procession around *all* the church except the original chapel; knocking at the west door; litany and Veni Creator, alphabet, consecration crosses on walls? Would anything further be required for chancel or high altar? Should it be combined with a solemn Eucharist celebrated by the Bishop in view of the fact that altars had been dedicated? Would it be in accord with medieval precedent to defer the final ceremony until the building was absolutely complete?

To all the questions Frere gave the following valuable reply:

So far as the consecration is concerned there are really two elements in it to be considered. The altars ought to be consecrated, and in fact they ought to be consecrated if in use at all even if the rest of the Church is not consecrated. Therefore if you have any unconsecrated altars those should be consecrated before their use. Secondly, there is the consecration of the Church, of really a different kind and relatively unimportant; that is to say it can be taken at almost any stage. There is a great deal to be said for waiting till the end, and keeping the big ceremony for then. But the question in your mind is, I gather, when your direct end is to be. I doubt whether it would be suitable to wait till you got all the decorations done; it is the public mainly that wants to be considered; when you have your completed fabric I should have thought you want a complete consecration of the Church itself. As a matter of policy I should have thought that there was a good deal to be said for getting everything you can into the plans and getting the plans passed for all under one faculty; then you can go on adding fresh ornaments according to the plans as you have the opportunity. If the

---

[1] Dr. John Wordsworth, Bishop of Salisbury, *On the Rite of Consecration of Churches especially in the Church of England together with the Form of Prayer and Order of Ceremonies used at the Consecration of Churches, Chapels, and Burial Grounds in the Diocese of Salisbury,* 1899. (Published for the Church Historical Society.)

ornaments are in any sort of sense dubious or might be objected to, it is probably easier to get them passed as part of the comprehensive plans for the Church than to get them individually at a later stage.

As regards forms of service there have been a good many put out recently, more or less good; a great deal depends upon how much ceremonial and ritual music you expect to be able to use profitably. I suppose the most elaborate of recent years has been the dedication of the chapel of the Sisters of All Saints by the Bishop of St. Albans. Probably that is more than would be desirable in the case of a parish church and probably also more than would be possible in a parochial choir. There is a very good form of consecration put out by F. L. Cobb for the consecration of St. Cyprian's Church when that was built by Comper, so he will know all about that, for he probably had a hand in it. I expect he will have a copy of it and could show it to you; or you could get one from Cobb for he is interested in the whole matter and I think himself is very largely responsible for the service, and that follows in the main the old medieval lines. The first modern line in England was quite a different one—quite good in its way but quite distinct—for it follows Bishop Andrewes's scheme of consecration. The whole point of that is going round the church and saying appropriate prayers at various places that may be used in the services. This is, of course, quite a different idea and scheme from the medieval one, which was rather a hallowing of the building itself; hence the procession, the crosses, and all the rest. We look upon the building as unclean until it is hallowed, cleaning it all like a child with a great deal of baptismal washing, in order to bring it into grace.

These few ideas don't sound very well. It is done in some places, however, and I have seen it done myself even in churches which were quite new—agreeing to keep the two services quite separate, a sort of evening service with a post-Reformation scheme, and then the solemn Eucharist in medieval form for the consecration of the altars on the morning following. The difficulty is that nowadays the evening popular sort of service is wanted as well as the real consecration service; and this seems to me the best way of meeting both kinds of congregations. But probably you will hardly want that. You have got so much of the Church consecrated already; and you will probably rely upon the bulk of the people who matter to rally to the big consecration service with Mass in the morning. I hope these brief suggestions will meet what you want.

Appendix I

10. THE BISHOP'S THRONE

The Bishop of Bombay (Dr. Acland) to Frere   9 *September* 1930

My dear Bishop,

I am taking advantage of having made your acquaintance to ask the following questions. If it is too much trouble to answer please do not feel obliged to do so.

A new throne is being put up in our Cathedral here in memory of one of my predecessors. The old throne was on the south side, east of the choir stalls. This is the customary position I think in England. It is suggested to put the new throne on the north side exactly opposite the present stall. The old stall, slightly altered, is to become the Archdeacon's stall.

What I want you to tell me is whether there is any authority for putting the Bishop's throne on the north side and also whether the traditional position of the throne in all our Cathedrals on the south side is due to some reason so strong and good that it would be a pity to break with it.

The only advantage in having the throne on the north side is that it gets me away from the organ and its noisy electric blower. I think it would be rather fun to have something peculiar about our Cathedral but not at the cost of breaking with a really valuable tradition.

I believe the present suggestion to put the throne on the north side is due to a muddle between the seat which in this letter I have called the Bishop's throne—because it always is so called, though it is really only his stall in choir I suppose, and his throne technically so called, i.e. his seat within the sanctuary which I believe is always on the north side. For a sanctuary throne of this sort we have no room for anything except a chair and a *prie-dieu*. I see from a photograph that Amiens Cathedral has a very fine sanctuary throne on the north side.

I should be very grateful if you would let me know whether it would be a stupid mistake to put my stall in choir on the north side.

Then I have a second question. I cannot from my books discover what caused the removal of the Bishop and Clergy from their seats in the apse behind the altar. Can you refer me to any book describing when and why this change took place? Was its cause architectural or liturgical?

With apologies for troubling you.

I am, Yours very sincerely,

R. D. Bombay.

Frere to the Bishop of Bombay 18 *December* 1930

My dear Bishop,

Your letter I am afraid was written on 9 September and ought to have had an answer before this; but until a bit of Christmas lull comes it is difficult to do anything but the most immediate correspondence, especially when I have been accumulating arrears more or less all the summer through ill-health. I hope your problem has already settled itself by now; if not, here are one or two remarks, I am afraid very casual and what comes into my head at the moment.

The old seat of the Bishop, as you know, was in the semi-circle behind the altar in the apse. When he moved from there his seat as celebrant moved as a rule to the north side of the sanctuary; this I suppose was determined more or less by the fact that the seats on the south side were wanted by the ordinary celebrant and his attendants. This remains in foreign churches as a rule. On the other hand in a collegiate church or a cathedral where there is a chapter or other body to deal with, the relations of the Bishop to that have been various, and he is seated consequently according to various relationships. When the Bishop authorized the Chapter to elect a Dean as their own president, he could not quite sit in the presiding place in the choir, for the Dean must do that. I suppose it was that that drove the Bishop to erect a throne for himself outside the choir at the east end of the south side. This seat, as you see and as far as I understand, has quite a different origin and character. Moreover, these changes, at any rate among ourselves are of relative importance; the Bishop's throne is in the sanctuary at times, while the Bishop's throne in the choir arose in the same sort of proportion as the Eucharist declined in importance compared with the choir office in the post-Reformation days. When this Roman custom was transferred elsewhere, it was the usual custom for the celebrant to stand the other way, with his back to the people; and from the point of view of that position a throne behind the altar was most unsuitable; it was therefore placed on the north side instead. This is partly the cause therefore, and partly architectural.

I don't know anything where the whole matter is put out at full length. There are references to it in some of the histories of Gothic art; but most of these are without adequate knowledge of the liturgical side of the matter. I have dealt partly with that, but again not at all completely in a book about the *Principles of Religious Ceremonial*. You might look up the bit about the tenth-century presentation of the

Service. If you haven't got it, the amount it contains bearing upon this subject is too small for you to bother about; I have only dealt with it to get in a note or two. So far as principles and precedents are concerned, I think there is something to be said for maintaining the ground that the bishop has his seat in the choir, but it is a separate seat. As to the choir seating, there are various plans according to the English churches and cathedrals; the chief difference being as to whether all the principal persons sit at the west end of the choir in the return stalls, or whether two of them are put to occupy the extreme ends. In any case the Bishop sits outside, and his throne should not be part of the choir stalls if the tradition counts for anything.

The shifting of the Bishop's seat from behind the altar I should think was mainly in origin caused by architectural considerations—either that they ceased to have an apse or pierced the apse as an entrance from outside. In either case the place behind the altar was no longer suitable. There is a certain amount also to be said for liturgical reasons; the throne behind the altar went naturally with the position of the celebrant facing the people, such as was customary in churches in Rome, where there was a 'Confessio' and therefore no place for the celebrant between the altar and the people....

11. THE DEDICATION OF ALTARS

Prebendary H.E. Bishop, the Librarian at Exeter Cathedral, sought Frere's advice on the dedication of altars in Exeter Cathedral.

Frere to Prebendary Bishop   16 March 1932

My dear Bishop,

... Now about your new query, which is rather an intricate one. The question of the patron saint I think stands apart from the question of any dedication of altars; at any rate in theory. The high altar is dedicated in any case to the Holy Trinity whatever supplementary names may have been added. The monastery or ecclesiastical body was not so dedicated, but had its patron. As you know in the early days the patron saint was treated as being a legal person who could hold property on behalf of those under his patronage. It was the legal fiction on which in the early days the holding of such property depended. There might, of course, be more than one patron saint, and then the institution would be called by more than one patron's name; which I think is what the St. Mary in your charter would probably mean. Similarly,

All Saints in your next charter is merely a sort of extra added on I think like '&c.' With Edward the Confessor you seem to get the clear recognition of the dedication of the Church to St. Peter, and that I suppose is its tradition since, in spite of the reference in 1225 to the Church of St. Mary and St. Peter. I think in strict theory Grandisson's action may be described thus—when he dedicated the high altar, he added to the dedication the names of Our Lady and St. Peter; the principle being as I have stated already that the high altar is dedicated to God simply. The custom begins to be complicated when the fashion for lady chapels began to come in, and the Cistercians I believe began regularly to dedicate their high altars to the Virgin, and on that account as a rule had no separate lady chapel. But I don't say they were right. I think that was a novelty, and really infringed a general rule—or custom at any rate if not a general rule. . . .

12. EPISCOPAL CEREMONIAL

The Revd. J. A. Hollis, Bishop-designate of Taunton to Frere
21 *December* 1930

My dear Bishop,

My Consecration is fixed for 11.30 a.m. on the Epiphany in Lambeth Palace Chapel. Shall you be in London then? It would be a real pleasure if you could assist. Mr. Dashwood is writing to know if I can tell him which bishops will be there.

I have been wishing I could see you and learn something of 'how to behave'. Is there any book you can recommend me which gives reliable instructions for a Bishop at various services? . . .

Yours very sincerely,
J. Arthur Hollis.

Frere to the Revd. J. A. Hollis 27 *December* 1930

My dear Hollis,

Thank you for your letter and for your kind wish that I should be at your Consecration. I wish indeed I could but I am afraid I am right away in Yorkshire for our Chapter at Mirfield and couldn't well go away then, much as I should like to be there.

Also I should like to have a talk about 'how to behave'. I know no decent book on the subject; I tried to stop the publication of a very bad one on the subject the other day but didn't succeed. Bit by bit I have been trying to build up a scheme, but very little of it has got on to paper yet; but Bishop Nash and I are hoping to work something together now he has come home and has leisure at Mirfield. Meanwhile I don't know what to suggest; but let me put down one or two obvious things that probably you will recognize at once.

First: the Mitre. The rule is very simple. Never say a prayer with it. That is to say, take it off for your prayers; and personally I find it much more convenient to take it off myself than to have a chaplain around trying to take it off; it is convenient, however, to have one to hold it during prayers and to hold the Staff also and to give it back when wanted. In prayers to be said standing, there is not the same necessity for keeping strictly to this rule as there is for prayers when said kneeling. Personally I make exception therefore in services, where, for example, there is a collect and a blessing to be said at the end: it is not worth while to take off the Mitre for a single collect and to have to put it back again for the Blessing which is said standing; and I think the exception justifies itself.

Secondly: the Staff. As a common rule one holds it, but there are cases when it is handy to have a chaplain by or some way of leaving one's hands free. Let me add I believe there is no reason why a Suffragan should not carry his Staff everywhere. I think it is merely a piece of Roman innovation that the Staff should be regarded as having anything to do with the exercise of jurisdiction. The English tradition certainly is that the Bishop has his Staff when he has his Mitre as a sign of his Episcopal Order; all the more so because the Staff was given to him at his Consecration whereas his Mitre was not. But, of course, for this we depend upon one another's doings; personally I always fit out a Bishop who comes here without a Staff, but I know that in many places elsewhere they have practically adopted the Roman Custom and regard the Staff as belonging specially to the Diocesan.

Next I put down a note or two about customs: you will understand it is only a personal exposition or personal experience. I generally confirm in Cope and Mitre in nearly all churches; in some I confirm in Chimere and no Mitre, where that is preferred. The tendency is in parishes where it is acceptable to wear Cope and Mitre; but here in fact we have not got very many where that is not preferred. I generally sit in the Sanctuary for any opening hymn and for the Service: I think a little movement rather valuable, especially in an unfamiliar church. Then I come down for the prayer normally at the Chancel steps to put the 'Questions'; chiefly we use the three questions rather than the one. Then I get rid of the Mitre and Staff and say the prayers, pointing down to the candidates with extended hands for the prayer for the sevenfold gifts. I then resume Mitre and Staff; I find the Staff in the left hand is a very good thing to rest on when I am tired, and one hand is much better to lay on than two; it makes the position of the hand much simpler. I make a Cross on the head or on the forehead, and after that give a short imposition of hands again at the closing words; it really is valuable to individualize the act. We generally have an Invocation of the Holy Spirit by a hymn after the answer to the questions. We usually, at any rate in small congregations, keep a short time in private prayer before the Lord's Prayer. At a Sunday Confirmation generally where there is a biggish collection of people and a more formal kind of sermon, I go to the end of the Confirmation Service and then have a hymn, the address, another hymn, and final collect and blessing of the congregation. At weekday Confirmations I am generally content with three hymns—one at the beginning, one after the answer to the questions, and one either before or after the address.

In celebrating I ordinarily follow the first part of the service at the appointed episcopal spot, that is from a seat near the altar. Special pontifical Celebrations take place mainly here at the Cathedral, where we have our own scheme for High Mass of a simple kind, generally without incense. But on Ordinations and great occasions like that I follow more elaborately the ancient episcopal plan. I don't usually use a Mitre at celebrating in ordinary Low Mass, but I should, of course, take one for occasions such as the consecration of an altar or chapel. I fight against the typical Roman custom of the Bishop being specially attended by two deacons; our English tradition of chaplains is very much better if their clothes are not varied too much, otherwise there is no reason why they shouldn't wear Copes; don't be put off with two deacons. If deacons attend at all they should be three, five, or seven in number. . . .

13. THE CONSECRATION OF OIL

Frere to the Revd. Fr. E. Symonds, C.R.　　　　　　　　　2 *April* 1928

My dear Edward,

I am afraid it can't be done. I do not think a Bishop has a right to consecrate oil for subjects of some other Bishop if the consecration of oil is given the importance of an episcopal character that it used to have. How many rows have I seen over a question as to whence you got your oils. So working on that line I don't see that it should be done.

For myself I prefer to work on the more modern lines, saying that the Anglican Bishops do not now restrict to themselves this office as they do the office of confirming, and that therefore oils for the sick should be consecrated by the clergy themselves, probably at the time of unction. That is what I have done here. It seems to me the wiser plan, especially in view of the half-hearted, to say the least, attitude which is at present the prevailing one with regard to unction generally. I have indeed consecrated oil; I did the other day for the Sisters here, but that was on the ground that they were directly under me and had no parish priest to do it for them. At other times I tell the parish priest to do it.

The net result: (*a*) I can't be consecrating holy oils on Holy Thursday, and (*b*) even if I were I don't believe it ought to be done for anyone except within the jurisdiction. I think you understand this and I hope your father will too, and you will understand also how sorry I am to say 'No', even though I think I have got a very good reason for doing so. . . .

14. A PART-TIME MINISTRY

The Bishop of Grahamstown (Dr. Phelps) to Frere   15 *November* 1927

My dear Bishop of Truro,

I am instructed by the Episcopal Synod of this Province to make inquiry whether the system of ordaining to Holy Orders men who would continue in the practice of their lay avocations during the week, is in your opinion legitimate under the Canonical rules of the Church; and whether it has been, within your knowledge, tried in any part of the Church, and if so, with what measure of success.

I shall be very grateful if you can give me an opinion on these points and any information which may be useful to our Bishops' Synod. I trust you will forgive my troubling you on this matter.

                                          I am,
                           Yours sincerely in our Lord,
                                   Francis R. Grahamstown.

Membra Disiecta

Frere to the Bishop of Grahamstown 6 *December* 1927

My dear Bishop,

It seems to me fundamental that Holy Orders as distinct from Minor Orders should demand wholetime service. I do not know that this principle has ever been seriously infringed since the clergy became an organized body in the second or third century. It seems to me a foundational point of the Ministry that it should be inconsistent with secular avocations. At any rate, I think our Ordinal would have to be modified considerably if any other views were taken. Besides, there is a whole range of Canon law, as you know, prohibiting this and that occupation as being incompatible with Holy Orders. The occupations that are compatible have no doubt varied and haven't always been very accurately defined; for example, at the present moment we consider the position of a schoolmaster quite compatible with that of a priest. Medical work we recognize as being valuable and especially when done by a priest in the Mission Field. I am not quite so clear what our view is of a man exercising both the medical and pastoral functions as a doctor in England, though lately I myself have sanctioned that here in the case of a man who has given up his priesthood for doctoring, and then subsequently wished, while earning his living as a doctor, to exercise his priesthood by helping his parish priest.

I do not know of any part of the Church where this experiment has been tried. It has been talked about a great deal in England, but it has always broken down before the fundamental difficulties. Convocation has toyed with the idea; in recent times the Lower House has rejected all this with a view to establishing a sub-diaconate such as you have already in South Africa, while the Upper House, I think both in Canterbury and York, has still flirted with the idea of a non-clerical deacon. Personally I hope that you will have nothing to do with anything of the sort in South Africa. It is a bold venture to have a subdeacon administering the chalice on Sundays after doing his secular avocation on a weekday; but I think it is justifiable in principle and practice, though no doubt it is an innovation. I wouldn't be prepared to go farther than that and deal in any such way with the diaconate. Nor do I think it is part of the lines which we quite wisely, I think, took up at the Reformation of drawing our line between the major and minor orders below the deacon. The Roman line drawn below the subdeacon for this purpose is really, comparatively speaking, modern—just temporary, I think—and has more to do with the question of celibacy than anything else: it is therefore no valuable precedent, in my judgement, for the present discussion. Lastly, to treat the diaconate in this way would seem to me to be particularly undesirable in the present state of things, because we have as it is a degraded diaconate in Presbyterianism and in various sorts of nonconformity, to say nothing of Sweden, where I think it is the case. The difference between what I venture to call a degraded diaconate and a sound diaconate seems to me to be all the more reason for preventing us from taking any step in that direction. I am afraid I am more expressing myself in an opinion than giving you what you want, namely history and authority, but this is what I can send at the moment and it is the result of having worked at it to a certain extent.

Yours sincerely,
Walterus Truron.

15. THE INDELIBILITY OF ORDERS

The Bishop of North China (Dr. Norris) to Frere   10 *February* 1928
My dear Walter,

   ... I should much like your views upon: What *I think* we mean by the 'Indelibility of Orders'. How far the difficulty is common in the Mission Field I don't know: but here in China there is a distinct leakage from the ranks of our clergy—for one reason or another—often money. Tommy is a small boy from a very poor home. He gets into a mission school where he makes friends with Dick and Harry. Quite honestly he says he wishes to be ordained—the salary of our clergy is princely compared to anything he ever knew in his own house. But by the time he's thirty, he finds Dick with three times and Harry with five times his salary, one in the customs service, the other in business perhaps; and they are members of his congregation, and apt to forget that his salary is not the same as theirs. So trouble arises, and they offer a way out, in the direction of a well-paid job either as schoolteacher or in an office. Tommy is by this time married, and is tempted to chuck his clergyman's job and, as he put it, 'Just for a few years try to save a little money for the family: then of course he will come back,' &c. What should Tommy's bishop do? When remonstrance and exhortation fail and Tommy goes off to the job, is Tommy to be disciplined as a wilful sinner? to be encouraged to live as a good lay Churchman? or what, and *why*, i.e. on what grounds? The question does not seem to me a very simple one to answer!!

Yours ever,
Frank L. Norris. Bishop.

Frere to the Bishop of North China   27 *December* 1928

My dear Frank,

   . . . [Re the indelibility of orders] technically I do not know how much it comes into your problem; of course it is also a problem of ours, namely of clergy who laicize themselves by taking work that is incompatible with the ministry. The theory I think merely means this, that however much they may overlay the marks set upon them by ordination, it is always there; and this of course is the safeguard—that they must not be ordained again if and when they revert to ministerial work. I am not sure that the theory of indelibility carries you any further than that, or is meant to do so. The practical problem is really one of discipline and not of orders, and I think we had best feel it has to be treated as a disciplinary matter. So we may give a minister two or three years penance for evil doings and tell him to live as a layman with a prospect of being restored to his ministry at the end of such time: that is I think obviously a justifiable course, imposed by authority, and is therefore all along quite regular. These other people put a discipline upon themselves or incur a discipline by their own act if they cease from clerical work and take up secular work instead; I think they have to be treated in the same sort of way as people who through their action have put themselves under discipline and are adopting really a penitential action in not continuing their ministry; that is to say practically that they should be suspended by the Bishop simultaneously on the grounds that they deserted the ministry; and that suspension he should only withdraw from them when they show good signs of repentance and come back to it. That is, I think, the Church's reply to the man's intimation that he is going off. I expect that is what you do, if you do anything as I hope you do; for you have a much clearer view in the mission field than we have at home of these disciplinary matters, and of who is inside and outside the Church and who is on the border-land of penitence between the two. . . .

16. THE MINISTRY

(In connexion with the proposed United Church of Persia.)

The Archbishop of York (Dr. Temple) to Frere   7 September 1932

My dear Bishop,

I promised the Bishop of Persia that I would draw up a memorandum on his suggestions for an advance to union in Persia, and after getting comments and modifying it in the light of them, send it to Cantuar. I enclose a copy of his own scheme and of my draft. If it is not too much trouble, would you be so very kind as to glance through these and return them to me with any comments that you would wish to make. I know that Cantuar's first inclination was to say that the two bodies must not only declare their intention of seeking unity; but, after full discussions of Faith and Order, actually inaugurate a United Church; otherwise there will only be a qualification of ministers to officiate in two separate churches. But I doubt whether the means for the 'full discussion,' &c., exists in Persia. I don't think they have at hand theologians such as were available in India; and the scheme avoids any recommendation or formal permission for Anglicans to receive Holy Communion from non-episcopally ordained ministers.

The difficulties of Christians in Persia are very great; there is much persecution; and every step towards unity has a special value.

Yours ever,
William Ebor.

Frere to the Archbishop of York   17 September 1932

My dear Archbishop,

I must send a brief line in answer to your letter and memorandum to say that I have not been able to give it any full consideration as I am just off abroad. The two outstanding things in my mind are these:

1. The episcopal duty of Ordination is not really separate from other matters of general Church policy in which the Bishop acts as the representative of the Church; in other words, Church policy must be unified as well as Ordination. Any other clear restrictions would be quite intolerable and the work of the Bishop in Ordination a set of superstitious beliefs rather than the action of the Church as a whole trailing behind the Bishop as its representative, and conferring orders and their restrictions accordingly. In other words, in Persia there seems to be a

need for bringing North and South into one form of Church polity. The subject is not an impossibility. I should welcome a Church policy in which the presbyters have a much larger place in conjunction with the Bishops than is customary with us in Anglican circles as at present. I think this, therefore, would have to be the first thing to be considered and the question of Ordination could not be considered apart from that.

2. The difficulty does not seem to arise so much if that were accomplished with regard to men ordained in the country as distinct from men sent out by missionary bodies at home of an unepiscopal character. The difficulty would be presented in that case of men of unepiscopal ordination coming out to the Mission Field of the Persian area with non-episcopal orders. If not, I suppose it would be possible in some cases to stipulate that men who were to be devoted to that field of work should be ordained out there and not at home before they go out: this would probably limit it very seriously and I don't know whether the authorities of the Nonconformists would agree to it. Alternatively it might be possible to arrange that they should have the same position as those already out there who are non-episcopal. It seems to me a much easier thing to deal with those already in the field and give them a position in a United Church than it is to give the same position to newcomers.

3. This leads to a further consideration. If the Church policy should take place and there is a synodical government of which the Bishops should be the head, what should be done with the non-episcopal ministry upon the spot? This is the situation which I think is capable of being dealt with though not so satisfactorily on the lines of South India. What seems to be desired is that ministers of non-episcopal orders already existing on the spot should come into the arrangement, should have their pathetic situation recognized, and as such should have their place: but they must recognize that they would be debarred from a full participation because as long as they continue in non-episcopal orders they cannot be counted as having the full ministry, and must be debarred from ministering the sacraments—Holy Communion and Absolution in particular. In other words, if they wished to move they would have to come into the position of full priesthood, though their present position would be condoned as long as it lasts unchanged. This I think is the real way of getting over the difficulty with regard to non-episcopal ministers and congregations.

But I write all this hurriedly; as you see, it is only a note on one or two of the main points which seem to me to be outstanding. . . .

17. PAPAL CLAIMS

Professor Whitney to Frere   19 *June* 1927

My dear Frere,

About the Roman *v.* Anglican controversy, which is very much disturbing Yorkshire, and also people in the South—do you think that Figgis's two lectures in 'Our Place in Christendom' (Longmans, 1916) could be republished? They are so good and the book as a whole got too little notice.

Longmans gave me leave to republish mine (which I am now going to do) with additions.

Something ought to be said about the Eastern Church. What of your lecture in the same book?

Please forgive my troubling you but your brother of York is anxious for something to be published.

                                            I am,
                                                Yours truly,
                                                    J. P. Whitney.

Frere to Professor Whitney   21 *June* 1927

My dear Whitney,

This controversy is very troublesome—the less we have of it, I think, the better. I come more and more to feel that it is not any good controverting the Roman system of Papalism in any century later than the time of Leo; by then the papist claims were formulated in a sufficiently developed sense for us not to be able to accept them now. We accepted them naturally as a Roman mission from the coming of Augustine down to the Reformation; seeing then how they lacked a proper basis we very rightly went back to our history to repudiate them. That's how I view the case. If that is so, then all the medieval history—interesting as it is as a study of the Papacy and a gradual development of unreasonable claims—is not of first-class importance in the discussion between us and Rome; for our point is, that already by the time of Leo the papal claim had been put forward in an exaggerated form. Beyond that I think the only thing worth saying is that we have as much right to repudiate mistakes as anybody else has; and in fact we are all doing that all the time as the world grows older, they no less conspicuously than we. Therefore, so far as controversy is concerned, I should myself think it needed mainly to be carried on in those early centuries, and that is exactly the point where I think at any rate the book that you mention was weakest. The biblical essay in particular, if I remember rightly, was very poor. I am not at all pleased with my own efforts with regard to the East; so much has been written about it since that it would all have to be reconsidered. But I agree that we want a restatement of our Anglican position with regard to the Papacy. I think Armitage Robinson would admirably state the biblical situation and Kidd the early Patristic one. If anything is done I would suggest applying to those two people to provide for publication the sort of reasoned statement of the Anglican position which we really need. Your articles were very good stuff and I am sorry they were used in that rather stifled book: but I think we lose ground rather than gain it if we let anybody think that the medieval history is vital or anything else but a by-product in the real Roman controversies. . . .

Yours sincerely,
Walterus Truron.

18. THE CHURCH OF ENGLAND AND COMPREHENSION

The context of the following letters is best expressed in a paragraph from the biography of Archbishop Lang (p. 379).

'A minor but tedious controversy of the early days (at Lambeth) was the dispute over St. Aidan's, Small Heath, Birmingham, where the patrons had presented an incumbent whom the Bishop of Birmingham (Dr. Barnes) refused to institute. The patrons, among whom was the Bishop of Truro (Dr. Frere), eventually applied for a declaration that their candidate, the Rev. Doyle Simmonds, had been duly presented and asked for an order compelling the Bishop to accept him. This they obtained, but the Bishop continued contumacious, refusing either to admit the authority of the High Court of Chancery in such a matter or even to appear before it. In the end the Archbishop was driven to admit Mr. Simmonds himself. The incident involved him in an argument with the Bishop of Birmingham, who took the opportunity to attack the doctrines of the Real Presence in a letter which made it plain that he did not really understand what the doctrine was. Lang, like Davidson before him, dealt politely but firmly with Dr. Barnes and so closed a rather unedifying incident.'

Sir Michael Sadler (Master of University College, Oxford) to Frere
25 December 1929

My dear Bishop,

This, please, is not a letter which needs acknowledgement. I should hate to add to the burden of your writing. But I am moved to say how great and growing is the debt which I feel that I owe to you for your courage, consistency, example. Very little time goes by without my thinking of what you are and what you have done, and without my feeling that you embody for me a way of life and a fabric of belief. Especially at times of crisis, like these.

If you (who know so much better than I do, how the battle really rages) think that at any cost the case for Catholic Doctrine, Worship, and Observance must be now fought out in the Church of England; and that without a fight, the issue of which may mean disruption (or non-juring in a new sense), the claims of Catholic doctrine to a recognized place in the Church of England will go by default; I have nothing else to say, except that, though I don't feel called upon to join in it, the fight ought to go on and be pressed to a conclusion.

But if there is any hope of comprehension, any prospect of our keeping in the same communion the descendants of Nelson, Baxter, and Ken, I pray that some accommodation may be found. What was published on Monday is the final act of a tragedy—the conflicts of two Rights. Forgive me if I have written when I should not....

Frere to Sir Michael Sadler   *28 December* 1929
My dear Master,

It is delightful to have a letter from you and I am grateful to you for all that you say. Of the two alternatives that you put, my whole heart and soul is on the side of comprehension. I believe that what the little English Church can contribute to the world is the conviction that Churchmen can live together resting on a deep basis of the fundamentals of the faith, whilst at the same time differing markedly as to superstructure. When I say 'faith' I may, perhaps also ought to, say 'faith and discipline', because I think it is becoming more and more clear that not only is a fundamental agreement in faith required if there is to be real unity, but that for different reasons and of quite a less important character there must be agreement of system and discipline. My hope is that we go on patiently getting to understand others and helping them to understand one another, hastening slowly; because of divisions in the Church of England which always distresses me—they are diversities rather than divisions—and the talk about the possibility of a new non-juring distresses me beyond words.

The Barnes episode is unfortunate, but it will never do that Bishops should get the idea that they can force presentees to make promises, by threatening not to institute unless they do. This novel idea of Barnes's spread elsewhere would speedily become disastrous; all Bishops would impose their own terms upon the unfortunate people who have been accepted for a benefice. The law quite rightly defines what the Bishop's duties are and what rights he has to do the institution; it gives him large powers of inquiry and of rejection; but it nowhere authorizes him to impose conditions for the future. This move therefore I think is one to be resisted, or our Bishops will become tyrants like the French ones, and hold all their clergy in terror....

19. THE TRANSFERENCE OF SISTERS TO DIFFERENT COMMUNITIES

The Bishop of Bombay (Dr. Palmer) to Frere   21 *November* 1927

My dear Bishop,

I am rather suddenly faced with difficulties in the Bombay Affiliation of the All Saints Sisterhood. Two of the younger Sisters have come home to have operations, which will take place at the end of this week. In the meantime they have come to me to explain that they cannot possibly go on with the Community which they find in Bombay, and that they want to be transferred to some other Community or to set up a teaching Sisterhood of their own elsewhere in India. Mike Furse tells me that you are the best person to consult about this question, so I write to you this letter.

Could you write down in a few sentences what are the general conditions for the transfer of a sister from one Community to another? If you could and would, would you tell me whether there is any book dealing with religious communities in the Church of England which would give me information about the practice in this matter and the principles on which it has been based? If I could have an answer on this point before 11 a.m. on Thursday, when the two sisters see me again, it would help greatly.

While I have been at home, Bishop Lloyd, acting on a commission from me, dispensed another young sister of the same Community from her vows. He satisfied himself after careful inquiry that she never ought to have been professed, and that the consequent misfit was doing her immense harm spiritually and mentally. I have not any doubt that he judged correctly. Father Bull of Cowley, on the other hand, has written to me to the effect that as the vows were taken under a constitution, which is drawn up without any reference to dispensation and therefore not in view of possible dispensation (which is one of the conditions of all vows in the Roman Church), the Bishop of the diocese has no right to dispense from the vows of the All Saints Community, and any Sister must either keep her vows or break them on her own responsibility. It appears to me to be absurd that this should be the only choice. There have always been occasional cases when life vows have been wrongly taken. Whether they were wrongly taken or not, the person who took them is the least able to judge of all men, and it ought not to be put on his or her conscience. I find that as a matter of fact two Bishops in England have dispensed two Sisters of this very Community in England, so I suppose they did not accept Father Bull's reasoning. He has another argument as follows: 'It is said in the Statute (of the All Saints Community) that the vows are not enforced by ecclesiastical authority, and by the same reasoning they are not the subject of ecclesiastical authority.' Will you tell me please what you think about this abtruse argument of Father Bull's? I am not worried at all about the essential justice or equity of what Bishop Lloyd did, but I should like to give Father Bull an answer which he would understand. Perhaps you could supply me with one. Anyhow, it would be of great interest and help to me to hear your opinion on what is really his general thesis, that as the Church of England has not officially recognized Religious Orders, its Bishops have no right to dispense members of those Orders from their vows.

I am, Yours very sincerely,
Edwin James Bombay.

Frere to the Bishop of Bombay   22 *November* 1927

My dear Bishop,

I think the general custom has been that it was recognized that there was good reason to proceed from one religious community to another of strict observance, not otherwise. How that exactly would at present affect our situation I don't know, for we are not as clearly marked in differences of observance as elsewhere, or in ancient days. But this represents a consideration which naturally comes in any question of facts. In practice, in England, I think, customs vary; some Communities practically never accept anyone from elsewhere; some accept them as novices if they are willing to come in that capacity; others more easily receive them and receive them possibly after a short time of probation as professed Sisters. If it was merely a question of transfer from one Order to a more strict one, there ought not to be much difficulty in this; but I don't like the idea of their setting up a teaching Sisterhood of their own. So many people think they can manage it and much better themselves than their superiors can. The Community of the Holy Family (which you probably know as being one which is already teaching in England) is one which I think is not so stiff as many with regard to accepting Sisters from elsewhere. So that this seems possibly the first thing to turn to, if you are satisfied whether they are right in wishing to be transferred.

Secondly, with regard to the question of dispensation. There seems to me to be three distinctions to be borne in mind first of all.

(*a*) The distinction between temporary and permanent vows.

(*b*) The distinction between the vow viewed as an obligation to a Community and as an obligation to God.

(*c*) The distinction between simple vows and solemn vows. The third is perhaps the most important to get clear first. A vow I take it has value according to the sanction that is given to it; that is to say when one is considering its external and objective value; anyone taking a private vow has merely that measure of sanction for it. A vow taken before a Director would have more. A vow taken in conjunction with a Community would have more still; but all these would be of the nature of private vows or simple vows. The solemn vow is the vow which the Church authorizes definitely through the authority of the Bishops; the Church then intervenes and gives the sanction which one of the others have got, and undertakes to regulate and if necessary dispense, no less an authority being able to regulate or dispense in that case.

The first question therefore to ascertain about any vow is by what authority this was taken. If it is a simple vow it is *ipso facto* dispensable, and of course ecclesiastical authority can intervene to dispense a vow that has been made without its authority, because it hasn't an equivalent claim to authority behind it. It must intervene if anyone is to do so in dispensing solemn vows. If the vow was made with episcopal authority through the Bishop or Diocesan as a solemn and permanent vow, then the Bishop can, and only he can, dispense it; whether this is quoted in the conditions or not. Father Bull, I think, didn't deny a vow taken without authority is an authoritative vow; in every properly regulated Community where vows are taken these are meant to be solemn and lasting vows, and should only be taken with the authority of the Episcopate or formal Diocesan Visitor. No Community should expect the Church to recognize, still less to support, vows taken clandestinely. I should say to Father Bull that the Church people don't contract out of their obligations and can't contract out of the Episcopate and still remain Catholic, although I am still aware that there are many trying hard to do it at the present moment. Our Bishops, I think, now on the general question require a Visitor for a Community, and they also require that the statutes of the Community should contain a provision for dispensation with the very purpose of avoiding the kind of thing in question. That is to say, that the Episcopate recognizes the Communities now and correspondingly takes its measure of control.

Lastly, there is the point with regard to the dual nature of the obligation, whether temporary or permanent, being obligations partly to God and partly to the Community. In any case of dispensation, the dispensing Bishop should, I think, make clear what exactly the dispensation includes. There should be in any case a formal document of dispensation, given to the person dispensed and to the Community; and this should state whether the dispensation is merely a dispensation from the obligations to the particular Community, so that the person goes out free from vow but remains otherwise tied by the personal obligations of the vow; or whether the dispensation includes a relief from the personal obligations. For example: I have recently dispensed a Sister of our Community here; she desired a dispensation and the Community was willing to release her. That made that part clear. I also ascertained from consultation with her that she did not desire, at any rate as at present, to be dispensed from her personal obligations, but hoped to lead a life of poverty, chastity, and obedience somewhere and in some measure. She is to report to me later on if she finds this is not what she can manage, and desires to be released from personal obligations. I do not think, probably, she will wish to be. But anyhow, that illustrates the case. I have written rather at length, because I don't know of any book to which to refer you. I have also written hastily, because you want a speedy reply; so please forgive obscurities and crudities. . . .

20. THE APPOINTMENT OF DEANS

Frere to the Dean of Lichfield (Dr. Savage)   30 *January* 1929
My dear Dean,

Can you tell me offhand when your predecessors ceased to be elected by their Chapter and were appointed as at present? Did the system of election go on till the Act of 1840, or whatever it was that changed the situation? I can't quite make out how far elections were carried on in the matter of Deans in the Cathedrals of the older foundation: probably you know the whole thing backward. I run into it merely in editing

Parker's Register, when I get a licence from him during a vacancy to the Chapter of Exeter to elect their Dean, and a similar approval of the election and mandate to install at a later vacancy. But I imagine that that, in one form or another, was supposed to go on in all that group of Cathedrals. So far as I can see also, the Bishop was the patron so to speak who made the licence to elect when there was a licence, so Chapters proceeded without it, and gave approval and confirmation when all was over. The Law Books, however, say that the Crown did this: I haven't so far found in my small investigation any confirmation of this. I don't like to bother you to write a reply. If you are going to be up in London next week for the Assembly, we perhaps might have a word about it sometime, and you can probably tell me easily all that I need to know in a few sentences upon the Parker situation. But if this bothers you don't do anything about it; I merely write on the chance of your carrying it all in your head. . . .

The Dean of Lichfield to Frere 2 *February* 1929

My dear Bishop,

The following quotation from Gibson's *Codex* (173) will probably give you all that is necessary at the moment: 'Deans of the Old Foundation come in by Election of the Chapter upon the King's *congé d'élire*, with the Royal Assent and Confirmation of the Bishop, much in the same way as the Bishops themselves do. But the Deans of the New Foundation come in by the King's Letters Patent upon which they are instituted by their Bishop, and then installed upon a Mandate directed to the Chapters' (i.e. in 1761).

But I may add one or two brief notes concerning the ancient method of appointment of a Dean in the Cathedrals of the Old Foundation.

1. In the Black Book of Lincoln (*Linc. Cath. Stat.* Bradshaw and Wordsworth i. 279).

'Decanus Lincolniensis sic creatur.
quando decanatum vacare contingit; capitulum hoc episcopo per litteras suas denunciat
et non petita ab eo eligendi decanum licentia; convocantur omnes persone ecclesie et archidiaconi et canonici in anglia commorantes ut certo die lincolniam conveniant decanum electuri.'

2. At Lichfield (as I suppose elsewhere) the Dean was originally under the Norman reconstruction appointed by the Bishop. But in 1214, during vacancy of the See and of the Deanery, King John claimed the right

of appointment to the Deanery. The Chapter, however, had already made arrangements to elect a Dean. Under pressure from Nicolas the Legate they accepted the King's nomination of Ralph de Neville 'but without prejudice to their right of election in the future'. Shortly afterwards when William de Cornhull became Bishop, he conferred on the Chapter by a Charter the right of electing a Dean; and this was ratified by a decree of Pope Honorius in 1221. From that time onwards the Dean was always elected by the Chapter, except when the Pope arrogated to himself the right of nomination: sometimes, but not always, when the Dean had been promoted by Papal action to a Bishopric.

There were also frequent incursions of royal interference and domination. And this domination was emphatic and unabashed under Henry VIII and his immediate successors.

In the time of James I (I have not the exact date at hand) the system of Royal Appointment of a Dean by a *congé d'élire* was instituted; thus impounding the right to the Crown, but maintaining the form of capitular election.

This system held until the Cathedrals Act of 1840 which definitely placed all appointments of Cathedral Deans in the hands of the Crown. The last Dean of Lichfield elected on a *congé d'élire* was appointed 1833.

I imagine that this outline would practically apply to the other Cathedrals of the Old Foundation. But I have not worked it out.

3. With regard to the Exeter case to which you refer, the Chapter there was almost entirely depleted by deprivation. Therefore the Archbishop set himself to fill up such vacancies. At Exeter he appointed Gregory Dodds Dean in 1560, in succession to T. Reynolds, deprived; and within the next two years he also appointed a Sub-Dean and nine prebendaries under similar conditions. (See Gee, *Elizabethan Clergy*, App. II, p. 277.)

The precedent for the Archbishop intervening in local appointments autocratically had been set by Cranmer during the nominal reign of Edward VI.

Yours always,
H. E. Savage.

Frere to the Dean of Lichfield   21 *February* 1929

My dear Dean,

Thank you very much for your kind reply to my query about the Deans of the Old Foundation. I expect the extract that you quote from

Gibson is the source from which all the modern law books draw their assertion that the ancient method of appointing a Dean was by the King's licence and afterwards the King's confirmation. That, however, is quite untrue, as you show from Lincoln and Lichfield, and it was also the same elsewhere—London and Hereford, for example, as I have ascertained. Isn't it worth while, therefore, that some historical dealing with the matter could be put out so as to prevent the false idea to which Gibson has given rise? At the same time if it is possible to ascertain the stages by which the Crown ousted the Bishops from their office of licensing, election, and confirming, it would be a gain also. I gathered from your notes that it came about temp. James I, and such little of the evidence as I have come across seems to show the same thing, but I doubt whether it was done by any official act; more probably by a mere series of aggressions as opportunity offered. It looked to me as if Dean Donne was the first Dean at St. Paul's who got in merely through the Crown, but I haven't looked up the accounts that there are in the London Registers, so that is merely a guess. I am inclined to go further and ask *you* to clear up the whole thing for us. It is a nice bit of constitutional history on a small scale. Archbishop Parker definitely gave a licence for the election of Gregory Dodds at Exeter (see the Register on p. 214) and compare a similar action later on in his episcopate also at Exeter. That is the ground of my inquiries. But as I say, the evidence wants collecting and sifting, and a nice bit of history might emerge from it. For myself I must leave it where it is; only putting a little comment upon the passages in Parker's Register when dealing with the matter in saying a few words in the Introduction.

Grateful thanks for your help....

21. EPISCOPAL SIGNATURES

The Archbishop of Canterbury (Dr. Lang) to Frere   24 *May* 1934

My dear Bishop,

I send you in confidence the enclosed letter from the good Canon Ollard. I think there is a great deal in what he says and I have told him that I think such a Monograph as he proposes would be of great interest and of some value. I would naturally have told him to do it himself but I note what he says in the first page of his letter. As you are mentioned more than once I venture to write to ask whether in such few moments of leisure as you may have, you might do what he suggests. Though it would be a sort of πάρεργον it might entertain you, and the field is, so far as I know, largely unoccupied. Tell me what you think and return the letter with your comments. I should really be most grateful if you thought it was possible for you to amuse yourself by these inquiries.

Yours affectionately,
Cosmo Cantuar.

Frere to the Archbishop of Canterbury   1 *June* 1934

My dear Archbishop,

I return Ollard's letter; the question is how much is supposed to be wanted. A scholarly treatise on the subject of episcopal style and signature would, of course, be an interesting and fairly laborious work to compile, if it was to have any completeness or historical authority. On the other hand, if what is wanted is guidance to the present-day issues, the matter is much simpler, I think; for surely the outline of the affair is not at all complicated.

First: the episcopal signature goes back behind the stage at which there were any surnames or signatures in our sense of the word. Episcopal style began much as follows: 'so and so by divine (whatever it was) Bishop of so and so, to so and so, Greeting'; then the document would start. If the Bishop was not the chief person making the grant, or whatever it was, but only one of those attesting it, he signed 'Thomas, Bishop', as somebody else signed 'Thomas, Presbyter' or 'Thomas, Monk' and might put a cross against his name, to make for clearness. He as chief granter added his seal and all was in Latin. In a later stage when people were acquiring surnames, the Bishop might have one; but it was more a nickname than anything else in a good many cases, and didn't appear as part of the episcopal signature. But his having a surname tended to reduce the importance of his Christian name: so he signed with an initial instead of a Christian name in full, followed by the adjective of his see instead of a surname. If the Bishop had a Christian name that was easily Latinized and had a see with the name of the same sort, all was well: he could sign then with his Christian name which was the really important part, together with the Latin name of his see. Here in England we have kept up this custom; it has been dropped elsewhere, but it was once widespread, foreign ecclesiastics have not kept the same continuity of custom as we have.

The practical question then that arises is this. Should the Bishops be encouraged to sign their Christian name in full instead of being satisfied with an initial? and with the see name?

Secondly: should they sign in Latin? if so, should their Latin signature be really Latin or else a jumble of English and Latin? In the case of new sees where there is no Latin tradition of the place and especially where there is no obviously suitable Latin available to the Bishop's signature, I would suggest that it should be in English.

Yours sincerely,
Walterus Truron.

APPENDIX II

THE ENTHRONEMENT OF DR. LANG AS ARCHBISHOP OF CANTERBURY

(The Bishop of Chichester, Dr. Bell, very kindly offered to place at my disposal not merely Dr. Frere's letters but the whole of the correspondence dealing with this question. Its value was considerable and I felt justified in going beyond the recognized scope of the book in including material not immediately concerned with Frere. The offer was therefore gratefully accepted. R. C. D. J.)

When Dr. Lang became Archbishop of Canterbury in 1928 the Dean of Canterbury, Dr. G. K. A. Bell, solicited the help of a number of experts in drawing up the Service of Enthronement. One of these was Dr. Brightman, and in one of his letters he remarked that as it had been the right of the Priors of Christ Church to enthrone Archbishops, he assumed that the Dean would enthrone him in this instance. This was, of course, contrary to precedent, for since the Reformation the Archdeacon of Canterbury had normally enthroned Archbishops. Dr. Bell thereupon consulted Maskell's *Monumenta Ritualia* and found support for Dr. Brightman's contention; while the Archdeacon did in effect enthrone Diocesan Bishops in the Southern Province, it had been the Prior who had enthroned Archbishops in pre-Reformation times. Further advice was sought from the Dean of Wells, Dr. Armitage Robinson. He professed to have no exact information on the subject but felt that it was illogical for the Archdeacon to enthrone the Archbishop. It did not seem likely that the Prior, if present, would have deputed the Archdeacon to act for him; though, of course, it was not inconceivable. It was his own opinion, though given 'with hesitation and reserve', that the Prior's part in this matter should belong to the Dean as the representative (if present) of the Mother Church of England. Finally he suggested that the Bishop of Truro should be consulted.

Frere agreed that the medieval practice was for the Prior to enthrone and cited the *Pontifical of Lacey*, the *Salisbury Pontifical*, and *Clifford's Pontifical* in support. The present position of the Archdeacon was certainly illogical; and without having definite proof he suspected that the Archdeacon's intervention only came in as a piece of false analogy. The Archdeacon of Canterbury was the Archbishop's representative and was in no way specially connected with the Convent or Chapter. Logically, therefore, he could not step into the position of representative of the Chapter or natural successor of the Prior: that was unquestionably the function of the Dean. The precedent for enthronement by the Archdeacon had undoubtedly started with Parker, for in his case the Archdeacon had been commissioned to enthrone him. It was a question of precedence prevailing over logic. Frere suggested that it might be interesting to find out what had happened in the case of Parker's predecessor, Pole. The Chapter records of the Reformation period might provide valuable information as to what had happened when the Prior ceased to exist.

Unfortunately the Chapter records revealed nothing, so Dr. Bell wrote to Dr. Claude Jenkins, Librarian of Lambeth Palace, to see whether the Lambeth records could throw any light on the matter. The quest was successful, and Dr. Jenkins was able to furnish information about the enthronement of both Pole and Parker. Pole had been too busy to go from Lambeth to Canterbury to be enthroned and had given a proxy to Robert Collins, the Commissary General, to go there and take over corporal possession. The Dean of Canterbury did not instal Pole's proctor, for although he was Dean of both Canterbury and York at the same time, his religious duties rested very lightly upon his shoulders. His real occupation was that of Ambassador at the French Court and it was therefore impossible for him to be present at Canterbury. No doubt the Archdeacon, Nicholas Harpsfield, would be regarded as a suitable person to act in his place. In any case the matter was not considered to be of great importance beyond the necessity of getting seisin as the result of induction.

When Parker was enthroned Wotton was still Dean of Canterbury and York and again failed to perform the ceremony. Indeed there is every indication that he was still occupied with his diplomatic work in France and the Netherlands.[1] The matter was taken in hand by Archdeacon Gest, although Dr. Jenkins claimed that Frere was wrong in saying that he undertook the enthronement. In effect he issued a long mandate stating that he was too busy to enthrone Parker and commissioned others to do it for him, although their actual names were not given.

Dr. Bell, in the light of this information, succeeded in effecting a compromise, whereby both Dean and Archdeacon enthroned the

[1] It seems that he was absent from England from Sept. 1558 to May 1559. Parker was consecrated on 17 Dec. 1559.

Archbishop. The Mandate for the enthronement was issued to the Chapter, who then asked both the Dean and the Archdeacon to take part. The Dean enthroned the Archbishop in the marble chair of St. Augustine and the Prior's seat in the Chapter House, while the Archdeacon enthroned him in the Archbishop's throne and in the Dean's stall. Enthronement in the marble chair involved a significant departure from previous custom. Hitherto this chair had been situated in the Corona, where the last three Archbishops had been enthroned out of sight of the congregations both in choir and nave. Now it was placed in full view on a platform at the top of the steps at the east end of the nave, thereby changing the enthronement from a private ceremony into one in which the whole congregation played a part. So, to quote J. G. Lockhart, 'The new arrangement, by the closer association of Church and people with the proceedings, symbolized the changed status of the Archbishop. He was more than the Bishop of a Diocese or the Metropolitan of a Province; he was the first spiritual leader of the land, the senior Bishop of a world-wide communion.'[1]

The Dean of Canterbury to Dr. Brightman   20 *September* 1928

My dear Dr. Brightman,

... As you intimate, the enthronement of the Archbishop is rather complex, in fact threefold.... I have been looking at Maskell (1882), vol. 2, and the enthronement service there appears to contemplate two enthronements for the Archbishop of Canterbury, but of course not the enthronement in the Dean's stall. I believe that the Archbishop is enthroned first in the Bishop's throne, then in St. Augustine's Chair as Metropolitan, then in the Dean's stall as head of the Cathedral Body. Would that be right? ...

You will notice from the printed form that the Prior no longer enthrones the Archbishop, but the Archdeacon of Canterbury, who receives a Mandate from the Vicar General. I should like to see the Archdeacon embrace the Archbishop as you suggest the Prior should, but I am not sure that I should be able to persuade either him or the victim. ...

                                         Yours very sincerely,
                                                     G. K. A. Bell.

[1] J. G. Lockhart, *Cosmo Gordon Lang*, 1949, pp. 313–14.

The Dean of Canterbury to Dr. Dearmer 20 *September* 1928

My dear Dearmer,

... I have been thinking over the service and have looked up various ancient books as well as the official description of various enthronements in the Chapter Act Books. If you have Hook's *Lives of the Archbishops* you would be most interested by the very full account of Winchelsey's enthronement. ...

You will notice the proposal to have the marble throne in the nave so as to give that congregation a part in the service instead of leaving it entirely in the cold. But all the antiquarians I fear will hold up holy hands of horror at the thought of taking the marble throne out of the choir; nothing as yet has been settled. But I don't think—wherever else this throne is put—we can leave it in the little corner where it is now, for such an occasion. Nobody sees anything of the ceremony in that position.

Yours ever,
G. K. A. Bell.

The Dean of Wells (Dr. Armitage Robinson) to the Dean of Canterbury
27 *September* 1928

My dear Dean of Canterbury,

... The marble seat has been moved about so much that I see no reason against your putting it where you like for a particular occasion. The platform in front of the choir door is an ideal position from the spectacular point of view and at least as suitable as Becket's Crown for an enthronement. I say this in ignorance of what upholders of tradition may have to say on the other side.

Enthronement signifies the public investing of the Prelate in his legal or customary rights, after due guarantee that he will use them in accordance with law and custom: ...

As to the Archdeacon of Canterbury's intervention, I take it to be grounded on the claim of the Prior and Convent of Christ Church to be 'the Mother Church of England'. They claimed that no Bishop should be consecrated in any church but their own except with their express permission. They carried their claim further in requiring that their Archdeacon should be representative in admitting the Bishop to his local rights by enthronement in his cathedral church. I presume that the Archdeacon so acted on their mandate or at their request.

We have then to ask what became of this claim of the Prior and Convent of Canterbury after the Reformation. Are we to suppose that the Archdeacon of Canterbury continued to act through custom? Or did the Dean and Chapter authorize him? I cannot say. I do not know what authority he acts on now (though perhaps I ought to know), but no doubt he can inform you.

As to the enthronement of the Archbishop of Canterbury, I have no information apart from your statement that it used to be done by the Prior. It seems unlikely that the Prior if present would depute the Archdeacon to act for him—though it is not inconceivable. . . . I can only speak with hesitation and reserve—for you may have documents or traditions which would suggest caution—but I conceive that the Prior's part in this matter should belong to the Dean as the representative (if present) of 'the Mother Church of England'.

I venture to suggest that before taking action on either of the matters raised in your letter, you should place what I have written before the Bishop of Truro, who has far more knowledge in these things than I have.

Yours very sincerely,
J. Armitage Robinson.

The Dean of Canterbury to Frere   28 *September* 1928

My dear Lord Bishop,

I should be very grateful if you would help me in one or two important matters connected with the enthronement of the new Archbishop in Canterbury Cathedral at the end of November or beginning of December. The Chapter and I are very anxious that the enthronement should be worthily and faithfully carried out, so far as depends upon us. I write to you—venturing so far to trouble you—because the Dean of Wells urges me to refer certain special points to your judgement. I enclose the letter which I have just received from him. I asked him three questions.

1. What does enthronement mean?
2. Is there any strong reason against placing the marble throne for this occasion at the east end of the nave?
3. How is it that the Archdeacon of Canterbury, and not the Dean, has in recent years enthroned the Archbishop?

He answers (1) clearly.

I would amplify (2) thus. The marble throne is now in Becket's Crown, and in that position, all hidden from the congregations in choir and nave, the last three Archbishops have been enthroned. But it was only moved there, our Chapter minutes show, in 1883 from the south choir transept. On the occasion of the Lambeth Conference 1920, the marble throne was placed just in front of the high altar. The main point of placing it at the east end of the nave at the enthronement is that the very large nave congregation may be brought into active and visible connexion with the enthronement. The enthronement on the Bishop's throne (opposite the pulpit) and the installation in the Dean's stall, *must* take place in the choir.

The point about (3) is this. The Archdeacon of Canterbury installs—and did so long before the Reformation—Diocesan Bishops of the Southern Province. But before the Reformation, as Maskell's *Mon. Rit.* specimen of the enthronement service of an Archbishop indicates, the Prior enthroned the Archbishop. How is it that the Archdeacon enthrones him today and not the Dean? Does some historical reason lie behind the recent practice by which the Archdeacon enthrones? And whom does the Archdeacon represent? Not the Archbishop clearly. Is it the Dean and Chapter? Would the Chapter *if they desired*, without injustice to the Archdeacon, depute someone else, e.g. the Dean? It is an historical problem; no personal problem is involved between the Archdeacon and myself!

As to the enthronement service, we are (at present) proposing to make it an independent service after the Eucharist and Mattins—not part of Mattins as in recent years. Is there any objection to this? Any hints, advice, or warning you can give me on the question of the service would, I need not say, be deeply appreciated.

Yours very sincerely and dutifully,
G. K. A. Bell.

Frere to the Dean of Canterbury   1 October 1928

My dear Dean,

I am very much interested in your letter and in these problems as well as the Dean of Wells's reply to them. I have been looking at such records as I have under my hand at the moment of medieval practice in the matter, where, of course, it is clear that the Prior did the enthronement. You probably know the forms which are most easily accessible—the one in the *Pontifical of Lacey*, and a very similar form printed from a *Salisbury Pontifical* at the end of the *York Pontifical* published by the Surtees Society. These give the forms which were customary then and, of course, there is no doubt about the position of the Prior. There are some further details with some rather more local references to Canterbury itself in the manuscript Pontifical called Clifford's which is at Cambridge. The main thing that is added there is that the Prior and ministers present make a station with the Archbishop on his entry before the marble throne under the feretory of St. Blaise, turning to the east; all this while the responds are being sung; and then come the prayers and the enthronement by the Prior; after all this comes the Mass of the Holy Trinity. It is interesting to compare the position with York which is fairly clearly set out in the appendixes to the same volume of the Surtees Society—several documents from the York Registers; there, of course, the Dean enthrones. If these things were recorded in the Chapter House at York probably similar records have been made by your Chapter at Canterbury, and if you have any such records of the Reformation time those would, of course, be especially valuable as showing what happened when the Prior ceased to exist. I can't help suspecting that the Archdeacon's intervention comes in only as a piece of false analogy; but of course it is merely a guess. I don't know what precedent has to say in the matter. But further, whatever there is of precedent for the Archdeacon acting, it seems to me to require something of a logical justification as well, and I cannot say that I see any logical justification for it whatever. No doubt there were monastic Archdeacons in places (and the Archdeacon of Westminster is the survival of one of them), but I do not think that there was ever a monastic Archdeacon, so far as I know, for the Chapter or Convent at Canterbury. Certainly the Archdeacon of Canterbury is clearly the Archbishop's representative, is he not, and in no way specially connected with the Convent or Chapter. I cannot see, therefore, that he could logically step into the position as representing the Chapter, or as being the natural successor of the Prior; from every logical point of view the Dean must be that. Logically, therefore, I should have thought present custom is not defensible and it ought to cease unless the force of tradition behind it is an overwhelming one. I should agree, as the Dean does, that the archiepiscopal throne should be put in the most convenient place, and there is no doubt, as he says, what the best place is. I can't identify, for lack of knowledge, the place which *Clifford's Pontifical* indicates, but probably you can. If it can be identified it would probably be clear whether there was any other purpose than stage management indicating the place where the chair should be for the purpose. As to the position of the service, I should have some sort of historical desire to keep the position of the ceremony before the Eucharist, most probably after Mattins, not merely on historical grounds. I think I should be inclined to add that there might be a good many practical reasons for the same thing. Of course, I recognize that modern conditions have altered things and to a certain extent have to be deferred to. ...

Yours ever,
Walterus Truron.

P.S. Yes, I see now the Archdeacon has good precedent. He was commissioned to enthrone Parker. See *Parker Reg.*, p. 34. Did he also Pole? The *Pole Reg.* or the *Sede Vacante* should tell. I don't fancy they do—anyhow my notes on them don't tell *me*—but Parker I expect set the precedent and it has probably prevailed over logic—alack!

The Dean of Canterbury to the Revd. C. E. Woodruff, Hon. Asst. Librarian to the Chapter of Canterbury 4 October 1928

Dear Mr. Woodruff,

You were kind enough to offer help in connexion with enthronement matters. One rather interesting point on which I have been in correspondence with the Bishop of Truro and the Dean of Wells is the question how the Archdeacon of Canterbury has come to enthrone the Archbishop. The Archdeacon, of course, enthrones the Diocesan Bishops in this Province. But it is clear that while the Archdeacon in pre-Reformation days enthroned the Bishops, it was the Prior who enthroned the Archbishop. Please do not imagine that I am going to do anything dreadful. But Frere, who is very decided in thinking that the Archdeacon is an illogicality for this purpose, says that our Chapter Acts and perhaps some Registers would throw a good deal of light on what happened in the past. I gather that the Royal Commissioners issued a Mandate to the Archdeacon and they were Bishops present to confirm the Archbishop. Who enthroned Pole? Frere says that Parker was enthroned by the Archdeacon. If you can throw any light on the early post-Reformation practice it would be very interesting, and I should be very grateful.

Yours sincerely,
G. K. A. Bell.

Appendix II

The Dean of Canterbury to Frere   5 October 1928

My dear Lord Bishop,

Very many thanks for your letter about the enthronement and for your most kind help. I have got hold of the Surtees Society *York Pontifical*, which is very interesting, and I am trying to get hold of Lacey's from the London Library. Mr. Woodruff is kindly investigating our Chapter records and any registers that we may have here. I will certainly let you know what discoveries we make.

As to the place of the marble throne, I am very glad to get your approval of the Dean of Wells's suggestion. I enclose a plan of the Cathedral from which you will see the proper and original place on which it stood. This is the place referred to as near the feretory of St. Blaise. The difficulty of putting it there, whether for the enthronement or permanently, is very much a practical one, though other difficulties have been felt by the present Archbishop, viz. the displacement of about 100 seats for members of the congregation; and our congregations are such that we cannot, so fas as I can see, do without these seats.

I note what you say about the celebration in close connexion with the enthronement. For many reasons I should like to have it. But when we have a congregation of over 4,000, as we had for the last enthronement, there are certainly difficulties, as you will agree.

Yours very sincerely and dutifully,

G. K. A. Bell.

In reply Frere sent the following postcard.

Don't bother about *Lacey's P*; you won't get more out of that than out of Surtees Soc.

The extra in *Clifford* is:

R⁊ Deum time *ad introitum chori* Archiep Prior Ministri faciant stationem coram sede marmorea archiepi sub feretro Blasii versi ad orientem. Finito.

R⁊ *Prior subjunget Or.* Deus qui excelso col. . . .
Perducat arch/em ad cath. Or OSD qui oim sis altissimus.
Enthrone in dei n. . . . authoritate eiusdem. *Eight monks sing:*
Bnes Deus. *Prior* OSD qu. . . . de summo. *Missa de Trin.*
Statio: Simply means they take up their position there to do the things specified.
The R⁊ is sung as they go there for entry to choir.

W. T.

The Enthronement of Dr. Lang

Mr. Woodruff submitted the following notes.

1. Our Registers do not record the enthronization of Pole or Parker. In Register V, ff. 166–70 there is a copy of the *Instrumentum sive processus installacionis et intronizacionis domini Edmundi Cantuar' archiepiscopi*, 1575.

Grindall was installed, i.e. by proxy, in the person of Thomas Godwyn, Dean of Canterbury. The mandate to induct, &c., was issued by the Bishops of London, Winchester, Ely, and Hereford, the royal commissioners *ad hoc*, and was delivered by the Public Notary, Robert Whithorne LL.B., appointed specially as scribe of acts and registrar by the Dean and Chapter, to the Archdeacon if the office should be full, or if it should be vacant, to the Dean and Chapter. The Archdeaconry being vacant, by the cession of Edmund Freke, the D and C appointed William Darell, the Vice-Dean, to install the Archbishop.

On 16 February 1575, Dr. Darell administered the oath to the Archbishop's proxy—that he should observe the customs and liberties of the cathedral and metropolitical Church, &c., as far as they were not repugnant to the word of God, the statutes of the realm and the royal prerogative.

The said W. Darell and Mr. Thomas Willoughby, the senior Canon, proceeded to the Chapter House and conducted Master Thomas Godwyn, the Archbishop's proxy, to the great west door of the nave of the Cathedral Church 'et abinde per medium chori usque ad sedem episcopalem inter eundem chorum et mensam Domini ibidem constitutum et ornatum. Ceteris vero canonicis maioribus et minoribus ac aliis ministris eos ordine precedentibus et ad solita loca respective se conferentibus et dirigentibus, ibique ad pedem dicte sedis eodem procuratore stante, (procuratorium?) procuratoris reverendissimi patris antedicti per me notarium publicum predictum iterum publice recitatum et perlectum fuit (   )[1] prenominatus magister Willelmus Darell eundem procuratorem in eadem sede archiepiscopali collocavit et (sedere?) fecit, ipsumque vice et nomine antedicti reverendissimi patris Edmundi Cant' archiepiscopi et eum in persona ei(usdem?) procuratoris sui in archiepiscopatum et dignitatem archiepiscopalem Cant' et in realem actualem et to(talem?) possessionem eiusdem inducebat intronizavit et installavit tunc ibidem publice et aperte sic dice(ns?) Ego auctoritate mihi concessa induco installo et intronizo reverendissimum patrem Edmundum Cant (   ) in persona tua et

---

[1] The blanks are due to burns at the edge of the manuscript.

te eius nomine et Dominus custodiat introitum suum et exitum suum ex hoc nunc (et in?) seculum, &c.

Quo facto et transcurso et cantato 73° psalmo a toto choro et intercantandum (   ) concionator in suggestu ac facta ibidem concione per discretum virum magistrum Nicholaum Symps(on) (artium?) magistrum accipiens pro themate Amen, dico, vobis: qui non intrat per ostium in ovile ovium, sed ascendit aliunde: ille fur est, et latro, &c. Jo. cap x°. Iidem seniores canonici produxerunt more predicto eundem (   ) per mensam Domini ad sedem marmoream tunc ibidem decenter preparatam in qua dicti seniores (   ) etiam collocarunt et sedere fecerunt, dicto magistro Willelmo Darell verba installacionis et (   ) modo quo supra dictante et recitante. Et tunc dictis et effusis per eundem procuratorem precibus (   ) de stanno [sic MS., for stallo?] sive sede marmorea huiusmodi surgebat quem prefati seniores ad stallum (   ) per medium chori modo quo supra conducebant qua in signum realis possessionis huiusmodi ass(   ) dicto magistro Willelmo Darell vicedecano antedicto stare sive sedere fecerunt. Et tunc su(ccentor?) dicte ecclesie cath' et metropolitice incepit decantare ympnum *Te Deum laudamus* in lingua (vulgari?) viz anglicana quem chorus cum organis solemniter persequebatur usque finem eiusdem (   ) psalmi.

The Archbishop's proxy was then conducted to the Chapter House where the said Master Darell placed him *in loco eminentiori*; and the whole Cathedral body made promise of canonical obedience.

2. Chapter Acts 1711–26. (Double sheet of paper inserted A45–6.)

Archbishop Wake's enthronization 15 June 1716, Mandate to install, &c., addressed to Dr. Thos Green, Archdeacon of Canterbury, or his sufficient deputy.

The Archdeacon with the Vicar General went to the west end of the nave while the Archbishop was robing in the Consistory Court, at that time under the north-west tower. When the Archbishop was ready Dean George Stanhope and Charles Elstob, Vice Dean, escorted the Archbishop through the choir, the Dean walking on the right hand and the Vice Dean on the left hand of the Archbishop to the Archiepiscopal seat between the choir and the Lord's Table.

Archidiacono immediate praecendente et Canonicis majoribus et minoribus ceterisque ministris superpelliciis et habitibus gradui compententibus indutis eos ordine praeuntibus et hymnum e psalmis desumptum cantantibus, ad stallum Archidiaconi Cant' se respective conferentibus, ubi totus conventus adstabat, et dictus dns Archiepus stallum dicti Archidiaconi sedi Archiopali adjunctum intrabat et in eodem per modicum temporis spatium sedebat. The Vicar General then delivered to the Archdeacon the royal mandate who received it humbly and gave it to the public notary to read; which done, the Archdeacon made the Archbishop sit in the Archiepiscopal seat and inducted and enthroned him into the real, actual, and corporal possessions of the Archbishopric by the following words:

Ego Thomas Greene S.T.P. Archidiaconis Cant. authoritate qua fungor induco installo et inthronizo vos reverendissimum in Christo patrem Gullielmum providentia divina Cant' Archiepiscopum in archiepiscopatum et dignitatem Archiepiscopalem Cant' ac in realem actualem et corporalem possessionem dicti archipiscopatus Cant', juriumque dignitatum honorum. praeeminentiarum et pertinentium eiusdem universorum, et Dominus custodiat introitum tuum et exitum tuum ex hoc nunc et usque in seculum. Amen.

After which, Morning Prayer was said by the Dean. Prayers ended, part of Psalm 135 was sung and Dr. Ralph Blomer preached a sermon on a text taken from Acts ix. 15–16. Then the Dean and Vice Dean escorted the Archbishop to the *sedem marmoream tunc decenter praeparatam*, in which they made the Archbishop sit down using the same words of installation as before. Then the Archbishop rose from his seat and knelt in private prayer after which he was conducted by the Dean and Vice Dean to the Dean's stall in the choir where again the Archdeacon installed him with these words: 'In signum realis possessionis Vos Reverendissime Pater in hac sede collocamus.' Then the Precentor began to chant the Te Deum in English, which was taken up and sung through by the choir with organ accompaniment. When this was finished the Archdeacon read and chanted certain versicles and suffrages, to which the choir of singers responded. Then the Archdeacon recited a collect for the Archbishop. This done, the Dean and Vice Dean conducted the Archbishop to the Chapter House where he was placed in the chief seat (*in loco eminentiore*) by the Archdeacon with these words: 'Vobis Reverendissime in Christo pater hanc sedem assignamus.' Then the Archdeacon administered the oath to the Archbishop 'sub hac verborum serie ... viz. Reverendissime Pater praestabis juaramentum corporale ad haec sancta Dei Evangelia per te hic corporaliter tacta quod jura et libertates huius Ecclesiae Cathlis et Metropol' Christi Cant' tueberis approbatasque et approbandas eiusdem ecclesiae consuetudines observabis et quantum ad te attinet facies ab aliis observari quatenus consuetudines huismodi non sunt contrariae et repugnantes verbo Dei ac statutis legibus provisionibus et ordinationibus huius regni aut praerogativae coronae serenissimi Dni Regis et non aliter neque alio modo.'

The promise of canonical obedience by the whole body of Ministers follows.

The Dean of Canterbury to the Revd. Claude Jenkins   17 *October* 1928

My dear Jenkins,

You have kindly helped me already with suggestions for the enthronement service. A very interesting problem has arisen. Brightman, writing to me, said that the Prior of Christ Church always enthroned archbishops, and assumed that the Dean would enthrone him in this instance. This caused me some thoughtfulness. I looked up some of the old services in Maskell, and I found that while the Archdeacon of Canterbury always enthroned the diocesan bishops in the Southern Province, it was always the Prior, and never the Archdeacon, who enthroned the Archbishop. I wrote to the Dean of Wells and the Bishop of Truro on the matter and they were both of one accord that the Archdeacon's position was quite illogical, and had probably been introduced by accident and false analogy. The Bishop of Truro went so far as to say that unless there were overwhelming practice against it, the mistake should be corrected now, and the Dean enthrone. Unfortunately, there is, so far as we can tell, unbroken historical precedent in favour of the Archdeacon. And Grindall, and it seems all successors, have been so enthroned. The Bishop of Truro wondered, however, what happened about Pole. Woodruff can find nothing here which throws any light on the matter. I wonder if there is anything at Lambeth?

I have talked it over with the Archdeacon and also with the Archbishop. We are proposing to place the marble throne in the nave, just in front of the choir screen. A proposal under consideration is that the Archdeacon shall enthrone in the choir, while the Dean enthrones in the marble chair in the nave. The Archbishop himself thinks there is a great deal to be said for this, and the Archdeacon actually suggested it off his own bat in a very nice way. But before I go further in the matter, I should be greatly helped if you have any light with regard to Pole.

Yours ever,

G. K. A. Bell.

The Revd. Claude Jenkins to the Dean of Canterbury 18 October 1928

My dear George,

It may seem very shocking but it is purely a modern fashion to attach any particular importance to the enthronement, nor is any special mention of it made as a rule in the Provincial Registers, though it ought to be in the Capitular Registers.

Pole was too busy to go from Lambeth to Canterbury to be enthroned and gave a proxy to Robert Collins, the Commissary General, to go there and take over corporal possession, &c. In the case of Parker's consecration, when owing to the importance of the occasion, every stage is represented by a record in the Provincial Register, the Archdeacon of Canterbury describing himself as the person to whom inductions and enthronizations of *Bishops of the Province of Canterbury* by long custom belongs, issues a long mandate stating that he is too busy to enthrone the new Archbishop, and commissioning other people (it has not even been thought worth while to fill in the names) to do it. I do not therefore understand Frere's statement, unless in the sense that *qui facit per alium facit per se*. All the evidence in hand is that at any rate Archdeacon Gest did not in person enthrone Parker. It is true that the Prior enthroned the Archbishop in pre-Reformation days, but it is quite certain that your eminent predecessor, the first Reformation Dean, Nicholas Wotton, did not instal Pole's proctor, since though he was Dean both of Canterbury and York at the time (as also at the time of Parker's advent) his real occupation was that of Ambassador at the French Court. In the circumstances Nicholas Harpsfield the Archdeacon would be a person whose performance of the functions would seem quite appropriate: he enthroned other Bishops. The Dean was not and could not be there, and the matter was in any case not one to which any special importance was attached beyond the necessity of getting seisin as the result of induction. When Parker was enthroned, Wotton was still holding both Deaneries and there were not the same obstacles to his performance of the function; but your acquaintance with his history will suggest a good many reasons why he should prefer that someone else should do it.

There, so far as I can see, is the origin of the whole matter. As to the double enthronement—well, there is no reason why, if you should want to have it, you should not, but it means *in the second case in the Cathedral*, if you have two enthronements there, absolutely nothing whatever from the point of view of secular or canon law. It is an opportunity no doubt for saying some prayers, but you will have to be very careful what you do as to the form of words.

Yours affectionately,
Claude Jenkins.

The Dean of Canterbury to Frere   17 November 1928

My dear Lord Bishop,

... You will be glad to learn that the Archdeacon of Canterbury and the Dean and Chapter have come to an agreement whereby the Mandate for the enthronement is to be issued to the Chapter, who will ask the Archdeacon to take certain parts, and the Dean certain parts, of the enthronement. . . .

Yours very sincerely and dutifully,
G. K. A. Bell.

INDEX

ABLUTIONS, 96, 232–4, 251, 255
Accession Service, 106, 108–9
Acland, Dr., Bp. of Bombay, 274–6
Act of Uniformity, 5, 11
Acts of the Church (Joyce), 134, 136
Alcuin Club, 95, 187
All Saints Sisterhood, Bombay, 289–91
Altars, Dedication of, 276–7
Anamnesis, 66–69, 71–74, 84–86, 105–6, 162–3
Anaphora, The, (W. H. Frere), 189–90
Angelus, 265
Anglo-Catholics, 95, 106, 114, 116, 129–30, 139–40, 143, 150, 162, 168, 172, 239, 262, 269
Antiphons, 54
Aquinas, St. Thomas, 88, 91
Arnold, Dr. J. H., 185
Ash Wednesday, 270–1
Aumbry, 99, 101–2, 125, 145–6

BAPTISM, 25, 46, 48, 106, 112–14, 121–2, 196
Barnes, Fr. Bertram, C.R., 179, 231, 237–42
Barnes, Dr. E. W., Bp. of Birmingham, 129–33, 167, 177, 183, 287–9
Barry, Revd. F. R., 94
Bason, 12, 17
Bell, Dr. G. K. A., Dean of Canterbury, later Bp. of Chichester, 95, 298–303, 305–6, 310–12
Benedicite, 7, 198–200
Benedictus, 8, 199, 203–5, 230, 254
Bishop, Preb. H. E., 276–7
Bishops, ceremonial behaviour of, 277–9
Black Letter Days, 8, 119
Book of Common Prayer, 1549, 11, 14, 18–21, 38, 39, 73, 85, 138; American, 60, 62 n., 66, 89, 214; Scottish, 1637, 50, 59, 66, 73, 89, 209, 212, 214, 218 n., 220 n.

Boutflower, Dr., Bp. in S. Tokyo, 198, 202
Brightman, Dr. F. E., 26, 42, 44, 46–47, 49–51, 53, 57, 215, 228, 298, 300, 310
Briscoe, Revd. J. F., 120
Browne, Dr., Bp. of Bristol, 10
Bull, Fr. H. P., S.S.J.E., 120, 289–91
Bullock-Webster, Canon, 129
Burial Service, 25, 46, 54, 92–94
Burrows, Dr. W., Bp. of Chichester, 83, 103, 123–4, 142

CALENDAR, REVISION OF, 24, 45, 48, 94–95, 122
Canon, Eucharistic (*see also* Communion, Holy), 25, 56–60, 62 n., 63–65, 67–81, 84, 95–99, 104–6, 114–15, 117–20, 138–41, 147, 150, 163, 173, 185–90, 203–11, 242–3, 250–3
Canons, 4–6, 89, 135
Carr, Dr., Bp. of Coventry, 144
Cecil, Lord Hugh, 83, 121, 124, 134–5
Cecil, Lord Wm., Bp. of Exeter, 183
Censer (*see also* Incense), 6, 11–12, 14–16
Ceremonial, Caroline, 17
Ceylon, Liturgy of, 253–5
Chandler, Bp, 185
Chase, Dr., Bp. of Ely, 10, 26, 40, 82
Chavasse, Dr., Bp. of Liverpool, 82
Church Assembly, 82–83, 93, 129, 138, 140, 145, 159, 171, 173, 175–6, 184
Church Association, 183
Church Times, The, 138, 171, 187–8, 261
Church Quarterly Review, The, 24, 210, 226–7
Collects, 24, 27–30, 36, 45, 50–51, 95, 228–30, 237–8, 240, 242, 245, 270–1
Comfortable Words, 58, 66–67, 74, 76, 96, 200, 209, 238, 242
Commission on Ecclesiastical Discipline, Royal, 3

Index

Committee on Liturgical Questions, Advisory, 26, 32–37, 39–42, 51, 53–57
Communion, Holy (*see also* Canon), 5, 9, 25–26, 38, 45, 48, 52, 54, 62, 65–82, 95, 103–6, 114, 117–18, 121–2, 194–7, 202, 209–12, 226, 230–2
Communion on Good Friday and Easter Eve, 267–9
Communion of the Sick (*see also* Reservation), 97–98, 100–2, 107, 120, 124, 150, 154–5, 262–4
Comper, Sir J. N., 273
Compline, 9, 10, 25, 27, 29–30, 55
Comprehension, 287–9
Conference on Reservation, 99, 102, 264
Conference on Revision of Canon, 74–76
Confession and Absolution, 7, 29–30, 45, 53, 200, 230, 238, 242–3, 250, 254 n.
Confirmation, 43, 46, 48, 50 n., 53–54, 269–70, 279
Consecration, Second, 80–82, 88–92, 211, 217, 226
Consecration, theories of, 56, 60, 64, 117–18
Consecration of a Church, 54, 271–3; of Bishops, 277–9; of Oil, 279–80
Convocation, 6, 33–34, 38–41, 47, 51, 53–55, 58–61, 80–83, 94, 108–14, 134–8, 151–4, 161, 166, 168–72, 174–5, 180
Cooper, ● Canon S., Chancellor of Truro Cathedral, 147–51, 153, 155–6, 158–9, 161
Cranmer, Abp., 67, 216–17, 295
Creed, Athanasian, 5, 8, 36, 54, 55, 94; Apostles, 7–8, 29, 48; Nicene, 43, 46, 48, 53–54, 109, 200, 226, 230, 242
Cremation, 46
Cross, Processional, 14
Crosses, 18–19

DALTON, CANON J. N., 26, 52, 57–58
Darragh, Canon, of Durban, 212–26
Davidson, Dr. R., Abp. of Canterbury, 26, 32–34, 52, 72, 75, 87, 95, 126–7, 129–38, 153–8, 167, 172, 177, 180, 246–54, 287
Deacon, 255, 281–2
Deans, appointment of, 292–5
Dearmer, Dr. Percy, 26, 94, 301
Devotions (*see also* Reservation), 100–2, 107, 125, 265
Donaldson, Dr. St. Clair, Bp. of Salisbury, 116, 266–7
Drury, Dr. T. W., Bp. of Ripon, 26, 54, 62, 65–83, 95
Duncan Jones, Very Revd. A. S. Dean of Chichester, 120–1, 187

EASTER EVE, 24, 31–32, 267–9
English Church Union, 94, 166, 174–5, 185–6
English Sacred Synods (Joyce), 136
Epiclesis, 61, 62 n., 66, 72–73, 76–80, 98, 104, 106, 114, 119–24, 126, 138–41, 146, 162, 185–8, 205–8, 211–26, 234
Episcopal Signatures, 295–7
Epistles, 24, 36, 45, 95, 230, 238, 240, 242, 245
Evangelicals, 62–63, 67, 69, 75, 94, 97, 114, 129, 150, 162, 262
Evening Prayer, 7–10, 24, 26, 28–29, 31–32, 45

FARNHAM CANON, 102–6
Fasting, 146–8, 150–1, 159, 268
Figgis, Fr. Neville, C.R., 286
Fortescue, Adrian, 218, 220, 225
Furse, Dr. M., Bp. of St. Albans, 116, 160–1

GARBETT, DR. C., BISHOP OF SOUTHWARK, 99–102, 116, 144
Gelasius, 216, 221
Gibson, Dr. E. C. S., Bp. of Gloucester, 3–4, 10–11, 13, 26, 53–55, 77–78, 82–83, 86–88
Gloria in excelsis, 96, 122, 209, 231, 234, 239, 240, 243, 254
Good Friday, 267–9
Gore, Dr. C., Bp. of Birmingham, 26; Bp. of Oxford, 61

Index

Gospels, 2–3, 36, 45, 95, 230, 238, 240, 242, 245
'Green' Book, 94, 96–99
'Grey' Book, 94, 96–99, 104

HANDBOOK OF THE CONVOCATIONS (Joyce), 137
Headlam, Dr. A. C., Bp. of Gloucester, 139–44, 154
Hebrew Christians, 246–8
Henson, Dr. H., Bp. of Durham, 133
Hicks, Sir W. Joynson, 138, 239
History of the Book of Common Prayer (Proctor and Frere), 3, 269
History of the York Convocation (Trevor), 136
Hollis, Revd. J. A., Bp.-designate of Taunton, 277–9
Humble Access, Prayer of, 56–59, 62 n., 68, 71, 74, 76, 96, 208–9, 231

INCENSE (*see also* CENSER) 11–12, 14–17
India, Church of, 259–60
Innocent, Pope, 88, 91
International Missionary Council, 266–7
Intinction, 88–91, 102, 233
Invocation (*see* Epiclesis)

JAPAN, LITURGY IN, 198–202
Jenkins, Revd. Claude, 26, 35, 41–42, 44, 47–49, 51, 53, 233, 299, 310–12
Jus Liturgicum, 259–62

KEMPTHORNE, DR. J. A., BP. OF LICHFIELD, 116, 265
Kidd, Dr. B. J., 120–1, 170–1, 287
King, Prayers for the, 9, 96, 144
Knox, Dr. E. A., Bp. of Manchester, 62 n., 82

LANG, DR. C. G., ARCHBISHOP OF YORK, 25, 82, 106, 116, 154; Archbishop of Canterbury, 180–2, 287; enthronement of, 298–312
Law, Summary of the, 46, 48, 50, 54–55
Lectionary, 36–39, 41, 44, 48, 54
Leeke, Revd. C. H., O.G.S., 231, 240–2

Legge, Dr., Bp. of Lichfield, 6–7
Letters of Business, Royal, 4–5, 35, 61, 83, 134–8
Levertoff, Dr. P. P., 246–8
Litany, 5, 8, 24, 26, 30–31, 45, 55, 201–2
Liturgical Sub-committee of Lambeth Conference, 193–7, 237, 242–4
Liturgy and Worship, 247–8
Lloyd, Dr., Bp. of Nasik, 289–90
Lockhart, J. G., 300
Lyttleton, Revd. E., 269–70

MACLEAN, DR. A., BP. OF MORAY, ROSS, AND CAITHNESS, 26, 33, 36–39, 41, 44, 46–47, 51, 53, 54, 128–9, 164
Matrimony, Holy, 46, 106, 111–14, 121
May, Dr. A., Bp. of Northern Rhodesia, 231, 234–7, 241–5
Ministry, Part-time, 280–2; in Persia, 284–5
Mitre, 278–9
Morning Prayer, 5, 7–9, 24–25, 27–28, 30, 54, 198, 200–1

NASH, DR. J., C.R., COADJUTOR BP. OF CAPE TOWN, 214–18, 278
Norris, Dr. F., Bp. of N. China, 180, 267–9, 282–3
Northern Rhodesia, Liturgy in, 230–45

OBLATION, PRAYER OF, 56–60, 62 n., 68–72, 74–76, 96, 98, 186, 205, 226–7
Offertory, 251, 254
Ollard, Canon, 270, 296
'Orange' Book, 95–99, 106, 108–9, 124
Orders, Holy, 280–5
Ordinal, 95, 281
Ordination, 129, 279, 284–5
Ornaments of the Church, 10–18
Ornaments Rubric, 3–6, 11, 16, 19, 23, 36

PALMER, DR. E. J., BP. OF BOMBAY, 249–52, 289–92
Papal Claims, 286–7
Parliament, 4–6, 134–8, 149, 170, 177, 179

Index

Parochial Church Council, 145–7, 149–50, 159–60, 167, 174
Parsons, Dr. R. G., Bp. of Middleton, 94, 104, 148
Pearce, Dr., Bp. of Worcester, 167
Persia, Proposed United Church of, 284–5
Phelps, Dr., Bp. of Grahamstown, 280–2
Phillimore, Lord, 167–70, 173–6
Pinchard, Revd. A., 120–1, 166
Pollock, Dr. B., Bp. of Norwich, 52 n., 164–5, 167, 177
Practical Manual for the Clergy (Nichaef), 90
Prayer Book Measure, 1922, 94; 1927, 107–9, 129, 138, 147–9; 1928, 170, 174, 177–8
Prayer for the Church, 9, 57, 254–5
Prefaces, Proper, 50, 52–55, 122, 231, 253
Presbyterians, 252
Presence, Real, 129, 263, 287
Principles of Religious Ceremonial (W. H. Frere), 275
Psalms, 7, 10, 24, 36–41, 44, 46–48, 54, 94, 253
Pyx, Hanging, 99–102, 125

QUICK, CANON O. C., 267

RACKHAM, FR. B., C.R., 198
Raven, Dr. C. E., 267
Rawlinson, Revd. D., 120–1
'Reconstruction of Worship' (C.Q.R., October 1912), 24
Red Letter Days, 7
Report 487B (Canterbury Convocation), 35, 41, 53; 487C (Cant. Convoc.), 55; 504, 515 (Cant. Convoc.), 55; CA 252 (Church Assembly), 144–6; NA 60 (Ch. Assem.), 86, 88, 91, 94; NA 84 (Ch. Assem.), 95–99, 112–13; of Farnham Conference, 120–3
Reservation (*see also* Communion for the Sick, and Devotions), 86–88, 97–102, 106, 114–16, 118–19, 121–5, 145–6, 150–1, 169, 262–4

Reservation, Southwark Regulations for, 102, 124–5; Bishops' Regulations for, 106, 124–5
Riley, Athelstan, 83, 89–91, 94
Robertson, Dr. A., Bp. of Exeter, 10, 26–27, 32–36, 38–41, 49–52, 58
Robinson, Dr. Armitage, Dean of Wells, 127, 173, 224, 287, 298, 301–3, 310
Robinson, Canon A. G., 104, 161–3
Robinson, Canon C. L., 261–2
Rogers, Canon Guy, 114
Rubric, Black, 144
Rubrics, 3–6, 14–16, 18, 24, 81–82, 98, 122
Ryle, Bp. H. E., Dean of Westminster, 83, 92–94

SACRING BELL, 12–13, 17
Sadler, Sir Michael, 287–9
St. Mark, Liturgy of, 75
Saint, Patron, 276–7
Sanctus, 56, 203–4, 206, 209, 251, 254
Sarum Gradual, The, 3
Sarum Missal, The, 12, 15, 88, 91
Savage, Dr. H. E., Dean of Lichfield, 292–5
Scott Holland, Canon, 262–4
Selwyn, Revd. E. G., 104, 120, 122–4
Shaftesbury, Earl of, 120–1, 166
Shaw, Revd. C. P., 120, 165–6
Shedden, Dr. R., Bp. of Nassau, 176
Shortened Services Act, 10
Simpson, Dr. Sparrow, 114
Some Principles of Liturgical Reform (W. H. Frere), 3–4, 24, 33, 37, 56–57, 187–9
South Africa, Liturgy of, 81, 203–29
South India, Liturgy of, 249–52
Spens, W., 120–1
Srawley, Dr. J. H., 83–86, 89–91, 104, 114–16, 124 n., 253
Staff, bishop's, 278–9
Stevenson, Canon Morley, 26, 53
Stone, Dr. Darwell, 114, 120, 152
Strong, Dr. T. B., Bp. of Oxford, 103 n., 116, 142–4, 270–1
Symonds, Fr. E., C.R., 279–80

TABERNACLE, 99, 152, 169
Talbot, Fr. E. K., C.R., 147, 151-3, 170-1
Talbot, Dr. N., Bp. of Pretoria, 171, 228-9
Te Deum, 7, 25
Temple, Dr. W., Bp. of Manchester, 116; Abp. of York, 181-4, 267, 284-5
Thanksgiving, Prayer of, 20, 59, 251
Throne, Bishop's, 274-6
Transference of Sisters, 289-92
Truro Diocesan Gazette, The, 138

UNCTION, 25, 54, 94, 122, 279-80
Underhill, Revd. F., 116, 120
Uses, diocesan, 241-4

VENITE, 7, 25, 55
Vespers, 9, 10, 31-32
Vestments, 4, 10-11, 16, 19-23, 98
Vigils, 45
Visitation of the Sick (*see also* Unction) 94, 122
Vows, 289-92

WAGGETT, FR., 176
Warman, Dr. G., Bp. of Truro, 26, 83; Bp. of Chelmsford, 95, 103 n., 116, 142-4
Westcott, Dr. F., Metropolitan of India, 195, 259-61
Weston, Dr. F., Bp. of Zanzibar, 243-4, 249
Whitney, Prof. J. P., 286-7
Wild, Dr., Bp. of Newcastle, 82
Wilson, Canon H. A., 114-15
Wilson, Revd. H. A., 26, 33, 41-43, 53, 57
Winchester Troper, The, 3
Winnington-Ingram, Dr. A. F., Bp. of London, 52, 264
Woodruff, Revd. E. C., 305-7, 310
Woods, Dr. T., Bp. of Winchester, 99, 103-4, 106, 116-21, 142, 154, 264
Wordsworth, Canon C., 26, 49-50
Wordsworth, Dr. J., Bp. of Salisbury, 10, 271-2

YORK MISSAL, THE, 15

www.ingramcontent.com/pod-product-compliance
Lightning Source LLC
Chambersburg PA
CBHW052052300426
44117CB00012B/2088